RELIGION AT WORK IN A NEOLITHIC SOCIETY

This book tackles the topic of religion, a broad subject exciting renewed interest across the social and historical sciences. The volume is tightly focused on the early farming village of Çatalhöyük, which has generated much interest both within and outside archaeology, especially for its contributions to the understanding of early religion. The chapters discuss contemporary themes such as materiality, animism, object vitality, and material dimensions of spirituality while exploring broad evolutionary changes in the ways in which religion has influenced society. The volume results from a unique collaboration between an archaeological team and a range of specialists in ritual and religion.

Ian Hodder is Dunlevie Family Professor of Anthropology at Stanford University. He previously taught at Leeds University and Cambridge University. His main large-scale excavation projects have been at Haddenham in the east of England and at Çatalhöyük in Turkey, where he has worked since 1993. He has been awarded the Oscar Montelius Medal by the Swedish Society of Antiquaries and the Huxley Memorial Medal by the Royal Anthropological Institute, has been a Guggenheim Fellow, and has Honorary Doctorates from Bristol and Leiden Universities. His main books include *Spatial Analysis in Archaeology* (Cambridge, 1976), *Symbols in Action* (Cambridge, 1982), *Reading the Past* (Cambridge, 1986), *The Domestication of Europe* (1990), *The Archaeological Process* (1999), *The Leopard's Tale: Revealing the Mysteries of Çatalhöyük* (2006), and *Entangled: An Archaeology of the Relationships between Humans and Things* (2012).

RELIGION AT WORK IN A NEOLITHIC SOCIETY

Vital Matters

Edited by

IAN HODDER
Stanford University

CAMBRIDGE UNIVERSITY PRESS

CAMBRIDGE
UNIVERSITY PRESS

32 Avenue of the Americas, New York NY 10013-2473, USA

Cambridge University Press is part of the University of Cambridge.

It furthers the University's mission by disseminating knowledge in the pursuit of education, learning and research at the highest international levels of excellence.

www.cambridge.org
Information on this title: www.cambridge.org/9781107671263

© Cambridge University Press 2014

First published 2014

Printed in the United States of America

A catalog record for this publication is available from the British Library.

Library of Congress Cataloging in Publication data
Religion at work in a neolithic society : vital matters / [edited by] Ian Hodder.
   pages   cm
Includes bibliographical references and index.
ISBN 978-1-107-04733-4 (hardback) – ISBN 978-1-107-67126-3 (paperback)
1. Çatal Mound (Turkey)   2. Neolithic period – Turkey.   3. Religion, Prehistoric –
Turkey.   4. Excavations (Archaeology) – Turkey.   5. Turkey – Antiquities.
I. Hodder, Ian.
GN776.32.T9R43   2014
939'.2–dc23   2013035748

ISBN 978-1-107-04733-4 Hardback
ISBN 978-1-107-67126-3 Paperback

This volume is dedicated to the memory of Alejandro Garcia-Rivera.

Contents

Figures

Tables

Contributors

Quentin D. Atkinson is Senior Lecturer in the School of Psychology at the University of Auckland and a visiting research Fellow at the Institute of Cognitive and Evolutionary Anthropology at the University of Oxford. His research uses method and theory from evolutionary biology to understand the evolution of human culture. This includes work on the evolution of religious beliefs and practices and the application of phylogenetic methods to linguistic data, linking the spread of language families with archaeological and genetic evidence of expansion.

Anna Belfer-Cohen is Professor of Prehistoric Archaeology at the Institute of Archaeology, The Hebrew University of Jerusalem. Her main interests of research relate to cultural "beginnings" observed in the archaeological record, namely, the appearance and evolution of the first modern human cultures and the incipient and sometimes subtle changes during Pre-Neolithic times in the Levant, developing into the full-fledged Neolithization processes, culminating in the world we are living in today. She has been engaged in fieldwork at various sites in Israel and in Georgia and published numerous archaeological reports as well as comprehensive papers drawing from the data at hand on cognitive and spiritual aspects of human existence.

Victor Buchli lectures with the material culture group in the Department of Anthropology, University College London. He works on architecture, domesticity, the archaeology of the recent past, critical understandings of materiality, and new technologies. He has conducted fieldwork in Russia, Britain, and Kazakhstan. His books include *An Archaeology of Socialism* (Berg 1999) – an ethnohistorical study of a constructivist housing block in Moscow – and *Archaeologies of the Contemporary Past* (Routledge 2001) with Gavin Lucas – an examination of the critical issues that arise when the archaeological method is applied to the study of contemporary material culture.

Alejandro Garcia-Rivera who was Professor of Systematic Theology, Jesuit School of Theology of Santa Clara University, California, passed away in 2010 and it is to him that this book is dedicated. His research interests included interfaith aesthetics, theology and the arts, theological aesthetics, suffering and the human person, the intersection between science and theology, fundamental theology. He had won several awards for his writings, which included spiritual essays in publications such as *U. S. Catholic and Momento Catolico* and scholarly works such as *St. Martin de Porres: The Little Stories, The Semiotics of Culture, The Community of the Beautiful: A Theological Aesthetics, A Wounded Innocence: Sketches for a Theology of Art, Living Beauty: A Liturgical Aesthetics.*

Nigel Goring-Morris is Professor at the Institute of Archaeology, The Hebrew University of Jerusalem. His primary research interests concern the investigation of changing settlement and adaptive patterns during the transformation of mobile hunter-gatherer groups through to and including the emergence of early settled farming communities and pastoral societies in the Middle East. His current field research focuses on the Pre-Pottery Neolithic B cult and mortuary site of Kfar HaHoresh in lower Galilee. His publications include "The Quick and the Dead: The Social Context of Aceramic Neolithic Mortuary Practices as Seen from Kfar HaHoresh" in *Life in Neolithic Farming Communities: Social Organization, Identity, and Differentiation* (edited by Ian Kuijt 2000).

Stewart Elliott Guthrie, Professor Emeritus of Anthropology at Fordham University, received his PhD from Yale University in 1976. His first book, *A Japanese New Religion* (Michigan 1988), was based on fieldwork in a Japanese mountain hamlet. He began writing on cognitive and evolutionary aspects of religion with "A Cognitive Theory of Religion" (*Current Anthropology* 1980), which held that religion can best be understood as systematized anthropomorphism. His *Faces in the Clouds* (Oxford 1993) extends that paper's key arguments, which are now widely adopted in the cognitive science of religion.

Lori D. Hager is a bioarchaeologist studying the biology of ancient people and their burial customs from sites in the Americas, Europe, and the Near East. She is a Research Associate at the Archaeological Research Facility, UC Berkeley, and a Senior Osteologist at Pacific Legacy, Inc., Berkeley. Dr. Hager considered evolutionary narratives in *Women in Human Evolution* (edited by L. D. Hager 1997) and in *Sex Matters: Letting Skeletons Tell the Story* (edited by L. Schiebinger 2008). As a participant in the human remains team at Çatalhöyük for more than a decade, Dr. Hager has written on the burial practices of these Neolithic people on the basis of her lengthy involvement in the excavation and analysis of the burials.

Ian Hodder is Dunlevie Family Professor in the Department of Anthropology at Stanford University. His main large-scale excavation projects have been at Haddenham in the east of England and at Çatalhöyük in Turkey, where he has worked since 1993. His main books include *Spatial Analysis in Archaeology* (Cambridge 1976), *Symbols in Action* (Cambridge 1982), *Reading the Past* (Cambridge 1986), *The Domestication of Europe* (Blackwell 1990), *The Archaeological Process* (Blackwell 1999), *The Leopard's Tale: Revealing the Mysteries of Çatalhöyük* (Thames and Hudson 2006), and *Entangled: An Archaeology of the Relationships between Humans and Things* (Wiley-Blackwell 2012).

Anke Kamerman is a freelance sociologist and interior architect. She did her MA on the relation between movement patterns and the articulation of material culture in de Krimpenerwaard, a "traditional" farmer community in Holland. She worked on material culture and spatial ordering in working-class neighborhoods in the Hague supported by the Hague Municipal Museum. She graduated as an interior architect from the Rietveld Academy of Fine Arts and has worked since 1995 as an interior architect on rebuilding and furniture design specializing in the relation between behavior patterns and spatial organization. From 2007 she combined her work as an architect with working at the Foundation for Papua Cultural Heritage, doing research on changing oral and material culture by migration of Dutch Papuans.

Camilla Mazzucato is a member of the Çatalhöyük Research Project and a researcher on the Ritual, Community and Conflict Project in the Centre for Anthropology and Mind at the University of Oxford. She began her studies at the University of Bologna, first obtaining a BA in Middle Eastern archaeology, followed by an MA on the Bronze Age–Iron Age transition on the Levantine coast and Iron Age Mediterranean archaeology. She then obtained an MSc degree in geographic information systems (GIS) and spatial analysis at the Institute of Archaeology, University College London. She has been working as a professional archaeologist in Italy and England since 2000 and as a GIS specialist for the Giza Plateau Mapping Project in Egypt and for the Çatalhöyük Research Project in Turkey since 2007.

Barbara J. Mills is Professor of Anthropology at the University of Arizona. She has conducted most of her archaeological research in the Southwest United States, focusing on ancestral and historic Puebloan societies, especially the Zuni, Chaco, and Mogollon Rim areas. She currently directs the Southwest Social Networks Project, focusing on the application of social network analysis to archaeological data across the region. Her research interests include the intersection of material culture with social questions relating to migration and identity, ritual and religion, and different dimensions of inequality and prestige. Professor Mills is the editor or author of eight books and monographs and dozens of articles and book chapters. She is the recipient of the Gordon Willey Award for her 2004 *American Anthropologist* article "The Establishment and Defeat of Hierarchy: Inalienable Possessions and the History of Collective Prestige Structures in the Puebloan Southwest."

Carolyn Nakamura is a postdoctoral researcher at Leiden University, where she coordinates the Global Interactions research profile. She obtained her PhD in anthropology from Columbia University. She specializes in the archaeology and material culture of the Near East and has worked with museum collections and done fieldwork in Turkey, Romania, and the United States. Her research has focused on the sociomaterial ecologies of ritual and magic. More recently, she has become interested in studying the histories/heritage of informal communities in Mumbai.

Kimberley C. Patton is Professor of the Comparative and Historical Study of Religion at Harvard Divinity School. She specializes in ancient Greek religion and archaeology, with research interests in archaic sanctuaries and in the iconography of sacrifice. She is the author of *The Sea Can Wash Away All Evils: Modern Marine Pollution and the Ancient Cathartic Ocean* (Columbia 2006) and *Religion of the Gods: Ritual, Paradox, and Reflexivity* (Oxford 2009). She is also coeditor of and contributing author to three other books: with Benjamin Ray, *A Magic Still Dwells: Comparative Religion in the Postmodern Age* (Berkeley 2000); with John Stratton Hawley, *Holy Tears: Weeping in the Religious Imagination* (Princeton 2005); and with Paul Waldau, *A Communion of Subjects: Animals in Religion, Science, and Ethics* (Columbia 2006).

Peter Pels has been Professor in the Anthropology of Africa at Leiden University since 2003. He earned his PhD in 1993 at the University of Amsterdam with a dissertation that appeared in 1999 as *A Politics of Presence: Contacts between Missionaries and Africans in Late Colonial Tanganyika* (Harwood Academic). Since then he has published work on the anthropology of religion and magic, the anthropology of colonialism, the anthropology of politics, the anthropology of modernity, the history of anthropology, social science ethics, material culture, and interpretation in archaeology. He is working on a book with the provisional title *The Spirit of Matter: Religion, Modernity, and the Power of Objects* and on essays on science fiction and the future, heritage, and qualitative methodology.

F. LeRon Shults is Professor of Theology and Philosophy at the University of Agder in Kristiansand, Norway, and Senior Research Fellow at the Institute for the Biocultural Study of Religion at Boston University. He has doctorates in philosophical theology (Princeton) and educational psychology (Walden). Shults is the author (or coauthor) of eleven books and more than sixty scientific articles and book chapters. His current research interest is on philosophical issues surrounding the cognitive science of religion.

J. Wentzel van Huyssteen is the James I. McCord Professor of Theology and Science at Princeton Theological Seminary. His area of special interest is religious and scientific epistemology. He earned a doctorate in theology from the Free University of Amsterdam in 1970 and was ordained a minister in the Dutch Reformed Church the next year. He was named Professor and Chair of Religious Studies at South Africa's University of Port Elizabeth in 1972, a post he held until going to Princeton. The author of some fifty articles published in academic journals, he is the editor (with Niels Henrik Gregersen) of *Rethinking Theology and Science* (Eerdmans 1998) and the author of eight other books, including *Essays in Postfoundational Theology* (Eerdmans 1997) and *The Shaping of Rationality: Towards Interdisciplinarity in Theology and Science* (Eerdmans 1999).

Mary Weismantel is Professor of Anthropology at Northwestern University and Director of the Gender and Sexuality Program. She has done ethnographic research in the Andean region of South America since 1980. Her first book was *Food, Gender and Poverty in the Ecuadorian Andes* (University of Pennsylvania Press 1989), an ethnographic study of the diet, cuisine, and kitchen practices of an indigenous agricultural community. She has also written about race and racism, gender, sex and sexuality, adoption, and kinship and is currently writing about pre-Columbian art. Her more recent book, *Cholas and Pishtacos: Tales of Race and Sex in the Andes* (University of Chicago Press 2001), won several awards. Her articles have been published in *American Anthropologist, American Ethnologist, Bulletin of Latin American Research, Identities, Modern Language Notes*, and *Food and Foodways*, as well as in edited volumes.

Harvey Whitehouse is Professor of Anthropology at Oxford University. He obtained his PhD from Cambridge in 1991. A specialist in Melanesian religion, he carried out two years of field research on a "cargo cult" in New Britain, Papua New Guinea, in the late 1980s. In recent years, he has focused his energies on the development of collaborative programs of research on cognition and culture. His books include *Inside the Cult: Religious Innovation and Transmission in Papua New Guinea* (Oxford 1995), *Arguments and Icons: Divergent Modes of Religiosity* (Oxford 2000), *The Debated Mind: Evolutionary Psychology versus Ethnography* (Berg 2001), and *Modes of Religiosity: A Cognitive Theory of Religious Transmission* (AltaMira 2004).

Preface

This volume results from a seminar funded by the John Templeton Foundation that took place at the Neolithic tell site of Çatalhöyük in Turkey over three years (2009–2011). The processes of engagement that led to the volume are described in Chapter 1. At the end of 2010, one of our original group, Alejandro Garcia-Rivera (Professor of Systematic Theology, Jesuit School of Theology of Santa Clara University, California), passed away at fifty-nine. This volume is dedicated to his memory.

Alejandro was mischievous, warm, brilliant, and creative, a wonderful mix of reverence and irreverence. He insisted that he and I should edit a "Journal of Irresponsible Archaeology," and at the same time he came up with a whole series of wonderful ideas about Çatalhöyük that he had only begun to explore. With the permission of his wife, Kathryn, I have included as a postscript a note he sent me after his visit to the site in 2009. Preliminary as the text is, the writing is, on the one hand, remarkably prescient – picking up already the themes that have become dominant in this volume, such as vitality and the symbolic importance of flesh – and, on the other hand, his text shows what a long way we as a project have still to go. Alejandro was already well ahead of us and he raised issues and ideas, such as devotion and the dramatic horizon, that I hope others may be stimulated to pursue.

I am deeply grateful to the John Templeton Foundation for its long-term support of the Çatalhöyük research initiatives, and in particular to Paul Wason. I am also deeply indebted to all the many members of the Çatalhöyük team who have, with great forbearance and goodwill over

The project participants and friends at Çatalhöyük in July 2011. Clockwise starting at top left: Paul Wason, Ofer Bar-Yosef, Ian Hodder, Shahina Farid, Harvey Whitehouse, J. Wentzel van Huyssteen, F. LeRon Shults, Barbara Mills, Mary Weismantel, Nigel Goring-Morris, Victor Buchli, Peter Pels, Veysel Apaydin, Anna Belfer-Cohen, Kimberley Patton, Rosemary Beck, Rob Swigart, Anke Kamerman, Stewart Guthrie, Çakan Tanıdık, Serap Özdöl, Sadrettin Dural, and Banu Aydinoğluğil.

the years, welcomed and engaged with the Templeton scholars. And finally I wish to thank the Templeton project members for making this such a pleasant and rewarding experience.

The John Templeton Foundation provided a grant in support of the project on which this book is based.

1

The Vitalities of Çatalhöyük

Ian Hodder

This book describes new work on the role of religion at the nine-thousand-year-old site of Çatalhöyük in Turkey. It follows on from a volume entitled *Religion and the Origin of Complex Societies: Çatalhöyük as a Case Study* (Hodder 2010) that resulted from a seminar funded by the Templeton Foundation. The new volume results from a larger and more ambitious Templeton seminar that took place at Çatalhöyük over three years (2009–2011). All the contributors to this volume participated in the seminar, spending a week at the site each year, talking to the excavators and laboratory researchers, developing their own chapters in dialogue with archaeologists. Each chapter in this volume thus results from in-depth engagement with the archaeological data from the site as well as from intense discussions with other contributors.

The contributors were charged with writing about the role of religion at Çatalhöyük from the point of view of their own experience but engaging with the detailed data from the site. The contributors come from philosophy and religious studies, anthropology and sociology, and from archaeological contexts in different parts of the world. The interactions between the various scholars and with the archaeologists at the site were fruitful, and the group as a whole moved toward an understanding of religion at Çatalhöyük in terms of "vital matter," that is, in terms of the ways in which materials and substances that were seen to have a vital force played active roles in forming and transforming societies. Bodies and bones, flesh and horns, surfaces and interfaces all in their various ways became marked as constitutive of social life. Such matters had vitality but were also vital in producing and reproducing social life. They constituted the religious by drawing numinous forces into the interstices of daily life.

General Introduction

Undoubtedly the most significant aspect of the culmination of the recent three years of Templeton work at the site has been the realization that religion should not be viewed solely in instrumentalist terms. We had started the recent project with the title "Religion as the Basis for Power and Property in the First Civilizations." In other words, we had assumed that religion came into play to allow the accumulation of power and property. As will be discussed later, many commentators on the origins of settled agricultural life in the Middle East have followed in the footsteps of Gordon Childe, and indeed of authors such as Rousseau, Marx, and Engels, in arguing that the accumulation of surplus made possible by agriculture allowed the emergence of property and social differentiation. Religion played an ideological role in creating community and justifying power, and various forms of these ideas have continued in much recent work (see later and Bender 1978; Kuijt 2000, 2008).

However, as will be described, the data amassed from Çatalhöyük and discussed in the Templeton seminar did not find evidence for clear relationships among power, property, and religion. And the same can be said of many other earlier sites in the Middle East, as will be argued later. The data and our discussions suggested that religion is not something that appears because it is useful in the organization of power, property, and society. Rather, the need for the transcendent can be argued to be an integral part of the human process, as central and ever-present as the need for food and the social. This is one aspect of the term "vital" – that religion is a vital aspect of being human. It can be manipulated, as can food and social relations, in order to obtain power, but it is not something that is produced through these instrumental processes, and it is not something humans can do without. Of course, much depends on how religion is defined. In the earlier volume, religion was described in terms of that which is marked and transcendent, relating to ultimate boundaries and the beyond. In this volume various definitions are used, but to some degree the term "religion" refers to any notion that there is vitality in matter – that there is an agentful 'beyondness' to the world. Such a definition is at the same time hopelessly vague (since it includes a scientific belief in physical forces that shape the universe) but also usefully inclusive, since the commonalities among science, religion, and spirituality perhaps do need exploring. "Vital matter" is thus a term that can draw attention to the ways in which we as humans try to make sense of the world. We see agency in the world, often in our own image, as Guthrie's discussion of anthropomorphism in Chapter 4 makes clear. So a second meaning of the term "vital" refers to the ways in which humans attribute causal powers to things.

Humans at Çatalhöyük lived religion in all parts of their lives as part of a seamless world. In everything they did there was an understanding that the world had vitality and power. The world was replete with substances that flowed and transformed and with surfaces that could be passed through. According to this view, religion was an ever-present component of the life process. For example, both ancestors and wild bulls were necessary for daily life, and they protected each other in the context of the home. Many substances were seen as vitally productive, whether they be collections of obsidian or natural crystals placed beneath floors, the symmetrical designs on walls, the plaster surfaces of houses, or the death of a woman during childbirth (as seen in Chapter 9, written by the religious scholar Kimberley Patton and the archaeologist Lori Hager; see also Rollefson 1984).

As an integral part of life, religion played varying roles in instigating and producing change. In the early part of the sequence at Çatalhöyük from 7400 to 6500 BC, the vital forces at play were productive of transformative change. Religion was central to a complex world in which the community was constituted by sodalities akin to mystery cults, dominated by symbols such as the leopard and the bear. But in particular, the ancestors and the wild bull were the foci around which social groups formed and developed relations with each other. But around 6500 BC, this system became restrictive and constraining, preventing change. The social focus on wild bulls and ancestors worked well for a long time. It allowed resilience and flexibility in a society based on a diversity of resources. But around 6500 BC, as society became more dependent on the more intensive herding of sheep and domestic cattle, the older system broke down. Religion now became part of a new way of life in which separate productive entities were linked by common religious doctrines and by the circulation of religious tokens and beliefs. These claims will be explored in detail later and in the chapters that follow.

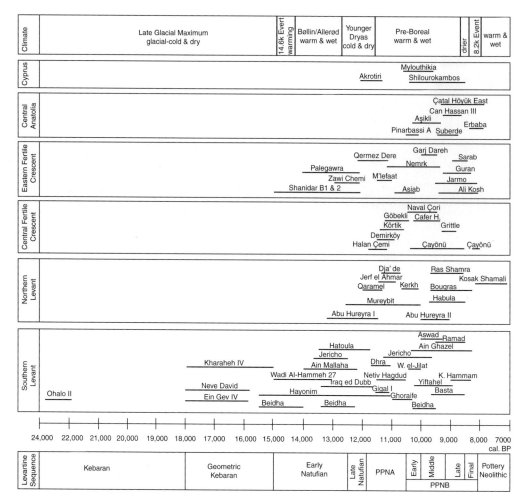

1.1. The chronological relationships between sites in the Middle East and Turkey. *Source*: Zeder 2011.

History and Background to the Project

The focus of this project, Çatalhöyük East (7400–6000 BC) in central Turkey, is one of the best known Neolithic sites in Anatolia and the Middle East, roughly contemporary with later Pre-Pottery and the following Pottery Neolithic in the Levant (see Figures 1.1 and 1.2). It became well known because of its large size (thirty-four acres and thirty-five hundred to eight thousand people), with eighteen levels inhabited over fourteen hundred years and dense concentrations of "art" in the form of wall paintings, wall reliefs, sculptures, and installations. Within Anatolia, and particularly within central Anatolia, recent research has

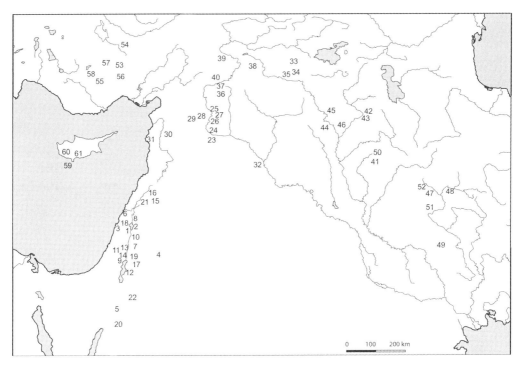

1.2. Distribution of main Late Epipaleolithic and Neolithic sites in the Near East. 1, Ohalo II; 2, Ein Gev IV; 3, Neve David; 4, Kharaheh IV; 5, Beidha; 6, Hayonim; 7, Wadi al-Hammeh 27; 8, 'Ain Mallaha; 9, Jericho; 10, Iraq ed Dubb; 11, Hatoula; 12, Dhra'; 13, Netiv Hagdud; 14, Gigal I; 15, Aswad; 16, Ghoraife; 17, Wadi el-Jilat 7; 18, Yiftah'el; 19, 'Ain Ghazal; 20, Basta; 21, Ramad; 22, Khirbet Hammam; 23, Abu Hureyra; 24, Mureybit; 25, Dja'de; 26, Jerf el Ahmar; 27, Kosak Shamali; 28, Halula; 29, Qaramel; 30, Tel el Kerkh; 31, Ras Shamra; 32, Bouqras; 33, Hallan Çemi; 34, Demirköy; 35, Körtik; 36, Göbekli Tepe; 37, Nevalı Çori; 38, Çayönü; 39, Cafer Höyük; 40, Gritille; 41, Palegawra; 42, Shanidar cave; 43, Zawi Chemi Shanidar; 44, Qermez Dere; 45, Nemrik; 46, M'lefaat; 47, Asiab; 48, Ganj Dareh; 49, Ali Kosh; 50, Jarmo; 51, Guran; 52, Sarab; 53, Pınarbaşı A; 54, Aşıklı Höyük; 55, Suberde; 56, Can Hasan III; 57, Çatalhöyük; 58, Erbaba; 59, Aetokremnos; 60, Mylouthikia; 61, Shillourokambos.
Source: Zeder 2011.

shown that there are local sequences that lead up to and prefigure Çatalhöyük (Baird 2007, 2008; Gérard and Thissen 2002; Özdoğan 2002). In southeast Turkey, the earlier sites of Çayönü (Özdoğan and Özdoğan 1998) and Göbekli Tepe (Schmidt 2001, 2006) already show substantial agglomeration and elaborate symbolism. In central Anatolia, Aşıklı Höyük (Esin and Harmankaya 1999) has dense packed housing through the millennium prior to Çatalhöyük. There are many other sites contemporary, or partly contemporary, with Çatalhöyük that are known in central Anatolia and the adjacent Burdur-Lakes region (Duru 1999; Gérard and Thissen 2002). Yet Çatalhöyük retains a special significance because of the complex narrative nature of its art, and many syntheses

1.3. View of the Çatalhöyük excavations undertaken by James Mellaart in the 1960s. *Source*: Ian Todd and Çatalhöyük Research Project.

(e.g., by Cauvin 1994 or Mithen 2003) give it a special place. Much of the symbolism of the earlier Neolithic and later (into historic times) periods of the Middle East can be "read" in terms of the evidence from Çatalhöyük, and the rich evidence from the site enables interpretation of the evidence from other sites.

The site was first excavated by James Mellaart in the 1960s (e.g., 1967) (Figures 1.3 and 1.4). After 1965 it was abandoned until a new project began in 1993 (Hodder 1996, 2000, 2005a, b, c, 2006, 2007). Through both projects, only 5 percent of the mound has been excavated, but the whole mound has been sampled using surface survey, surface pickup, geophysical prospection, and surface scraping (see reports in Hodder 1996). More than two hundred houses have so far been excavated by Mellaart and the current project. The main architectural components of the site are densely clustered houses, with areas of refuse or midden between them. The art and symbolism and burial all occur within houses. There is evidence of productive activities in all houses, in midden areas, and on partial second stories. None of the sampling has found evidence of large public buildings, ceremonial centers, specialized

1.4. Building with leopard relief, excavated by James Mellaart.

areas of production, or cemeteries. The population of the settlement at any one time (between thirty-five hundred and eight thousand) has been conservatively estimated (Cessford 2005b) by using a variety of techniques, and making a variety of assumptions about how many houses were inhabited at any one time.

Although more than two hundred houses have been excavated at Çatalhöyük, a relatively small number have been fully excavated by the present project using modern scientific techniques. Many other buildings have been partly excavated by the present project, but the buildings have been put on public display and so have not been completely excavated. All of the extensive excavation in the 1960s took place without screening, and with limited recording and no scientific analysis (except radiocarbon dating). It remains the case that only 5 percent of the mound has been excavated, and a very small proportion of that excavation using modern scientific techniques resulted in fully excavated houses.

In the earliest phase of the current project (1993–1995), we concentrated on regional survey and on planning and studying the surface of the mounds, conducting surface pickup, drawing eroded profiles of the

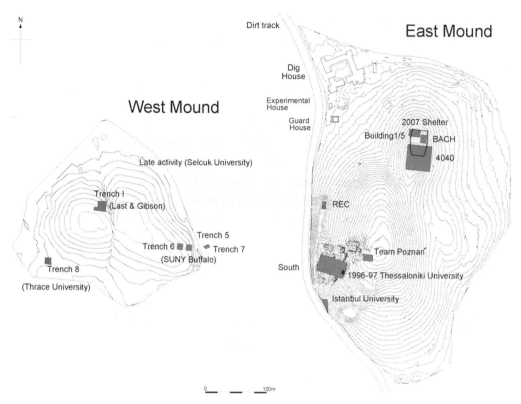

1.5. Excavation areas at Çatalhöyük.
Source: Camilla Mazzucato and Çatalhöyük Research Project.

earlier excavation trenches, and using geophysical prospection. We also undertook a reevaluation of the material in museums that had been excavated by Mellaart (Hodder 1996).

In the second phase of fieldwork and publication (1996–2002) the research aim focused on individual buildings. We excavated in two main areas on the East Mound (Figure 1.5). In the northern area of the East Mound we concentrated on excavating buildings (Buildings 1 and 5 and Building 3 in the BACH Area) in great detail in order to discern depositional processes and in order to understand how individual houses functioned. In the South Area we continued the trenches that had been started by Mellaart in order to understand the overall sequence of the site and to see how individual houses were rebuilt and reused over time. At the same time paleoenvironmental work was conducted, regional survey continued (Baird 2002) and excavations were undertaken on the later Chalcolithic mound at Çatalhöyük West (Figure 1.5). Publication of the monographs for this second phase of work was completed in 2007 (Hodder 2005a, b, c, 2006, 2007). The methods used by the project were published in an earlier volume (Hodder 2000).

The research aims for the third phase of the project (2003–2012) turned from individual houses to the social geography of the settlement as a whole and larger community structure. Excavation took place from 2003 to 2008, with postexcavation from 2009 to 2012. Extensive excavation took place in a new area of the site, specifically in the 4040 Area in the northern part of the mound (Figure 1.6), and in 2008 a shelter was erected over part of this area (Figure 1.7). Excavation also continued in the South shelter (Figure 1.8) so that we could explore the organization of architecture in the upper levels of the site and link our results to the work done by Mellaart in this area of the site. Excavations by other teams, especially the TP Team led by Arek Marciniak of Poznan University and Lech Czerniak from the University of Gdansk in Poland, and by the IST Team led by Mihriban Özbaşaran from Istanbul University, allowed further exploration of the upper levels. And on the following Chalcolithic West Mound, excavation by three teams (University of Thrace at Edirne led by Burçin Erdoğu, Selcuk University at Konya led by Ahmet Tırpan and Asuman Baldıran, and Berlin University and SUNY Buffalo led by Peter Biehl and Eva Rosenstock) allowed an increased understanding of the developments in the sixth millennium BC.

In the 4040 Area the focus has been on understanding the variation among contemporary buildings. The new buildings and midden areas excavated here have allowed increased understanding of the social makeup of the mound. In particular, we have now clear evidence for the grouping of houses into small clusters that probably share ancestral burial houses termed "history houses" (discussed later), as well as larger-scale groupings into sectors of clustered houses bounded by midden areas and/or alleyways. In the South Area of the site our focus has been on a sequence of buildings in one "column" of houses (from the base of the column these are Buildings 65, 56, 44, and 10). This sequence of houses stacked one on top of the other over time has provided much clear evidence for strong microtraditions and repetitive practices that almost certainly indicate long-term occupancy of a "history house" by the same group. The recirculation of human body parts is certainly part of this occupancy (see later discussion). For the chronological relationships among different parts of the site see Table 1.1.

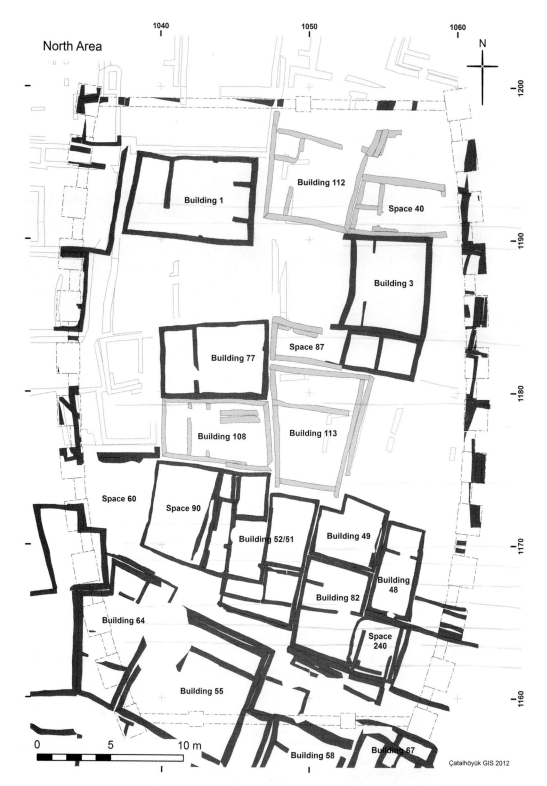

1.6. Map of buildings excavated in the North or 4040 Area of Çatalhöyük.
Source: Camilla Mazzucato and Çatalhöyük Research Project.

1.7. The 4040 or North shelter at Çatalhöyük.
Source: Jason Quinlan and Çatalhöyük Research Project.

1.8. Excavations in the South Area at Çatalhöyük.
Source: Jason Quinlan and Çatalhöyük Research Project.

Table 1.1. Chronological relations between occupation levels excavated by James Mellaart and the current project and their approximate radiocarbon dates BC

	Levels	
0,I,II	TP6	
	South T- 4040.J	
	South S- 4040.J	
	South R- 4040.I	6400–6000
	South Q- 4040.H	
(V)	South P- 4040.H	
VIA	South O- 4040.G	
VIB	South N- 4040.G	6500–6400
VII	South N- 4040.G	
VIII	South L- 4040.F	6700–6500
IX	K	
X	J	
XI	I	7300–6800
XII	H	
Pre XII	Gi,G2,G3,G4	

Development of Research Questions

Toward the end of the third phase of research identified previously, targeted funding from the John Templeton Foundation allowed the scope of the analysis and postexcavation work to be expanded so as to include consideration of the following four research questions: (1) At Çatalhöyük what is the relationship between religious and other symbolism and the control of production in the different house types? (2) Is there secure evidence that important symbolic and religious objects were handed down in houses, and preferentially in "history houses" at Çatalhöyük? (3) Through time how does the "history house" system change, and is there a concomitant decline in the role of religious symbolism? (4) Is religion related to power and property elsewhere in the emergence of civilization in the Neolithic of the Middle East?

In other words, we were asking instrumentalist questions, assuming that religion could be explained in terms of its usefulness in creating power and property. Not that we argued that religion only existed after the adoption of agriculture and settled life. Çatalhöyük has always been identified with a rich symbolism that invites interpretation in terms of religion, and recent remarkable discoveries such as at Göbekli Tepe (Schmidt 2006) and Körtik Tepe (Özkaya and Coşkun 2011) have only emphasized the role of symbolism and religion in the gradual transition to farming. So religion may always have existed in some form, but it seemed possible to argue that the heightened focus on temples, carved stele, skull cults, and wild animal symbolism during the late Epipaleolithic and Neolithic could be explained in relation to social differentiation. The feats of labor and construction seen at Jericho, Göbekli, and Tell Qaramel (Mazurowski 2004) have suggested to many that elites may have been involved. Social differentiation is often seen as a key feature of this period (Belfer-Cohen 1995; Belfer-Cohen and Bar-Yosef 2000; Bender 1978; Byrd 1994; Byrd and Monahan 1995; Flannery 1972, 1993; Goring-Morris 2000; Hayden 1990; Hole 2000; Kuijt 2000; Rosenberg and Redding 2000; Wright 1978, 1984). Religion may have played a role in relation to differentiation, power, and the control of production, land, and property.

So it seemed reasonable to expect that social differentiation at Çatalhöyük would be related to the control of resources and to religious practices. As noted previously, to date large public buildings, ceremonial centers, and specialized areas of production have not been found at the site despite extensive sampling of the entire mound. On the other hand, the large population size suggests that some degree of social control may have existed. And certainly we had found differences between houses at the site. Some houses at Çatalhöyük are more elaborate than others. Elaboration is defined in terms of the sum, for any one phase of a building, of the number of floor segments, basins, benches, installations (including bucrania), pillars, and paintings in the main room. Some houses also have more burials beneath the floors than others; some have no burials, whereas Building 1 had sixty-two. Some houses are rebuilt over longer periods than others such as the 65–56–44–10 sequence referred to previously (see Figure 1.9). Some houses are built on midden and are replaced by midden when abandoned, but other houses are rebuilt in the same place at least six times. These three ways of differentiating buildings (elaboration, numbers of burials, and numbers of rebuilds) do not necessarily correlate, and in many cases we have not excavated deeply enough to know how many times buildings were rebuilt in the same place. But we have noted, as previously did Düring (2006), that multiply rebuilt buildings often contain many burials at some point in their sequence and are elaborate. We have come to term these buildings "history houses" (Hodder and Pels 2010). The term "history house" refers both to an individual building and to the larger community of people that used that building for burial.

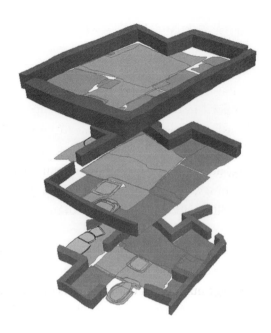

1.9. The sequence of buildings 65-56-44 in the upper levels at Çatalhöyük. *Source*: Camilla Mazzucato and Çatalhöyük Research Project.

We can thus define four types of building at Çatalhöyük, elaborate buildings, multiple burial buildings, history houses, and other buildings, although there is much overlap among the first three of these categories. The variation in building type can then be used to explore the question of whether religion was linked to the control of resources. The elaborate houses contain more of the symbolism that is used to refer to religion at the site and in the Neolithic – bucrania, wild animal parts, wild animal representations, reliefs, and paintings. The houses with multiple burials engaged with religion in the sense of being repositories for the dead and being involved in the retrieval and circulation of human heads and other body parts. So, is there any evidence that these special buildings, often coincident with what Mellaart (1967) would have called "shrines," controlled production, storage, and property or that the inhabitants had better diets and health than in other houses? The data collected from the site could be scrutinized during the Templeton project in order to explore the four questions about the relationships among power, property, and religion at Çatalhöyük.

(1) *At Çatalhöyük what is the relationship between religious and other symbolism and the control of production in the different house types?* In fact, correlations were hard to find in the data studied within

this project. Many different types of data, including botanical data, obsidian point densities, and numerous health and diet markers for those buried beneath the floors of buildings, did not show correlations with the measures of architectural elaboration, numbers of burials, and longevity of buildings. There were not good correlations with storage or with overall building size (Hodder and Pels 2010). Mazzucato (2013) plotted logged density of finds per building, number of individuals buried in each building, the area of the buildings, the amounts of obsidian projectile points found, and building elaboration indices with the objective of trying to find correlations among these variables. No correlations were observed. No correlation was found between the number of burial goods and the size or elaboration of buildings (Nakamura and Meskell 2013a). The average numbers of burial artifacts per person for history houses and nonhistory houses were not different (2013a). While some differences between house types were found in some markers of disease and workload, the overall impression was of a fierce egalitarianism.

Tung (2013) argued that elaborate houses were not built with more elaborate materials. Love (2013) found that builders of architecturally elaborate buildings were not intentionally using mudbrick materials as an indicator of status or value. Nakamura and Meskell (2013b) discovered a lack of correlation between the presence of elaborated architectural features and the presence of figurines. Figurine frequencies also did not correlate with building size and with numbers of burials. In terms of the differences among history, elaborate, and other buildings, the plant material did not suggest differences in densities and storage of crops (Bogaard et al. 2013).

Biodistance work based on human dental morphology found that history houses did not emerge as distinctive in expressions of relatedness (Hillson et al. 2013). In a study of the rate of growth and development of children it was found that there were no differences between history houses and other houses (2013). Similarly, studies of the growth rates of adolescents could find no differences between history and nonhistory houses. Variation in the teeth wear of adults showed no differences between history and nonhistory houses. Ontogenetic bending strengths for the bones of children recovered from history houses and other locations suggest that these children experienced indistinguishable loading environments and probably similar nutritional and health status.

There is some slight evidence of incipient specialization in some aspects of material culture, especially in the later levels of occupation at the site, perhaps associated with some of the later elaborate houses; these changes will be discussed later. Overall there is a lack of evidence for the control of production or storage in specific house types. The inhabitants of some houses seem to have been "successful" in that they lasted longer (were rebuilt more times), had more burials (perhaps largely as a by-product of longevity), and collected many bull and other animal parts that were installed in houses as part of architectural elaboration (again perhaps as a by-product of longevity). But these houses did not seem able to convert their roles in relation to ancestors and religion into other forms of social power and status. In the early and middle levels of occupation at the site at least it was inappropriate to show wealth differences. Accumulations of obsidian were hidden in caches beneath floors. Stored food was hidden away in side rooms. Elaborate buildings with much evidence of feasting and special deposits (e.g., B.49) were small. Up until South M and N there was a great emphasis on living in clustered neighborhoods rather than on marking social difference.

(2) *Is there secure evidence that important symbolic and religious objects were handed down in houses, and preferentially in "history houses," at Çatalhöyük?* This question has been answered unequivocally by the discovery within this Templeton project of clear cases in which parts of human bodies were taken from earlier graves and incorporated into later graves. These human parts include limbs, but mainly teeth and skulls. For example, in Building 65 teeth were missing from a skeleton buried within the east central platform in the main room. In the house built above it, Building 56, loose teeth were placed beneath the floors of the central east platform, directly over the earlier platform. These teeth were found to fit exactly into the earlier skull.

We also now have several examples of burials from which heads had been removed during the occupation of the site. Of the 350 burials excavated at the site only 18 had their heads removed, usually about one year after initial burial of the whole body. Of the 18 headless bodies (Boz and Hager 2013), all 11 that were found in completely excavated buildings that can be assigned a category occurred in either history houses (Buildings 1, 6, 44, 60) or the multiple burial Building 49. None occurred in fully excavated buildings that can be classified as "other." The only possible exception is Building 42, which has not been fully excavated but is a new foundation and cannot be classified as a history house. A larger number of heads have been found without bodies. The 29 excavated (Boz and Hager 2013) were found in a wider range of contexts including both history houses and other houses (e.g., Building 3). The heads were sometimes deposited in foundation, abandonment, and other rituals. In one case, in Building 42, a skull of a woman was placed in the arms of another woman in a foundation burial. This skull had been plastered and painted red four times, suggesting that the skull had been kept and passed down over a period of time. We know that sculptural components were retrieved from the west wall of the main room in Building 1 after abandonment (Hodder 2006) and that large numbers of cattle horns were amassed, perhaps over time, in Building 52 (Farid 2013).

There is substantial evidence that in sequences of buildings built on top of each other over up to five hundred years, specific practices were passed on, suggesting repetitive practices and routines. Thus in the 65–56–44–10 sequence of houses, neonates were always buried in the southwest corner of the building, a pot was repeatedly placed at the base of the ladder, and a small grindstone was twice placed on the hearth at abandonment of the building. Such evidence suggests a continuity of social-religious practice and the continuity of memory.

Thus, while history houses did not control production in the "classic" early and middle levels at Çatalhöyük, they and the other special types of house did have some special role in the passing down of important symbolic objects and ritual practices. We know, from biodistance work conducted on the human teeth, that those buried beneath houses were not close kin (Pilloud and Larsen 2011). Rather, house membership was itself constructed through rituals and the passing down of objects of symbolic importance. All those connected to a particular history house or elaborate or multiple burial house were thus tied together by social and religious connections and the passing down of important objects. The function of these various types of special house seems to be less concerned with amassing power and controlling production and more with creating networks and close webs of interdependence (Watkins 2008). In Chapter 7 in this volume, Mills argues that the ritual and symbolism at Çatalhöyük were involved in creating cross-cutting sodalities.

This argument seems plausible (see Hodder 2013), but presumably connections could have been set up among the inhabitants of Çatalhöyük without complex rituals. The fact that complex rituals were involved in making connections between people in the settlement suggests that symbolism and religion were part of lived experience. Symbolism and ritual regarding notions of an agentful beyond do not seem to be explainable in terms of the function of creating connections, any more than they can be explained by the exercise of power.

(3) *Through time how does the "history house" system change, and is there a concomitant decline in the role of religious symbolism?* This question has again been unequivocally answered by a large amount of archaeological evidence that shows gradual change throughout the sequence at Çatalhöyük, but a marked change at 6500 BCE around levels South O and P. In the upper levels after this change, history houses invested less in ritual ties between clustered neighborhoods and focused more on independent production and the buildup of their own surpluses. The increased focus on domestic production was seen in the heavier investment in sheep herding and in the adoption of domestic cattle and the processing of milk. There were greater mobility and use of the landscape for a wider range of resources. Personhood became less based on membership of the house within its larger history house cluster and on membership of cross-cutting ritual communities; rather it became more associated with individual ties of exchange. Because the focus was more on individual house production, the dependence on large cohesive populations to provide a safety net declined: population decreased and dispersed. The emphasis on egalitarian relations continued throughout the occupation of the site, but as the close ties weakened within the community, houses had to depend more on their own production and on relations of dependence with others based on exchanges of labor and goods.

In the upper levels, houses often became larger and multiroomed and they started to take over adjacent midden areas for use as yards and a range of activities linked to household production. This expansion of house-based production spread out into the landscape. The adoption of domestic cattle and an intensification of sheepherding were associated with a broader use of the landscape and greater human mobility. This wider use of the landscape was associated with and perhaps facilitated by a shift in social organization. While many social and ritual practices continued from the lower levels, there was a shift in emphasis. Bucrania installations and reliefs of bears and leopards were less common in the upper levels, but bull heads appeared as reliefs on pottery and bulls are shown in paintings. Leopards and bears appeared on mobile stamp seals. There seems to be a change from the stable fabric of the house to the mobile elements of material culture. A possibly related shift is seen very clearly in a decreased focus on house continuity. Düring (2006) has noted that there is less continuity of buildings in the upper levels, and Cessford (2005a) has shown that the use lives of houses decreased. In her discussion of the phasing of the site, Farid (2007) notes that it is from Level VI (South N and O) upward that the problems in assigning buildings to levels became more acute. In the upper levels the steady incremental constructions based on preceding plans declined. For example, there was a phase of midden and pitting above B.67 and before B.47, suggesting a lack of concern with continuity. While some of the walls of B.47 in 4040 J were founded on the walls of B.67, the construction and plan were quite different. The walls were thicker, the internal features and configuration were unfamiliar, and there was a central oval hearth. As we have seen, there were frequent open spaces around houses in the upper levels, suggesting a lack of concern with continuous placement. The decrease of installations in the upper levels and the decreased continuity of house fabric may suggest a decreasing concern with history making. It is true that the 65–56–44–10 sequence has much evidence of continuity and history making, but many of the building phases in this sequence seem short-lived (Regan and Taylor 2013).

There is other evidence that the community was increasingly less dependent on cohesive ritual ties and increasingly engaged in exchanges between independent productive units. In the upper levels, the amounts of sheep and goat remains increased in both daily and special consumption contexts. This is a shift from earlier periods, in which sheep and goat were mainly used in daily consumption, and there was a preference for wild bulls to be used in special consumption. While the numbers of cattle stayed relatively constant into the upper levels, the use of wild animals was diluted by the introduction of domestic cattle. The dependence on wild cattle therefore decreased. While cattle (and perhaps still especially bulls) continued to be used in special deposits in the upper levels, the degree of fragmentation of cattle bones in middens increased post South P, suggesting that cattle were also increasingly involved in daily consumption as well.

There is also a significant decrease in the material elaboration of burials in the upper levels. The long-term trend is that the prevalence of house burial and ancestry making declined and transformed in the upper levels: in TP multiple burials and a "tomb" have been found, and by the West Mound adult burial in buildings seems to have ceased. One possible interpretation is that this overall trend is linked to the decreasing emphasis on house-based history making in the upper levels.

In the upper levels at the site there is in a way a decrease in the material remains of religious symbolism. This is because the symbolism in the lower part of the site was literally built into the house – as part of the process of creating house histories (see also Banning and Byrd 1987). In the upper part of the site, symbolism became more mobile (on stamp seals and on pottery) and distributed, and thus less engrained into the architecture of the house. But this is not a decline in religious symbolism itself, since religion was ever-present in new modes, and certain houses became very invested in both greater production and the control of religious narrative. This shift is similar to that described by Harvey Whitehouse, Camilla Mazzucato, Ian Hodder, and Quentin D. Atkinson (see Chapter 6) as the shift from imagistic to doctrinal modes of religiosity. While religion seems to have changed in relation to other variables, it remained an ever-present component of social life throughout the sequence at Çatalhöyük.

(4) *Is religion related to power and property elsewhere in the emergence of civilization in the Neolithic of the Middle East?* We have seen that in answering the first three questions it is possible to argue that religious symbolism had a potent force at Çatalhöyük that resulted in its being involved in many aspects of social and economic life. But the presence of religion and the centrality of ritual and symbolism at the site do not seem fully explainable in instrumentalist terms. In particular, religion at the site does not seem to be linked to the control of power and property. But is this conclusion a peculiarity of Çatalhöyük and its specific focus on egalitarian relations? What are the relations among religion, power, and property at other Neolithic sites in the Middle East?

This question was explored in the international conference that took place at Çatalhöyük in 2010. Excavators attended from many of the major sites in Turkey and adjacent areas. Most participants agreed that power and property were collectively held during early farming settlements and towns without significant individual ranking or private property. As noted at Çatalhöyük, religion was a pervasive and important component of all social and economic life, both productive of change and at times producing constraint.

Çatalhöyük acts as a bridge between societies in the "Fertile Crescent" to the east where agriculture and settled life began earliest, and societies in western Anatolia, Greece, and southeast Europe where agriculture and settled life did not begin until the seventh millennium BCE with economies that quickly included domestic cattle. To the east, there is more evidence of collective ritual and there are more claims for social differentiation related to ritual. But for most participants in the conference, the major monuments of this area and period from the tenth to the seventh millennia BCE, such as the temples of Göbekli Tepe (Schmidt 2006), the towers of Jericho (Kenyon 1981) and of Tell Qaramel (Mazurowski 2004), the large circular buildings at Jerf el Ahmar (Stordeur 2000) and the Skull Building of Çayönü (Özdoğan and Özdoğan 1998; Özdoğan 2002), indicate collective rituals. There is little clear evidence of concentrations of power that depend on or are related to the control of production. (Differences between parts of the settlement at Çayönü (Özdoğan and Özdoğan 1998) perhaps offer an exception.)

To the west of Çatalhöyük, there is less evidence for large-scale rituals, temples, or religious monuments. Indeed, early Neolithic sites to the west of Çatalhöyük are more similar to Çatalhöyük in that the symbolism is often house-based and associated with clearly egalitarian villages. These societies had a fully fledged agriculture in which domestic cattle and sheep played key roles, allowing smaller-scale societies to spread over a diversity of environmental zones. It seems that the shifts made at Çatalhöyük around 6500 BCE contributed to the ability of societies to break out of "history making" toward more flexible and individual house-based production.

From Instrumental Function to Material Vitality

We had started with an expectation that religion and ritual at Çatalhöyük would be linked in some way to the control of production and the attainment of power and property. As we worked through the data it became clear that, while religion was embedded in many components of social and economic life and played important roles in establishing links between individuals and communities, it could not be explained in such instrumentalist terms. Religion and ritual may have been transformed in different contexts, but they seemed to have a potent force that could not be explained functionally. The distinctive symbolic elaboration at Çatalhöyük, the intense use of human and animal skulls and body parts, the complex art and architectural elaboration all had social functions that varied through time. And yet questions remained as to why and how material symbols could have played these roles. Rather than being produced by society and economy, the religious symbolism seemed to have a force of its own that required it to be drawn into social, economic, and political life. Rather than there being any evidence for a separate religious sphere at Çatalhöyük, religion seemed to have been an ever-present aspect of life linked to important objects such as human skulls, bull horns, leopards, and vultures.

The Templeton group thus found itself taking different routes. One route, dominant in the papers in the first part of the volume, explores the cognitive and evolutionary aspects of religion in its relation to other aspects of life. In these contributions religion is seen as a vital aspect of being human, and this vital component of life is seen as including cognitive and universalist dimensions. A second route, dominant in the second part of the volume, explores the specific ways in which many material things at Çatalhöyük had a vitality that was productive of social life and necessary to it. The materiality of Çatalhöyük seemed composed of substances and surfaces that were vital to the conduct of the inhabitants of this settlement. Thus the term "vital" in the subtitle of this book has a dual meaning, one related to the ways in which religion is a vital and universal part of being human, and the other to the ways in which matter appears to humans to have agency of a spiritual or religious kind. These two senses of the word are closely connected. As Guthrie notes succinctly in Chapter 4, "The collective vitality that many scholars of Çatalhöyük ascribe to [the] world ... is a universal human phenomenon." Or as Whitehouse et al., note in Chapter 6, the "two aspects of religion are intimately interconnected – stripped of its vitality religion's social functions could hardly be fulfilled."

In the concluding chapter in this volume I will summarize some of the main themes that have emerged in these papers regarding the ways in which vital matter plays a role in producing the sacred in the midst of daily life. Some authors in this volume (in Part 1) explore this question through an evolutionary perspective, asking whether religion is an evolutionary adaptation related to reproductive fitness, or whether it is a by-product of various cognitive capacities of the human mind (such as an overactive human tendency to detect agency). Other authors (in Part 2) take a more contextualist perspective and explore the varieties of ways in which substances are experienced as having vital force.

Aims of the Book

The aims of this book are threefold. First, the book contributes to contemporary debates in archaeology and the social sciences about "materiality" – the ways in which, for humans, matter comes to have agentful power. Many authors, often influenced by Gell (1998), have explored the ways in which things appear to have a sort of agency: not the primary agency of conscious human intentionality, but a secondary agency given to things by humans (Robb 2005; Dobres and Robb 2000). Spiritual and other forms of presence, almost by definition, need things to exist and flow through (Miller 2010). There is much recent work that explores how materials are construed in different social settings (e.g., Meskell 2005a, b) and historical contexts (Joyce 1998, 2000, 2005; Pauketat 2001, 2007; Pels 2008). Things, matter, fluids – all these are construed differently in different historical contexts. The study of materiality explores these cultural relationships, and the biographies of objects are pursued through varying social contexts (Keane 2003; Pels 2008). Following authors such as Georg Simmel, who argued (1979: 65) that "subject and object are born in the same act," Meskell (2004: 7) notes how in Egypt past and present "persons exist and are constituted by their material world: subjects and objects could be said to be mutually fashioning and dependent." As Johnson (2010: 264) notes, materiality includes "the proposition that things create people as much as people create things."

   This volume results from a concerted effort by a distinguished interdisciplinary group of scholars to work through ideas about materiality in the context of a single site. The result is a nuanced and multidimensional account that refracts the concept of materiality through a number of different perspectives. Materiality comes into view as radically diverse and relational, and recent developments are included such as the "vibrant matter" discussed by, for example, Jane Bennett (in her 2010 book subtitled *The Political Ecology of Things*), who argues that matter is not inert but actively engages humans in the production of life.

The second aim of the book is to contribute to wider discussions of religion. The earlier Templeton volume (Hodder 2010) discussed the ways in which archaeologists can identify religion at the same time that it critiqued many established definitions of the term. That volume recognized the dangers in using the term "religion" at all but in the end defined it as a dimension of social life dealing with the marked and transcendent. Religion often has little to do with belief and doctrine and more to do with embodied practices. But the earlier volume paid scant attention to the ways in which religions emerge and change or how they make use of material culture in those changes. Religion had a diversity of functions at Çatalhöyük. It was vital for the development of settled life because it created the sociality that was needed for village life, because it gave humans the authority to intercede in the natural and social world in order to domesticate plants and animals, and because it helped to create the time depth that was needed to support the long-term investments that are the hallmarks of agriculture (Bloch 2010). But religion cannot be fully explained by these functions. It is also a vital and necessary part of what it is to be human, a cognitive and emotional by-product of human interactions with the world.

The third aim is to showcase some remarkably innovative new interpretations of the site of Çatalhöyük. The experiment of assembling a large cadre of interdisciplinary scholars at the site itself aimed to open up debate and to broaden interpretive horizons. In this way the project has been successful, as many new interpretations have emerged as a result of the Templeton projects at Çatalhöyük. The new interpretations involve the role of vital matter as a religious force. As the chapters in this volume demonstrate, there are many ways in which houses and the materials within them seemed to have vital lives that interacted with humans and other things across the community. The vital matter in houses created sodalities (Mills Chapter 7) and histories (Whitehouse et al., Chapter 6). In contrast to most interpretations of Neolithic societies it is clear that the houses at Çatalhöyük did not represent biological kin groups (Pilloud and Larsen 2011). Rather they were machines vital for creating social relations between people: the wall surfaces were involved in the interactions between persons (Buchli Chapter 11), and

Kamerman (Chapter 12) argues that two of the most distinctive symbols at the site, the leopard and the bear, drew people into transcendent relations. These radical new perspectives derive from the close interactions of an interdisciplinary group and they offer new avenues for the interpretation of early societies in the Middle East and Europe.

This volume differs from the previous volume (Hodder 2010) in a number of ways. As already noted, it deals more with change – that is with long-term evolutionary change, but also with change during the occupation of the site. The previous volume had represented Çatalhöyük as rather static and stable, and this interpretation turns out to be incorrect. The volume also differs in being more archaeological. More of the authors are archaeologists and many of the authors from other disciplines engage very thoroughly with the archaeological data from the site. The volume also has a greater focus on materiality and the vitality of things in contrast to the earlier volume, which focused more on definitions of religion and on how religious practices could be observed at Çatalhöyük. Overall, the papers in the new volume are less diverted by issues of definition and abstract theorizing about the nature of religion and come to grips more with how religion actually had force in these early societies.

Organization of the Book

After this Introduction, the book is divided into two main parts. The first part describes the organization of Çatalhöyük and its ritual and symbolic components in relation to wider themes regarding the evolution of human religious capacities. Chapters in this part describe the organization of the site in comparison to other Neolithic sites in the Levant (Goring-Morris and Belfer-Cohen). The papers by van Huyssteen, Shults, and Guthrie situate Çatalhöyük within a longer-term evolutionary framework and show that the data from the site can be used to address broader issues – such as the relations between the self and religion, between religion and anthropomorphism, and between religion and sociality. An underlying and foundational question is whether religion can be explained in evolutionary adaptational terms or whether it should be understood as a by-product of other cognitive capacities. More specific social evolutionary processes are explored by Whitehouse et al. with regard to changes in modes of religiosity.

The second part of the book explores the role of vital materials in the production and transformation of society at Çatalhöyük. The chapter by Mills focuses on the comparison of village societies in the Neolithic Middle East and the ethnohistoric Southwest in order to examine how networks of objects and rituals actively created communities of practice at Çatalhöyük. The chapter by Nakamura and Pels shows how social materials obtain their significance by the way they punctuate the social process and create temporalities, while the particular case of the burial discussed by Patton and Hager leads to discussion of how death at childbirth seems to have become drawn into a broader temporal and religious field. Weismantel examines the material vitality of the house at Çatalhöyük in terms of the construction of "dividual" persons, partible and embodied within the walls of the building. For Buchli it is more the surfaces of things that are important in linking persons and things in powerful combinations, often crossing material registers. Kamerman, too, in her chapter, shows how the decoration and inscription of surfaces create complex relations and intersections within the social fabric.

A final chapter summarizes the substantive results of the project in terms of its aims and in terms of its impact on the understanding of the development of settled life in the Middle East. The chapter also includes comments from the project participants on the scholarly and intellectual process involved in this interdisciplinary experiment. In particular, the participants comment on their responses to the process of engagement with archaeological data "at the trowel's edge" at Çatalhöyük, and on how their views changed as a result. The archaeological data, too, seemed to have a vitality that engaged with and affected the project participants in novel and unexpected ways, and notions of "assemblage" seem relevant to the ways in which knowledge was produced in the interdisciplinary group.

Acknowledgments

I am very grateful to the John Templeton Foundation for their support of the project on which this book is based, and to the participants in the project who so willingly took on such an unusual task. I am also grateful to all the members of the Çatalhöyük Research Project, on whose long years of research this project was able to build, and in particular to Shahina Farid. Several anonymous reviewers provided helpful suggestions, and I am grateful to Lynn Meskell for her advice and guidance.

BIBLIOGRAPHY

Baird, D. 2002. Early Holocene settlement in Central Anatolia: Problems and prospects as seen from the Konya Plain. In *The Neolithic of Central Anatolia. Internal Developments and External Relations during the 9th-6th Millennia cal BC, Proceedings of the International CANeW Round Table, Istanbul 23–24 November 2001*, eds. Gérard, F. and Thissen, L. Ege Yayınları. Istanbul 139–152.

    2007. Pınarbaşı: From Epipalaeolithic camp site to sedentarising village in central Anatolia. In *The Neolithic in Turkey: New Excavations and New Discoveries*, eds. M. Özdoğan and N. Başgelen. Istanbul: Arkeoloji ve Sanat Yayınları, 285 – 311.

    2008. The Boncuklu project: The origins of sedentism, cultivation and herding in central Anatolia. *Anatolian Archaeology*, 14: 11–12.

Banning, E. B. and Byrd, B. F. 1987. Houses and the changing residential unit: Domestic architecture at PPNB 'Ain Ghazal, Jordan. *Proceedings of the Prehistoric Society* 53: 309–325.

Belfer-Cohen, A. 1995. Rethinking social stratification in the Natufian culture: The evidence from burials. In *The Archaeology of Death in the Ancient near East* eds. S. Campbell and A. Green, pp. 9–16. Oxbow Monograph 51, Oxford: Oxbow.

Belfer-Cohen, A. and Ofer Bar Yosef. 2000. Early sedentism in the Near East: A bumpy ride to village life. In *Life in Neolithic Farming Communities: Social Organization, Identity, and Differentiation*, ed. Ian Kuijt. New York: Kluwer Academic/Plenum, 19–38.

Bennett, J. 2010. *Vibrant Matter: A Political Ecology of Things*. Durham, NC: Duke University Press.

Bender, B. 1978. Gatherer-hunter to farmer: A social perspective. *World Archaeology* 10:204–222.

Bloch, M. 2010. Is there religion at Çatalhöyük…. or are there just houses? In *Religion in the Emergence of Civilization. Çatalhöyük As a Case Study* ed. I. Hodder. 146–162. Cambridge: Cambridge University Press.

Bogaard, A., Charles, M., Livarda, A., Ergun, M., Filipovic, D. and Jones, G. 2013. The archaeobotany of mid-later Neolithic Çatalhöyük. In *Humans and Landscapes of Çatalhöyük: Reports from the 2000–2008 seasons*, ed. I. Hodder. Los Angeles: Cotsen Institute.

Boz, B. and Hager, L. 2013. Intramural burial practices at Çatalhöyük. In *Humans and Landscapes of Çatalhöyük: Reports from the 2000–2008 Seasons* (ed) I. Hodder. Los Angeles: Cotsen Institute.

Byrd, B. 1994. Public and Private, Domestic and Corporate: The Emergence of the Southwest Asian Village. *American Antiquity* 59:639–666.

Byrd, B. and C. M. Monahan. 1995. Death, Mortuary Rituals and Natufian Social Structure. *Journal of Anthropological Archaeology* 14:251–287.

Cauvin, J. 1994. *Naissance des divinités, Naissance de l'agriculture*, Paris: CNRS.

Cessford C. 2005a. Absolute dating at Çatalhöyük. In *Changing Materialities at Çatalhöyük: Reports from the 1995 – 1999 Seasons*, ed. I Hodder, pp. 65 – 100. Cambridge, UK: McDonald Inst. Archaeol. Res./Br. Inst. Archaeol. Ankara Monogr.

Cessford, C. 2005b. Estimating the Neolithic population of Çatalhöyük. In *Inhabiting Çatalhöyük: Reports from the 1995–1999 Seasons*, ed. I. Hodder Cambridge: McDonald Institute for Archaeological Research/British Institute of Archaeology at Ankara Monograph.

Dobres, M. A. and J. Robb (eds.) 2000. *Agency in Archaeology*. London: Routledge.

Duru, R. 1999. The Neolithic of the Lake District. In *Neolithic in Turkey: The Cradle of Civilization. New Discoveries*, eds. M. Özdoğan and N. Başgelen Istanbul: Arkeoloji ve Sanat Yayınları 165–191.

Düring, B. S. 2006. *Constructing Communities: Clustered Neighbourhood Settlements of the Central Anatolian Neolithic, ca. 8500–5500 Cal. BC.* Leiden: Nederlands Instituut voor het Nabije Oosten.

Esin, U. and Harmanakaya, S. 1999. Aşıklı in the frame of Central Anatolian Neolithic. In *Neolithic in Turkey: The Cradle of Civilization. New Discoveries*, eds. M. Özdoğan and N. Başgelen Istanbul: Arkeoloji ve Sanat Yayınları 115–132.

Farid, S. 2007. Level IX relative heights, Building 2, Buildings 22 & 16 and Building 17. In *Excavating Çatalhöyük: South, North and KOPAL Area Reports from the 1995–1999 Seasons*, ed. I. Hodder. British Institute of Archaeology at Ankara Monographs. Cambridge: McDonald Institute for Archaeological Research, 139–226.

Farid, S. 2013. Buildings 51 and 52. In *Çatalhöyük Excavations: The 2000–2008 Seasons*, ed. I. Hodder. Los Angeles: Cotsen Institute.

Flannery, K. 1972. The origins of the village as a settlement type in Mesoamerica and the Near East: A comparative study. In *Man, Settlement and Urbanism*, edited by Peter Ucko, Ruth Tringham, and Geoffrey Dimbleby, pp. 23–53. Duckworth, London.

Flannery, K. 1993. Will the Real Model Please Stand up: Comments on Saidel's "Round House or Square?" *Journal of Mediterranean Archaeology* 6:109–117.

Gell, A. 1998. *Art and Agency*. Oxford: Clarendon.

Gérard, F. and Thissen, L. 2002. *The Neolithic of Central Anatolia. Internal Developments and External Relations during the 9th-6th Millennia CAL BC*, Istanbul: Ege Yayınları.

Goring-Morris, N. 2000. The quick and the dead: The social context of Aceramic Neolithic mortuary practices as seen from Kfar HaHoresh. In *Life in Neolithic Farming Communities: Social Organization, Identity, and*

Differentiation, ed. Ian Kuijt. Kluwer Academic/Plenum Publishers, New York, 13–36.

Hayden, B. 1990. Nimrods, piscators, pluckers, and planters: The emergence of food production. *Journal of Anthropological Archaeology* 9(1), 31–69.

Hodder, I. ed. 1996. *On the Surface. Çatalhöyük 1993–95,* Cambridge: McDonald Institute for Archaeological Research/British Institute of Archaeology at Ankara Monograph.

2000. *Towards Reflexive Method in Archaeology: The Example at Çatalhöyük,* Cambridge: McDonald Institute for Archaeological Research/British Institute of Archaeology at Ankara Monograph.

2005a. *Inhabiting Çatalhöyük: Reports from the 1995–1999 Seasons,* Cambridge: McDonald Institute for Archaeological Research/British Institute of Archaeology at Ankara Monograph.

2005b. *Changing Materialities at Çatalhöyük: Reports from the 1995–1999 Seasons,* Cambridge: McDonald Institute for Archaeological Research/ British Institute of Archaeology at Ankara Monograph.

2005c. *Çatalhöyük Perspectives: Themes from the 1995–1999 Seasons,* Cambridge: McDonald Institute for Archaeological Research/British Institute of Archaeology at Ankara Monograph.

2006. *The Leopard's Tale: Revealing the Mysteries of Çatalhöyük,* London: Thames and Hudson.

2007. *Excavating Çatalhöyük: Reports from the 1995–1999 Seasons,* Cambridge: McDonald Institute for Archaeological Research/British Institute of Archaeology at Ankara Monograph.

2010. *Religion in the Emergence of Civilization. Çatalhöyük As a Case Study.* Cambridge: Cambridge University Press.

Hodder, I. 2013. The social geography of Çatalhöyük. In *Integrating Çatalhöyük: Themes from the 2000–2008 seasons,* ed. I. Hodder. Los Angeles: Cotsen Institute.

Hodder, I. and Pels, P. 2010. History houses: A new interpretation of architectural elaboration at Çatalhöyük. In *Religion in the Emergence of Civilization. Çatalhöyük as a Case Study,* ed. I. Hodder. 163–186. Cambridge: Cambridge University Press.

Hole, F. 2000. Is size important? Function and hierarchy in Neolithic settlements. In *Life in Neolithic Farming Communities. Social Organization, Identity, and Differentiation,* ed. Ian Kuijt. New York: Kluwer Academic/ Plenum, 191–210.

Johnson, M. 2010. *Archaeological Theory: An Introduction.* Oxford: Wiley-Blackwell.

Joyce, R. A. 1998. Performing the body in prehispanic Central America. *Res* 33:147–165.

2000. Girling the girl and boying the boy: The production of adulthood in ancient Mesoamerica. *World Archaeology* 31:473–483.

2005. Archaeology of the body. *Annual Review of Anthropology* 34:139–158.

Keane, W. 2003. Self-interpretation, agency, and the objects of anthropology: Reflections on a genealogy. *Studies in Society and History* 45(2):222–248.

Kenyon KM. 1981. *Excavations at Jericho.* Vol. 3: *The Architecture and Stratigraphy of the Tell.* London: Br. Sch. Archaeol. Jerus.

Kuijt, I. ed. 2000. *Life in Neolithic Farming Communities: Social Organization, Identity, and Differentiation,* New York: Kluwer Academic/Plenum.

2008. The Regeneration of Life: Neolithic Structures of Symbolic Remembering and Forgetting. *Current Anthropology* 49(2):171–197.

Hillson, S. W., Larsen, C. S., Boz, B., Pilloud, M. A., Sadvari, J. W., Agarway, S. C., Glencross, B., Beauchesne, P., Pearson, J., Ruff, C. B., Garofalo, E. M., Hager, L. D. and Haddow, S. C. 2013. The human remains I: Interpreting community structure, health and diet in Neolithic Çatalhöyük. In *Humans and Landscapes of Çatalhöyük: Reports from the 2000–2008 seasons,* ed. I. Hodder. Los Angeles: Cotsen Institute.

Love, S. 2013. An archaeology of mud-brick houses. In *Substantive technologies at Çatalhöyük: Reports from the 2000–2008 seasons* ed. I. Hodder. Los Angeles: Cotsen Institute.

Mazurowski, R. F. 2004. Tell Qaramel excavations 2003. *Polish Archaeology in the Mediterranean* 15:355–370.

Mazzucato, C. 2013. Sampling and mapping Çatalhöyük. In *Humans and Landscapes of Çatalhöyük: Reports from the 2000–2008 seasons,* ed. I. Hodder. Los Angeles: Cotsen Institute.

Mellaart, J. 1967. *Çatal Hüyük: A Neolithic Town in Anatolia,* London: Thames and Hudson.

Meskell, L. 2004. *Object Worlds in Ancient Egypt: Material Biographies Past and Present.* Oxford: Berg.

2005a. *Archaeologies of Materiality.* Oxford: Wiley Blackwell.

2005b Introduction: Object orientations. In *Archaeologies of Materiality,* ed. L. Meskell. Oxford: Wiley Blackwell, 1–17.

Miller, D. 2010. *Stuff.* Cambridge: Polity Press.

Mithen, S. 2003. *After the Ice: A Global Human History, 20,000–5000 BC,* London: Weidenfeld and Nicolson.

Nakamura, C. and Meskell, L. 2013a. Burial associations. In *Humans and Landscapes of Çatalhöyük: Reports from the 2000–2008 seasons,* ed. I. Hodder. Los Angeles: Cotsen Institute.

2013b. Figurines. In *Substantive Technologies at Çatalhöyük: Reports from the 2000–2008 Seasons,* ed. I. Hodder. Los Angeles: Cotsen Institute.

Özdoğan, M. and Özdoğan, A. 1998. Buildings of cult and the cult of buildings. In *Light on Top of the Black Hill: Studies Presented to Halet Cambel,* eds. G. Arsebük, M. Mellink and W. Schirmer. Istanbul: Ege Yayinlari 581–593.

Özdoğan, M. 2002. Defining the Neolithic of Central Anatolia. In *The Neolithic of Central Anatolia. Internal Developments and External Relations during the 9th-6th Millennia cal BC, Proceedings of the International CANeW Round Table, Istanbul 23–24 November 2001*, eds. F. Gérard and L. Thissen. Istanbul: Ege Yayınları 253–261.

Özkaya, V. and Coşkun 2011. Körtik Tepe. In *The Neolithic in Turkey*, eds. M. Özdoğan, N. Başgelen and P. Kuniholm. Istanbul: Archaeology and Art, 89–127.

Pauketat, T. R. 2001. Practice and history in archaeology. An emerging paradigm. *Anthropological Theory* 1:73–98.

2007. *Chiefdoms and Other Archaeological Delusions.* Lanham, MD: AltaMira.

Pels, P. 2008. The modern fear of matter: Reflections on the Protestantism of Victorian science. *Material Religion* 4(3):264–283.

Pilloud, M. A. and Larsen, C. S. 2011. 'Official' and 'practical' kin: Inferring social and community structure from dental phenotype at Neolithic Çatalhöyük, Turkey. *American Journal of Physical Anthropology.* http://onlinelibrary. wiley.com/doi/10.1002/ajpa.21520/abstract. Accessed 24 June 2011.

Regan, R. and Taylor, J. 2013. The sequence of Buildings 75, 65, 56, 69, 44 and 10 and external Spaces 119, 129, 130, 144, 299, 314, 319, 329, 333, 339, 367, 372 and 427. In *Çatalhöyük Excavations: The 2000–2008 Seasons*, ed. I. Hodder. Los Angeles: Cotsen Institute.

Robb, J. E. 2005. The extended artifact and the monumental economy. In, *Rethinking Materiality: The Engagement of Mind with the Material World*, eds. E. DeMarrais, C. Gosden, and C. Renfrew. Cambridge: McDonald Institute for Archaeological Research. 131–139.

Rollefson, G. O. 1984. ʿAin Ghazal: An Early Neolithic Community in Highland Jordan, near Amman. *Bulletin of the American Schools of Oriental Research* 255:3–14.

Rosenberg M, Redding, R. W. 2000. Hallan Çemi and early village organization in eastern Anatolia. In *Life in Neolithic Farming Communities: Social Organization, Identity, and Differentiation*, ed. I Kuijt. New York: Kluwer Academic/Plenum, 39 – 61.

Schmidt, K. 2001. Göbekli Tepe, Southeastern Turkey: A preliminary report on the 1995–1999 excavations. *Paléorient* 26(1):45–54.

2006. *Sie bauten die Ersten Tempel*, Munich: Beck.

Simmel, G. 1979. *The Philosophy of Money.* Boston: Routledge and Kegan Paul.

Stordeur D. 2000. New Discoveries in Architecture and Symbolism at Jerf el Ahmar (Syria), 1997 – 1999. *Neo-Lithics* 1/00:1 – 4.

Tung, B. 2013. Building with mud: An analysis of architectural materials at Çatalhöyük. In *Substantive technologies at Çatalhöyük: Reports from the 2000–2008 seasons*, ed. I. Hodder. Los Angeles: Cotsen Institute.

Watkins, T. 2008. Supra-Regional Networks in the Neolithic of Southwest Asia. *Journal of World Prehistory* 21:139–171.

Wright, G. A. 1978. Social differentiation in the Early Natufian. In *Social Archaeology, Beyond Subsistence and Dating*, eds. Charles Redman, M. J.

Berman, E. V. Curtin, W. T. Langhorne Jr., N. M. Versaggi and J. C. Wanser. New York: Academic Press, 201–223.

Wright, H., ed., 1984. *On the Evolution of Complex Societies.* Malibu, CA: Undeena.

Zeder, M. 2011. The Origins of Agriculture in the near East. *Current Anthropology* 52:S221–S235.

PART I

VITAL RELIGION: THE EVOLUTIONARY CONTEXT OF RELIGION AT ÇATALHÖYÜK

2

Different Strokes for Different Folks: Near Eastern Neolithic Mortuary Practices in Perspective

Nigel Goring-Morris and Anna Belfer-Cohen

Introduction

How can one begin to address the questions pertinent to the ongoing discussion on religion, property, and power at early Neolithic Çatalhöyük? It seems that a productive avenue is to stand back and consider how Çatalhöyük integrates within the broader perspective of Southwest Asian (Near Eastern) Neolithization processes. Nevertheless, such an effort with regard to every aspect of human existence is a mighty endeavor, and certainly well beyond the scope of a single article, not to mention the humble competence of its authors. Given the special nature and prominence of burials at Çatalhöyük, we have chosen to focus specifically on that aspect of community behavior. We shall provide a background based on data from earlier periods within the broader region of Southwest Asia (the Near East), and most especially the southern Levant.

Burial practices are generally considered to reflect aspects of the symbolic/spiritual worldview of the populations involved. It has often been suggested that with the advent of sedentism and the beginnings of agricultural production (plant and animal domestication) there were significant changes in social organization and cohesion. Yet from the very beginning of our essay, we can state that the description of burial practices from the Late Epipaleolithic Natufian (as well as the scarce earlier evidence) through the Pre-Pottery Neolithic A (PPNA) (and even Pre-Pottery Neolithic B [PPNB] and later) in the southern Levant indicates "business as usual," in the sense that we can observe the same marked variability (of the same components more or less) continuing unchanged all through the period considered as revolutionary, encompassing changing paradigmatic worldviews. We shall attempt to relate

to this issue of variability in the discussion following the presentation
of the data.

Burial Practices in the Southern Levant (Terminal Pleistocene/ Early Holocene)

THE EPIPALEOLITHIC

Following virtually nonexistent evidence for burial practices during the
Upper Paleolithic (Belfer-Cohen and Goring-Morris in 2013a), the
number of documented burials increased during the Early and Middle
Epipaleolithic (starting at ca. 22,000 up to ca. 15,000 years cal BP). These
were mostly single, primary burials, in shallow pits. However, as data
accrue it is becoming increasingly clear that there is some degree of variability, foreshadowing that observed in the following Late Epipaleolithic
(ca. 15,000 up to 11,500 years cal BP), Natufian entity. At Ein Gev I the
inhumation is located below the floor of a *fond de cabane*, while at Ohalo
II the burial is located away from the huts (Arensburg and Bar-Yosef
1973; Hershkowitz et al. 1995). Though most of the burials are single
and extended (e.g., Ohalo II, Wadi Mataha – Hershkowitz et al. 1995;
Stock et al. 2005), there are also other positions, for example, the sitting
burial from Early Epipaleolithic Ain Qassiya (Richter et al. 2010) and
the flexed burial, among the extended ones, at the Middle Epipaleolithic
cemetery at 'Uyyun al-Hammam (Wadi Ziqlab 148) (Maher et al. 2011).
From the Middle Epipaleolithic there is some evidence for marking of
the grave by the placement of stone mortars/bowls on top of the burials, as at Neve David (Bocquentin et al. 2011) and Wadi Mataha (Stock
et al. 2005; and see later discussion). At the 'Uyyun al-Hammam (Wadi
Ziqlab 148) cemetery most graves were of single individuals with no
grave goods, but at least one grave contained the remains of two individuals, and a couple of burials included intentionally deposited animal
remains, most spectacularly, those of a fox – until recently considered a
uniquely Natufian characteristic, and see later discussion (Maher et al.
2011). A polished pebble is reported from the single burial at Moghr al-
Awal in the Lebanese mountains (Garrard and Yazbeck 2003). Of interest
are the Early Epipaleolithic burned human remains from Kebara Cave;
deriving from Turville-Petre's (1932) excavation in the 1920's, these
were long thought to be Natufian, yet both detailed osteological studies (Smith 1972) as well as 14C dates obtained much later on the bones

themselves indicate that these burned skeletons (N = 23) more likely relate to the earlier, Kebaran Epipaleolithic levels (Bar-Yosef and Sillen 1993). Unfortunately, no data are available as regards the interment details there, that is, position, single or multiple, and so on. Whatever the case, cremation has not been documented elsewhere in the Levant during the Epipaleolithic and Neolithic (but see Wadi Hammeh 27 during the early Natufian) (Webb and Edwards 2002).

The shift to the Late Epipaleolithic Natufian complex coincides with evidence for larger, more permanent settlements, especially in the Mediterranean zone (Belfer-Cohen and Goring-Morris 2013b). Recently, with advances in radiometric calibration, the duration of the Natufian has been extended significantly (at least thirty-five hundred years), and differentiation between the Early and Late phases relates also to the nature and patterning of the burials. A significant increase in the numbers of burials as compared to the preceding period is indicated by the approximately four hundred fifty Natufian individuals identified to date. This actually reflects the fact that burials become an integral part of the Natufian social identity (and see discussion later). Burials become incorporated within settlements, both inside and outside structures (residential or other), for example, at Hayonim Cave (Belfer-Cohen 1988), as well as in areas specifically designated as burial grounds or cemeteries, such as at Nahal Oren (Stekelis and Yizraeli 1963), or even more obviously at Hilazon Cave (Grosman, Munro, and Belfer-Cohen 2008). In certain cases the burials were marked, whether by breached basalt mortars incorporated in the grave as at Nahal Oren (Stekelis and Yizraeli 1963), or with cup-marked slabs, or with both, as at Hayonim Cave and Raqefet Cave (Belfer-Cohen 1988; Nadel et al. 2008, 2009).

Natufian graves comprise interments in every imaginable combination, including single and multiple burials (of various ages and genders), primary and secondary, sometimes together, and in a wide array of burial positions (Belfer-Cohen 1988, 1995; Bocquentin 2003; Webb and Edwards 2002; Garrod 1936–1937; Garrod and Bate 1937; Lengyel and Bocquentin 2005; Perrot and Ladiray 1988 and references therein). Graves with primary burials were sometimes reopened, and certain skeletal parts, mostly the skull and limbs, were removed to be interred elsewhere; such practices clearly reflect considerable manipulation of the human remains, as illustrated by some primary burials missing parts of the skeleton (and not simply as a consequence of taphonomic factors), accompanied by secondary burials, comprising but limbs (sometimes still articulated), and skulls. Through the course of the period both extended and flexed burials are documented, with a greater emphasis upon extended burials during the Early Natufian. It is of interest to note that tightly flexed, contracted burials are more common in the Late/ Final Natufian. These are commonly considered to represent burials that were moved from some distance away to be interred in sacks or bundles, at "sanctioned" sites, such as Ain el-Saratan (Azraq 18) and Eynan (Garrard 1991; Perrot and Ladiray 1988). Some of the burials at various sites were "pinned down" (literally and figuratively) by large stones, sometimes crushing the skeleton. On other occasions stones were placed on both sides of the head to hold it in place, for example, H15 at Eynan and H2 at Raqefet (Lengyel and Bocquentin 2005; Nadel et al. 2008; Perrot and Ladiray 1988). Approximately 10 percent of the burials – all, but with rare, and often controversial exceptions, being assigned to the Early Natufian phase – are decorated (Belfer-Cohen 1995). The decorated specimens are of different ages (from children to adults), and of all sexes. There are also significant contrasts in the intensity of decoration, ranging from single beads up to lavish adornments.

Although there is some evidence for local mortuary patterns in the nature and form of the decorative elements represented – that is, the beads and pendants, mostly shaped of bone, teeth, and shells – they differ from one site to the other; for instance, dentalia decorated caps and headbands are reported only from el-Wad (Garrod 1936–1937). Yet these local, sometimes site-specific patterns are never exclusive; for instance, beads of a variety dominant at one site are found in only single numbers in another, such as Eynan versus Hayonim (Belfer-Cohen and Goring-Morris 2013b). Other "grave-goods" sometimes comprise unique bone and stone tools, whether an elongated spatula/"bone dagger" or large flint bifaces, such as Graves XII, XIII, XVII at Hayonim Cave (Belfer-Cohen 1988, pers. obs.).[1] Notable is the use of ochre daubed on skull bones at Ain el-Saratan and Wadi Hammeh 27, and flowers on burials at Raqefet (Webb and Edwards 2002; Garrard 1991; Nadel et al. 2013). In addition and, most interestingly, there are also parts of animals, such as the tortoise carapaces, as well as the human/ dog burials at el-Wad, Eynan, and Hayonim terrace (Davis and Valla

---

[1] Without going into a discourse of what is meant or considered as "grave-goods."

1978; Garrod and Bate 1937; Perrot and Ladiray 1988; Tchernov and Valla 1997). Here, we should also recall the "shaman" burial of an old woman at Hilazon Cave, where we have an outstanding example of *pars pro toto* – whether through parts of animals or a fragment of a basalt mortar (Grosman, Munro, and Belfer-Cohen 2008). Another instance of animal parts incorporated in a grave are two pairs of gazelle horns, one pair adorning the skull of H25, the upper burial, and the other, found admixed with the disturbed burial of H27 beneath the former in Locus 10, Eynan (Perrot and Ladiray 1988). It should also be stressed that there are instances of isolated human remains outside obvious grave contexts, such as a calvaria "chalice" on the floor of Locus 131 at Eynan, together with half a mandible of a fox (Perrot and Ladiray 1988), or scattered skull fragments, some with evidence of burning at Wadi Hammeh 27 (Webb and Edwards 2002). Such remains indicate most clearly rituals that were likely part of the mortuary practices taking place on-site. At Raqefet the possible presence of a "perishable" cushion to support the head of H17 (Nadel et al. 2009: 45) may presage more common "pillowing" during the PPNA (see later discussion).

Last, but by no means least, in terms of Natufian mortuary practices is the tradition of postmortem skull removal.[2] This long-lasting tradition, which was never ubiquitous, was already sporadically documented during the Early Natufian. The skulls appear both as single items, such as H37, as opposed to the cache of eight skulls in Tomb 9 at Eynan (Perrot and Ladiray 1988). In addition there is considerable evidence for skulls being modified, for example, H102 on the floor of Locus 131 at Eynan (perhaps used as a chalice?) (Perrot and Ladiray 1988) and/or burned, as at Wadi Hammeh 27 (Webb and Edwards 2002). At some Late/Final Natufian sites, though, all burials retain their skulls, as at Raqefet Cave (Nadel et al. 2009). However, recent claims (Valla et al. 2010) for a complete absence of skull removal in the Final Natufian phase at Eynan are problematic, in light of both Perrot's previous observations (Perrot and Ladiray 1988), as well as Valla et al.'s descriptions of the human remains they recovered.

Within and associated with graves there is evidence for feasting. The most detailed account available to date derives from the Late/Final Natufian cemetery site of Tachtit, where species representation and

---

[2] Here it is important to differentiate between the terms "decapitation" and "postmortem skull removal."

contextual associations are interpreted as indications for feasting on both
aurochs and tortoise (Grosman and Munro 2007; Munro and Grosman
2010). Of interest to note is the interpretation given to the "stone pipes"
(breached mortars) incorporated within graves at the Late Natufian cemetery of Nahal Oren as ways to channel libations to the dead (Stekelis and
Yizraeli 1963). Yet, in general, the direct evidence for feasting during the
Natufian is rather meager (Hayden 2011); it is mostly based on concentrations of bones within confined localities, such as the bird bones from
the two constructed hearths within Locus 131 at Eynan (Valla 1988), or
in the shear amount of bones within the occupational level in general as
well as the presence of large hearths, as at Nahal Oren (Goring-Morris
and Belfer-Cohen 2011).

THE PPNA

Relatively few PPNA (ca. 11,500–10, 500 years cal BP) sites provide reliable data about mortuary practices; this stems to a large degree from issues
associated with the history of research. Thus, at Jericho, the site with by far
the greatest number of burials, little attention appears to have been paid to
differentiating between PPNA and PPNB burials (and see Cornwall 1981;
Kenyon 1957; Kurth and Rohrer-Ertl 1981; Kuijt 1995, 1996, 1997).

Generally during the PPNA, the vast majority of burials appear to
have been single, primary, and articulated. However, there are indications that secondary burials may have been present at Jericho as well as
at Netiv Hagdud (Belfer-Cohen et al. 1990; Kenyon 1981). Graves seem
to have been concentrated in the area of the tower at Jericho (perhaps
a sacred precinct), yet elsewhere there is little in the way of evidence for
separate cemetery areas within habitation sites, or as dedicated mortuary
sites. There is also little evidence for grave goods, apart from single finds
reported from various sites (and see later discussion).

At Hatoula, where there are both Khiamian and Sultanian PPNA burials (Le Mort 1994; Le Mort, Hershkovitz, and Spiers 1994), most burials are complete – with but one instance (H04) just a single skull – tightly
flexed or contracted on the stomach or back (but rarely on the side),
and often with stones placed on the joints, for example, Sultanian H08,
comparable to Natufian practices (Le Mort, Hershkovitz, and Spiers
1994). "Pillowed" heads have been observed in five (out of nine) burials at Hatoula (Le Mort 1994) (as well as at Wadi Faynan 16; see later
discussion), again a feature observed first in the Natufian. Grave goods

sometimes comprise single stone beads (in two cases at Hatoula – H07 and H04 – both adult males). There is also an aurochs skull associated with an old female, H09 (Le Mort 1994).

A very different pattern is reflected by the human remains at Netiv Hagdud, notwithstanding the great affinity of various material culture realms to those at Hatoula. Thus at Netiv Hagdud fifteen of twenty-seven individuals have the skull missing, but usually the mandible present; four of the individuals are represented only by the skull and mandible. There are a number of instances of cached skulls, sometimes in pairs. Skull removal was applied to male and female adults and young children (Belfer-Cohen et al. 1990). Furthermore, where the position of the burial could be ascertained, they were contracted on one side (for the others it was not possible to determine the orientation or they are disturbed/secondary burials).

Only preliminary reports are currently available for the PPNA occupation at el-Hemmeh in Transjordan (Makarewicz and Rose 2011). There is evidence for the use of carefully built grave cists/pits in one structure (Structure 6) for primary as well as secondary burials; interestingly, the arms, legs, and torso of a young adult placed in a sitting position in one cist (Feature 14) had been covered with lime or gypsum plaster; a similar position and treatment were afforded to a young child in an adjacent pit (Feature 15).

At Wadi Faynan 16 the total skeletal remains reported to date appear to represent three immature individuals and three adults (Roberts, in Finlayson and Mithen 2007). Detailed examination of the report reveals that only some of them can be treated as burials, while others are represented by single bones or teeth. One grave (Pit 247) is interpreted as a disturbed foundation deposit and included a "mixture of partially articulated, disarticulated and arranged bones" (Finlayson and Mithen, 2007, fig. 6.47), mostly of an adult, but also including the fragmented skull of a seven- to eight-year-old juvenile. The skull of the adult was resting on a stone "pillow." Another burial, undisturbed, is of an articulated and flexed adult, with his skull resting, once again, on a stone "pillow" (Context 332, Finlayson and Mithen, 2007, figs. 6.61, 6.62).

In some sites burials seem to have been rare, and only sporadic remains have been described; such is the case at Abu Madi I, Bir el-Maksur, Nahal Oren, Gilgal, Iraq ed-Dubb, Dhra, and Zahrat ad-Dhra 2 (Edwards et al. 2004; Kuijt 2004; Malinsky-Buller, Aldjem, and Yeshurun 2009; pers.

obs.; Stekelis and Yizraeli 1963).[3] But, inasmuch as they do appear, they accord with the patterns observed in other PPNA sites throughout the southern Levant.

THE PPNB

The PPNB (ca. 10,500 to 8,400 years cal BP) represents the floruit of social developments, including burial practices. The period is of rather a long duration and is subdivided into at least four subperiods, each with its own distinct characteristics. As the numbers of burials and the variety of ways to treat the dead diversified, it is not possible to provide a detailed inventory and description here without vastly exceeding the framework of the current paper. Accordingly, we shall present only a general overview, while emphasizing those points we want to discuss as regards the role of the dead in the world of the living.

Though both PPNB settlements and burial grounds/cemeteries grew in size, it is widely accepted that there are insufficient burials relative to the assumed numbers of inhabitants within villages, the settlement sizes, and the relative areas excavated, such as 'Ain Ghazal and Beidha (Rollefson 2000; Kirkbride 1966). There is, however, some debate as to the nature and locations of supposedly normative PPNB burial practices. Burials do occur within walls and beneath the floors of residential structures (Kuijt 2001; Stordeur and Khawam 2007, 2008), although significant numbers occurred as "trash burials" in pits within open areas (and see Rollefson 2000). There were also obviously special, designated areas at the edges of villages for cultic and/or funerary practices, as at Aswad, Atlit Yam, and Jericho (Galili et al. 2005; Kenyon 1981; Stordeur and Khawam 2008). Additionally, the specific location of some sites as well as contextual evidence indicate that they were designated primarily for ceremonial-cum-burial purposes, such as Nahal Hemar and Kfar HaHoresh (Bar-Yosef and Alon 1988; Goring-Morris 2000, 2005).

Many graves comprise single articulated burials, although multiple primary, as well as multiple secondary, burials are found, including combinations of primary and secondary interments within the same grave. Some of this variability appears to reflect geographical and/or chronological trends; for example, "cist" burials appear to be the norm in

---

[3] At Gilgal a couple of burials (both adult, primary, articulated, with skulls) were recovered in an open area, although these were not reported in the final report (Bar-Yosef, Goring-Morris and Gopher 2010; pers. obs.).

southern Transjordan, as at Shaqaret Msiad and Baja (continuing a tradition first noted at PPNA el-Hemmeh), and southern Sinai, at Ujrat el-Mehed (Gebel, Hermansen, and Kinzel 2006; Hermannsen et al. 2006; Hershkovitz, Bar-Yosef and Arensberg 1998; Kinzel et al. 2011). Indeed, Building F at Shaqaret Msiad is a large (circa seven meters in diameter) circular structure, centrally placed within the settlement, and, although only partially excavated, yielded in excess of fifty-five individuals in stone-lined cists (Kinzel et al. 2011). The structure thus appears to have served as a dedicated charnel house in its later phase – perhaps akin to the memory houses of Çatal (and see discussion later).

Postmortem skull removal continued to be practiced selectively, whether on males, females, adults, or immature individuals. In some instances these skulls were embellished by sophisticated modeling of the facial features or heads, as in 'Ain Ghazal, Aswad, Jericho, Beisamoun, Kfar HaHoresh, Nahal Hemar, and Yiftahel (Goren, Goring-Morris, and Segal 2001; Khalaily et al. 2008; Kuijt 2008; Stordeur and Khawam 2007). After their secondary "death," skulls, modeled or not, were disposed of, sometimes as caches. Although long claimed to be absent, grave goods are present on occasion, whether in the form of beads, pendants, flint artifacts, animal bones, marine molluscs, or other items (Goring-Morris 2000, 2005).

There is continuity from the Natufian in the presence of human/animal associations during the PPNB; sometimes this appears to be in the form of certain specific faunal elements being included within or placed adjacent to graves, as at Kfar HaHoresh, Shaqaret Msiad, and Basta (Becker 2002; Goring-Morris 2005; Goring-Morris et al. 1998; Hermansen et al. 2006; Horwitz and Goring-Morris 2004). In other instances, there are indications that this reflects actual feasting activities (Goring-Morris and Belfer-Cohen 2011; Goring-Morris and Horwitz 2007; Twiss 2008).

Contemporaneous Burials in the Northern Levant

Without providing detailed descriptions of each site, one can state that the mortuary patterns observed in the areas to the south of the Taurus-Zagros (corresponding to the very end of the Natufian, the PPNA, and the PPNB in the south) are broadly similar to those observed and described for the Southern Levant, even though most reports are preliminary and fragmentary. There is considerable variability in the numbers of individuals in different sites, mirroring the situation farther south. Suffice it to note that at Çayönü more than four hundred fifty individuals were counted (Özbeck 1982, 1988; Croucher 2006a, b, 2010, 2012). Indeed, Çayönü is quite unique in that many of the burials are primarily associated with the "skull building," a long-lasting (PPNA–PPNB) special function architectural complex, associated with animal remains including aurochs bucrania. At PPNB Dja'de a charnel house was exposed (Coqueugniot 2008). Furthermore, the human remains in many northern sites comprise burials of both complete skeletons, as well as separate skulls and postcrania, such as the six human crania placed in the northwest half of a "house" at PPNA Qermez Dere (Watkins, Baird and Betts 1989); while at Mureybet in Structure 21 of Level IIIB one may note a skull and long bones burial, together with, a little distance to the east, another burial comprising only the spine, pelvis, chest, and articulated hands and feet (Ibanez 2008).

The reports of all sites with human remains detail variations in the positions of interments: contracted to loosely flexed, on the back, stomach, and side, as at PPNA Nemrik (Kozlowski 2002) and Qaramel (Kanjou 2009). The situation at PPNB Tell Halula is locally unique in the systematic placement of the deceased seated in pits beneath the floors at the front of residential structures (Guerrero et al. 2009; Ortiz, Chambon and Molist 2013). However, the striking similarities in burial practices to those at PPNA el-Hemmeh in Edom, Transjordan, are intriguing (see earlier).

Generally there are few grave goods in most sites, but at PPNA Körtik Tepe on the Tigris the situation is quite different and the majority of burials were interred with numerous grave goods comprising jewelry, decorated and undecorated bone objects, stone figurines, as well as stone vessels, pestles, mace heads, and axes (Özkaya 2009; Özkaya and Coşkun 2009). Additionally, quite a number of burials are covered by fragments of broken stone vessels, which may have been intentionally broken as part of the funerary practices (a variation of an old tradition, and see discussion later).

Furthermore, in the northern areas there are phenomena that have not, to date, been recognized (or only rarely) in the south. These include violence, sometimes on an individual level, as at PPNA Jerf el-Ahmar (Stordeur and Abbès 2002), but sometimes seemingly on a more systematic scale, as at Nemrik (though here it is difficult to distinguish between

PPNA and PPNB and see Kozlowski 2002) and, especially, at Shanidar Cave. In the latter, the "Proto-Neolithic" occupation represents a cemetery site with the remains of twenty-nine individuals (Solecki, Solecki, and Agelarakis 2004). Of interest here is the high number of individuals with evidence of traumatic injuries to the skull, perhaps from mace heads (quite common among the material culture remains).

Another pattern in the north appears to be the ceremonial closure of structures using human burials. This may be the case of the headless skeleton of a circa fifteen- to eighteen-year-old female, sprawled on the floor of the burned communal structure EA 30 at PPNA Jerf el Ahmar (Stordeur and Abbès 2002): speculatively, the young woman had apparently been killed immediately before the structure was intentionally burned, and her head subsequently removed after the roof had collapsed. A similar situation may be indicated by a tightly contracted burial used for the "closure" of the lowermost "kiva-type structure" in the PPNA levels of Dja'de (Coqueugniot 2008, 2013).

Gypsum plaster was smeared on many of the skeletons at PPNA Körtik Tepe (Özkaya 2009; Özkaya and Coşkun 2009) – this practice occurs later, during the PPNB at Tell abu Hureyra (Moore, Hillman, and Legge 2000), and perhaps presages the practices at Tell Sabi Abyad (Akkermans 1996; and see discussion for comparisons with the southern Levant). Several skulls at Körtik Tepe display parallel bands of red and black pigments. Such color traces are also seen on grave goods; this is interpreted by the excavator as evidence for several stages of treatment of the dead, as first they were interred; later, after defleshing (natural or intentional), covered with plaster; and then painted (Özkaya 2009). Red coloring is implied also in Çayönü in the form of red ochre pieces scattered over and besides the burials (Croucher 2006a, b).

Discussion

In appraising the nature of burial practices in the Levant during Neolithization processes as briefly described previously, it should be quite obvious that there are few, if any, definite and/or enduring patterns, spatially and/or chronologically. For example, "grave goods" do occur from the Natufian onward, but they are rarely numerous, and there is often difficulty in distinguishing between genuine grave goods and personal jewelry and adornments on clothing of the dead, not to mention simple background "noise" of grave fill. Indeed grave goods are oftentimes difficult to identify as such; for example, how should we consider the incorporation of animal bones within graves – a sporadic occurrence from the Middle Epipaleolithic all through the Pre-Pottery Neolithic, whether as complete animal carcasses, or as single bones. These may be interpreted as purely emblematic, representing a symbolic system (*pars per toto*) that we have yet to decipher or simply as evidence for ceremonial feasting as part of the burial rites (and see earlier examples). Should the burial of a fox together with human remains at the Middle Epipaleolithic site of the 'Uyyun al-Hammam (Wadi Ziqlab 148) cemetery be considered as a precursor of the (rare) Natufian canid burials? And what should we make of the ground-stone utensils found in association with burials? Such associations are documented since at least the Middle Epipaleolithic, through to the Natufian, and even to the PPNB in the southern Levant. Do these "presage" the burials at Körtik Tepe on the Upper Tigris, which were lavishly covered by the intentionally broken shards of stone utensils (and see earlier discussion)? Is this simply a matter of independent evolution and convergence? Or, do such practices reflect ties of some sort, which are otherwise undetected?

Some traditions were more spectacular than others, most especially that of postmortem skull removal. This custom, which was never ubiquitous, was first documented during the Natufian, continuing in the PPNA and PPNB, lasting through to at least the Pottery Neolithic in the southern Levant. Subsequent modification and embellishment, as in the form of plastering, are associated only with the Middle and Late PPNB, four thousand years *after* the Natufian. Skulls were curated or reburied after their "secondary" death. They appear both as single items as well as in caches. Indeed, it seems that skulls have been of special importance from the proverbial "beginning" (i.e., Epipaleolithic) since there is evidence of special treatment – decapitation, modification, and burning (?) of skulls, with skulls being cached, stored, or reburied after their "secondary" deaths. The unique treatment of the skull overrules the caution one normally has to exercise when excavating a prehistoric occurrence taking into consideration problems of taphonomy; in other words, when does a missing skull actually reflect skull removal, and when does it represent poor preservation?[4] Last, but not least, we do find material evidence for long-distance

---

[4] And, tongue in cheek, we should not forget "Moshe," the headless Mousterian Neanderthal from Kebara cave (Bar-Yosef et al. 1988).

connections between the southern Levant and central Anatolia in the form of one of the plastered skulls from Kfar HaHoresh in Lower Galilee, the pigment on which proved to be cinnabar deriving from sources in the Taurus region of central Anatolia.[5] Furthermore, various aspects of the mortuary practices at PPNB Shillourokambos in Cyprus (Guilaine, Briois, and Vigne 2011) also closely mirror similar practices at Kfar HaHoresh. Another convergence(?) is the practice of smearing gypsum/lime plaster on many of the skeletons at PPNA Körtik Tepe (Özkaya 2009; Özkaya and Coşkun 2009) – this practice also occurs later, during the M/LPPNB at Tell abu Hureyra (Moore, Hillman, and Legge 2000), and perhaps presages the practices at Late Neolithic Tell Sabi Abyad (Akkermans 1996), all sites located in the northern Levant. Recently it has also been documented at PPNA el Hemmeh, in the southern Levant (Makarewicz and Rose 2011)! So, one may ask, which area has precedence?

Another interesting and hardly commented upon practice concerns the use of "pillows" placed to raise the head of the deceased above the rest of the body. Sometimes this seemingly involved "perishable" cushions (e.g., Late Natufian Raqefet); or, and more commonly, stone "pillows," as at PPNA Hatoula and Wadi Faynan 16 (Le Mort, Hershkovitz, and Spiers 1994; Nadel et al. 2008; Finlayson and Mithen 2007).

So, ultimately, how can we explain the observed variability in burial practices as regards the community behaviors that they reflect through this long period? And how do those burial practices relate to the broader picture of the socioeconomic transformations occurring concurrently? Burials as a constant phenomenon start to appear during the Early Natufian, crossing the "Rubicon" of domestication processes, that is, the shift from small foraging bands to large sedentary communities. All in all, it seems to us that the changes in burial practices were gradual rather than abrupt – apparently these aspects pertain to the core of society's fabric, relevant to the very identity of the specific human group. Accordingly, each of the cultural entities during the terminal Pleistocene and Early Holocene displays evidence for continuity in some aspects of the burial practices, in tandem with considerable variability in others.

The variation observed is indeed amazing, and it is already very obvious during the Natufian, when a plethora of burials and wide range of burial types are documented through the length of the long Natufian

---

[5] Interestingly, cinnabar is mentioned as one of the pigments associated with skulls at Çatal (Boz and Hager 2013; Nakamura and Meskell, 2013).

chronological sequence. We cannot resist yet another illustrative example: Tomb 23 at Eynan has one individual in articulation associated with grave goods (a small basalt bowl, a biface, and a few bones of a "large" animal [aurochs?]). The burial also has a "tombstone" and other large stones embedded in the grave to "pin down" the deceased and demarcate the grave's perimeter. And above this grave is yet another grave, this time represented only by a single mandible (Perrot and Ladiray 1988: 51, fig. 29). This seems to be another instance of extended memory and *pars per toto*, at the same time reflecting the inherent variability of Natufian funerary practices.

Obviously we have to take into consideration those changes induced through time, as well as the particular, evolving histories of each settlement/area/region within Southwest Asia (i.e., the Near East). Such a statement is clearly valid for every period in human history. However, what is specific to the Neolithic in the region is that the changes involved in Neolithization processes were unprecedented occurrences in human history – aggregation, sedentism, cultivation, domestication, and so on, all for the first time (Belfer-Cohen and Goring-Morris 2009). Aggregation, for example, meant that the traditional separation into small hunter-gatherer bands broke down as various such groups, because of the new circumstances involving economic and spiritual shifts, began to **live** together, as evidenced through the archaeological data. These were indeed first-time phenomena and individual groups were grappling with unfamiliar "territory," in the sense that there was still no real canonization of social mutuality, even if the basics of social behaviors and ritual practices derived from a general, shared sociocultural milieu. All of these were constantly changing, while individuals and communities tried to adhere to what was familiar and had been accepted practice/agency for many millennia.

Undoubtedly, the pronounced chronological and regional variability observed, occurring during these "troubling" times of profound changes in the fabric of human existence, can accommodate the uniqueness of the findings from Çatalhöyük. Çatalhöyük is geographically located at the very northwestern edge of Neolithization processes and was founded relatively late within PPN developments. Yet, we may assume that the initial founding and development of Çatalhöyük likely reflect Neolithization processes somewhat akin to those encountered earlier within the Levant, namely, that Çatalhöyük represents the amalgamation of disparate groups from within the general region – and see Bonçuklu (Baird 2006, 2010). The contexts of the human remains recently described and summarized for the Çatal sequence (Boz and Hager 2013; Nakamura and Meskell 2013) incorporate almost all the mortuary elements described for the Levant from the Natufian onward. The detailed studies revealed some local patterns, such as the emphasis on primary burials, on grave goods being mostly associated with infants and children, and, to a lesser degree, with older women; differing proportions (through time) between burials outside and inside houses; but none of these is really unique or exceptional relative to the variability in the mortuary repertoire elsewhere in the Near East. Rather, we can observe differences on the basis of individual burials (e.g., Patton and Hager, this volume). Each internment and its context tell a story that incorporates both personal and societal aspects, reflecting the private history of the deceased in tandem with the customs and beliefs of the community at large. Indeed, the rather opaque diachronic and synchronic trends and tendencies displayed at Çatalhöyük broadly parallel those in the Levant. Accordingly, it is against the backdrop of the developments detailed earlier that the burials in Çatalhöyük and their chronospatial contexts represent yet another unique social experiment that developed, flourished, and gradually transformed into something else during the course of its circa-fifteen-hundred-year history. As such it parallels other distinctive and unique experiments during Neolithic transformations elsewhere in Southwest Asia.

Neolithization processes entailed profound changes in all spheres of human existence, prominent among which was the manner that the living accommodated their dead. In examining the inventory of mortuary practices detailed, it is quite clear that we are facing processes influenced by changes taking place in other realms; the most obvious is the aggregation of people into sedentary settlements, sharing space (in life as in death) with strangers ("nonkin"). The diachronic differences observed among subregions throughout the Near East reflect innovations that developed in situ or that were acquired through contacts with "outside" groups. The Neolithic as a whole was a period of flux and communities were constantly pushed into contacts with the outside (through trade, exchange, craft specialization, migration, etc.), at the same time trying to retain and define their own identities. Treatment of and attitudes toward the dead were undoubtedly influenced by this duality. Thus we can observe the adoption of traditions, originating in one particular place, diffusing

all over the Near East in no time at all, or at least at a pace that archaeology today can hardly measure (e.g., skull removal, plastered skulls, the
inclusion of animal remains). Mortuary practices played an important
role in defining community identity. Even if one acknowledges the prob-
lematics of imposing present-day as well as recent and subrecent ethnographic values on prehistoric mortuary behavior, it is obvious that there
was a continuous "discourse" between the living and the dead, with the
former trying to continue and impose their *Weltanschauung* on the latter;
the changes and variability reflecting the turbulent nature of Neolithic
times and the "for the first time" circumstances of groups and individuals merging to create a "brave new world." With all the intricacies and
difficulties involved in identifying the complex patterning of mortuary
practices observed at Çatalhöyük, this simply reflects the situation elsewhere within the Near East through most of the Neolithic sequence.
Indeed the similarities in the treatment of the dead can be considered as
one of the reasons that the concept of "the PPNB Koine" came about;
concurrently it is obvious that each community was feeling its own way
in order to promote cohesion and solidify group identity, drawing from
the realms of both the living and the dead.

BIBLIOGRAPHY

Akkermans, P. M. M. G., eds. 1996. *Tell Sabi Abyad: The Late Neolithic Settlement.*
    Leiden/Istanbul: Nederlands Historisch-Archaeologisch Instituut.
Arensburg, B., and Bar-Yosef, O. 1973. Human Remains from Ein Gev I, Jordan
    Valley, Israel. *Paléorient* 1:201–206.
Baird, D. 2006. The Bonçuklu Project: The Origins of Sedentism, Cultivation
    and Herding in Central Anatolia. *Anatolian Archaeology* 12:13–16.
    2010. Was Çatalhöyük a centre: The implications of a late Aceramic Neolithic
    assemblage from the neighbourhood of Çatalhöyük. In *The Development of
    Pre-State Communities in the Ancient Near East*, eds. D. Bolger and L. C.
    Maguire. Oxford: Oxbow Books.
Bar-Yosef, O., and Alon, D. 1988. *Nahal Hemar Cave.* 'Atiqot 18. Jerusalem:
    Israel Department of Antiquities.
Bar-Yosef, O., Goring-Morris, A. N., and Gopher, A., eds. 2010. *Gilgal:
    Excavations at Early Neolithic Sites in the Lower Jordan Valley. The
    Excavations of Tamar Noy.* Oakville, CT: ASPR Monograph Series & David
    Brown/Oxbow.
Bar-Yosef, O., Laville, H., Meigen, L., Tillier, A.-M., Vandermeersch, B.,
    Arensberg, B., Belfer-Cohen, A., Goldberg, P., Rak, Y., and Tchernov, E.

1988. La Sépulture neandertaliènne de Kebara (unité XII). In *La Pense*, ed., M. Otte. Liège: ERAUL, 17–24.

Bar-Yosef, O., and Sillen, A. 1993. Implications of the New Acclerator Date of the Charred Skeletons from Kebara Cave (Mt. Carmel). *Paléorient* 19:205–208.

Becker, C. 2002. Nothing to do with indigenous domestication? Cattle from Late PPNB Basta. In *Archaeozoology of the Near East*, eds., H. Buitenhuis, A. M. Choyke, M. Mashkour and A. H. Al-Shiyab. Groningen: ARC, 112–137.

Belfer-Cohen, A. 1988. The Natufian Graveyard in Hayonim Cave. *Paléorient* 4(2), 297–308.

1995. Rethinking social stratification in the natufian culture: The evidence from burials. In *The Archaeology of Death in the Ancient Near East*, eds. S. Campbell and A. Green. Edinburgh: Oxbow Monographs, 9–16.

Belfer-Cohen, A., Arensburg, B., Bar-Yosef, O., and Gopher, A. 1990. The Human Remains from the PPNA Site of Netiv Hagdud, Jordan Valley, Israel. *Mitekufat Haeven – Journal of the Israel Prehistoric Society* 23:79–85.

Belfer-Cohen, A., and Goring-Morris, A. N. 2009. For the First Time. Comments on Papers in "Conversation on the Origins of Agriculture". *Current Anthropology* 50(5), 669–672.

2013a. The Upper Palaeolithic and earlier Epi-Palaeolithic of Western Asia (ca. 50–14.5 k calBP). In *The Cambridge World Prehistory*, Volume 3, eds. A. C. Renfrew and B. G. Bahn. Cambridge: Cambridge University Press, 1381–1407.

2013b. Breaking the mold: Phases and facies in the Natufian of the Mediterranean Zone. In *The Natufian Culture in the Levant II*, eds. O. Bar-Yosef and F. R. Valla. Ann Arbor, MI: Monographs in Prehistory, 543–561.

Bocquentin, F. 2003. Pratiques funeraires, parametres biologiques et identités culturelles au Natoufien: une analyse archéo-anthropologique. Thèse de Doctorat en Anthropologie Biologique, Université Bordeaux 1.

Bocquentin, F., Crevecoeur, I., Arensburg, B., Kaufman, D., and Ronen, A. 2011. Les hommes du Kébarien géométrique de Neve David, Mont Carmel (Israël). *Bulletins et Mémoires de la Société d'anthropologie de Paris* 23(1–2):38–51.

Boz, B., and Hager, L. 2013. Intramural burial practices at Çatalhöyük. In *Humans and Landscapes of Çatalhöyük: Reports from the 2000–2008 Seasons*, ed. I. Hodder. Los Angeles: Cotsen Institute.

Coqueugniot, E. 2008. Diversified funerary practices: the case of Dja'de (Syria, Euphrates valley, 9th millenium cal. BC, late PPNA and EPPNB). In *Proceedings of the 5th International Congress on the Archaeology of the Ancient Near East*, eds., J. M. Córdoba, M. Molist, M. Pérez, I. Rubio and S. Martínez. Madrid: Centro Superior de Estudios sobre el Oriente Próximo y Egipto.

Coqueugniot, E. 2013. Dja'de (Syria) and the 9th millenium cal. BC symbolic representations. In *Transitions en Mediterranée ou Comment des Chasseurs Devinrent Agriculteurs (Epipaléolithique, Mésolithique, Néolithique Ancien)*, eds. J. Guilaine, C. Manen, and T. Perrin. Le Museum d'Histoire Naturelle de Toulouse, le Centre de Recherche sur la Préhistoire et la Protohistoire de la Mediterranée (EHESS/UMR Traces du CNRS). Toulouse.

Cornwall, I. W. 1981. The pre-pottery Neolithic burials. In *Excavations at Jericho*. Vol. 3: *The Architecture and Stratigraphy of the Tell*, ed. T. A. Holland. London: The British School of Archaeology in Jerusalem, 395–406.

Croucher, K. 2006a. Death, display and performance: A discussion of the mortuary remains at Çayönü Tepesi, Southeast Turkey. In *The Archaeology of Cult and Death*, eds. M. Georgiadis and C. Gallou, pp. 11–44. Budapest: Archaeolingua.

2006b. Getting ahead: Exploring meanings of skulls in the Neolithic Near East. In *Skull collection, modification and decoration*, ed. M. Bonogofsky. Oxford: Archaeopress, 29–44.

2010. Tactile engagements: the world of the dead in the lives of the living … or 'sharing the dead'. In *The Principle of Sharing – Segregation and Construction of Social Identities at the Transition from Foraging to Farming*, ed. M. Benz. Berlin: SENEPSE 14, ex oriente, 277–300.

2012. *Death and Dying in the Neolithic Near East*. Oxford: Oxford University Press.

Davis, S. J. M., and Valla, F. R. 1978. Evidence for Domestication of the Dog 12,000 Years Ago in the Natufian of Israel. *Nature* 276:608–610.

Edwards, P. C., Meadows, J., Sayej, G., and Westaway, M. 2004. From the PPNA to the PPNB: New views from the southern Levant after excavations at Zahrat adh-Dhra' 2 in Jordan. *Paléorient* 30(2), 21–60.

Finlayson, B., and Mithen, S., eds. 2007. *The Early Prehistory of Wadi Faynan, Southern Jordan*. Oxford: Oxbow Books & CBRL.

Galili, E., Eshed, V., Gopher, A., and Hershkovitz, I., 2005. Burial practices at the submerged Pre-Pottery Neolithic site of Atlit-Yam, northern coast of Israel. *Bulletin of the American School of Oriental Research* 339:1–19.

Garrard, A. N. 1991 Natufian settlement in the Azraq Basin, Eastern Jordan. In *The Natufian Culture in the Levant*, eds. O. Bar-Yosef and F. R. Valla. Ann Arbor, MI: International Monographs in Prehistory, 235–244.

Garrard, A. N., and Yazbeck, C. 2003. Qadisha Valley Prehistory Project (Northern Lebanon): Summary of First Two Seasons Investigations. *Baal* 7:7–14.

Garrod, D. 1936–1937. Notes on Some Decorated Skeletons from the Mesolithic of Palestine. *Annual of the British School in Athens* 37:123–127.

Garrod, D. A. E., and Bate, D. M. A. 1937. *The Stone Age of Mount Carmel. Excavations at the Wadi-Mughara*, vol. 1. Oxford: Clarendon Press.

Gebel, H. G., Hermansen, B. D., and Kinzel, M. 2006. Ba'ja 2005: A Two-Storied Building and Collective Burials. Results of the 6th Season of Excavation. *Neo-Lithics* 1/06:12–19.

Goren, Y., Goring-Morris, A. N., and Segal, I. 2001. Skull Modeling in the Pre-Pottery Neolithic B: Regional Variability, the Relationship of Technology and Iconography and Their Archaeological Implications. *Journal of Archaeological Science* 28(7), 671–690.

Goring-Morris, A. N. 2000. The quick and the dead: The social context of Aceramic Neolithic mortuary practices as seen from Kfar HaHoresh. In *Life in Neolithic Farming Communities. Social Organization, Identity, and Differentiation*, ed. I. Kuijt. New York: Kluwer Academic/Plenum, 103–135.

2005. Life, death and the emergence of differential status in the Near Eastern Neolithic: Evidence from Kfar HaHoresh, Lower Galilee, Israel. In *Archaeological Perspectives on the Transmission and Transformation of Culture in the Eastern Mediterranean*, ed. J. Clark. Oxford: CBRL & Oxbow Books, 89–105.

Goring-Morris, A. N., and Belfer-Cohen, A. 2011. Evolving human/animal interactions in the Near Eastern Neolithic: Feasting as a case study. In *Guess Who'S Coming to Dinner: Feasting Rituals in the Prehistoric Societies of Europe and near East*, eds. G. Aranda, S. Montón and M. Sanchez. Oxford: Oxbow Books, 64–72.

Goring-Morris, A. N., Burns, R., Davidzon, A., Eshed, V., Goren, Y., Hershkovitz, I., Kangas, S., and Kelecevic, J. 1998. The 1997 Season of Excavations at the Mortuary Site of Kfar HaHoresh, Galilee, Israel. *Neo-Lithics* 3/98:1–4.

Goring-Morris, A. N., and Horwitz, L. K. 2007. Funerals and Feasts in the Near Eastern Pre-Pottery Neolithic B. *Antiquity* 81:902–919.

Grosman, L., and Munro, N. 2007. The Sacred and the Mundane: Domestic Activities at a Late Natufian Burial Site in the Levant. *Before Farming: The Archaeology and Anthropology of Hunter-Gatherers* 4:1–14.

Grosman, L., Munro, N. D., and Belfer-Cohen, A. 2008. A 12,000-year-old Shaman burial from the southern Levant (Israel). *Proceedings of the National Academy of Sciences* 105(46), 17665–17669.

Guerrero, E., Molist, M., Kuijt, I., and Anfruns, J. 2009. Seated Memory: New Insights into Near Eastern Neolithic Mortuary Variability from Tell Halula, Syria. *Current Anthropology* 50:379–391.

Guilaine, J., Briois, F., and Vigne, J. D., eds. 2011. *Shillourokambos. Un eétablissement néolithique pré-ceramique à Chypre. Les fouilles du secteur 1*. Paris: Editions Errance/Ecole Française d'Athenes.

Hayden, B. 2011. Feasting and social dynamics in the Epipaleolithic of the Fertile Crescent: an interpretive excercise. In *Guess Who's Coming to Dinner: Feasting Rituals in the Prehistoric Societies of Europe and the near East*, eds. G. Aranda Jimenez, S. Monton-Subias and M. Sanchez Romero. Oxford: Oxbow Books, 30–63.

Hermansen, B. D., Thuesen, I., Jensen, C. H., Kinzel, M., Petersen, M. B., Jorkov, M. L., and Lynerrup, N. 2006. Shkarat Msaied: The 2005 Season of Excavations. A Short Preliminary Report. *Neo-Lithics* 1/06:3–7.

Hershkovitz, I., Bar-Yosef, O., and Arensburg, B. 1994. The Pre-Pottery Neolithic Populations of South Sinai and Their Relations to Other Circum-Mediterranean Groups: An Anthropological Study. *Paléorient* 20(2), 59–84.

Hershkovitz, I., Spiers, M. S., Frayer, D., Nadel, D., Wish-Baratz, S., and Arensberg, B. 1995. Ohalo II – a 19,000 Years Old Skeleton from a Water-Logged Site at the Sea of Galilee. *American Journal of Physical Anthropology* 96(3), 215–234.

Horwitz Kolska, L., and Goring-Morris, A. N. 2004. Animals and Ritual during the Levantine PPNB: A Case Study from the Site of Kfar Hahoresh, Israel. *Anthropozoologica* 39(1), 165–178.

Ibañez, J. J., ed. 2008. *Le Site Néolithique de Tell Mureybet (Syrie du Nord). En hommage à Jacques Cauvin.* Oxford: BAR International Series 1843 (I–II).

Kanjou, Y. 2009. Study of Neolithic Human Graves from Tell Qaramel in North Syria. *International Journal of Modern Anthropology* 2:25–37.

Kenyon, K. M. 1957. *Digging Up Jericho.* London: Benn.

   1981. *The Architecture and Stratigraphy of the Tell: Excavations at Jericho III.* London: British School of Archaeology in Jerusalem.

Khalaily, H., Milevski, I., Getzov, N., Hershkovitz, I., Barzilai, O., Yaroshevich, A., Shlomi, V., Najjar, A., Zidan, O., Smithline, H., and Liran, R. 2008. Recent Excavations at the Neolithic Site of Yiftahel (Khallet Khalladyiah), Lower Galilee. *Neo-Lithics* 2/08:3–11.

Kinzel, M., Abu-Laban, A., Hoffman Jensen, C., Thuesen, I., and Jorkov, M.-L. 2011. Insights into PPNB Architectural Transformation, Human Burials, and Initial Conservation Works: Summary on the 2010 Excavation Season at Shkarat Msaied. *Neo-Lithics* 1/11:44–49.

Kirkbride, D. 1966. Five Seasons at the Prepottery Neolithic Village of Beidha in Jordan. *Palestine Exploration Quarterly* 98:8–72.

Kozlowski, S. K. 2002. *Nemrik: An Aceramic Village in Northern Iraq.* Warsaw: Institute of Archaeology, Warsaw University.

Kuijt, I. 1995. New Perspectives on Old Territories: Ritual Practices and the Emergence of Social Complexity in the Levantine Neolithic. Unpublished Ph.D. Dissertation, Harvard University.

   1996. Negotiating Equality through Ritual: A Consideration of Late Natufian and Pre-Pottery Neolithic A Period Mortuary Practices. *Journal of Anthropological Archaeology* 15:313–336.

   1997. Jericho. In *The Oxford Companion to Archaeology*, eds. C. Beck, G. Michaels, C. Scarre and N. A. Silberman. New York: Oxford University Press, 363–364.

2001. Place, death, and the transmission of social memory in early agricultural of the Near Eastern Pre-Pottery Neolithic. In *Social Memory, Identity, and Death: Anthropological Perspectives on Mortuary Rituals*, ed. M. S. Chesson. Washington, DC: Archeological Papers of the American Anthropological Association: 80–99.

2004. The Pre-Pottery Neolithic A and Late Natufian Occupations at 'Iraq ed-Dubb, Jordan. *Journal of Field Archaeology* 29:291–308.

2008. The Regeneration of Life: Neolithic Structures of Symbolic Remembering and Forgetting. *Current Anthropology* 49(2):171–197.

Kurth, G., and Rohrer-Ertl, O. 1981. On the anthropology of the Mesolithic to Chalcolithic human remains from the Tell es-Sultan in Jericho, Jordan. In *Excavations at Jericho*, vol. 3, ed. T. A. Holland. Oxford: Oxford University Press, 409–499.

Le Mort, F. 1994. Les sepultures. In *Le Gisement de Hatoula en Judée Occidentale, Israel*, eds. M. Lechevallier and A. Ronen. Paris: Association Paléorient, Mémoires et Travaux du Centre de Recherche Français de Jérusalem, 39–57.

Le Mort, F., Hershkovitz, I., and Spiers, M. 1994. Les restes humains. In *Le Gisement de Hatoula en Judée Occidentale, Israel*, eds. M. Lechevallier and A. Ronen. Paris: Association Paléorient, Mémoires et Travaux du Centre de Recherche Français de Jérusalem, 59–72.

Lengyel, G., and Bocquentin, F. 2005. Burials of Raqefet Cave in the Context of the Late Natufian. *Journal of the Israel Prehistoric Society* 35:271–284.

Maher, L. A., Stock, J. T., Finney, S., Heywood, J. J. N., Miracle, P. T., and Banning, E. B. 2011. A Unique Human-Fox Burial from a Pre-Natufian Cemetery in the Levant (Jordan). *PLoS ONE* 6(1).

Makarewicz, C. A., and Rose, K. 2011. Early Pre-Pottery Neolithic settlement at el-Hemmeh: A survey of the architecture. *Neo-Lithics* 1/11:23–29.

Malinsky-Buller, A., Aldjem, E., and Yeshurun, R. 2009. Bir el-Maksur. A New Pre-Pottery Neolithic A Site in Lower Galilee. *Neo-Lithics* 2/09:13–17.

Moore, A. M. T., Hillman, G. C., and Legge, A. J. 2000. *Village on the Euphrates. From Foraging to Farming at Abu Hureyra*. Oxford: Oxford University Press.

Munro, N. D., and Grosman, L. 2010. Early Evidence (ca. 12,000 BP) for Feasting at a Burial Cave in Israel. *Proceedings of the National Academy of Science* 107(35):15362–15366.

Nadel, D., Danin, A., Power, R. C., Rosen, A. M., Bocquentin, F., Tsatskin, A., Rosenberg, D., Yeshurun, R., Weissbrod, L., Rebollo, N.R., Barzilai O., and Boaretto, E. 2013. Earliest floral grave lining from 13,700–11,700-y-old Natufian burials at Raqefet cave, Mt. Carmel, Israel. *Proceeding of the National Academy of Science (PNAS)*.

Nadel, D., Lengyel, G., Bocquentin, F., Tsatskin A., Rosenberg, D., Yeshurun, R., Bar-Oz, G., Bar-Yosef Mayer, D., Beeri, R., Conyers, L., Filin, S., Hershkovitz I., Kurzawska, A., and Weissbrod, L. 2008. The Late Natufian at Raqefet Cave: The 2006 Excavation Season. *Journal of the Israel Prehistoric Society* 38:59–131.

Nadel, D., Lengyel, G., Cabellos, T., Bocquentin, F., Rosenberg, D., Yeshurun, R., Brown-Goodman, R., Tsatskin A., Bar-Oz, G., and Filin, S. 2009. The Raqefet cave 2008 excavation season. *Journal of the Israel Prehistoric Society* 39:21–61.

Nakamura, C., and Meskell, L. 2013. Figurines. In *Substantive Technologies at Çatalhöyük: Reports from the 2000–2008 Seasons*, ed. I. Hodder. Los Angeles: Cotsen Institute.

Ortiz, A., Chambon, P., and Molist, M. 2013. "Funerary bundles" in the PPNB at the archaeological site of tell Halula (middle Euphrates valley, Syria): Analysis of the taphonomic dynamics of seated bodies. *Journal Archaeological Science*.

Ozbek, M. 1988. Cults des crânes humains à Çayönu. *Anatolica* 15:127–135.

1992. The Human Remains at Çayönu. *American Journal of Archaeology* 96:374.

Özkaya, V. 2009. Excavations at Körtik Tepe: A New Pre-Pottery Neolithic A Site in Southeastern Anatolia. *Neo-Lithics* 2/09:3–8.

Özkaya, V., and Coşkun, A. 2009. Körtik Tepe, a New Pre-Pottery Neolithic A Site in South-eastern Anatolia. *Antiquity* 83(320).

Perrot, J., and Ladiray, D. 1988. *Les Hommes de Mallaha (Eynan), Israel*. Mémoires et Travaux du Centre de Recherche Française de Jérusalem, No. 7. Paris: Association Paléorient.

Richter, T., Stock, J. T., Maher, L., and Hebron, C. 2010. An Early Epipalaeolithic Sitting Burial from the Azraq Oasis, Jordan. *Antiquity* 84:321–334.

Rollefson, G. O. 2000. Ritual and social structure at Neolithic 'Ain Ghazal. In *Life in Neolithic Farming Communities. Social Organization, Identity, and Differentiation*, ed. I. Kuijt. New York: Kluwer Academic/Plenum, 163–190.

Smith, P. 1972. Diet and Attrition in the Natufians. *American Journal of Physical Anthropology* 37:233–238.

Solecki, R. S., Solecki, R. L., and Agelarakis, A. P. 2004. *The Proto-Neolithic Cemetery in Shanidar Cave*. College Station: Texas A&M.

Stekelis, M., and Yizraeli, T. 1963. Excavations at Nahal Oren – Preliminary Report. *Israel Exploration Journal* 13:1–12.

Stock, J. T., Pfeiffer, S. K., Chazan, M., and Janetski, J. 2005. F-81 Skeleton from Wadi Mataha, Jordan, and Its Bearing on Human Variability in the Epipaleolithic of the Levant. *American Journal of Physical Anthropology* 128(2):453–465.

Stordeur, D., and Abbès, F. 2002. Du PPNA au PPNB: mise en lumière d'une phase de transition à Jerf el-Ahmar (Syrie). *Bulletin de la Société Préhistorique Française* 99(3):563–595.

Stordeur, D., and Khawam, R. 2007. Les crânes surmodelés de Tell Aswad (PPNB, Syrie). Premier regard sur l'ensemble, premières réflexions. *Syria* 84:5–32.

2008. Une place pour les morts dans les maisons de Tell Aswad (Syrie). (Horizon PPNB ancien et PPNB moyen). In *Proceedings of the 5th International Congress on the Archaeology of the Ancient Near East*, eds., J. M. Córdoba, M. Molist, M. Pérez, I. Rubio and S. Martínez. Madrid: Centro Superior de Estudios sobre el Oriente Próximo y Egipto, 561–590.

Tchernov, E., and Valla, F. R. 1997. Two New Dogs, and Other Natufian Dogs, from the Southern Levant. *Journal of Archaeological Science* 24(1):65–95.

Turville-Petre, F. 1932. Excavations at the Mugharet El-Kebarah. *Journal of the Royal Anthropological Institute* 62:270–276.

Twiss, K. C. 2008. Transformations in an Early Agricultural Society: Feasting in the Southern Levantine Pre-Pottery Neolithic. *Journal of Anthropological Archaeology* 27:418–442.

Valla, F. R. 1988. Aspects du sol de l'abri 131 de Mallaha (Eynan). *Paléorient* 14:283–296.

Valla, F. R., Khalaily, H., Samuelian, N., and Bocquentin, F. 2010. What Happened in the Final Natufian? *Journal of the Israel Prehistoric Society* 40:131–148.

Watkins, T., Baird, D., and Betts, A. 1989. Qermez Dere and the Early Aceramic Neolithic in Northern Iraq. *Paléorient* 15(1):19–24.

Webb, S. G. and Edwards, P. C. 2002. The Natufian Human Skeletal Remains from Wadi Hammeh 27 (Jordan). *Paléorient*, 28(1), 103–123.

3

Excavating Theogonies: Anthropomorphic Promiscuity and Sociographic Prudery in the Neolithic and Now

F. LeRon Shults

Introduction

Where do babies come from? Archaeologists do not need to dig around for an answer to this question as they attempt to understand and explain the empirical data uncovered at Çatalhöyük, other sites in the Neolithic, or elsewhere. They certainly need to search for plausible hypotheses to illuminate the vital kinship structures, pregnancy rituals, birthing practices, and neonatal health care policies of any specific community. However, if the community was composed of *Homo sapiens*, archaeologists can appropriately assume that infants appeared within the population as a result of the same basic procedures that produce them today, when – well, you know. The inhabitants of Çatalhöyük were anatomically modern humans and naturally reproduced in the same way that we do.

Where do *gods* come from? In this chapter I will argue that archaeologists (as well as other scientists, philosophers, and theologians) can now also appropriately assume that the reproduction of supernatural agents in Çatalhöyük occurred in much the same way that it does today, at least in small-scale societies. Although we have known where babies come from for several millennia, only within the last few decades have we come to understand more fully why gods appear (and are cared for) in human populations. As with the process of bearing children, one finds an astonishing variety of ways of ritually surrounding and socially manipulating the process of bearing supernatural agents. Beliefs about and behaviors toward the latter are regulated and transmitted differently in the major religious traditions that were forged within complex literate states during the axial age and now dominate the global landscape. Nevertheless, all members of our species share a phylogenetic heritage that includes sets of cognitive and coalitional tendencies, which together help to explain why gods are so easily born(e) across cultures in time and space.

This is the first purpose of this essay: to offer an integrated reconstruction of theoretical advances in the biocultural study of religion, pointing to the convergence of insights from a variety of disciplines around two conceptual attractors that I will call *theogonic* mechanisms (anthropomorphic promiscuity and sociographic prudery) and demonstrating their potential illuminative power in relation to the empirical findings at Çatalhöyük. In the field of archaeology I am an amateur (in both senses of the word) and will not pretend to offer expert analyses of the data. And so this essay has a second, more philosophical, and perhaps even more daring, purpose: to explore some of the implications of the unearthing of these theogonic mechanisms for the shared global future of the human race, attending to the adaptive challenges and opportunities that must be faced today in light of our new understanding of the impact that bearing gods has on our mental and social well-being.

In my earlier analysis of the material, social, and spiritual entanglement at Çatalhöyük (Shults 2010), I used the term "religion" in a broad sense to indicate the way in which humans symbolically engage what they take to be of ultimate value. In the current context, however, I am focusing more narrowly on a particular feature of human life that also appears across cultures: *shared imaginative engagement with supernatural agents*. In this sense, "religion" was entangled within and developed alongside all of the other vital matters that shaped human evolution. In the conclusion (part 5), I will emphasize the philosophical, psychological, and political significance of the unveiling of the mystery of god-bearing mechanisms, which, like Girard's scapegoat mechanism, only work well when they are hidden.

The bulk of the chapter (parts 2–4) is a conceptual excavation and reconstruction of ways in which anthropomorphic promiscuity and sociographic prudery may have operated at Çatalhöyük. How was their shared imaginative engagement with supernatural agents (such as the spirits of ancestors and aurochs) vitally entangled with the material and social dimensions of their lives? To what extent were their production of food and artifacts and their regulation of communal property shaped by their perception of the causal power and social relevance of such agents? It seems to me that bulls, burials, and proprietary production were all mixed together at Çatalhöyük. The first step, however, is to provide a brief introduction to the general conceptual framework that will guide my archaeological and philosophical observations.

"Bearing Gods" in the Neolithic

It should be clear enough that my use of the term *bearing* has a double function, indicating the naturally evolved processes by which gods are *born* in human cognition (by the overactive detection of agency) and *borne* in human culture (by the overactive protection of coalitions). The term *god*, however, calls for further clarification. Although in common parlance it typically evokes images of Zeus, Yahweh, or Vishnu, one increasingly finds scholars within the biocultural study of religion using "gods" as shorthand for all kinds of culturally postulated disembodied entities such as animal spirits, ghosts, ancestors, jinn, angels, and others (e.g., Guthrie 1993, Atran 2002, Tremlin 2006, Boyer 2010). This practice is adequate for the purposes of this essay, and so in what follows *gods* should be understood as a virtual synonym for "supernatural agents."

Supernatural agents are disembodied (or dis-embodi-able) intentional forces that are perceived to have some interest in and causal power over the members of the coalition that imaginatively engage them. Despite – or because of – their discarnate status these *agents* are believed to be capable of playing some kind of constitutive and/or regulative role in the social life of a particular human coalition. In this sense, the monotheistic idea of "God" also falls within this category, although it has distinctive features that need to be parsed out in other contexts for different reasons (cf. Shults 2012a). My interest here is in uncovering the general mechanisms that condition all kinds of *theogonies*. I am using this latter term not in the narrow sense of popular literary accounts of the genesis of the gods, such as Hesiod's graphic portrayal of Cronos's swallowing of divine offspring and mutilation of titanic genitals, but more broadly as a way of referring to any narrative imaginative engagement that reinforces the detection and protection of a specific supernatural agent coalition.

Accepting the risk of blurring still other important distinctions within and across disciplines, I want to offer a heuristic model of the integration of these mechanisms, which is based on my reconstructive reading of recent empirical findings and theoretical reflections across a variety of fields including archaeology, cognitive science, evolutionary neurobiology, moral psychology, social anthropology, and political theory. I do not

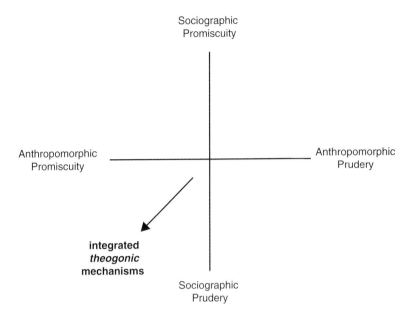

3.1. Conceptual scheme for terms used in this chapter.

have the space here to review all of the various trends in these disciplines that bear on the biocultural evolution of religion (for a more detailed reconstruction, cf. Shults 2011, 2012b, In press).

However, it seems to me that many of these trends converge in supporting the general hypothesis that gods are born(e) as a result of evolved human tendencies to overdetect agents in the natural environment and to overprotect coalitions in the social environment. These cognitive and cultural strategies contributed to the survival of hominid groups before, during, and after the Neolithic. The big question today is whether they are still healthy strategies for adapting in our rapidly changing, pluralistic environment. Are there other directions we could or should pursue? The conceptual framework depicted in Figure 3.1 can help clarify the options.

The level of generality at which human tendencies are depicted on this grid does not allow us to capture all of the nuances within the various theories on offer within the many disciplines we will explore. However, it does capture precisely what is needed to accomplish the general purpose for which the framework has been constructed: clarifying the relation between two basic sorts of proclivity found among *Homo sapiens* the integration of which leads to the reproduction of shared imaginative engagement with supernatural agents.

The horizontal line represents a spectrum on which we can mark the tendency of persons to guess "humanlike intentional force" when confronted with ambiguous phenomena in the natural environment. The anthropomorphically *promiscuous* are always on the lookout, jumping at any opportunity to postulate such agents as causal explanations even – or especially – when these interpretations must appeal to disembodied intentionality. The anthropomorphically *prudish*, on the other hand, are suspicious about such appeals. They tend to reflect more carefully before giving in to their intuitive desire to grab at agential explanations.

The spectrum represented by the vertical line registers how a person holds on to conventional modes of inscribing the social field, that is, to the proscriptions and prescriptions that regulate the evaluative practices and boundaries of the coalition(s) with which he or she primarily identifies. Sociographic *prudes* are strongly committed to the authorized social norms of their in-group, following and protecting them even at great cost to themselves. They are more likely to be suspicious of out-groups and to accept claims or demands that appeal to authorities within their own coalition. The sociographic *promiscuity* of those at the other end of the spectrum, on the other hand, leads them to be more open to intercourse with out-groups about alternate normativities and to the pursuit of new modes of creative social inscription. Such persons are also less likely to accept restrictions or assertions that are based only or primarily on appeals to convention.

It is important to emphasize that these spectra indicate proclivities within the mental and social space of human life, rather than judgments about the accuracy or adequacy of specific interpretive engagements. The horizontal axis is not about particular objects of detection, but the intentional capacities or *tendencies* of detecting subjects. Many of the most important things that happen to us are indeed a result of embodied human (or humanlike) agents, and so the anthropomorphic guess often turns out to be correct. Similarly, the vertical axis refers not to particular actions but to dispositional *tendencies* in attending to social inscriptions. Following coalitional authorities can be the safest and healthiest thing to do, and so sociographic prudery often promotes the wisest course of action.

The evolutionary default is toward anthropomorphic promiscuity and sociographic prudery. In other words, human beings today are intuitively and naturally drawn into the biocultural gravitational force of the integrated theogonic mechanisms into the lower left quadrant. Why? In the early ancestral environment the selective advantage went to hominids whose cognitive capacities enabled them quickly to detect relevant agents (such as predators, prey, protectors, and partners) in the *natural* environment, and whose groups were adequately protected from the dissolution that could result from the presence of too many defectors and cheaters in the *social* environment.

A growing body of evidence, which we will explore in more detail later, suggests that the chance of survival was increased for those small groups of *Homo sapiens* who developed beliefs and rituals related to supernatural agents around ninety thousand to seventy thousand years ago. Shared imaginative engagement with disembodied agents (who might be watching) protected the cohesion of these coalitions, in which descendants who easily detected such agents by interpreting ambiguous phenomena in anthropomorphic terms were naturally selected. The integration of these mutually reinforcing theogonic mechanisms was highly adaptive. Sometime around sixty thousand years ago it appears that some of these "god-bearing" groups left Africa, out-competing all other hominid species and spreading out across the Levant and into Europe and Asia.

All living humans are the genetic offspring of these groups and so share a suite of inherited traits that support the tendency to detect supernatural agents and protect supernatural coalitions. These naturally evolved traits were tweaked differently in various contexts, leading to the diversity of manifestations of religious life today. In other words, supernatural agent conceptions are never immaculate; the particular features of our gods betray our religious family of origin. In the study of *sexual* reproduction, it was once claimed that ontogeny recapitulates phylogeny. In *religious* reproduction, theogony capitulates to ethnogeny. Nevertheless, in both cases we can acknowledge that there are underlying mechanisms characteristic of our species.

The Neolithic is a particularly fertile period for the purposes of excavating theogonies. Ancestor worship (or at least imaginative engagement with dead ancestors) had probably already emerged sometime between fifty thousand and thirty thousand years ago, and the Upper Paleolithic was characterized by an explosion of innovations in toolmaking, art, and burial elaboration. However, the Neolithic was "revolutionary" in many ways, most notably the shift toward sedentism and the domestication of plants and animals. For most of the twentieth century these developments were interpreted as the result of human responses to environmental changes and new modes of controlling material production and social organization, which in turn provided the conditions for the emergence of religion. Today, however, theoretical reflections on empirical research from a variety of disciplines are converging to suggest that symbolic engagement with supernatural agents played a generative and primary role in the Neolithic "revolution."

Published at the turn of the century, Jacques Cauvin's *The Birth of the Gods and the Origins of Agriculture* (2000) provides an illuminative example of this trend. He includes an assessment of Çatalhöyük within a broad overview and analysis of a variety of finds from earlier in the Natufian to the diffusion and eastern spread of agriculture later in the Neolithic. Cauvin argues that the key to the transformation was the development of symbolic imagination and a mythical interpretation of the natural world. In other words, religion was not an aftereffect of changes in managing the material world (as in Marxist hypotheses), but ingredient to the transformation of the human mind that made the Neolithic revolution possible. To put it bluntly, in some sense "religion" was a causal factor in the rise of domestication and sedentism, or at least, as Ian Hodder would put it, "entangled" within the rise of these developments.

Despite his provocative title, which fits nicely with the metaphor guiding the reflections of this chapter, Cauvin's analysis does not really deal with the origin of the *gods* per se, but with the emergence of symbolic and mythical interpretations of the world. I agree that religion played a creative role in this revolution, but want to suggest that closer attention to the actual mechanisms by which *supernatural agents* are born(e) can complement these broader reflections. Given my interest in the fertility of the mental and social fields of Çatalhöyük during the Neolithic, one might expect me to focus on the well-known imagery of the "goddess" (Figure 3.2). Unlike Cauvin, however, I do not find the "Goddess and Bull" mythology inspired by Mellaart's earlier interpretations compelling. As Hodder and Meskell argue (2010), it seems more likely that Çatalhöyük was characterized more by the kind of phallocentrism typical of other sites in the region such as Gobekli Tepe. My interest is not primarily in the perceived sexual antics performed – or the alleged reproductive assistance provided – by any female or male divinities in the mythological "spirit world" of Çatalhöyük, but in the mechanisms by which the god(desse)s themselves were born(e) within the embodied

3.2. Female statuette found by James Mellaart in A.II.1.
Source: Jason Quinlan and Çatalhöyük Research Project.

and encultured cognition of its inhabitants. Moreover, that interest itself is driven not only by a fascination with the original revolutionaries of the Neolithic but also with the *current* "inhabitants" of Çatalhöyük, that is, the interdisciplinary and international team of researchers who ritually descend upon it every summer.

Unlike those whose bones, belongings, and abodes they study, for the most part these scientists are anthropomorphically prudish (suspicious of causal explanations that appeal to supernatural agents) and sociographically promiscuous (seeking out the insights of other disciplinary coalitions). In the conclusion I will return to the conceptual apparatus of Figure 3.1 and examine the tension this creates among the various shareholders interested in the revelations of those who dig the site Now. In the next three sections, however, my focus will be on the current team's research questions related to power, production, and property in Çatalhöyük during the Neolithic, exploring the extent to which these dynamics may have been entangled with the theogonic mechanisms outlined briefly earlier.

Burials, Bulls, and Proprietary Production

Perhaps there were no "goddesses" at Çatalhöyük, but there is strong evidence in the data that supports the claim that its original inhabitants engaged in behaviors intended to engage supernatural agents whom they considered to be socially and causally relevant to their coalition. In his analysis of the site in *The Leopard's Tale,* Ian Hodder suggests that "as people, society and crafted materials increasingly became entangled and codependent, so the codependent material agents were further enlisted and engaged in a social world in which spirits were involved" (1996, 195). He also explicitly proposes a link between "control of knowledge about and the objects of the spirit world" and the acquisition and maintenance of rights, resources, status, and prestige in the community (250). In this context, I take terms like "spirits" and "spirit world" to be roughly synonymous with what I have been calling supernatural agent coalitions.

My concern is with the role played by theogonic mechanisms in this entanglement. We could point to many instances of material objects that indicate shared imaginative engagement with "gods" in the broadest sense. For example, the polishing and caching of obsidian mirrors may have been conceived as a way of seeing or divining the "spirit world" (Hodder 2006, 229, 239). More speculatively, one might argue that the making of figurines could be an expression of a growing awareness of and interest in detecting or even controlling humanlike agents, that is, anthropomorphic promiscuity. Moreover, the repetitive patterns of architecture and art within houses and across levels suggest a rather prudish sociography. At any rate, I want to focus here on the two types of supernatural agents that seem particularly prevalent within the socius: aurochs and ancestors.

I see dead people. But like most of my cosmopolitan colleagues, I see them rarely, briefly, mostly at funerals, usually once and only one at a time. The original inhabitants of Çatalhöyük, on the other hand, saw dead people much more often. Indeed, one of the most distinctive

3.3. Burial platform from Building 49.
Source: Jason Quinlan and Çatalhöyük Research Project.

features of the "town" is the burial of some of the dead within the houses, often immediately under the main sleeping area (Figure 3.3). It is hard to know whether this was comforting or as creepy to them as it is to us. Whatever the case, the removal, burial, and long-term retrieval of skulls as well as other forms of treating the skeletons indicate that their manipulation was perceived as an engagement with supernatural agents who played some sort of causal role in the coalition. But human ancestors were not the only, and perhaps not even the most important, disembodied intentional entities around which the thoughts and actions of their daily lives were herded.

Holy cow. What is one to make of all the bull at Çatalhöyük? There are many types of dangerous animals represented in the painting and decoration of the houses, including bears and leopards. However, bulls (aurochs) seem to have played a particularly significant role. It would be anachronistic to call them "sacred" cows, but it appears that the aurochs were indeed set apart as dominant agents within the shared imagination of the coalition. Their bucrania in particular were a prominent part of the décor, as Figure 3.4 illustrates. Moreover, their positioning sometimes suggests that they bear some relevant relation to the human burials within the homes. We will return later to the possible connection between aurochs and ancestors within what Ian Hodder calls the

3.4. "Shrine 8" as reconstructed by James Mellaart.
Source: Alan Mellaart.

"prowess–animal spirit–hunting–feasting" nexus that seems so important in life at Çatalhöyük.

At this point I want to emphasize two things. First, as Hodder points out, both of these types of disembodied agents within the spirit world appear to have played a special role in mediating power related to proprietary production, that is, in providing access to the fruit of communal labor. He hypothesizes that the power of dominant groups such as elders or shamans may have been based partly on their capacity to intercede in relation to *wild animals and ancestors* (204). There may have been competition between forms of power based on the control of knowledge about ancestral ties and auroch behavior and forms of power based on domestic production and accumulation, but Hodder suggests all of these dimensions (material, social, spiritual) were entangled and mutually conditioned one another. "It seems most likely that much of the variation in elaboration of buildings, and in the number of burials, relates to the ability of household members (perhaps especially elders) to mobilize ritual, symbolism, revelation and their performance, even though exchange and production played their part" (183).

Second, the remains of both ancestors and aurochs played a special role in the ongoing process of hiding and revealing that characterized so much of the ritual behavior at Çatalhöyük. The sharp parts of animals (including bulls) were placed in walls, covered, and uncovered over and over again. Human skulls (as well as sculptures and other artifacts) were buried, dug up, kept over time, and reburied. Hodder proposes that this process of material circulation played a role in maintaining social continuity within the houses and had some bearing on status and power. "Things are hidden and then revealed. And often they are hidden in places where the *ancestors and animal spirits* are – beneath floors and behind walls. So when things return, revealed, they bring with them an aura from that other world. They have been magnified in their hidden journey" (Hodder 2006, 170, emphasis added). These repetitive and apparently ritual (un)covering processes appear to be linked to both ancestry and exchange.

In what follows I hope to contribute to the ongoing unearthing of the mysteries of the Çatalhöyük community by exploring ways in which our current knowledge of the naturally evolved human tendency toward anthropomorphic promiscuity and sociographic prudery, which together help to explain why and how gods are born(e) in the mental and social space of human life, could lead to new hypotheses about the role of supernatural agents within their daily lives in general and proprietary production in particular. Both dead ancestors and aurochs clearly qualify as *supernatural agents*, in the sense defined previously. The way in which their remains were engaged indicates shared beliefs about the causal power and intentionality of these disembodied entities within the coalition. What role did the integration of theogonic mechanisms play at Çatalhöyük?

Anthropomorphic Promiscuity at Çatalhöyük

There is a massive and rapidly growing literature supporting the claim that human beings have a naturally evolved tendency to overdetect agency, intentionality, and purposiveness. Neurological, psychological, and ethnographic research across cultures has demonstrated that human cognition automatically seeks out (more or less humanlike) agents (cf. Pyysiainen 2002, 2009; Barrett 2004; Tremlin 2006; Rossano 2010; Boyer 2010). Even the random movement of dots on a computer screen will be quickly interpreted as "intentional," and, especially under stress, most subjects will immediately guess "agent" with little or no priming when confronted with ambiguous phenomena. Humans seem to have evolved with a "hair-triggered" cognitive mechanism for detecting agents.

In my view Stewart Guthrie's *Faces in the Clouds* (1993) is still the best place to start for an introduction to the issue of anthropomorphism. Although a great deal of scientific research in the intervening decades has clarified the cognitive and cultural mechanisms involved, Guthrie's book provides a clear exposition of its prevalence and a daring philosophical assessment of its importance. His cognitive theory of religion is built on the reasonable hypothesis that the survival of early humans depended on their ability to perceive any other agents – especially other people – who might be around (cf. Guthrie 1980). Hypersensitivity to humanlike agents leads to many false alarms (e.g., seeing faces in the clouds) but it also makes it more likely that hidden agents will be perceived when it is really important (e.g., a camouflaged enemy). For Guthrie, anthropomorphism is by definition the failure of a naturally evolved perceptual strategy, and religion is systematized anthropomorphism.

Religious anthropomorphism is often understood as consisting of the attribution of humanity to gods, but Guthrie turns this around: "Gods consist of attributing humanity to the world" (1993, 3–4). In this sense all religions have gods or a god; they all involve "ostensible communication with humanlike, yet nonhuman, beings through some form of symbolic action" (197). The example of Buddhism is often raised as a counterexample, but although some philosophical streams of that tradition resist anthropomorphism (as do minority streams within all the axial age traditions), the vast majority of Buddhists are deeply entangled in shared imaginative engagement with all kinds of supernatural agents such as devas, bodhisattvas, and, of course, Buddhas. The question before us is what communication with "gods" such as the spirits of aurochs and ancestors may have looked like at Çatalhöyük.

To my knowledge the most explicit application of the research on (what I am calling) anthropomorphic promiscuity to Çatalhöyük is in the work of David Lewis-Williams and David Pearce (2005). They emphasize the *neurological* basis of belief in supernatural agents, which they interpret as the result of mistakenly attributing reality to iconic hallucinations experienced during altered states of consciousness. On the basis of neurological studies and ethnographic work in many contemporary small-scale societies, they argue that religion evolved as those who were particularly susceptible to or adept at having such experiences (shamans) came to be understood as capable of mediating between the human coalition and the spirit world.

Building on Lewis-Williams's earlier analysis of upper Paleolithic cave art (2002), they argue that the similarity between images found in the latter, such as handprints and geometric designs reminiscent of entopic phenomena in altered states, and the images found at Çatalhöyük suggest that the houses were a "built cosmos" replacing caves as the *axis mundi* within which mediation with spirit worlds can occur. Long before sedentism, human groups were participating in shared engagement with supernatural agents, especially human-animal hybrids perceived during hypnagogic states as hovering above or emerging from other worlds below. "The domestication of animals was already conceptually embedded in the worldview and socio-ritual complex we have described before people began actually herding the aurochs" (2005, 141). Here we have another example of the claim noted earlier, defended in different ways by Cauvin and Hodder, that symbolic imaginative engagement with "spirits" contributed to the revolution(s) of the Neolithic.

This interpretation of Çatalhöyük, whatever its other weaknesses or strengths, does not adequately incorporate some of the other popular hypotheses surrounding the phenomena of anthropomorphic promiscuity. Without downplaying the neurological basis of the overactive perception of agency, we should also note that one of the most important reasons for the hypersensitivity of this cognitive mechanism is the adaptive value of quickly detecting *predators and prey* (cf. Atran 2002). The predominance of dangerous animals in the art and décor of Çatalhöyük, including reliefs of leopards and bears as well as the teasing and hunting of bulls suggests that they were particularly interested in perceptual strategies related to these agents.

It makes sense, then, that the spirits of powerful predators would have been attributed power in the spirit world as well, and that the inhabitants of Çatalhöyük would have been primed to detect them. Whatever the details, we can plausibly conclude that their evolved hypersensitivity to seeking out agents was operative in their growing attempts to find, control, respond to, and manipulate dangerous agents even or especially in the spirit world. Shared engagement with such imagined agents may well have led to new strategies for finding and controlling actual agents in the natural environment and contributed to domestication and sedentism.

But of course predators and prey are not the only agents that are important to detect; for the species to survive, humans also need to find *protectors and partners*. Here is where the ancestors come in. *Homo sapiens* in the Neolithic, like their forebears and descendants, were born with a tendency to seek out protectors (usually parents) and developed an interest in seeking out partners (potential sexual mates). Our attachment to these embodied human agents does not suddenly disappear when they are not around; even after their death we feel emotionally connected to them. The powerful cognitive mechanics of anthropomorphic promiscuity continue to grind away and, given the significance of our attachment to such caregiving figures within the working models by which we navigate life, it is easy to understand why we remain predisposed to perceive their presence.

In the "attachment theory" developed by John Bowlby (1969) and others, the dynamics of the human behavioral system are described in explicitly evolutionary terms. Systems in which infants actively sought attachment with caregivers, and caregivers quickly detected and responded to the needs of infants, were naturally selected, and such dispositions became stronger over phylogenetic time. More recently, researchers have demonstrated that the attachment styles developed in infancy and childhood continue to affect adult life, especially in close and romantic relationships (e.g., Mikulincer and Shaver 2007; Rholes and Simpson 2004). Moreover, this deeply embedded drive for attachment also shapes people's relation to their perceived divine attachment figures, at least in the case of images of "God" (cf. Kirkpatrick 2005).

In other words, our naturally evolved hyperactive longing for attachment with embodied human agents easily spills over into a promiscuous seeking for and imaginative engagement with supernatural partners and protectors. Of course gods are not always (or even usually) nice, and supernatural agent coalitions are just as (if not more) likely to include fearsome predators as they are potential caregivers. For our purposes, however, the main point is that the data at Çatalhöyük could be illuminated in light of such theories. In my view, the most compelling example is the woman embracing the plastered skull in Figure 3.5. However, we could also point to the burials of infants, figurines, or even animals as examples of evidence that our Neolithic ancestors continued to detect the presence of their own dead ancestors with whom they had developed significant attachments.

We should be suspicious, as always, of overly speculative interpretations of the archaeological evidence, but if the inhabitants of Çatalhöyük were anatomically modern humans with the same basic cognitive mechanisms that we have today, we have good reasons to suspect that the data

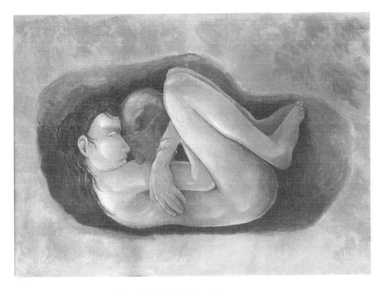

3.5. Reconstruction of burial in Building 42.
Source: John Swogger and Çatalhöyük Research Project.

are at least susceptible to such explanations. However, this is not the whole story. Supernatural agents may be born through overly sensitive cognitive mechanisms for detecting relevant intentional forces, but this does not explain why human families continue to bear responsibility for taking care for them. It takes the overly sensitive protection of a village to raise a god. Or, in the case of Çatalhöyük it took a Neolithic "town."

Sociographic Prudery at Çatalhöyük

The claim that religion plays a role in holding together human groups is hardly new. In fact, for much of the twentieth century, theories (like Durkheim's) that posited a social function at the root of religion were more influential than views (like Tylor's) that posited belief in "spiritual beings" as its essential characteristic. In the last two decades, however, empirical findings and theoretical reflection across the disciplines that study religion have contributed to an integration of these intuitions. The cognitive mechanisms that give rise to belief in supernatural agents and the coalitional mechanisms that hold groups together are mutually reinforcing. While one finds a natural and healthy competition among hypotheses for this mutuality, they are for the most part complementary and even convergent (cf. Shults 2011).

But how have these developments affected the interpretation of Çatalhöyük? Lewis-Williams and Pearce have proposed that shamans played a key role in regulating the "social contract" of its inhabitants as a way of dealing with their shared interpretations of the introverted end of the consciousness spectrum (2005). In other words, like all societies, they had to develop a "consciousness contract" as a way of dealing with their experiences of altered states of consciousness. The presence of entopic patterns and other representations in the art and architecture of Çatalhöyük that are reminiscent of shamanic cultures suggests to Lewis-Williams and Pearce that their social organization was structurally similar to that of others across the world. However plausible this may be, it does not go very far in explaining the actual mechanisms that produced and maintained the sociographic prudery of this particular Neolithic town.

Whitehouse and Hodder (2010) have pressed further by applying Whitehouse's "modes of religiosity" theory to Çatalhöyük. They point to evidence that suggests a slow shift from primarily "imagistic" toward more "doctrinal" modes of transmission during the sixteen-hundred-year settlement. The former mode is characterized, among other things, by emotionally intense rituals with low frequency, while the latter mode involves more frequent but less intense rituals (cf. Whitehouse 2004). They take the transition from extensive use of bucrania in the lower levels to a growing presence of stamp seals and pictorial narratives in the upper levels to indicate that the coalition became increasingly "doctrinal" over the centuries.

They suggest that as shamans (loosely defined) came to develop discursive and narrative strategies for transmission the settlement became characterized by more standardized ways of engaging and more authoritative interpretations of the spirit world. This highlights the importance of Çatalhöyük as a transitional site, which may have "paved the way for more centralized, large-scale and hierarchical patterns of political association" (Whitehouse and Hodder 2010, 142). One of the values of this theory is the way in which it illuminates the link between cognitive and coalitional structures at Çatalhöyük. The social morphology of the town became more complex as a result of the relation between divergent modalities of ritual transmission. Examining the archaeological data in this light will likely lead to new insights about the impetus for such change, identifying patterns that would otherwise have been missed.

It seems to me that there are at least two other types of theories related to sociographic prudery that could complement this proposal and lead to additional insights about the actual mechanisms at work at Çatalhöyük. The first type has to do with the role of supernatural agents in *moral evolution*. If organisms survive by taking care of themselves, why do we find apparently altruistic behavior in human life, such as actions in which an individual sacrifices her needs for the group? Some of the most popular scientific answers to this question these days are variants of the claim that the imagined presence of "gods" helped to solve the problem of cooperation within coalitions. It is often in the best interest of an individual to defect or cheat, especially if he or she can do so without being caught. However, if one is convinced that supernatural agents, who have fuller access to knowledge about socially relevant human actions and the power to bring or hinder misfortune, may be (or always are) watching, one is more likely to follow the rules that hold the group together.

To my knowledge, such hypotheses (e.g., Boyer 2001; Hauser 2006; Rossano 2010) have not been extensively applied to the Çatalhöyük material. This may be due in part to the fact that so little is known (or knowable) about the ethical codes or norms that guided their daily lives. Nevertheless, we do know that once supernatural agents have emerged within the human imagination, they are automatically attributed qualities that are common to the category PERSON, such as thoughts, intentions, and desires. We also know that the way in which they minimally violate intuitions about this category, such as embodiment, actually makes them easier to remember; that is why ideas of gods are such socially contagious concepts. Given our shared phylogenetic heritage, which includes such cognitive tendencies, it is reasonable to postulate that shared belief in "spirits" played a similar role in enhancing cooperation among the inhabitants of this Neolithic community. Like all other groups of *Homo sapiens*, the members of the Çatalhöyük coalition would have naturally and automatically wondered what their supernatural agents thought or desired.

What do goddesses want? For that matter, what did any of the gods of Çatalhöyük – animal spirits or deceased ancestors of either gender – want? At least during the period of the lower levels, the inhabitants of the houses would have been constantly confronted with images of bucrania (and other symbols) that would have activated the idea that animal spirits were watching them. Repeated burials and reburials within the houses would also have reinforced a sense that their ancestors may be listening. What are the animal spirits thinking about what they see? What are the ancestors feeling about what they hear? Whatever the specific answers, it is plausible to assume that this general sort of question had the effect of solidifying a willingness to cooperate in the ongoing rituals and moral conventions of Çatalhöyük. The ambiguity produced by the repeated hiding and revealing of bones and other artifacts would only have reinforced the detection and protection of the supernatural agent coalitions.

A second set of promising hypotheses, linked to what I have called sociographic prudery, that have not (to my knowledge) been applied to Çatalhöyük are those related to *costly signaling theory*. Here too the issue is explaining what appear to be anomalies within evolution, such as extravagant peacock tails, which require a high percentage of metabolic energy and weaken the capacity to evade predators. Such tails, however, are a signal to peahens that their carrier has genes strong enough to survive. In the case of religion, the phenomena to be explained include behaviors that are costly in terms of time and energy, often painful and also without any clear survival value. Richard Sosis, for example, points to the rituals of the Ilahita Arapesh, in which adult males dressed like boars pin down three-year-old boys and rub their genitals forcefully with stinging nettles (2006, 61). The descriptions of the molestations that must be suffered by males in this coalition, which continue in various forms throughout their lives, would make Hesiod blush.

Sosis argues that these and other religious behaviors, including the pursuit of badges and the acceptance of bans, neither of which provides (but often reduces) adaptive advantage, are actually forms of costly signaling. Participation signals commitment to the group, which strengthens the solidarity of the coalition and indirectly benefits the survival of the gene pool. For the most part, and over the long run, the most convincing displays are by those who are *really* committed to their beliefs and their promises to the coalition. People whose beliefs are internalized are willing to engage in displays of commitment that are (otherwise) so unreasonable that they would be very hard to fake. Scott Atran suggests that "collective commitment to the absurd is the greatest demonstration of group love that humans have devised" (2010, 450; cf. Bulbulia 2004). The most reliable signals of this love, which protects the coalition by reinforcing the willingness of its members to cooperate, are by those who truly believe that they are in coalition with supernatural agents.

How might this apply to Çatalhöyük? There is no strong evidence of excessively violent rituals, but the art depicts the teasing of wild animals which appears dangerous indeed. Moreover, there does not seem to be any survival advantage in having extremely sharp bulls' horns (cf. Figure 3.4) protruding from the walls of one's house. Using cognitive energy to remember how deeply ancestors are buried, and physical energy to dig them up and rebury them, have no obvious adaptive value. Given the explanatory power of costly signaling theory in so many other contexts, when *we* dig up something that indicates a widespread form of behavior that does not enhance fitness it seems reasonable to ask whether we have found evidence for shared imaginative engagement with supernatural agents. Participating in the various frequent rituals within the houses as well as the less frequent rituals connected with hunting, baiting, and feasting on bulls would have been ways of signaling commitment to the coalition, including those in the spirit world. This in turn would have strengthened the cohesion of the Çatalhöyük community.

Unfortunately, the other side of in-group cohesion is often out-group violence. Especially under difficult conditions, commitment to one's own group can reinforce discrimination against other groups. This is a natural evolutionary mechanism, but, as John Teehan points out, religion can intensify this discrimination by giving the moral differentiation between groups a divine sanction and raising the stakes of commitment to cosmic proportions (2010, 174). Teehan's analysis focuses on the Abrahamic religions, demonstrating how the ethical codes of these monotheistic traditions are expressions and extensions of, rather than exceptions to, the natural moral intuitions that emerged through the evolution of human brains in social groups.

The people of Çatalhöyük were clearly not monotheists, and there is not yet any clear evidence of violence toward in-group defectors or outgroups. This lack of evidence is itself one of the most fascinating features of the site, and its further exploration may shed light on the conditions that give rise to religious (or other) violence. In the meantime, there is much to ponder about our own propensity toward anthropomorphic promiscuity and sociographic prudery, which, on this side of the rise of the axial age religions and in this ever more complex space of global pluralism, may no longer have adaptive value for the human race. Seeking out and protecting supernatural agent coalitions with dead ancestors and aurochs may have helped keep the inhabitants of Çatalhöyük alive by providing a kind of emotional and social entangling force that held together their modes of proprietary production. But following similar strategies today could end up killing us.

Theolytic Mechanisms in Science and Theology

Digging at Çatalhöyük has revealed a great deal about the complex revolutionary changes that occurred in the evolution of humanity during the Neolithic. But can its physical and conceptual excavation disclose anything important about the difficult task our species faces today in learning to adapt to ever more complex intellectual and social challenges? If it is placed within the broader context of the phylogenetic emergence and psychological and political effects of god-bearing mechanisms, I believe it can. In this context I only have space for a few provocative suggestions.

As I have indicated, my primary interest as a philosopher and theologian is in how insights into the lives of the Neolithic inhabitants of Çatalhöyük can help us understand ourselves as we struggle to understand them. We too are entangled in particular ways of tending to proprietary production, but most of us live a quasi- or postsedentary life in which not just plants and animals but the natural environment itself is largely domesticated. We have become digital nomads, information hunter-gatherers roaming around a virtual global socius. The cognitive and coalitional tools that we still use in our navigation of this world, however, evolved in an environment with very different natural and social challenges. Tendencies toward anthropomorphic promiscuity and sociographic prudery served (some of) our ancestors well – but how are they working out for us?

Earlier I alluded briefly to the fact that scientists tend to be anthropomorphically prudish and sociographically promiscuous; let me now explain what I mean. Most scientists resist explanations of phenomena that appeal to the causal influence of disembodied intentional agents like the spirits of animals or ancestors. Regardless of academic discipline, such ideas are not welcome in the logical chains of their arguments or in the planning of their empirical experiments. For example, one will not find in archaeological journals any explanations of the data at Çatalhöyük that appeal to the actual causal efficacy of bull spirits (or goddesses) within the coalition. Most archaeologists would also be suspicious of any claims from their colleagues that their knowledge about the site had been revealed to them through angels or astrology. "The religious world increases the number and influence of intentional agents while science ultimately aims to minimize both by seeking alternative accounts of affairs in terms of underlying, predictable, non-intentional mechanisms" (McCauley and Lawson 1990, 162). In other words, scientists are (or try to be) anthropomorphic prudes.

Scientists are also suspicious of claims that appeal primarily or solely to authority or convention. Certainly they operate within a particular disciplinary tradition and must take much of what is handed down to them in trust, but scientists raise their eyebrows when a particular argument is immunized from critique because of the reputation of its source or the longevity of its popularity. For example, for many years the consensus of the archaeological community was that early hominin groups were violent. For the members of the Hodder team with whom I have interacted, actively seeking out new ways to organize the inquiry of their disciplinary socius in light of the new data at Çatalhöyük is more important than fidelity to such dominant conventions. Like most scientists, they pursue novel ways of inscribing the conceptual academic field with new hypotheses. In the case of the current (summer) inhabitants of Çatalhöyük, this also involves openness to intercourse with other disciplines – even philosophy and theology.

These two mutually reinforcing tendencies among scientists might be called *theolytic* mechanisms (cf. Figure 3.6) because of the way in which they loosen or dissolve (lysis) the hold of supernatural agents or gods (theos) on human minds and coalitions.

We do not have space here to deal with the other two quadrants of this diagram, which represent quite different ways of integrating the mechanism directions and, suffice it to say, lead to approaches that are either too prodigal or too penurious to work. For our purposes, the important point is the diametrical opposition between the direction sponsored by our evolved theogonic mechanisms (the lower left quadrant) and the direction represented in the upper right quadrant.

The integration of *theolytic* mechanisms unveils the hidden mechanisms by which supernatural agent coalitions are born(e). My rhetorical use of the phrase "unveiling theogonic mechanisms" is inspired by Rene Girard's well-known concept of the scapegoat mechanism (1977, 1986).

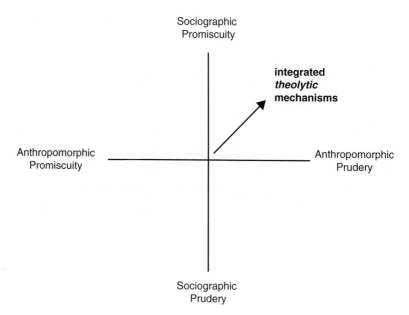

3.6. Theolytic mechanisms as defined in this chapter.

One might argue that the scapegoat mechanism is simply one (important) example of the integration of theogonic mechanisms, insofar as the former involves the detection of an ambiguous intentional force that must be dealt with in order to maintain the social cohesion of and psychological stability of an in-group. In this context, however, it is important to note some similarities and the differences between scapegoating and the integrated theogonic mechanisms we have been discussing. Here is perhaps the basic difference:

- The *scapegoat* mechanism creates weak victims, more or less vulnerable, who must be cursed, sent away, or destroyed in order to rid the community of violence, sin, or evil.
- The *theogonic* mechanisms, on the other hand, create powerful perpetrators, more or less invulnerable, who must be appeased in some way, in order to avoid misfortune or acquire blessing.

Both theogonic and scapegoating mechanisms "work," in the sense that persons within the in-group often feel better and their communities often survive longer because of them. One of the basic similarities between these mechanisms is that their "working" can actually make matters worse.

- Removing or destroying *scapegoats* reinforces the powerful belief that our problems can be solved by more violence.
- Detecting and protecting *gods* reinforce the powerful belief that our problems can be solved by our coalition with supernatural agents.

Another important similarity is that the very process of unveiling any of these mechanisms *weakens* their power. This is because they only work well when they are hidden to those within whom or upon whom they are operating. When we begin to recognize what we are doing to scapegoats, and what our scapegoating is doing to us, the process no longer automatically has the effect of (temporarily) calming us psychologically and politically. Similarly, as we begin to see how gods are born(e) in human cognition and culture, such conceptions can more easily become the objects of our critical reflection rather than surreptitiously shaping our subjectivity. For the reasons outlined in previous sections, evolution has predisposed us to think, act, and feel in ways that keep these mechanisms hidden.

This is why exposing the reproductive processes of god bearing can be so difficult and even frightening. We have evolved not to challenge beliefs in the things hidden in the walls and foundations of our coalitions. Challenging the beliefs or practices related to the supernatural agents of *other* traditions easily leads to conflicts that can quickly escalate and become dangerous. And so we avoid this too. This may not have been much of an issue at Çatalhöyük, with a relatively small and homogeneous population. There would be no reason to challenge the efficacy of engaging the spirit world by hiding and revealing skulls, the sharp parts of animals, and other artifacts. During the Neolithic, the ambiguity and mystery surrounding these processes would only have further activated the natural tendencies to detect humanlike agency and to protect one's place in the collective by costly signaling of commitment.

Now, however, we face very different adaptive challenges in an increasingly pluralistic and interconnected global environment in which we rely ever more deeply and are affected ever more intensely by scientific modes of inquiry and technological developments. During times of crisis, the same theogonic mechanisms that produce and maintain the supernatural agent coalition of a particular in-group also intensify its anxiety about and discrimination toward out-groups. Allowing these procreative urges to run wild in our current context is no longer productive. We can no longer afford to romanticize the human search for gods to protect and partner with us; it may once have been a harmless (or even helpful) romantic distraction, but today it is distracting us from the urgent task of developing new strategies for surviving in a rapidly changing environment.

Facilitating and strengthening theolytic mechanisms will not be easy. It will require great psychological and political sensitivity in relation to a wide array of shareholders with a stake in this endeavor, including not only scientists from diverse disciplines, but also laypeople and leaders associated with religious institutions, museums, educational groups, and funding agencies. Nevertheless, it is important to realize that, whether or not we mean it to, digging up Çatalhöyük has a theolytic effect. In my view it is best not to hide these mechanisms; we should move them out in the open for analysis and evaluation. Engaging in anthropomorphically prudish and sociographically promiscuous reflection on the processes by which gods are born(e) increases our capacity for adapting *intentionally*. Although this is not the job of archaeologists, anthropologists, or psychologists qua scientists, the kind of space created by international and interdisciplinary projects like this one provides an excellent opportunity for such intentional dialogue.

But what role could *theology* possible play in this endeavor? The vast majority of theologians have operated within the context of one of the religious traditions that can trace its roots to the axial age; for the most part, they have reinforced the detection and protection of particular supernatural agent coalitions. This direction within theology, which I call its *sacerdotal* trajectory, has by far been the most dominant and obviously contributes to theogonic reproduction. However, there have always been streams of dissent within these traditions, forces that push against anthropomorphic conceptions of the divine and push toward modes of sociography that do not inscribe harsh boundaries between groups. Pressing in this direction, which I call the *iconoclastic* trajectory of theology, has the effect of breaking the power of particular images of gods whose detection protects a conventional way of inscribing the socius (cf. Shults 2012a).

Theologians who follow this latter course today are in a unique position to collaborate with scientists in the unveiling of theogonic mechanisms. For example, demonstrating the logical incoherence of the notion of *an* infinite Supernatural Person, for which there are a wealth of resources even within the monotheistic traditions, can complement scientific challenges to the plausibility of appeals to the intervention of finite supernatural agents in the natural world (cf. Shults 2012b). In my view the best strategy here is not to attempt to disprove the possibility or even to weaken the probability of such causation through deductive or inductive arguments, but to challenge the plausibility of such religious hypotheses by offering abductive arguments that more adequately explain the phenomena without appealing to hidden revelations, thereby making it easier to disentangle the gods from the material and social dimensions of our proprietary production.

To an extent hardly imaginable even a century ago, we have gained significant control over the processes of childbirth. Developing effective means of divine birth control may prove to be much more difficult. It may turn out to be impossible. Perhaps theogonic mechanisms are so deeply embedded in our phylogeny that we can never escape the ontogenetic delivery of the gods. If so, the supernatural population will continue to grow within the natural mental and social space of *Homo sapiens*. The planet already feels overcrowded – physically, emotionally, cognitively. Given the potentially destructive effects of psychological strategies that are based on detecting divine attachment figures and political strategies that are driven by protecting supernatural coalitions, it seems to me that we can no longer avoid the challenge all parents must face. Some ways of caring for our offspring can become addictive and unhealthy; holding on to them too long is not good for us. Can we learn to let go of our supernatural progeny? It may become easier as the processes behind their mysterious arrival within our families of religious origin are increasingly unveiled.

BIBLIOGRAPHY

Atran, Scott. 2002. In *Gods We Trust: The Evolutionary Landscape of Religion*. Oxford: Oxford University Press.

2010. *Talking to the Enemy: Faith, Brotherhood, and the (Un)Making of Terrorists*. New York: Harper Collins.

Barrett, Justin. 2002. "Dumb gods, petitionary prayer and the cognitive science of religion." In *Current Approaches in the Cognitive Science of Religion*, eds. I. Pyysiainen and V. Anttonen. New York: Continuum, 93–109.

2004. *Why Would Anyone Believe in God?* New York: AltaMira Press.

Bowlby, John. 1969. *Attachment*. New York: Random House.

Boyer, Pascal. 2001. *Explaining Religion: The Human Instincts That Fashion Gods, Spirits and Ancestors*. London: Random House.

  2010. *The Fracture of an Illusion: Science and the Dissolution of Religion*. Gottingen: Vandenhoeck & Ruprecht.

Bulbulia, Joseph. 2004. "Religious Costs as Adaptations That Signal Altruistic Intention." *Evolution and Cognition* 10/1:19–42.

Cauvin, Jacques. 2000. *The Birth of the Gods and the Origins of Agriculture*. Trans. T. Watkins. Cambridge: Cambridge University Press.

Girard, Rene. 1977. *Violence and the Sacred*. Trans. P. Gregory. Baltimore: Johns Hopkins.

Girard, Rene. 1986. *The Scapegoat*. Trans. Y. Freccero. Baltimore: Johns Hopkins.

Guthrie, Stewart. 1980. "A Cognitive Theory of Religion," *Current Anthropology* 21/2:181–203.

  1993. *Faces in the Clouds: A New Theory of Religion*. New York: Oxford University Press.

Hauser, Marc. 2006. *Moral Minds: The Nature of Right and Wrong*. New York: Harper Collins.

Hodder, Ian. 2006. *Catalhoyuk: The Leopard's Tale*. London: Thames & Hudson.

Hodder, Ian and Lynn Meskell, "The Symbolism of Catalhoyuk in its regional context," In *Religion, Violence and Spirituality at Çatalhöyük*, ed. Ian Hodder. Cambridge: Cambridge University Press, 32–72.

Kirkpatrick, Lee A. 2005. *Attachment, Evolution and the Psychology of Religion*. New York: Guilford.

Lewis-Williams, David. 2002. *The Mind in the Cave: Consciousness and the Origins of Art*. New York: Thames & Hudson.

Lewis-Williams, David and David Peirce. 2005. *Inside the Neolithic Mind*. New York: Thames & Hudson.

McCauley, Robert N., and E. Thomas Lawson. 1990. *Rethinking Religion*. Cambridge: Cambridge University Press.

  2002. *Bringing Ritual to Mind: Psychological Foundations of Cultural Forms*. Cambridge: Cambridge University Press.

Mikulincer, Mario and Phillip R. Shaver. 2007. *Attachment in Adulthood: Structure, Dynamics, Change*. New York. Guilford Press.

Pyssiainen, Ilkka. 2009. *Supernatural Agents: Why We Believe in Souls, Gods and Buddhas*. Oxford: Oxford University Press.

Pyssiainen, Ilkka and Veikko Anttonen, eds. 2002. *Current Approaches in the Cognitive Science of Religion*. London: Continuum.

Renfrew, Colin and Iain Morley, eds. 2010. *Becoming Human: Innovation in Prehistoric Material and Spiritual Culture*. Cambridge: Cambridge University Press.

Rholes, W. Steven and Jeffry A. Simpson, eds. 2004. *Adult Attachment: Theory, Research and Clinical Implications*. New York: Guilford Press.

Rossano, Matt J. 2010. *Supernatural Selection: How Religion Evolved*. Oxford: Oxford University Press.

Schaller, Mark et al., eds. 2010. *Evolution, Culture and the Human Mind*. New York: Taylor & Francis.

Shults, F. LeRon. 2010. "Spiritual entanglement: Transforming religious symbols at Çatalhöyük." In *Religion, Violence and Spirituality at Çatalhöyük*, ed. Ian Hodder. Cambridge: Cambridge University Press,73–98.

— 2011. "Bearing Gods in Mind and Culture." *Religion, Brain & Behavior* 2/2 (2011) 1/2: 154–167).

— 2012a "The problem of good (and evil): Arguing about axiological conditions in science and religion." In *Science and the World's Religions*, eds. Wesley Wildman and Patrick McNamara. New York: Praeger, 39–68.

— 2012b. "Science and religious supremacy: Toward a naturalist theology of religions." *Science and the World's Religions*, eds. Wesley Wildman and Patrick McNamara. New York: Praeger, 73–100.

— In press. *Iconoclastic Theology: Gilles Deleuze and the Secretion of Atheism*. Edinburgh: Edinburgh University Press.

Simpson, Jeffry A., and W. Steven Rhodes, eds. 1998. *Attachment Theory and Close Relationships*. New York: Guilford Press.

Sosis, Richard. 2006. "Religious behaviors, badges and bands: signaling theory and the evolution of religion," In *Where God and Science Meet*. Vol. I: *Evolution, Genes and the Religious Brain*, ed. Patrick McNamara. London: Praeger, 61–86.

Teehan, John. 2010. *In the Name of God: the Evolutionary Origins of Religious Ethics and Violence*. New York: Wiley-Blackwell.

Tremlin, Todd. 2006. *Minds and Gods: the Cognitive Foundations of Religion*. Oxford: Oxford University Press.

Whitehouse, Harvey. 2004. *Modes of Religiosity*. New York: Alta Mira Press.

Whitehouse, Harvey and Ian Hodder. 2010. "Modes of religiosity at Çatalhöyük." In *Religion in the Emergence of Civilization: Çatalhöyük as a Case Study*. ed. Ian Hodder. Cambridge: Cambridge University Press, 122–145.

4

Religion As Anthropomorphism at Çatalhöyük

Stewart Elliott Guthrie

Introduction

The first question put to the 2006–2009 Templeton scholars was, How can archaeologists recognize the spiritual, religious, and transcendent in early time periods? The question is difficult, not least because the very meanings of the terms "spiritual," "religious," and "transcendent" are contested. The initial question thus immediately devolves to theoretical issues both broad and hoary. That question was not addressed to our cohort; yet the issues are so central, rich, and refractory as to merit further comment. I therefore wish to offer another answer to the question What is religion? and to apply it to a few topics at Çatalhöyük. These include the nature of ancestral remains, the house, leopards, and teeth and claws in walls. More specifically, my answer helps account for the vitality – that is, the animacy – that these objects apparently had for the people who created or curated them.

In addressing the question of what is religion, I assume that religion is a concept, not a real thing in the world, and that this concept originated at a particular time in a particular part of the world. In contrast, in most of the ancient and modern world, including Çatalhöyük (Hodder 2010a: 16, Hodder this volume), religion does not stand out as a separate concept but is part of the cultural fabric. As Pels (2010: 233) writes, we should not look for a "distinct practice, with institutional and doctrinal unity or coherence" at Çatalhöyük. Nonetheless, religion there as elsewhere can be given a particular, substantive definition, one based on a category of human thought and action that is even broader than religion, yet still distinctive.

My aim here exemplifies both Bloch's (2010) sketch of the predicament of the nonarchaeologist at Çatalhöyük, who wishes to contribute but risks speaking from ignorance, and the observations by Hodder (2010a) and Hodder and Meskell (2011: 243) that outsiders tend to arrive with their theories ready-made. Alerted by these writers, I shall try to adapt my theory to the Çatalhöyük data.

Definitions and Theories of Religion

Views of religion among the first Templeton-Çatalhöyük cohort diverge fundamentally. Hodder (2010a: 13) remarks that tension arose from the start, for instance, over whether the term "religion" denotes something culturally universal or is culture bound. Van Huyssteen (2010: 102 and 105), for example, writes that "every human society … possessed religion" and that the religious imagination is central to both paleoanthropological and theological definitions of humanness. Bloch (2010: 161), in contrast, sees religion as culture bound and is "confident that there was no religion in Çatalhöyük."

In our own cohort, similar disagreements arose concerning explanations appropriate for religion. "Instrumentalist" explanations (Braithwaite 1970), some of which are implicit in the questions asked of our cohort (Hodder Ch. 1, this volume), account for religion by its supposed purposes, such as reducing anxiety or promoting ethical behavior. Instrumentalist explanations contrast with, for example, "spandrel" explanations (Gould and Lewontin 1979), which account for varied phenomena including religion as accidental by-products of evolution.

Instrumentalism is a kind of functionalism, the doctrine that a feature (the wings of birds, for example, or the incest taboo) may be explained by what it does for an organism or a society. I have argued elsewhere (e.g., 1993) against functionalism, on grounds that even if a feature "explained" by its ostensible purpose does fulfill that purpose, the feature first must come into existence – the very fact that is to be explained. Thus, for example, religion may (or may not) produce social solidarity or justify the concentration of wealth, but first it must arise and be plausible. Hence explaining natural phenomena (arguably including as a subset many social phenomena, such as crime rates) by their ostensible purposes is teleological (Bacon 1960) and hence anthropomorphic.

My own, evolutionary argument is of the spandrel kind, not the instrumentalist.

Disagreement on defining and explaining religion is of course chronic. Shults (2010: 90) remarks that the very term is notoriously difficult. So are related terms. Nakamura (2010: 304), noting that Pels (2010) considers magic "everyday" religion, says the concept of magic is slippery too. Nonetheless, we should continue "trying to make sense" (Shults 2010: 77) of the notion of religion.

Pursuing both such sense and a better understanding of Çatalhöyük, I explore here how a particular universalist, substantive, and family-resemblance view of religion may apply to the archaeological material. In this view, religion is an aspect of a broad, ramified, and panhuman cognitive phenomenon, anthropomorphism. As noted, this approach may help show why such inanimate materials as Çatalhöyük's human and animal burials, sharp and pointed animal parts, skulls in history houses, and not least houses themselves possess vitality and power.

My approach also constitutes a response to Bloch's (2008) assertion that anthropologists should study not religion but a human universal. By identifying a universal of which religion appears as one aspect, I hold, we can study both. The argument satisfies as well Durkheim's ([1912] 1995: 51) stipulation that "for a phenomenon as widespread as [religion] to be explained by an illusion, the cause of the very illusion ... invoked would have to be equally widespread."

A Cognitive Theory

The argument appeared decades ago (Guthrie 1980) and, despite refinements and updates, remains much the same. Cognitivist scholars of religion now generally accept at least three of its propositions: that we are especially concerned to detect intentional agents (prototypically humans) in our environments, that we search for them with high sensitivities and low thresholds, and that we necessarily overdetect. Doing so, we construct a world brimming with humanlike vitality.

Guthrie (1980) made three further assertions touching on religion. First (as Spinoza 1955; Hume 1957; Horton 1993; and others also hold), religious and secular thought and action are similar and continuous and spring from the same cognitive processes. Religion is not sui generis. Although this claim of continuity contradicts much traditional religious scholarship, it agrees with the 2006–2009 Templeton cohort that "religion and the secular cannot easily be distinguished" (Hodder 2010a: 14), and with Hodder that at Çatalhöyük "ritual and mundane activity [are] impossible to separate" and "every single act we can observe seems to blur the boundaries between the everyday and the sacred or special" (2010a: 16).

My second further assertion was that anthropomorphism, understood as the attribution of human characteristics to nonhuman things and events, pervades our thought and action, mostly unconsciously. It is more diverse and less accessible than we appreciate. Few are aware, for example, that we perceive landscapes in terms of the human body or that contemporary print advertisers pair bottles and glasses, respectively, as men and women (Guthrie 2007b). Hume (1957: 29–30) says even philosophers cannot help anthropomorphizing, and Goethe says, "The human *never* knows how anthropomorphistic he is" (Liebert 1909: 22, translation mine).

We anthropomorphize, largely involuntarily and unaware, not only artifacts and natural phenomena but also abstractions, such as liberty, death, and the seasons. Discussing magic at Çatalhöyük, for instance, Nakamura (2010: 305 and 316, emphasis added) bears out Hume on the spontaneity and generality of anthropomorphism by crediting magic with needs, character traits, goals, effort, companions, allies, adversaries, complicity, and strategy. Magic "often *needs* to push against something [and] *cunningly*, appears to belong to the very system it *labors* to subvert; it has been [a] *constant companion* [and] an *ally* and *agitator*.... [However,] magic need not be an *adversary* [but] might be more *complicit*.... Magic often *seeks out* isolated and hidden spaces, perhaps ... *to contain the force of its performance*."

Nor is Nakamura's passage idiosyncratic. Rather, we all produce endless representations of humans in nonhuman form. Most of these stem from intuitions: judgments that, for want of alternatives, proceed automatically. We anthropomorphize daily by hearing wind-slammed doors as intruders, apprehending illnesses as just deserts, or seeing design in leaves. The cognitive psychologist Wegner (2005: 22) notes our "compelling inclination to perceive even ... geometric figures" as agents, and Mar and MacRae (2006: 110) write, "We routinely view quite abstract nonliving representations as if they were intentional agents."

This inclination is ancient. The archaeologist Lahelma (2008: 135) notes that "some of the earliest ... paleoart feature[s] anthropomorphism" and that a jasperite pebble apparently carried into a South African cave by an Australopithecine two to three million years ago evidently was chosen because it had natural "eyes" and a "mouth." Similar tendencies appear throughout the history of art and occur even in science (Guthrie 1993).

At Çatalhöyük, objects probably seen as alive and humanlike include houses and ancestral remains. That ancestors should be so conceived may be self-evident; yet in the biological view, the skeletal and other remains with which they are associated are *not* persons. Thus treating them as persons, as the constant curation (and in one case, plastering) of skeletal materials suggests they were, anthropomorphizes them. Houses also are widely conceived as persons, especially in "house societies" (in which kin relations are based on residence as well as on descent and marriage), of which Çatalhöyük apparently was one.

The third additional assertion in Guthrie (1980) is that religion may best be conceived as anthropomorphism systematized and taken seriously. That religion is anthropomorphism is not a new idea, having been proposed by Feuerbach, Freud, Horton, Hume, Levi-Strauss, Spinoza, Tylor, and others. However, the analyses of anthropomorphism upon which these earlier proposals rest are divergent and incomplete.

Hume (1957), for example, like Spinoza (1955) before him, persuasively identifies religion as a product of ordinary cognition, namely, as mistakenly perceiving natural phenomena as human or humanlike. He describes such perceptions as spontaneous and involuntary. Yet although Hume is perhaps the preeminent theorist of religion and the precursor of cognitive science (Morris 2009), his view that such perceptions stem simply from our familiarity with humanlike models may usefully be amended by the addition of simple game theory, á la Blaise Pascal (Guthrie 1980, 1993).

Viewed through game theory, anthropomorphism stems from an interpretive strategy, as follows. In grasping the world, we must guess (Hume 1957: 28–29) how to construe phenomena. Perception is interpretation, because every stimulus has more than one potential cause (a tickle on the skin may be a loose thread or a spider; a thump in the night may be a door closed by wind or a burglar.) Ambiguity haunts even the simplest percepts, such as lines and edges. As Gombrich (1973, following Adelbert Ames Jr.) puts it, perception is betting. It may be considered betting about cause: what, or who, caused the tickle or thud? We predictably bet on the most significant possibility: the spider not the thread, the burglar not the wind.

The most significant possibilities (universally seen as the most animated and vital, Cherry 1992) usually are organisms, especially humans. Practically, humans are significant because they are complexly organized and powerful, able to generate, for example, an indeterminate range of effects including symbolic ones. Intellectually, as models for understanding the world, they again are most significant, generating endless inferences from the same power and complexity.

Human presence, however, may be hard to detect. As do other animals (famously including leopards, for instance) we exploit perceptual uncertainty by camouflage and deceit. Moreover, our behavior is so protean that almost nothing, from sea-level rise to earthquakes, can be excluded a priori as an effect. Thus our difficulty in discovering humans and similar intentional agents is not peculiar to the Pleistocene as some hold (e.g., Westh 2013), but ongoing. This difficulty compounds the intrinsic complexity of cognition. And thus as we bet high, on humanlike agents, we face long yet worthwhile odds.

The evolutionary basis of this strategy (evidently shared by other animals, Guthrie 2002; Foster and Kokko 2008) is, Better safe than sorry: better to mistake a stick for a snake or a boulder for a bear, and more generally to mistake an lifeless object for a vital one, than the reverse. The logic is that of Pascal's wager: if right, we gain much and, if wrong, lose little. The most salient default models resulting from this wager, humanlike ones, are endlessly diverse, general, and largely unconscious. Thus accidents appear as punishments, earthquakes as messages, and the universe as designed.

It is worth noting that the strategy described has nothing to do with "projection," a concept often said (e.g., by Freud 1990 [1912–1913]; Mithen and Boyer 1996; Boyer 2001: 143–144; and Descola 2009) to explain anthropomorphism. Although popular, the concept of projection as a mental process is muddled and has aptly been called a metaphor without a theory (Harvey 1995). No precise description of this purported mental process is available, and scrutiny reveals the metaphor as not merely useless but also misleading (Guthrie 2000).

A key question arises: What is "humanlike" in a model, and for what do we search? We search first (Guthrie 1980, 1993, 2007a, 2008) for minds and behavior resulting from them, notably symbolism. Wegner (2005:

22) similarly notes our "readiness to perceive minds behind events" and writes that our "faculty for mind perception is a strong guiding force in perception more generally." Human minds, in turn, include generalized capacities for language and other symbolism; so all events – taps on the window, comets, illnesses – seem to signify.

The complementary question is, What is *not* humanlike in gods, spirits, and other humanlike agents? No clear disjunction exists. Rather, they, we, and other animals appear on a continuum or, better, on various continua. Gods may, for example, share the travails of the human life course: being born, eating, drinking, growing old, getting sick, and dying (Thompson 1955; Ehnmark 1939).

These answers raise further questions: If gods, spirits, and other humanlike agents (central to religion, pace Keane 2010: 195), with their traces and messages, are anthropomorphisms, why are they frequently represented as invisible and/or intangible, when actual humans are neither? If invisible, why are they plausible? Can humans also be invisible and intangible, or do these qualities distinguish gods and spirits? Since spiritual beings and especially humans (Cherry 1992) arguably are for us the archetypical agents, to answer these questions is to say how we conceive agency.

Cognitive Science, Agency, and Spiritual Beings

Folk-psychological, that is, intuitive, concepts of agency, in fact, resemble our concepts of spirits in a number of ways (Guthrie 2008). Centrally, scholars in a number of disciplines (e.g., Lakoff and Johnson 1999 in linguistics and philosophy; Bloom 2004 in psychology; Lohmann 2003 and Descola 2006 in anthropology; and Koch 2008 in religious studies) say the concept of agency is informed by intuitive and even innate mind-body (or spirit-body) dualism. Bering (e.g., 2002, 2006) in psychology, for example, shows that children at the age of three or four understand physical death, but assume that a mind survives it. A neurobiologist (Stent 1998: 578), referencing Kant, writes, "To be human means to be a dualist." Even a critic of the view that dualism is intuitive (Hodge 2008) denies only that our dualism is Cartesian and absolute, and indeed attributes of mind and body constitute a continuum, not sharply divided poles (e.g., Cohen, Burdett, Knight, and Barrett 2011). Anthropologists and others report dualism, with material body and immaterial mind (or near-equivalents, often plural) in many world areas, and evidence for it at Çatalhöyük exists as well.

A second aspect of agency is that mind (or spirit, life, or person), widely conceived as the immaterial or ethereal basis of identity, sentience, and volition, and often as divisible, has priority over, and independence from, body. Writers in a number of disciplines describe something like this priority of mind. In philosophy, Shults (2010: 75), for example, notes that "spirit" was long used for "that which energized or moved things." Indeed mind or spirit is widely conceived as life itself, so this dualism is, at the same time, vitalism; as Kant remarks (1952: §29:131, in Drake 2008: 172), "The mind is all life (the life-principle itself)."

Despite the priority and relative independence of mind/spirit/life, its relation to body is complex, nuanced, and variable. Cherry (1992) gives book-length linguistic evidence that humans cross-culturally rank forms of life by degree of "animacy" (roughly, vitality), basing their ranking on degree of resemblance to humans. Cues for judging this resemblance include morphology, such as eyes, a mouth, and bilateral symmetry, but more importantly behavior, especially goal-directed action. The more like humans other forms of life are, the more alive they are; so Cherry's "animacy" really is anthropomorphism.

Thus our conceptions of spirit in animals and other life-forms apparently are (as Tylor 1964 [1878] held) variants of our conceptions of ourselves. This is consistent with the widespread attribution to animals of humanlike thought, language, and culture (e.g., Thompson 1955; Descola 2009). At Çatalhöyük, for instance, the horns, teeth, and bones embedded in houses may have "materialized an animistic society" in which the immured animals resembled and were continuous with the people buried below them (Weismantel, this volume). As Weismantel remarks, "Not all societies recognize the duality of man and beast."

That mind is independent of body usually means that it is free of physical limitations such as a single location (spirits often are compared to wind) and an inability to see through solid substances. At Çatal, freedom from that inability would mean that even bones and teeth within walls or covered with plaster would be perceptible to spirit beings. As Buchli (this volume, cited by Hodder, this volume) puts it, Çatal walls are "seething" with the forces of animal parts embedded in them. Their seething is forceful in part because it is perceptible, at least to spirits.

Regarding the freedom of location enjoyed by ideas, thoughts, and agency, Bloch (2007) writes that it results from our production of similar states of mind in each other. We see such states as located in one person, in several, as broadly collective, or as nowhere in particular. In any case, the indeterminate location of mind/spirit/life does not prevent its contingent association with, or attachment to, the body; witness the association of spirits with graveyards.

Spirit widely is associated especially with the most durable parts of the body: the skeleton and teeth. This obtains also at Çatalhöyük, where human bones evidently were agentful "partible vital substances" (Hodder Chapter 13, this volume), "delegates of the dead [who] intruded themselves into daily life" (Hodder 2006: 61). As skeletons, indeed, "the ancestors would not go away and they could be named and identified" (2006: 61). Patton and Hager (Chapter 9, this volume, cited by Hodder this volume) say that human bones were what animated the houses; and for Buchli, bones, together with images, are what is seething in the walls. Gillespie (2002) similarly interprets domestic burials in another putative house society, the pre-Hispanic Maya, where the ancestors were a carefully curated resource who were encouraged to "stay home," that is, inside the house.

Further opinion that intuitive conceptions of agency give mind/spirit/life priority over, and independence from, body arises from several disciplines. In anthropology, Lohmann (2003) finds this priority primordial, and Gell (1998) argues that human agency is "distributed," in that we act not only through our body but also, at a distance and over time, through artifacts. In archaeology Wason (2010: 277), among others, assumes that Çatalhöyük cosmology included "active spirit agents." In linguistics and philosophy, Lakoff and Johnson (1999) say humans consider their essential selves immaterial, and Leder (1990) says we think of ourselves as minds because we are aware of our bodies only when they trouble us.

Psychologists also widely find the mind preeminent in intuitive agency, and the body secondary, rudimentary, or even absent. A bounded body is unnecessary to conceptions of agency (Csibra, Gergely, Bíró, Koós, & Brockbank 1999; Scholl and Tremoulet 2000), and we perceive even a collection of dots moving together as an agent (Bloom and Veres 1999). By about age three or four, children represent immaterial agents (Kelemen 2004); and five-month old infants may not even see humans as material objects (Kuhlmeier, Bloom, and Wynn 2004; but see Saxe,

Tzelnic, and Carey 2006). Theory of mind may be domain-general, since people apply it to inanimate phenomena such as weather (Lillard and Skibbe 2005: 281).

The freedom of mind and person from a bounded body noted by psychologists again has analogs at Çatalhöyük. Meskell (2007: 280) reports figurines showing "amorphous bodies that defy the natural boundaries of the body" (her illustration resembles ghosts as depicted in both European and East Asian traditions), and Hodder (Ch. 1, this volume) writes that the "world had vitality and power" as in natural crystals, symmetrical wall designs, and plaster surfaces. Wason (2010: 292–293) similarly suggests that theory of mind was applied to inanimate things: paintings, pots, bucrania, teeth and claws, skulls, and obsidian blades.

A third aspect of agency is that teleology is central, almost by definition. However, teleology can also appear by itself, as in our sense that the natural world shows design, for example in the symmetry of Çatalhöyük's crystals. Csibra et al. (1999: 265) find that infants readily attribute goals to objects if they move, even by being pushed. Thus teleology also, like theory of mind generally, is domain independent and is, for infants, a basic way of understanding the world. Kelemen (2004, 2012) too writes that young children are teleologists and indeed natural theists, since they find purpose and design everywhere and assume there must be a designer.

A fourth aspect of agency is that we perceive it unconsciously. Neuroscientists and psychologists (Farah and Heberlein 2007; Hassin, Uleman and Bargh 2005; Lillard and Skibbe 2005: 282; Phelps 2007; and Scholl and Tremoulet 2000) write that detecting intentionality and animacy is perceptual and automatic. Seeing one geometric figure "follow" another on a screen, for example, we predictably infer agency. Similarly, agency may be evoked by parts as well as by wholes – at Çatalhöyük, by a jaw, a wolf paw, or a pair of horns.

A fifth and last aspect of agency is that our standards for judging it present are low (Mar and MacRae 2006: 118). As noted, even a moving collection of dots appears as an agent. We look for agency actively and, as Nietzsche noted (Cziko 2000: 13), automatically. These five intuitive aspects of agency – dualism, priority of mind, teleology, unconsciousness, and low threshold – together prime us to detect agents, embodied or not. Apparently, then, the reason that invisible and intangible spirits are believable is that they are the essence of how we conceive agency in daily life. The collective vitality that many scholars of Çatalhöyük ascribe to that world thus is a universal human phenomenon.

Why do we intuitively conceive agents so differently from modern biology? Such conceptions may constitute an evolved strategy for a perceptual problem (Guthrie 2008): identifying intentional agents in a world in which their embodiments are innumerable and camouflaged and defy easy identification. Compared to their embodiments, agents' goals and purposes are few and predictable. Indeed the central ones are only three: eating, reproducing, and avoiding being eaten. Perhaps in consequence, our notions of agents are built more around their goals and effects than around their bodily forms. At Çatalhöyük, for example, ancestors surely were characterized more by their interest in, and effects on, the well-being of their houses, and leopards more by their interest in and effects on domestic herds, than either was by their appearance. Both ancestors and leopards were difficult to see, but the actions of ancestors could be discerned in (for instance) the sickness or health of households, and those of leopards in missing goats.

A Neurology of Anthropomorphism

The preceding description of our readiness to find humanlike beings everywhere, in myriad forms or in no form at all, is supported by recent brain studies. These bear out, from another direction, Hume's description of anthropomorphism as spontaneous and inevitable.

Farah and Heberlein (2007), Phelps (2007), and Henshilwood and Dubreuil (2011) suggest that our perception of persons is produced by specialized perceptual and conceptual nervous circuitry constituting a social brain and, according to Farah and Heberlein, a dedicated person-representation system. The circuitry in question, associated, for example, with the fusiform gyri, the amygdala, the temporoparietal junction, and the medial prefrontal cortex, by several accounts constitutes a network producing representations of a wide variety of human physical and mental features.

Whether or not these brain areas constitute a dedicated network, some other neurologists agree that both "psychological and neurological evidence [shows we are predisposed] to create the illusion of personhood. We do this automatically, and it ... may be impossible to change this perception, even when we are ... aware that it is inaccurate" (Phelps 2007: 50).

This person-representation circuitry, then, is on a hair trigger. It produces human features both from endlessly diverse, often minimal, external stimuli (e.g., from humans and their communications and artifacts – such as the ambiguous clay figurines and sticklike paintings of humans at Çatalhöyük – and even from wind sounds and cloud shapes) and from internal reflection. Triggering one feature in this circuit lights up other features, forming indefinitely varying representations. The circuitry thus embodies the logic of Pascal's wager: better to guess mistakenly many times that something important is present than to guess mistakenly once that it is *not*.

Anthropomorphism and Houses

As anthropomorphism is involuntary and pervasive, few objects of perception or contemplation escape it. Architecture, however, displays especially complex interaction between, and comparison of, artifact, body, and whole person. This comparison is enduring and worldwide (Vitruvius 1931, 1960; Frascari 1987, 1991; Carsten and Hugh-Jones 1995; Forshee 2006: 101; Gillespie 2007: 33; Drake 2008) but is especially explicit in house societies, such as Çatalhöyük.

It is appropriate, then, that Hodder (this volume, Ch. 13) describes Çatal houses as having had particular vital force, citing Patton and Hager on house-foundation burials of infants and Weismantel on the house as "materially alive ... infused with spirit and being" (all this volume). He earlier describes houses as having "lives" (2006: 129, 165) and "potency" (2006: 132), and as "huddling" together. Houses "push and shove" (Whitehouse and Hodder 2010: 135) to be near ancestral houses. They are "born" in ritual including foundation burials of neonates (Hodder, personal communication) and "die" (2006: 129) but remain potent, requiring proper cleaning and burial. At Çayönu at least, and perhaps at Çatalhöyük, they are buried (Hodder 2006: 132), and Hodder and Meskell (2011: 249) describe Çatal wooden pillars, bearing bucrania and embedded in walls, as "suggesting ... a skeleton for the house." House demolition sometimes is associated with the meaty parts of bulls, suggesting that a funeral meal was held for the house. In house societies generally, a house is a "corporate body" and, at Çatalhöyük, "it is the life of the house which constructs social lives as much as the other way round" (Hodder 2006: 165).

The notion of house as person is intuitive, and, at Çatalhöyük, even observers from nonhouse societies adopt it readily. As Patton (citing Mills and others of our cohort) put it at our first meeting in 2009, Çatalhöyük "houses are people." The house is "a living entity … homologous to a human person" and must "be born, be animated, be fed and maintained throughout its life, and … buried when its time comes to die. [Houses have] a life cycle … that triggers all the ritual responses of a human life." Weismantel (this volume) similarly notes that "people at Çatalhöyük treated the house like they treated human skeletons" in dismembering and rearranging its parts.

Just as the Çatal house as a whole is alive, so are its contents and parts, each "of which had a material vitality of its own" and is "animate [and] alive with productive desire" (Weismantel, this volume). These contents and parts "act as material agents or delegates for people" (Hodder 2006: 189) and are "co-dependent" (2006: 257) with them. Nakamura (2010: 325–326) refers to features, rooms, and houses as "'forms of life'" and wonders whether people attributed agency to "ovens, bins, platforms and houses." People cannot complete their domestic schedules "unless pots help them" (Hodder 2006: 60). Over time, some parts of the house move animatedly: Hearths "seem to wander" (2006: 251) and ovens move "restlessly" (2006: 62). In Buildings 1 and 4, ovens sometimes are so carefully buried as to be preserved (Hodder 2006: 133), and Nakamura (2010: 310) also notes that ovens and heat installations are strongly emphasized. Such emphasis again is consistent with animacy, widely associated with heat and light. It also resembles conceptions in young children (and perhaps in adults) of human internal organs as having "initiative and effortful engagement in activity" (Inagaki and Hatano 1993: 1534).

The scope of anthropomorphism at Çatalhöyük is broadened still further by Hodder's (2010a: 23) remark that, if we know the association of the navel and the spiral meander, "the human form is everywhere at the site." In fact, there is virtually no phenomenon to which humans do not ascribe human features, either as persons or as artifacts of personal action. These features may be physical, but more importantly include theory of mind, with human linguistic and symbolic capacities; narrativity; teleology; and mind-body dualism.

Phallocentrism, Pointed and Dangerous Parts, and Piercing

I turn finally and briefly to several recent issues about Çatalhöyük and environs, to comment on a few interpretations given by scholars "closer to the trowel's edge." Hodder and Meskell (2011) identify three symbolic themes in the early Turkish Neolithic, based primarily on Çatalhöyük and Göbekli, and suggest that these themes may have been instrumental in the process of agricultural intensification.

The three themes are first, phallocentrism, with depictions of erect penises, both animal and human; second, a concern with wild and dangerous animals and especially their hard, pointed, and durable parts; and third, a concern with the piercing and manipulation of flesh connected with curating skulls, both human and animal. What these three themes may have meant and how they may have been related are, of course, hard to know, as the authors and respondents note. Nonetheless, I will offer a few thoughts, starting by recasting the issues as questions.

First, why is there apparent phallocentrism? Second, why are there sharp, dangerous animal parts in the walls (and why, to revive a question in Hodder 2006, do these not include leopard parts?) And third, why are there piercing of flesh and removal of human and animal heads? We can derive a few possible suggestions from the intersection of the notions of house society and of pervasive anthropomorphism, including its religious forms. That is, each question can be set in the context of people's presumed desire to maintain durable houses and their presumed belief that humanlike agency in the world is general.

Why, then, was there phallocentrism, as opposed (for example) to goddesses? Hodder and Meskell (2011: 237) note that phallocentrism privileges maleness as a cultural signifier and a "source of power and authority," and that this is echoed in choosing bulls for feasting at Çatalhöyük and in depicting male animals there and at Göbekli. In contrast, older interpretations of male-centered imagery, Hodder and Meskell note skeptically, link it with violence.

My first observation is that Hodder's and Meskell's connection of phallocentrism with power is consistent with an assumption that people at Çatalhöyük, as elsewhere, saw the penis as having its own anthropomorphic vitality. In relatively recent times, for example, Montaigne writes, "We are right to note the license and disobedience of this member which thrusts itself forward so inopportunely when we do not want it to, and which so inopportunely lets us down when we most need it. It imperiously contests for authority with our will" (Haidt 2006: 5). This organ is thus a locus of independent animacy and hence interest, both in humans and in animals. This observation admittedly is both ahistoric and acontextual; but the widespread presence of phallicism in European Upper Paleolithic art (Angulo and García-Díez 2009) as well as in the Turkish Neolithic means at least that we must cast our explanatory and comparative net wider than Çatalhöyük alone.

A second suggestion about phallocentrism is that if – as is likely – Neolithic people understood the male role in reproduction, then an interest in fertility could be expressed as an interest in male sexuality just as well as in female. At Çatalhöyük such an interest could also be tied to perpetuating the house, although similar imagery at Göbekli, where there may have been no houses to perpetuate, may undercut the plausibility of this connection.

The second question is, Why are sharp, dangerous animal parts in the walls – and why, in Hodder's (2006) question, do these not include leopard parts? Here I feel on firmer ground. Hodder and Meskell (2011) suggest that the embedded animal parts could have played several roles, indicating durability, significant events in house history, and piercing of the flesh. They again (rightly, to my mind) downplay violence.

Rather than violence, I suspect (as do several respondents as well as Hodder 2010a: 24, who refers to the "power or energy of wild animals") that, in addition to the roles suggested by the authors, the sharp animal parts embody animacy or vitality – that is, power, energy, and life – and contribute it to the house. They are physical intersections of special vitality with the world and, as Nakamura (2010: 321) puts it, may have been a "condensation of animal power." Carnivores and raptors, compared both to prey and to domesticated animals, are brighter, more independent, and more active and thus, in Cherry's (1992) terms, more animate and humanlike. Therefore, they are natural sources of animacy. Mindbody dualism, as described earlier, aided by similarity and contiguity, means both that this animacy survives the (fleshed) body and that the parts need not be visible to enliven the house.

In a related question, Hodder earlier (2006: 11) asked why there should be so many depictions of leopards at Çatalhöyük but "such a marked lack of leopard bones"; and Meskell, Nakamura, King, and Farid (2007: 281) similarly note the absence of leopard skulls within plastered forms. A possible reason for the depictions is that leopards were a threat, and depictions widely are thought to control or influence their subjects (as the sculpture of a woman seated upon two probable leopards suggests). If so, then depictions of leopards may have exercised power over real leopards.

In contrast to depictions, however, physical remains – especially bones, teeth, and claws – typically do not merely point to but, like relics of saints, *embody* agency, including its danger. In at least some hunting traditions, an intact skeleton can regenerate the animal; and at Çatalhöyük human bones likely were, as Hodder (2006: 61) notes, delegates of the dead. If so, then leopard bones likely were delegates too, but unwelcome ones. In the case of raptors and small carnivores, sharp parts could safely be kept and displayed because humans can cope readily with these animals. Leopards, in contrast, are wily, dangerous adversaries, neither to be hosted nor to be lightly invoked. Meskell et al. 2007: 280 note their "cunning," Kamerman (this volume, cited by Hodder Ch.13, this volume) notes their powerful ability to "merge into the environment," and Lewis-Williams (2000) offers a cautionary San account of two friends who hunt a leopard but are separately ambushed and killed by it.

Thus the taboo that Hodder thinks may have existed against taking leopard bones into town might well have been motivated by reasonable prudence (understandable to me as a resident of Boulder, Colorado, where mountain lions often enter town). What would require special explanation is, instead, the exception to the rule: the perforated leopard claw buried with a woman and a plastered skull.

Last, why are there piercing of the flesh and removal of human and animal heads? I assume that the "piercing of flesh" is not itself a goal but the means to obtain (particular) skulls, as skulls probably were the central loci of ancestral spirits. To explain the removal of heads, we again need the two notions of the durable house and of anthropomorphism: the former as the goal of the actions, and the latter as their rationale. Here the anthropomorphism lies in attributing human mental qualities to human remains, an attribution reflecting an aspect of the intuitive dualism described earlier: mind, or spirit, is independent of body and survives it.

The remains of ancestors (not necessarily adults, as Hodder and Meskell 2011: 246 point out, since in house societies "ancestors" often include all who have died in the house) probably played a role similar to that of sharp animal parts: they contributed their vitality, power (recall Patton's image of power "humming" under the floor), pedigrees, and authority to the house. Clearly, their descendants wanted them to remain close and, doubtless, in communication.

That the ancestors were in fact encouraged to stay is suggested not only by their location within the house but also by the lack of grave goods noted in Nakamura and Meskell's (2013) Çatalhöyük conference paper. Rather than tools or travel gear, graves here had only a very few personal items such as ornaments. I suggest that the reason that the deceased needed no equipment, travel or otherwise, is that they already were home and encouraged to stay. The importance of their presence probably was, as in most house societies, not only emotional but also political and economic, as the basis for rights to property both material and immaterial.

A similar view of keeping the ancestors home is advanced by Gillespie (2002) on the pre-Hispanic Maya. They were also a house society, indeed calling their corporate kin groups "houses," and similarly buried their dead under the floors or in the platforms of houses. "By continually curating the bones of deceased family members within their own domestic space" (2002: 67), Gillespie writes, descendants maintained their rights to both tangible and intangible property. Intangible property, judging from ethnohistorical and ethnographic sources, included the names and souls of the dead. These appear to have been passed down in perpetuity within the house, with the souls reincarnated in descendants.

Similar relationships may have underlain the concern with ancestors apparent in the Middle East Neolithic. The skull found at Çatalhöyük at the base of a house post, and infant foundation burials, reflect literally the foundational relation of ancestors to the house. Hodder (2010a: 26–27) writes similarly that social structure and dominance were created "not through the control of production but through the performance of rituals, links to ancestors and the animal spirits. ... Thus religion and spirituality at Çatalhöyük were closely linked to the house." Indeed, he writes (2010b: 345), "in house-based societies, houses *are* religion."

This apt phrase recalls the response of a new householder in the hamlet in which I worked in Japan (also a house society), to a question about his house's religion (*shūkyō*). "We are the first generation in this house," he replied, "so we have no ancestors here. So we have no religion" (Guthrie 1988: 65). Religion for him, that is, consists of relations with the ancestors, the source of pedigree and a major component of status. Religion at Çatalhöyük doubtless, as in Hodder's description earlier, similarly featured relations with deceased ancestors and other nonhuman persons.

Conclusion

Religion may be understood cognitively, I have claimed, as an instance of our bias to see all possible humanity, including traces and messages, in our environment. This bias is inevitable because, in an inchoate and uncertain world, we always must guess first at what matters most. That usually is humanlike agency, embodied or not. Errors in identifying such agency are inevitable, but this cognitive strategy has no good alternative. Religion consists in following this strategy by endorsing, elaborating, and promulgating an account of the world as having a particular vitality: one modeled on that of humans.

Unless the human epistemic condition has changed fundamentally since Çatalhöyük, people there also found humanlike agency in locations outside human persons. Arguably these locations included leopards, other animals, and the sharp and pointed parts of animals. Almost certainly they included, as they have in house societies at other times and places, ancestral remains and the material houses themselves.

WORKS CITED

Angulo, J., and Garcia-Diez, M. 2009. Male Genital Representation in Paleolithic Art: Erection and Circumcision before History. *Urology* 74(1):10–14.

Bacon, F. 1960. *The New Organon and Related Writings*, ed. F. H. Anderson. New York: Liberal Arts Press.

Bering, J. 2006. The Folk Psychology of Souls. *Behavioral and Brain Sciences* 29:453–498.

2002. Intuitive Conceptions of Dead Agents' Minds. *Journal of Cognition and Culture* 2 263–308.

Bloch, M. 2010. Is there religion at Catalhoyuk ... or are there just houses? In *Religion in the Emergence of Civilization*, ed. I. Hodder. Cambridge: Cambridge University Press, 146–162.

2008. Why Religion Is Nothing Special but Is Central. *Philosophical Transactions of the Royal Society*, 363(1499): 2055–62.

2007. Durkheimian anthropology and religion: Going in and out of each other's bodies. In *Religion, Anthropology and Cognitive Science*, eds. H. Whitehouse and J. Laidlaw. Durham, NC: Carolina Academic Press, 63–80.

Bloom, P. 2004. *Descartes' Baby: How the Science of Child Development Explains What Makes Us Human*. New York: Basic Books.

Bloom, P., and Veres, C. 1999. The Perceived Intentionality of Groups. *Cognition* 71:B1–B9.

Boyer, P. 2001. *Religion Explained*. New York: Basic Books.

Braithwaite, R. 1970. An empiricist's view of the nature of religious belief. In *The Philosophy of Religion*, ed. B. Mitchell. Cambridge: Cambridge University Press, 72–91.

Carsten, J., and Hugh-Jones, S. 1995. *About the House: Levi-Strauss and Beyond*. Cambridge: Cambridge University Press.

Cherry, J. 1992. Animism in thought and language. Ph.D. thesis, University of California, Berkeley.

Cohen, E., Burdett, E., Knight, N., and Barrett, J. 2011. Cross-Cultural Similarities and Differences in Person-Body Reasoning: Experimental Evidence from the United Kingdom and Brazilian Amazon. *Cognitive Science* 35(7):1282–1304.

Csibra, G., Gergeley, S., Biro, S., Koos, O., and Brockbank, M. 1999. Goal Attribution without Agency Cues. *Cognition* 72(3):237–267.

Cziko, G. 2000. *The Things We Do*. Cambridge, MA: MIT Press.

Descola, P. 2006. Beyond Nature and Culture. Radcliffe-Brown Lecture in Social Anthropology, 2005. *Proceedings of the British Academy* 139:137–155.

2009. Human Natures. *Social Anthropology / Anthropologie Sociale* 17(2):145–157.

Drake, S. 2008. *A Well-Composed Body: Anthropomorphism in Architecture*. Saarbrücken: VDM Verlag Dr. Müller Aktiengesellchaft & Co.

Durkheim, E. [1912] 1995. *The Elementary Forms of Religious Life*, trans. K. Fields. New York: The Free Press.

Ehnmark, E. 1939. *Anthropomorphism and Miracle*. Uppsala: Amqvist & Wiksells Boktryckeri.

Farah, M. J., and Heberlein, A. 2007. Personhood and Neuroscience: Naturalizing or Nihilating? *American Journal of Bioethics* 7(1):37–48.

Forshee, J. 2006. *Customs and Culture of Indonesia*. Westport, CT: Greenwood Press.

Foster, K., and Kokko, H. 2008. The Evolution of Superstitious and Superstition-like Behavior. *Proceedings of the Royal Society B*, doi:10.1098/rspb.2008.0981.

Frascari, M. 1991. *Monsters of Architecture: Anthropomorphism in Architectural Theory*. Savage, MD: Rowman & Littlefield.

1987. The Body and Architecture in the Drawings of Carlo Scarpa. *RES, Autumn*, 123–142.

Freud, S. 1990 [1912–1913]. *Totem and Taboo*, trans. and ed. J. Strachey. New York: Norton.

Gell, A. 1998. *Art and Agency: An Anthropological Theory*. Oxford: Oxford University Press.

Gillespie, S. D. 2007. When is a house? In *The Durable House: House Society Models in Archaeology*, ed. R. A. Beck. *Center for Archaeological Investigations, Occasional Paper No.35*. Copyright 2007 by the Board of Trustees, Carbondale: Southern Illinois University.

2002. Body and soul among the Maya: Keeping the spirits in place. *Archaeological Papers of the American Anthropological Association*, 11:67–78.

Gombrich, E. 1973. Illusion and art. In *Illusion in Nature and Art*, eds. R. Gregory and E. Gombrich. London: Gerald Duckworth, 193–243.

Gould, S. J., and Lewontin, R. C. 1979. The Spandrels of San Marco and the Panglossian Paradigm: A Critique of the Adaptationist Programme. *Proceedings of the Royal Society of London* 205B, 581–598.

Guthrie, S. E. 2008. Spirit beings: A Darwinian, cognitive account. In *The Evolution of Religion: Studies, Theories, and Critiques*, eds. J. Bulbulia, R. Sosis, C. Genet, E. Harris, and K. Wyman. Santa Margarita, CA: Collins Foundation Press, 239–245.

2007a. Anthropology and anthropomorphism in religion. In *Religion, Anthropology and Cognitive Science*, eds. H. Whitehouse and J. Laidlaw. Durham, NC: Carolina Academic Press, 37–62.

2007b. Bottles Are Men, Glasses Are Women: Religion, Gender, and Secular Objects. *Material Religion* 3(1):14–33.

2000. Projection. In *Guide to the Study of Religion*, eds. R. McCutcheon and W. Braun. London: Cassell, 225–238.

1993. *Faces in the Clouds: A New Theory of Religion*. New York: Oxford University Press.

1988. *A Japanese New Religion: Risshō Kōsei-kai in a Mountain Hamlet*. Ann Arbor: University of Michigan Center for Japanese Studies.

1980. A Cognitive Theory of Religion, with CA Comment. *Current Anthropology* 21(2):181–194.

Haidt, J. 2006. *The Happiness Hypothesis: Finding Modern Truth in Ancient Wisdom*. New York: Basic Books.

Harvey, V. A. 1995. *Feuerbach and the Interpretation of Religion* (Cambridge Studies in Religion and Critical Thought). Cambridge: Cambridge University Press.

Hassin, R. R., Uleman, J. S., and Bargh, J. A. eds. 2005. *The New Unconscious*. New York: Oxford University Press.

Henshilwood, C., and Dubreuil, B. 2011. The Still Bay and Howiesons Poort, 77–59 ka: Symbolic Material Culture and the Evolution of Mind during the African Middle Stone Age. *Current Anthropology* 52(3):361–400.

Hodder, I. n.d. The vitalities of Çatalhöyük. In *Religion and the Transformation of Neolithic Society: Vital Matters*, ed. I. Hodder. Cambridge: Cambridge University Press.

Hodder, I. n.d. Theories and their data: interdisciplinary interactions at Çatalhöyük. In *Religion and the Transformation of Neolithic Society: Vital Matters*, ed. I. Hodder. Cambridge: Cambridge University Press.

2010a. Probing religion at Catalhoyuk: An interdisciplinary experiment. In *Religion in the Emergence of Civilizatioln*, ed. I. Hodder. Cambridge: Cambridge University Press, 1–31.

2010b. Conclusions and evaluation. In *Religion in the emergence of Civilization*, ed. I. Hodder. Cambridge: Cambridge University Press, 332–355.

2006. *The Leopard's Tale: Revealing the Mysteries of Çatalhöyük*. London: Thames & Hudson.

Hodder, I., and Meskell, L. 2011. A "Curious and Sometimes a Trifle Macabre Artistry": Some Aspects of Symbolism in Neolithic Turkey, with CA Comment. *Current Anthropology* 52:235–263.

Hodge, K. M. 2008. Descartes' mistake: How afterlife beliefs challenge the assumption that humans are intuitive Cartesian substance dualists. *Journal of Cognition and Culture* 8:387–415.

Horton, R. 1993. *Patterns of Thought in Africa and the West: Essays on Magic, Religion and Science*, Cambridge: Cambridge University Press.

Hume, D. 1957 [1757]. *The Natural History of Religion*, ed. H. E. Root. Stanford, CA: Stanford University Press.

Inagaki, K., and Hatano, G. 1993. Young Children's Understanding of the Mind-Body Distinction. *Child Development* 64,1534–1549.

Keane, W. 2010. Marked, absent, habitual: Approaches to neolithic religion at Çatalhöyük. In *Religion in the Emergence of Civilization: Çatalhöyük as a Case Study*, ed. I. Hodder. Cambridge: Cambridge University Press, 187–219.

Kelemen, D. 2012. Teleological Minds: How natural intuitions about agency and purpose influence learning about evolution. In *Evolution Challenges: Integrating Research and Practice in Teaching and Learning about Evolution*, eds. Rosengren, K., Brem, S., Evans, M., and Sinatra, G. Oxford: Oxford University Press.

Kelemen, D. 2004. Are Children 'Intuitive Theists'? *Psychological Science* 15(5):295–301.

Koch, G. 2008. The cognitive origins of soul belief: Empathy, responsibility and purity. Ph.D. dissertation, Department of the Study of Religion, Aarhus University.

Kuhlmeier, V., Bloom, P., and Wynn, K. 2004. Do 5-Month-Old Infants See Humans as Material Objects? *Cognition* 94(1):95–103.

Lahelma, A. 2008. Communicating with "stone persons": Saami religion and Finnish rock art. In *A Touch of Red: Archaeological and Ethnographic Approaches to Interpreting Finnish Rock Paintings*, ed. A. Lahelma. Helsinki: The Finnish Antiquarian Society, 121–142.

Lakoff, G., and Johnson, M. 1999. *Philosophy in the Flesh: The Embodied Mind and Its Challenge to Western Thought*. New York: Basic Boods.

Leder, D. 1990. *The Absent Body*. Chicago: University of Chicago Press.

Liebert, A. 1909. Der Anthropomorphismus der Wissenschaft. *Zeitschrift fuer Philosophie und Philosophische Kritik* 136:1–22.

Lillard, A., and Skibbe, L. 2005. Theory of mind. In *The New Unconscious*, eds. R. J. Hassin, J. S. Uleman, and J. A. Bargh. Oxford: Oxford University Press, 277–305.

Lohmann, R. I. 2003. The Supernatural Is Everywhere: Defining Qualities of Religion. *Anthropological Forum* 13(2):175–186.

Mar, R., and MacRae, C. N. 2006. Triggering the intentional stance. In *Empathy and Fairness*, eds. G. Bock and J. Goode. London: Wiley, Chichester, 110–132.

Meskell, L., and Nakamura, C., with King, R. and Farid, S. 2007. Archive Report: Çatalhöyük Figurines. *Çatalhöyük Research Project*, 277–302.

Mithen, S., and Boyer, P. 1996. Anthropomorphism and the Evolution of Cognition. *The Journal of the Royal Anthropological Institute* 2(4):717–721.

Morris, W. E. 2009. *David Hume. The Stanford Encyclopedia of Philosophy*, ed. Edward N. Zalta (Summer 2009 Edition). http://plato.stanford.edu/archives/sum2009/entries/hume/.

Nakamura, C. 2010. Magical deposits at Çatalhöyük: A matter of time and place? In *Religion in the Emergence of Civilization*, ed. I Hodder. Cambridge: Cambridge University Press, 300–331.

Nakamura, C. and Meskell, L. 2013. The Çatalhöyük burial assemblage. In *Humans and Landscapes of Çatalhöyük: Reports from the 2000–2008 Seasons*, ed. I. Hodder. Los Angeles: Cotsen Institute.

Pels, P. 2010. Temporalities of "religion" at Çatalhöyük. In *Religion in the Emergence of Civilization*, ed. I. Hodder. Cambridge: Cambridge University Press, 220–267.

Phelps, E. A. 2007. The Neuroscience of a Person Network. *American Journal of Bioethics* 7(1):49–50.

Pilloud, M., and Larson, C. 2011. "Official" and "Practical" Kin: Inferring Social and Community Structure from Dental Phenotype at Neolithic Çatalhöyük, Turkey. *American Journal of Physical Anthropology* 145(5):519–530.

Saxe, R. T., Tzelnic, T., and Carey, S. 2006. Five-Month-Old Infants Know Humans Are Solid, like Inanimate Objects. *Cognition* 101:B1–B8.

Scholl, B., and Tremoulet, P. 2000. Perceptual Causality and Animacy. *Trends in Cognitive Sciences* 4(8):299–309.

Shults, L. 2010. Spiritual entanglement: Transforming religious symbols at Çatalhöyük. In *Religion in the Emergence of Civilization*, ed. I. Hodder. Cambridge: Cambridge University Press, 73–98.

Spinoza, B. 1955. *The Chief Works of Benedict de Spinoza: On the Improvements of the Understanding; The Ethics; Correspondence*, trans. R. H. M. Elwes. New York: Dover.

Stent, G. 1998. Epistemic Dualism of Mind and Body. *Proceedings of the American Philosophical Society* 142(4):578–588.

Thompson, S. 1955. *Motif-Index of Folk-Literature*. Bloomington: Indiana University Press.

Tylor, Edward B. 1964 [1878]. *Researches into the Early History of Mankind*, ed. P. Bohannon, Chicago: University of Chicago Press.

Van Huyssteen, W. 2010. Coding the nonvisible: Epistemic limitations and understanding symbolic behavior at Çatalhöyük. In *Religion in the Emergence of Civilization*, ed. I. Hodder. Cambridge: Cambridge University Press, 99–121.

Vitruvius, P. 1960. *The Ten Books on Architecture*. Mineola, NY: Courier Dover.

Vitruvius, P. 1931. *On Architecture*. Vol. 1: *Books 1–5* (Loeb Classical Library No.251) trans. F. Granger. Cambridge, MA: Harvard University Press.

Wason, P. 2010. The Neolithic cosmos at Çatalhöyük. In *Religion in the Emergence of Civilization*, ed. I. Hodder. Cambridge: Cambridge University Press, 268–299.

Waterson, R. 2010. *The Living House: An Anthropology of Architecture in South-East Asia*. Rutland, VT: Tuttle.

Wegner, D. 2005. Who is the controller of controlled processes? In *The New Unconscious*, eds. R. R. Hassin, J. S. Uleman, and J. A. Bargh. Oxford: Oxford University Press, 19–36.

Westh, P. 2013. Anthropomorphism in god concepts: The role of narrative. In *Origins of Religion, Cognition and Culture*, ed. A. Geertz. London: Equinox, 396–413.

Whitehouse, H., and Hodder, I. 2010. Modes of religiosity at Çatalhöyük. In *Religion in the Emergence of Civilization*, ed. I. Hodder. Cambridge: Cambridge University Press, 122–145.

5

The Historical Self: Memory and Religion at Çatalhöyük

J. Wentzel van Huyssteen

For a philosophical theologian deeply committed to interdisciplinary discourse with the sciences, the remarkable privilege of being involved in Ian Hodder's Çatalhöyük project has indeed been enriching as well as an extraordinary challenge. Most importantly, I have learned that archaeology presents us with a very unusual problem of semantic innovation: in looking back to the distant past, how does new meaning come to be, and, in doing so, how does interpretation enable us to reconfigure often long-forgotten meanings of the past? For the French philosopher Paul Ricoeur, this kind of hermeneutical venture always involved a radically interdisciplinary journey and the long route of multiple hermeneutical detours in direct dialogue with the human sciences, the natural sciences, philosophy, and theology (cf. Ricoeur in Kearney 2004: 124). In these boundary crossings or border exchanges between reasoning strategies, various disciplines transversally connect around shared problems. Therefore, in spite of the fact that the staple of archaeology has always been material culture, interpretations of the archaeological record are also profoundly anchored in the integration of input from other disciplines (Belfer-Cohen and Hovers 2010: 167). In the art of deciphering indirect meaning the past is indeed always mediated through an endless process of cultural, political, historical, and scientific interpretations. And it is this kind of hermeneutics that is fundamentally important for any approach to Çatalhöyük and will shape the interdisciplinary epistemology of what we can remember and know about this city.

At the heart of this paper lies the question of personhood, the idea of how we might think of the embodied human self in prehistory. Crucial for any understanding of Çatalhöyük is certainly the question of what kind of persons lived in this city. Were they people like us? Were their daily lives infused with symbolic, religious behavior, or not? I am convinced there is enough scientific evidence available today to believe that it is precisely through the long evolution of our embodied, symbolic minds that the evolution of our linguistic, aesthetic, moral, and religious dispositions was firmly embedded in our ancestral human bodies (van Huyssteen 2010). I believe this important case study of prehistoric selves at Çatalhöyük will confirm conclusions from my recent work on self-identity in the West European Upper Paleolithic (van Huyssteen 2006), and by discerning how cognitive/neurological links in the evolution of symbolic behavior might converge with contemporary archaeological data, it will be precisely in the embodied human self that we will find the key for overcoming contemporary challenges to the idea of multidimensional, holistic notions of self and personhood. I will briefly develop and integrate this idea into an interdisciplinary dialogue with remarkably convergent ideas of neuro- and cognitive scientists working today on notions of self, empathy, attachment, and symbolic/religious behavior. My collaboration on the Çatalhöyük project has convinced me that this central idea will be hugely helpful in discerning evolutionary and neurological links for an understanding of the evolution of symbolic behavior, specifically religious and ritual behavior. I also believe that as we "sail upstream toward our evolutionary origins," my recent work on the Upper Paleolithic will provide a necessary background for better understanding the Middle Eastern Neolithic and, quite specifically, the vanished culture of Çatalhöyük. Here too, as in the dark caves of western France, we have to wonder whether it makes any sense to ask about the "meaning" of prehistoric imagery, or even more challenging, what might have made the artifacts, wall paintings, sculptures, bucrania, and house burials meaningful for persons who lived at Çatalhöyük.

I trust, therefore, that this research project will be helpful in discerning evolutionary and neurological links for understanding the evolution of symbolic behavior, specifically religious and ritual behavior. If we can discern an evolutionary, neurological bridge to Neolithic culture, it might still be impossibly difficult to cross the vast interpretive bridge to prehistory and try to probe the beliefs and specific meaning systems of this ancient culture. From a cognitive science of religion point of view, however, a holistic approach to the imagistic material culture of Çatalhöyük would presuppose that whatever the symbolic context and enigmatic ritual practices meant for the people of the time, it seems to be unmistakably true that religious practices of all kinds have always presupposed worldviews, deep convictions, and beliefs of what empirical and ritual practices were about. In this sense beliefs and their accompanying rituals sacramentally integrate the natural and the supernatural, and thus ultimately define religion, even if we may never know exactly what those beliefs really represented.

A Sense of Self

Writing about the human self in prehistory, Ian Tattersall (2011: 33) states as follows:

> In the very broadest of meanings, every organism has a sense of itself. From the simplest unicellular creature on, all living things have mechanisms that allow them to detect and react to entities and events beyond their own boundaries. As a result, every animal may be said to be self-aware at some level, however rudimentary such responsiveness might appear. In sharp contrast, complex human self-awareness is a very particular possession of our species. We humans experience ourselves in a very specific kind of way – a way that is, as far as we know, unique in the living world. We consciously *know* we have interior lives.

The intellectual resource that allows us to have such knowledge is our symbolic cognitive style: it is indeed our unique symbolic ability that underwrites the internalized self-representation expressed in the peculiarly human sense of self. It is this extraordinary cognitive style that is the product of a long biological history. It seems, therefore, reasonable to conclude that the human sense of self and self-identity as we experience it has its roots precisely in human consciousness, self-awareness, and our symbolic capacities. Tattersall puts it even more strongly: we can be on fairly firm ground in proposing that a *fully developed* sense of self of the kind with which we are familiar today and that depends on internalized mental representations of self is a recent acquisition in human and hominid history (Tattersall 2011: 47).

In a recent essay on the prehistory of self and personhood, Ian Hodder (2011) focuses very much on the relationship between the self and its object world, and behind this approach lies the idea that archaeology can actually demonstrate transformations of self and personhood related to major social and economic changes in prehistory. For Çatalhöyük, in this early period, the effects of transformations of self are directly related to farming, settled life, and new forms of ritual behavior as exemplified in art and burial practices. What quickly become clear in Catalhöyük are new forms of agency, as well as changes in notions of self and personhood. New identities were molded as people settled down in stable houses and incorporated new ritual practices through plastered forms and especially secondary mortuary practices, and, of course, long-term social entanglements.

Hodder wants to explore the idea that the emergence of a sense of self in some ways was also a gradual process, closely tied to the increasing entanglement between humans and the material objects of daily life. It is especially true of the fact that as humans increasingly came to own things, they simultaneously developed a greater sense of self. As they increasingly separated objects that they owned from other objects, it seems likely that they would have increasingly separated themselves from others (Hodder 2011: 50f.). For Hodder the question rightly is whether there is any ethnographic and archaeological evidence to support such a hypothesis. In addition, he wants to ask whether or not there is a role for the spiritual and religious in this process (Hodder 2011: 52).

Hodder first looks at the principle of "property rights," that is, the basic principle that work/labor transforms material things into property. By looking carefully at concepts of ownership between immediate-return hunter-gatherers and delayed-return hunter-gatherers (Hodder 2011: 53ff), Hodder now wants to argue that as property rights became more clearly defined a sense of separate self gradually emerged. Against this background Hodder now asks two important questions: i) Was the human self at Çatalhöyük coincident with the body boundary? and ii) To what extent can the prehistoric self at Çatalhöyük be seen as an autonomous agent? These two are obviously interlinked.

Hodder further argues that the first burials associated with Neanderthals and with *Homo sapiens* that occurred from about 100,000 BP and the appearance of bodily adornment and human figuration (the Venus figurines and other forms of representations in the Franco-Cantabrian art) from forty thousand years ago onward all suggest a gradually increased concern with self, however continuous that self may have been with worlds around it (Hodder 2011: 54f), as do examples of huts and replastered floors that suggest some form of continued housing, and thus memory construction, in the fourteenth millennium BC as well as in the following Natufian. Thus by the eleventh millennium BC at least, there is good evidence of long-term investment in place, of the construction of "histories" through time, some evidence of storage, and a major extension of the human engagement with material objects like antler and bone tools, groundstone grinders, axes, and more stable housing. Hodder also argues that in the late Paleolithic period in Europe and the Middle East we increasingly see signs of greater use of burial, greater elaboration of the human body in the proliferation of beads and ornaments, and even more depictions of humans. Ownership at this time must have been both individual and collective, with some items (cf. arrowheads, beads) seen as personal items, and others as collective items or places. Thus in the Pre-Pottery Neolithic in the Middle East there emerged large round buildings at sites such as Göbekli that are clearly ritual in content and collective in scale (Hodder 2011: 54f).

The site of Göbekli is particularly interesting because here massive stone pillars encircle ritual enclosures (Schmidt 2006) in a society still without fully developed domestication of plants and animals. Intriguing is the fact that the giant pillars also have engraved arms, indicating that they "represent" or "are" humans in some form. For Hodder it is clear that we can talk here of a new sense of human agency – at least in relation to the animals engraved on the sides of the pillars (Hodder 2011: 55). At Göbekli humans or humanlike beings clearly dominate, and in the animals carved on their bodies we see the sort of domination of animals that was a prerequisite for their domestication (Cauvin 1994). The increased human agency that we see here may have been collective, and it may have been associated with a greater sense of ownership as people invested in more long-term relationships with each other, with animals, and with material things. From these examples discussed by Hodder it becomes clear that as humans became more entangled with material things through the Pleistocene and into the early Holocene, and as their relationship turned toward an increased sense of exclusive property, so the sense of self became more marked and visually expressed, both personally, in terms of bodily decoration and burial, and collectively, as in communal ritual enclosures (Hodder 2011: 55). Such an increase in a sense of self, and of memory, would necessarily have led to an increase of a sense of history.

The Self at Çatalhöyük

In contrast to earlier sites in central Turkey and the Middle East, at Çatalhöyük many activities were moved directly into the house. Hodder points out that there is no evidence for large ritual structures, but the houses are more heavily used for a range of domestic activities, including burials, which are now done exclusively in houses. What follows from this is a clear case for historical, house-based self-identities. At the same time there was an important focus on larger-scale community organization, and overt expressions of individual house differences were clearly not sanctioned. In addition there is very little in the way of individual burial variability, and houses are grouped into small clusters associated with ancestral houses in which people from the group are preferentially buried (Hodder 2011: 57).

People spent much of their time, especially in winter, in these small, seven meter by four meter houses. The houses contained, on their south sides, hearths and ovens, and much daily activity took place in these areas. This southern part of the main room was also where neonates and young infants were buried. In the northern part of the main rooms there were whiter and higher platforms on which people have slept and under which adults were buried. Importantly, we know that people in the houses remembered where they had placed individual bodies as they were able with great precision to dig down and retrieve bodies, and indeed later to retrieve skulls from bodies. So in the typical Çatalhöyük houses the prehistoric self was situated in complex webs of memories: not only would a person who moved around the house have known about who was buried where, but individuals who were buried were remembered and as such would acquire over time a very clear narrative identity (Hodder 2011: 58).

However, and very important for articulating a sense of the self in prehistoric Çatalhöyük, the remembered selves of those who had died were also mutable, or partible: Hodder here points to a grave that was found in Building 49 in which a fully articulated torso was discovered, but without legs, arms, or scapulae. Presumably the arms and legs were circulated, creating links with this body and Building 49. It is, however, mainly head removal that was practiced in Çatalhöyük, which is one of the most distinctive aspects of Neolithic mortuary practices in the Middle East, even if at Çatalhöyük skull removal remains relatively rare, however, and heads are usually deposited individually (Hodder 2011: 58).

There also clearly seems to be some continuity between the removal and circulation of human heads and animal heads. The installation of bull and ram heads is in fact a feature of the house walls at Çatalhöyük, and animal skulls not only were embedded in walls but were also kept while placing them on walls and on pedestals, with the facial features modeled in clay. And as is well known, many times the horns of bulls (bucrania) were installed into the walls. Even more interesting is that the art on the house walls at Çatalhöyük also shows headless bodies associated with vultures (Meskell 2008: 375). For Hodder this means that head removal was associated with myths and stories in which vultures were involved in the removal of heads and flesh from bodies (Hodder 2011: 60). Does this removal of heads now suggest nonintegrated and partible selves in Neolithic prehistory? For Hodder it is reasonable to argue that at Çatalhöyük individual heads became transformed into the heads of ancestors that were then used to hold up and found houses. So the overall evidence of personhood gained at Çatalhöyük from burials, figurines, and other imagery suggests not the atomized and highly individualized self of our own world, but rather a self that was mutable, that can be divided physically; a self that can transform; a self that can become an ancestor, and even a bird or other animal (Hodder 2011: 61).

All of this converges with the very prominent place that secondary mortuary practices have in certain Neolithic communities, including at Çatalhöyük. In a recent essay Ian Kuijt (2008) focuses particularly on secondary mortuary practices and on the fact that in the Neolithic the social construction of personal identity and memory is most often expressed through imagery and ritual. In the Middle Eastern Neolithic it is exactly mortuary practices, the repetitive use of imagery and figurines, and the long-term reuse of human skulls that most clearly illustrate how household ritual linked the living to the dead. This essay argues that, also at Çatalhöyük, it is secondary mortuary practices and the plastering and painting of human skulls as ritual heirlooms that functioned as a form of memorialization and finally erasure of identity within communities. The deliberate focus on the face in both construction and decoration seems to have been part of a shared system of ritual practices. In fact, skull caching and modification transcended the past, present, and future, reiterating the expectation of future mortuary events while recognizing continuity with the past through the crafting of memory. Collectively these patterns represent a complex web of interaction involving ritual knowledge, imagery, mortuary practices, and the creation of intergenerational memory and structures of authority (Kuijt 2008: 171). This essay by Ian Kuijt explores precisely the possible interweaving of social memory, ritual practice, and time, in Neolithic communities like Çatalhöyük.

A crucial question is, of course, how can objects and the rituals in which they may have been employed inform us about Neolithic perceptions of ancestry, memory, and commemoration? Memories are almost always linked to action, especially ritual action, and precisely as physical actions, ritual and commemoration are linked to the production of shared memories and experiences in specific communities (Kuijt 2008: 173). Ian Kuijt has argued that memory is directly linked to meaning and experience, and that experience itself can be spatially, temporally, and materially situated. Crucial to this concept of memory is that there are always general patterns in the development of social memory and commemoration. Kuijt argues that solemnization of commemoration involves four important factors: repetitiveness in observance, reenactment of some former circumstance, social sanction of the ceremony, and formality. It is, however, repetitiveness in ritual that is critically important, that is socially sanctioned and as such gives formality to the ritual (Kuijt 2008: 173). I want to argue that exactly this must have been true for the burial rituals, house architecture and buildings, and also art at Çatalhöyük, and that gave this historical depth to selves that were constructed in this particular space in Neolithic prehistory.

It is, then, the repetition of words, actions, and interactions that made these events and experiences coherent, understandable, and meaningful over time to participants. It is in this way that the past, present, and future dimensions of commemorative ritual are affirmed and made compatible with each other. It is, of course, very difficult to understand how past ritual actions and ceremony were exactly organized. Nevertheless, for Kuijt ritual should be seen as a rule-governed activity of a clear symbolic character that draws the attention of its participants to objects of thought and feelings that they hold to be of a special significance (Kuijt 2008: 173). Furthermore, memory, historical depth, and its materiality are generated through the actions of individuals and groups. And even highly formalized acts of commemoration are likely to have changed over time: it is, after all, through the act of remembering that memory is both crafted and maintained. In this sense memory and tradition alone do not preserve an object's identity, but it is the ongoing incorporation of that object into routinized practice that generates historical meaning (Kuijt 2008: 173). It is in this sense too that memory itself is transformed and modified through time.

It is, of course, this materiality of our embodied existence that has come about through the process of biological evolution and has given us what seems to be a unique human sense of self. The cognitive archaeologist Steven Mithen puts it well: one's self-identity is intimately related to the feeling that one has a suite of beliefs, moods, desires, and feelings that are quite unique to oneself (Mithen 2009: 214).

The most recent body of work by the French philosopher Paul Ricoeur provides us with a remarkable in-depth analysis of exactly this notion of self. Ricoeur has developed a striking notion of the self as defined, at the deepest level, by the depth of its historical dimension, that is, by time and narrative. For Ricoeur, the narrative dimension of human self-awareness and consciousness not only enables us to envision new projects, to evaluate motivations, to initiate viable courses of action, but to empathize and identify deeply with others. Ricoeur claims that a narrative understanding provides us with an ethics of responsibility, which then propels us, precisely through empathy, beyond self-reference to relationships with others (Ricoeur 1992: 113–139). It is this extension of the "circle of selfhood" that involves an enlarged mentality ultimately capable of imagining the self in the place of the other. In this way Ricoeur has revisioned the notion of narrative understanding – where one represents oneself as another – to the extent that it ultimately liberates us from all-consuming narcissistic interest without liquidating our identity as selves. Narrative understanding thus generates a basic act of empathy whereby the self flows from itself toward the other in a free variation of imagination. Thus narrative imagination transforms self-regarding into a self-for-another (Kearney 2004: 173).

In his Gifford Lectures, Paul Ricoeur (1992: 3f.) argued that our sense of self, our personal identity, should be understood precisely in terms of this narrative identity. Through the power of imagination the self (or as I would call it, the historical self) is able to weave together various elements of a life into a single story, just as we also maintain a sense of personal identity when we stay true to our promises over time. For Ricoeur there is a direct connection between this notion of personal, historical identity and self, which we model on the unity of various narratives and our imaginative capabilities. As he strikingly expresses it: in many narratives the self seeks its identity on the scale of an entire life (Ricoeur 1992: 115). By directly linking memory and imagination (Ricoeur 2004: 1–55), Ricoeur could argue that in this sense our memories retain within themselves a claim to faithfulness to the past and serve an integral role in shaping personal identity in the present and into the future. Ricoeur claims, then, that memory is in fact the "gateway to the self" and to personal identity, and since there is always a narrative component to memory, our remembering always implies narrative experience (Ricoeur and Homans 2008: 222).

In the philosophical framework on which Ricoeur builds, then, memory serves as the ultimate mediator between time and narrative, while imagination leads the way in forging an understanding of the human self as *oneself* only in and through the other person. As such, personal identity, or the historical "self," is both articulated *and* constructed solely through the temporal and relational dimensions of embodied human existence. On this view, self-identity rises out of our narrative identities, and in many narratives the self as a lived body seeks its identity for the duration of an entire lifetime (Ricoeur 1992: 152). In this way Ricoeur could anticipate contemporary multiple selves theories and could explicitly state, "to be a human being is to live at the same time at several levels of self-structuring, of the constitution of self-identity" (Ricoeur and Homans 2008: 229). Finally, it is the embeddedness of the self in time through memory and imagination that reveals the link of a sense of self also to the future: insofar as my personal identity is dependent on keeping my word, the act of promising binds me to the future.

Against this background it is very interesting indeed to see how closely Ian Kuijt's terminology converges with that of Paul Ricoeur. Kuijt also refers to *embodied* and *inscribed* memories (cf. Kuijt 2008: 173), the former including bodily rituals and behavior and the latter focusing on monuments and representations, which Ricoeur has called *souvenirs* (Ricoeur 2004: 24ff.). For the historical self at Çatalhöyük the question certainly is how memory is created, maintained, and modified in prehistoric, Neolithic communities between households and across generations. Distinguishing between experiential and referential meanings and memories allows us to develop a framework for modeling patterns of Neolithic social memory and to situate this framework in a theoretical context that moves us beyond a simple and static reference to ancestors. On this view memory is then time-sensitive and dynamic and is created through the actions of people who intersect at different social scales, such as those of the individual, the household, and the community (Kuijt 2008: 174). As such the genesis of memory is linked to the experiences and meanings that are created through the intersection of people at multiple levels. These short-term events and the interactions of people involved in them helped shape the long-term intergenerational meanings and memories into a form of collective memory.

What is fascinating for the Çatalhöyük context is that on some levels memory is clearly deeply personal and linked to the life histories of individuals, and on other levels it seems to be more public and intergenerational. Over time then memories may change from experiential and personal to abstract and referential (Kuijt 2008: 174). Direct experiential memory of individuals over time can then change from more personal to more indirect and referential, highlighting social membership rather than direct biological lineage. In this way, after two or three generations, the memories of individuals may become depersonalized and abstract and are merged into an ancestral memory that is anonymous and collective. Importantly, the social process of this transition, depending on the cultural context, is complicated and probably not always observable in archaeological data (Kuijt 2008: 174). At Çatalhöyük the association of ancestors and their skulls with individual houses is more marked than in the Levant.

Finally, in this dynamic of remembering and forgetting, the process of forgetting the dead is most probably linked to the decontextualization of the individual – the creation of a more collective identity that is shared and experienced by others. But among the living there certainly is a deep personal, experiential, and direct memory of the dead, creating tangible links between personhood in life, death, and memorialization. Kuijt also focuses on social memory, and the transition of social memory. Social memory is intimately interconnected with oral tradition, images, and location, and participation can indeed be seen as the core of commemorative events (Kuijt 2008: 175). As with all social memory the spatial context, organization, and images or mortuary practices are culturally defined and cannot be understood without reference to a worldview that integrates place, time, space, and imagery in the production of meaning. Against this background the following distinction becomes important for mortuary practices in Neolithic Çatalhöyük: primary mortuary practices center on the permanent burial of the dead after a relatively short period (often less than a week). In contrast, secondary mortuary practices are the socially sanctioned movement of part or all of the deceased individual and involve the intentional removal of skeletal materials from one location to some other location. Secondary mortuary practices are often also part of high-profile public ceremonies and can therefore be viewed as spiritual and symbolic acts that have social, political, or personal meanings (Kuijt 2008: 175). In this sense then the decapitation and modification of skulls or their placement in a highly visible location also represents an integrated act of social memory in both remembering and forgetting the dead.

Most important, however, for the theme of this paper: in secondary mortuary practices the identity of self and personhood become mutable and potentially open to multiple identities, and at the same time linked to narrativization and life histories as the practices help to structure the construction of memory and identity (Meskell 2008: 378). When first removed from their bodies, the skulls of the deceased would have been associated with specific individuals and households. With the passing of generations, the nature of these memories and relations would have changed from personal and experiential to abstract and referential (Kuijt 2008: 177). And where in some instances the plastering and painting of the faces of removed skulls focused so much on the face, it becomes even clearer that the secondary removal of skulls from human skeletons was part of a shared system of ritual practices. In any case, one of the most interesting aspects of ritual in early Neolithic agricultural communities was the circulation of skeletal elements. In fact, Neolithic ritual practices seem to have focused on the body as a signifier of social relations and involved a recirculation of these objects through what might have been multiple events (Kuijt 2008: 182). And specifically skull removal should be viewed as a delayed act that simultaneously linked people to their past and projected them into the future (Kuijt 2008: 184). The prominent place of secondary mortuary practices in certain Neolithic communities thus helps us to understand how individual and collective identities and memories were developed and sustained. These practices highlight cycles of remembrance and indicate that community members approached life and death as integrated and cyclical. The broad regional similarities in these practices also support the argument that they were part of a shared system of beliefs (Kuijt 2008: 185f.), although secondary burial is less common at Çatalhöyük and grouping of plastered skulls does not occur.

What is clear at Çatalhöyük, however, is that notions of self were directly bound up with the house and were continuous with ancestors and other beings and things. Secondary mortuary practices as well as increasing ownership would also have pointed to the increasing emergence of a personhood coincident with body boundaries in a densely packed agricultural settlement such as Çatalhöyük. For me this would suggest a notion of self that very closely anticipated contemporary notions of self: a self that is experienced as deeply embodied, and a very distinct, or individualized self. In this regard Hodder also refers to the work of Nerissa Russell and her analysis of pendants and beads worn around the neck, even in burials. This clearly seems to suggest that these pendants were part of personal possessions and were thus linked to individual and short-term memories, and thus to personal identities (Hodder 2011: 62). Possible evidence of an even stronger sense of self is also provided by the obsidian mirrors found at Çatalhöyük. Ian Hodder, following Jim Vedder, has argued that these mirrors would not have functioned well as signaling devices or means to start fires, but they do reflect images well. They may also have been used to "see" and "divine" the spirit world, but it is tempting to suggest that they could actually have been used to look at one's own face and body (Hodder 2011: 63). In his own extensive work on the role of obsidian at Çatalhöyük, Tristan Carter has provided an analysis of the temporal and spatial contexts within which one can locate the Çatalhöyük hoards and has also focused on the conceptual underpinnings of the very act of the burial and retrieval of obsidian. Within this context Carter has distinguished between obsidian hoards and obsidian grave goods, exploring the idea that there might be a conceptual or ritual/symbolic link between the burial and retrieval of obsidian and the burial and exhumation of people (Carter 2007: 352ff.). All this attention to facial and bodily presentation fits well with the focus on individual self-image. Certainly in the burials the focus is on individual body boundaries, even if bodies were sometimes removed later and transformed into more social, abstract selves.

I believe we can conclude then that the people of Çatalhöyük were very strongly and immediately socialized into social rules and roles, and their sense of self was primarily associated with the house and other social groups. This self, seen within the broader, ritualized context of Neolithic behavior, was indeed a transformable, historical self. But as part of this process, some clear sense of the individual self and the recognition of individual bodily boundaries became more marked (Hodder 2011: 640). I believe, however, that what we find at Çatalhöyük is certainly more than just that "the seeds of individual selves were being sown." From a neurobiological point of view, and therefore in terms of the definitions of consciousness and self-awareness, these people already were embodied, self-aware selves, even if there is clear evidence, through more adornment of burials in the upper levels, that culturally this process of emergence or individualization increased through time (Hodder 2011: 64). Could the historical selves of Çatalhöyük already be seen, however, as typifying what some scholars have called *Homo religiosus?* Ian Hodder has suggested that as human entanglement with material things increased, a greater sense of agency emerged, as well as a stronger sense of individual selves. These shifts were not solely concerned with a self-representational capacity of the brain, but much of the changing conception of self and personhood emerged directly from the practices of an embodied engagement with the entanglements of daily life (Hodder 2011: 67). In the practices of creating memories and histories in house sequences, heads and body parts were circulated, thus also partitioning and dispersing the body. And yet these circulated parts were from identifiable bodies whose locations beneath the house floors were remembered.

Hodder rightly alerts us to take note of how many of the practices at Çatalhöyük relate to interactions beyond the immediate practical world. So many of the actions at Çatalhöyük involve constructions of persons in relation to ancestors, to animal spirits, to birds associated with the mythical removal of flesh. They also involve burial, figurines, and the depictions of narrative wall art. It does indeed seem that the emergence of a stronger and more complex sense of personhood at this time was intimately bound up with the self as a transcendent category. The historical self is always a social category, bound up in the material and relational entanglements of everyday life. But this dependence on material things, and I would add the dependence on relationships with the other, always seem to require a transcendence (Hodder 2011: 67). And this transcendence inevitably seems to point to the primary role of religion, and some sense of transcendent meaning, in the emergence of the historical self at Çatalhöyük.

At this point, therefore, I want to return to my original thesis that any conversation with archaeology about the self in prehistory must inevitably involve a radically interdisciplinary journey. In spite of archaeology's focus on material culture, I believe it is precisely interdisciplinary conversation that protects us scholars from the lingering positivism and empiricism in which we are all too easily constrained by interpretative barriers of our own making (Clark 2008: 187). Ian Hodder is correct, of course, in arguing that it is indeed notable how many of the practices at Çatalhöyük also relate to interactions beyond the immediate practical, empirically experienced world. This religious dimension at Çatalhöyük cannot be ignored but must be addressed also by examining the ritualizing of behavior and the implications for understanding the self at Çatalhöyük in terms of the many dimensions of neural traits for religious faith of some sort. Only in this sense is Hodder's final statement understandable: the self is indeed always a social category, bound up in the entanglements of daily life. But exactly this dependence on material things seems to require a "transcendence": the more the self is dragged into things, the more it seems to seek some transcendent meaning (Hodder 2011: 67).

Interdisciplinary Perspectives on the Self

Much has been written over the years about humankind's apparent universal religiosity, and about the fact that no culture was ever discovered that did not have at least some form of religion. Much has also been written lately, especially in cognitive science of religion, about the evolution of religion and the question of whether or not religion should be seen as an adaptive trait or rather a by-product of some other universal neuropsychological traits. Much innovative work has also been done on rethinking the enduring problem of consciousness, which opens the way to think more holistically and complexly about the possibility of various traits or dispositions for religious belief.

Especially important for this specific interdisciplinary conversation is the German neuroscienticst Thomas Fuchs's recent development of an *embodied cognitive neuroscience* (Fuchs and Schlimme 2009). On this embodied cognition perspective the human mind and brain are seen as a biological system that is rooted in body experience and interaction with other individuals and with one's immediate environment. Embodiment here refers to both the embedding of cognitive processes in brain circuitry and the origin of these processes in an organism's sensory-motor experience. What emerges here is a human body that is connected to its environment and to other embodied human beings. Fuchs thus strongly opposes any view that would see the human mind, or consciousness, as somehow localized in, or caused by, or identifiable with, only the human brain: this kind of short-circuit between mind and brain leads to a conceptual and methodological impasse, for it misses the essentially embodied, relational, and biographical character of the human mind.

For Fuchs, then, consciousness does not develop in an isolated brain, *but only in a living organism enmeshed in its environment*. This could also be stated as follows: the human mind is not confined within the human head, but extends throughout the living body to the living world in which both mind and brain are embedded. The mind as such, therefore, includes the world beyond the membrane of the organism, especially the interpersonal world of self and other, which is also the world in which mind and brain are essentially formed. For Fuchs the brain is never the "origin" of the mind, but rather acts as a *transformer* that translates the stimuli (single elements of a given situation) into wholes or Gestalt units, and finally into three cycles of embodiment: the affective self, the ecological self, and, ultimately, the intersubjective self. But in this context the brain is only an organ, and it is not just the brain, but the whole organism of the embodied living person that has conscious access to the world.

Most importantly, Fuchs talks about our bodies as *transparent to the world*: human subjectivity is embedded in the world, with the body acting as its mediator. And consciousness as the luminosity which reveals the world to a subject is the direct result of this mediation. Miraculously, our bodies, as solid and material objects, are capable of a transformation that turns matter into mind and lets the world appear. In this way the body becomes transparent to the world and allows us to act in it (Fuchs and Schlimme 2009). For Fuchs this goes to the heart of emotional contagion and empathy, for we understand the gestures and facial expressions of others immediately: there is an implicit resonance with the expressions of others, while our own bodily and emotional reactions through emotional contagion show how the body works as a tacitly "felt mirror" of the other. And the discovery of "mirror neurons" in the premotor cortext seems to provide the core neural mechanism of this sensorimotor integration. But observing the other's movements and gestures implies a transmission of intentions as well: in theory of mind we use not just our brains, but the operative intentionality of our whole bodes as instruments for understanding the other's intentions (Fuchs and Schlimme 2009).

The psychologist Lee Kirkpatrick builds on a similarly enriched notion of consciousness, intentionality, and attachment when he turns to the evolution of religion. For Kirkpatrick religion is not itself an adaptation and humans do not possess, as part of our species-universal evolved psychological architecture, mechanisms designed by natural selection specifically for the purpose of generating religious belief or behavior as a solution to any particular adaptive problem (Kirkpatrick 2005: 238). For instance, attachment theory and its embodied empathetic dispositions, as outlined in Kirkpatrick's work, should rather be seen as simply one part of a much broader model in which the attachment system represents just one of many domain-specific psychological mechanisms that have been co-opted in the service of religion and religious belief. Religion activates attachment processes but also many other psychological processes as well, like Theory of Mind, empathy, altered states of consciousness, and it is probably this *combination* that is responsible for its widespread success and staying power (Kirkpatrick 2005: 239). The path from genes to religious belief is, therefore, clearly a very long and circuitous one (Kirkpatrick 2005: 327).

A radically different view from Lee Kirkpatrick's nonadaptive views on our very human propensity for religious awareness and religious belief, but one equally focused on human embodiment, is found in the work of the neuroscientist Patrick McNamara. For McNamara it is exactly the deep religious propensities of the human mind that cannot be explained by naturalistic evolutionary accounts of human nature and behavior only. An interesting and rather bold move in this direction was recently presented in his book *The Neuroscience of Religious Experience* (2009). As a neuroscientist McNamara wants to develop his own central conviction that religion is a defining mark of what it means to be human, as emblematic of its bearer as the web is of the spider (McNamara 2009: ix). The special focus of McNamara's work, however, is to examine the phenomenon of religion through the eyes of the human self. Strikingly, in spite of the self's great dignity and worth, it is still treated by religions as divided, conflicted, and in need of salvation. Most importantly, McNamara argues that there is a considerable anatomical overlap between the brain sites implicated in religious experience and the brain sites implicated in the sense of "self" and self-consciousness. This accounts for the crucial conclusion that religious practices often operate to support a transformation of self such that the self becomes more like an "ideal self" whom the individual hopes to become (McNamara 2009: xi). In this sense religious practices directly contribute to the creation of a unified self-consciousness and to what McNamara calls an ideal "executive self." So, when religions are operating normally they tend to create a healthy, unified, and integrated sense of self. Religions accomplish this feat by promoting a cognitive process that McNamara calls *decentering* (2009: 44f.), where religious practices help to build up a centralized executive self.

McNamara's bold claim, then, is that religion is irrevocably a central part of the evolution of symbolic and religious behavior and of the construction of a centralized, "executive" self. As for the evolutionary status of religion, this implies that religion is not, as is often argued, an unfortunate by-product of more useful cognitive capacities of the human mind. On the contrary, this implies that religion is indeed an adaptation, which is confirmed by the fact that the practice of religious rituals and belief in supernatural agents occur in virtually all human cultures (McNamara 2009: 249). And it is precisely religion's impact on the problems associated with the self and consciousness that could be seen as adaptive. The self and its default position, the divided self, should thus be taken into account when discussing the evolutionary history of religion (McNamara 2009: 253).

In Wesley J. Wildman's important book, *Science and Religious Anthropology* (2009), various strands from our conversation so far now flow together in an exciting and challenging way. The central argument of this work supports a naturalistic interpretation of the human self and of religion, but quite specifically the human self as *Homo religiosus*. Religion in this specific sense suffuses every aspect of human life, and Wildman makes it clear that our value commitments, our efforts at meaning construction, and our socially borne explorations of life possibilities, all reach far beyond the historically most prominent forms of religiosity. Wildman, in language reminiscent of Patrick McNamara, states it well: at an axiological level, beneath the most overt beliefs and practices of both religious and nonreligious people, we find *Homo religiosus*. From there on we can trace the impact of human religiosity in a more general sense on existential levels, on moral awareness, and on the social construction of reality (Wildman 2009: xvii). Wildman thus wants to present a religious anthropology by focusing on the embodied *Homo religiosus*, and by enlarging the scope of religious behaviors, beliefs, and experiences, to encompass everything relevant to human meaning and value.

Wildman also wants to ask about the *evolutionary status of religion*, and against this background Wildman considers two extreme views, namely, i) that religion has no genetic component, or ii) that religion is an adaptation arising on the back of one or two traits. In light of this Wildman now asks, is religion an evolutionary adaptation, increasing fitness in and of itself and originating because of the adaptive functions of religious behaviors, beliefs, and experiences? Or, is religion a side effect of a collection of adapted traits? Or is it possible that religion has no genetic component at all and finds its origin only in a long history of cultural expressions? In the end he develops his own, and in my view most plausible, view, *that religion in evolutionary terms is a combination of side effects of both adapted and nonadapted features of the human organism* (Wildman 2009: 37f.). And, whatever one's views of theological truth claims, the evolutionary story of the origins of religion is directly relevant to assessing the meaning and value of religion, as well as religious claims about human beings (Wildman 2009: 42).

There is indeed overwhelmingly strong evidence against the extreme view that no aspect of religion is genetically related or evolutionarily conditioned. Similarly, for Wildman it is clear that the evidence for religion as an adaptation so narrows the focus to one or two adapted "religion traits" that only a fraction of the varied phenomena of religion are registered in the explanation. He argues, therefore, in language reminiscent of that of Lee Kirkpatrick, that it seems highly likely that the evolutionary explanation for the origin of the multifaceted reality of religious behaviors, beliefs, and experiences must lie somewhere between these extremes. Religion, in other words, is evolutionarily conditioned, possibly in a few special respects by virtue of the adaptiveness of specifically religious traits, but in most respects by virtue of side effects of traits adapted for some other, primarily and originally nonreligious purpose (Wildman 2009: 48).

In the end Wildman does state that little is gained for the religionist or theologian by mastering the intricate cognitive science of religion debate over adaptations versus exaptations versus spandrels because little depends on the details of how religion evolved, once it is granted that religion is in fact partly the product of evolutionary processes. The general fact that religion is partly the product of evolutionary processes indeed proves to be the most salient point for any religious anthropology (Wildman 2009: 54–55). At this point Wildman directly refers to Lee

Kirkpatrick who, as we saw earlier, has argued that religion is indeed a complex combination of side effects that have a variety of adaptive functions. And as Wildman succinctly states: understanding religion in evolutionary terms predominantly as a combination of side effects of both adapted and nonadapted features of the human organism, possibly with a few directly adapted features, is the hypothesis that I regard as possessing the most prima facie plausibility (Wildman 2009: 56).

Crucially important from the perspective of this paper on notions of self in Neolithic Çatalhöyük is Wildman's consistent and enduring focus on human embodiment. Because the human brain furnishes the cognitive, emotional, and motor capacities underlying our extraordinary range of religious behaviors, beliefs, and experiences, it is reasonable to expect the neurosciences to have at least as much transformative importance for religious anthropology as the evolutionary sciences (Wildman 2009: 87). And important for the ongoing current discussion in the cognitive science of religion is Wildman's argument that biases exist in the human cognitive system either because they have been selected in the evolutionary process for their survival benefits, or because they are side effects of other traits selected for their usefulness (Wildman 2009: 94). This enables Wildman also to focus on three domains in which a sharp awareness of human bodies and their functions is vital for understanding the human being as *Homo religiosus*: sociality, morality, and, finally, religious and spiritual experiences. In all three of these areas it is *bodies* that make religion, in the broadest sense of the word, not only possible, but also inevitable. Bodies shape the cognitive and emotional form that religion takes in individuals, and the social and moral practices that religions manifest in groups. Our bodies do not completely determine who we are, but they do constrain without determining, and as such they directly shape what we are and do, how we think and interpret, how we love, and how we construct religions (Wildman 2009: 118). Thus our religious and spiritual experiences arise from a suite of bodily capacities with neurological and sensory roots that have vast existential and social impacts (Wildman 2009: 141).

Some scholars, of course, have argued that religion is an evolutionary phenomenon in a double sense, that is, on both biological and social/cultural levels. Scholars like David Lewis-Williams (2002), for instance, have claimed from very different disciplinary backgrounds that altered states of consciousness, ecstatic religious experiences, and forms of shamanism not only are neurophysiologically grounded but represent the earliest forms of prehistoric religion. McClenon and Lewis-Williams have also provided possible scenarios for how shamanic rituals could have evolved by natural selection in the human ancestral environment, perhaps as early as thirty thousand years ago. Lewis-Williams has also argued persuasively that beliefs in a supernatural realm persist worldwide. In addition it is exactly the persistence of religion into our modern, materialistic Western milieu that in fact points to the answer to the problem of the origin of religion: instead of religion being only an answer to social and psychological needs, and in place of a too linear conception of the evolutionary stages of religion, Lewis-Williams prefers to think of *origin-as-process*. On my view this is a helpful reframing of the important question of why religion persists today: the very human spectrum of neuropsychological dispositions for religious belief, wired into human consciousness, are in fact the reasons why religion persists today, and they are, in some fundamental ways, the same as those that explain why religion came into being in the first place. In this sense, one might conclude, the many dimensions of religion, or rather religious belief, played a primary role in the emergence of the historical self at Çatalhöyük.

Conclusion

Our reflections on the historical self and on various rituals, especially mortuary practices, invariably revealed how exactly these and other material entanglements always raise the question of "transcendence" as framed by Ian Hodder (2011: 67). In our thinking about religion or spirituality in the Neolithic, and our thinking of the historical self as also *Homo religiosus*, we should, therefore, not expect to discover some clearly demarcated, separate domain that we could identify as "religion" as such. What this means is that we should avoid making easy and uncomplicated distinctions between natural/supernatural and material/spiritual when trying to understand the prehistorical self at Çatalhöyük. The complex material culture of Çatalhöyük clearly demands a more holistic approach where not just special artistic objects and artifacts, but daily material life itself (houses and other structures) must have been deeply infused with spirituality for the people there. This implies that archaeologists can indeed recognize the spiritual or religious in early periods only through the material legacy of the people of that time. Imagery, sculptures, paintings, and other artifacts may not always be exclusively religious but may point to normal living spaces as symbolic realms.

A holistic approach to the world of Çatalhöyük thus enables us to link the art discovered at this Neolithic city to the archaeological legacy from daily life, that is, the houses, their structures, the unusual and complex burials with their ritual skull removal and replacement. It also enables us to see the history houses as ritualized living spaces where bucrania and vulture and weasel skulls are enigmatically embedded in the walls (Meskell 2008: 377), and where historical selves could emerge as constructed by memory and imagination. On this view it should not be far-fetched to link this symbolic material world, so typical of imagistic modes of religion, to the spectrum of neurasthetic abilities and religious dispositions of the uniquely symbolizing human mind. For me this sense of a deep material/spiritual entanglement does not at all imply only a generic "shamanistic" reading of the Neolithic material at Çatalhöyük. However, it would be safe to assume that the neurological functioning of the human brain, including important traits like HADD, empathy, attachment, Theory of Mind, and altered states of consciousness, like the structure and functioning of other parts of our bodies, is a human universal, and that at least some of the material from Çatalhöyük clearly suggests an early imagistic, deeply religious culture, of which important experiential and ritual elements would have been carried through to later, more doctrinal modes of religiosity.

By looking at the place of especially secondary mortuary practices we could better understand how individual and collective identities emerged and how crucially the role of memory and imagination shaped notions of self at Çatalhöyük. These burial practices par excellence highlight cycles of remembrance and clearly indicate that community members approached life and death as integrated and cyclical. In this context mortuary practices were communal actions that served not only to commemorate the individual identity of the deceased, but also to provide a conduit of collective memory and the reaffirmation of identity and communal membership (Kuijt 2008: 186). For Ian Kuijt this has important implications for understanding personal identity at Çatalhöyük: the low mean age of death in the Neolithic and the occurrence of secondary mortuary practices created the context for rapid shifts in identity and memory. Within two generations memories, events, and objects associated with named individuals would have been transformed from experiential and personal to referential and abstract. This also suggests that a city like Çatalhöyük would have been structured around the cyclical nature of practice, embodiment, and symbolism. In this sense the symbolic focus on the human face and head served as a center for memory, and in many ways as a shared system of ritual practices (Kuijt 2008: 186). In this way remembrance and forgetting formed an integrated and dialectic process in which Neolithic communities literally, visually, and symbolically dismembered and memorialized persons.

In this paper I have argued that the question of the emergence of the historical self in Neolithic Çatalhöyük can never be disentangled from the broader issue of the evolution of embodied human personhood, and, therefore, from evolution of religion and of religious behavior. This implies that the evolution of distinctive traits and aspects of personhood like morality, sexuality, and empathy (which I have not dealt with here), and the evolution of the religious disposition played a defining role in the evolution of human communication and interpersonal attachment and, along with the evolution of complex symbolic behavior, combine to give us important insights into the evolution of religion and religious behavior.

I believe that various scholars, as cited, have made good arguments for the fact that religion is not in itself adaptive. We humans do not possess, as part of our evolved neurological and psychological architecture, intuitive mechanisms designed by natural selection specifically for the purpose of generating religious beliefs or behavior as a solution to particular adaptive problems. However, distinctive neurological traits like empathy, Theory of Mind, attachment, altered states of consciousness, HADD, and the evolution of the moral sense/intuitive morality should all be seen as part of a much broader model in which many domain-specific mechanisms have been co-opted in the service of religion and religious belief. Religion thus activates attachment processes, but also many other processes such as altered states of consciousness and HADD, and it is most probably this combination that is responsible for the widespread success and staying power of religious belief.

Religion, in other words, is evolutionarily conditioned, possibly in a few special respects by virtue of the adaptiveness of specifically religious traits, but in most respects by virtue of side effects of traits adapted for some other, primarily nonreligious purpose. Understanding religion in evolutionary terms predominantly as a combination of side effects of both adapted and nonadapted features of the embodied human might be the most plausible hypothesis for beginning to understand the evolution of religion and religious behavior. Thus religious and spiritual experiences arise from a suite of bodily capacities with neurological and sensory roots and vast existential and social impacts (Wildman 2009: 56, 141). For my own research it is, therefore, significant to think through the theological implications of this debate where various scholars have argued (as we saw earlier) that cognitive approaches and adaptationist approaches can in fact be seen as complementary, and where we come to understand that religion is of primary importance for understanding the human self at Çatalhöyük.

BIBLIOGRAPHY

Belfer-Cohen, A. and Hovers, E. 2010. Modernity, Enhanced Working Memory, and the Middle to Upper Paleolithic Record in the Levant. *Current Anthropology* 51(1):167–175.

Carter, T. 2007. Of blanks and burials: Hoarding obsidian at Neolithic Çatalhöyük. In *Technical Systems and Near Eastern PPN Communities.* Antibes: Editions APDCA.

Cauvin, J. 1994. *Naissance des Divinités, Naissance de l'Agriculture.* Paris: CNRS.

Clark, J. 2008. Comments. *Current Anthropology* 49(2):187–188.

Fuchs, T., and Schlimme, J. E. 2009. Embodiment and psychopathology: a phenomenological perspective. *Current Opinion in Psychiatry*, 22(6), 570–575.

Hodder, I. 2011. An archeology of the self: The prehistory of personhood. In *In Search of Self: Interdisciplinary Perspectives on Personhood*, eds. J. W. Van Huyssteen and E. P. Wiebe. Grand Rapids, MI: William B. Eerdmans, 50–69.

Kearney, R. 2004. *On Paul Ricoeur: The Owl of Minerva.* Aldershot: Ashgate Press.

Kirkpatrick, L. A. 2005. *Attachment, evolution, and the psychology of religion.* Guilford Press.

Kuijt, I. 2008. The Regeneration of Life: Neolithic Structures of Symbolic Remembering and Forgetting. *Current Anthropology* 49(2):172–188.

Lewis-Williams, J. D. 2002. *The mind in the cave: Consciousness and the origins of art.* London: Thames & Hudson.

Lewis-Williams, D. (Ed.). (2000). *Stories that float from afar: ancestral folklore of the San of southern Africa* (Vol. 5). Cape Town: New Africa Books.

McNamara, P. 2009. *The neuroscience of religious experience.* Cambridge University Press.

Meskell, L. 2008. The Nature of the Beast: Curating Animals and Ancestors at Çatalhöyük. *World Archaeology* 40(3):373–389.

Mithen, S. 2009. *The Singing Neanderthals: The Origins of Music, Language, Mind and Body*. Cambridge, MA: Harvard University Press.

Ricoeur, P. 1992. *Oneself as Another*. Chicago: University of Chicago Press.

2004. *Memory, History, and Forgetting*. Chicago: University of Chicago Press.

Ricoeur, P., and Homans, P. 2008. Afterword: Conversations on Freud, memory, and loss. In *Mourning Religion*, eds. W. B. Parsons, D. Jonte-Pace, and S. E. Henking Charlottesville: University of Virginia Press, 221–238.

Schmidt, Ks. 2006. *Sie bauten die Erste Tempel*. DTV Deutsche Taschenbuch.

Tattersall, I. 2011. Origin of the human sense of self. In *In Search of Self: Interdisciplinary Perspectives on Personhood*, eds. J. W. Van Huyssteen and E. P. Wiebe. Grand Rapids, MI: William B. Eerdmans, 33–49.

Van Huyssteen, J. W. 2006. *Alone in the World? Human Uniqueness in Science and Theology*. Grand Rapids, MI: Wm. B. Eerdmans.

2010. When Were We Persons? Why Hominid Evolution Holds the Key to Embodied Personhood. *Neue Zeitschrift fur Systematische Theologie* 52:329–349.

Van Huyssteen, J. W., and Wiebe, E. P. 2011. *In Search of Self: Interdisciplinary Perspectives on Personhood*. Grand Rapids, MA: William B. Eerdmans.

Wildman, W. J. 2009. *Science and religious anthropology. A Spiritually Evocative, Naturalistic Interpretation of Human Life* (Farnham, UK: Ashgate).

6

Modes of Religiosity and the Evolution of Social Complexity at Çatalhöyük

Harvey Whitehouse, Camilla Mazzucato, Ian Hodder, and Quentin D. Atkinson

One of the greatest unsolved puzzles in the study of cultural evolution is the first emergence of large-scale, complex civilizations. Social scientists and historians have long puzzled over the dynamics of large hierarchical societies and the mechanisms responsible for their survival and spread. But less is known about the origins of complex societies, which first emerged in only a few places around the world, leaving behind no written records of the process by which this quantum leap in human social organization occurred. The excavations at Çatalhöyük may help solve the puzzle. We argue that a major factor driving the emergence of complex society was *religious routinization*. The frequency of rituals appears to have increased over the course of settlement at Çatalhöyük and this may have had major consequences for the scale and structure of Neolithic society.

This argument permits a conciliatory stance on the relationship between religion's "vitality," as conceptualized in much of this volume, and its "functionality" in bolstering a social order. In fact these two aspects of religion are intimately interconnected – stripped of its vitality religion's social functions could hardly be fulfilled. The evidence from Çatalhöyük suggests that the earliest functions of religion were not to legitimate political and economic inequalities. Initially religion's function was to bind together small tribal groups, but gradually, as agriculture intensified, this ancient function faded and religion became a means of reproducing much larger (if more diffuse) group identities. This entailed a change also in religion's vitality – a shift from esoteric mystery cult to something more ideologically uniform, in some ways less awe-inspiring and more controlling. The exploitation of this new kind of religion by elites occurred much later, however, entailing the evolution of new forms of religious vitality.

Modes of Religiosity at Çatalhöyük

The connection between ritual frequency and social morphology has been the subject of considerable research in recent years. A central hypothesis is that low-frequency, "dysphoric" (frightening and/or painful) rituals with others promote prosocial behavior in cooperative endeavors rather more than the sharing of either euphoric or neutral ritual experiences, and that the amount of reflection and rumination triggered by the experience and/or the fusion between the individual participant and the group will mediate this effect (Whitehouse 1996; Richert, Whitehouse and Stewart 2005). Dysphoric rituals are thought to bind small face-to-face groups based on networks of relational ties (Swann et al. 2012). Such rituals may be especially adaptive where survival depends on high levels of cooperation despite strong incentives to defect, such as chronic tribal warfare or systems in which meat is procured by hunting large and dangerous animals with simple weapons. This clustering of features (especially low-frequency dysphoric ritual and intense social cohesion in small groups) has become known as the "imagistic mode of religiosity" (Whitehouse 2004).

By contrast, participation in high-frequency (e.g., daily or weekly) religious rituals is thought to foster identification of group members within large "imagined" communities, efficient spread of authoritative dogma that is standardized by means of speech and text, and multiple levels of jurisdictional hierarchy (Whitehouse 1995). High-frequency religious rituals, like many other culturally shared behavioral conventions, are recalled as procedural scripts and semantic schemas (Baddeley 1997). Scripts and schemas specify what typically happens in a given ritual and what is generally thought to be its significance. In a group whose identity markers are composed mainly of scripts and schemas, what it means to be a member of the community may be generalized to everyone who performs similar acts and holds similar beliefs. This route to the construction of communal identity, based on routinization, may be especially conducive to the establishment of large populations sharing a common tradition and capable of behaving as a coalition in interactions with nonmembers, *despite* the fact that no individual in the community could possibly know all the others, or even hope to meet all of them in the course of a lifetime (Whitehouse 2000). Routinization also may also allow very complex networks of dogma and narrative to be learned and stored in collective memory, making it relatively easy to spot unauthorized innovations. High-frequency rituals would seem to be adaptive for large populations requiring standardized identity markers to facilitate trust among strangers, for example, when competing for partners in trading networks, or to facilitate participation in large-scale cooperation. This nexus of features (high-frequency ritual and large-scale, hierarchical social morphology) has come to be known as the "doctrinal mode of religiosity" (Whitehouse 2004).

Evidence for the theory of modes of religiosity was originally based on a large body of detailed historical and ethnographic case studies (e.g., Ketola 2002; Martin and Pachis 2009; Martin and Whitehouse 2005; McCauley 2001; McCauley and Lawson 2002; McCauley and Whitehouse 2005; Naumescu 2008; Whitehouse and Laidlaw 2004; Whitehouse and Martin 2004; Whitehouse and McCauley 2005; Xygalatas 2007). Qualitative evidence of this kind was useful in refining the theory but is inevitably vulnerable to the criticism of "cherry picking" examples that confirm the predictions and ignoring those that do not. To address the problem, more systematic data on this topic are now being assembled. For instance, in a recent survey of 644 rituals selected from a sample of 74 cultures Atkinson and Whitehouse (2010) found an inverse correlation between ritual frequency and levels of dysphoric arousal, with most rituals clustering around the high-frequency/low-arousal (doctrinal) and low-frequency/high-arousal (imagistic) poles of the continuum. One of the predictions of the modes theory supported by this cross-cultural evidence was that high-frequency rituals correlate with larger-scale farming societies while more dysphoric rituals prevail in smaller communities exhibiting lower reliance on agriculture. Extrapolating these findings to the transition from foraging to farming in the prehistory of the Middle East and Mediterranean, Atkinson and Whitehouse observed:

> The first appearance of the doctrinal mode in human prehistory would seem to presage the first appearance of large-scale, hierarchical political systems in Mesopotamia and Egypt. Was this seismic shift in social evolution driven by a change from imagistic to doctrinal practices? Although the question of causality cannot be determined here, the link between agriculture and relatively low arousal, high frequency rituals in our survey of contemporary societies offers support for this hypothesis. Whereas the exploitation of wild resources requires only sporadic group co-operation (e.g. in hunting larger game), the domestication of animals and plants fosters increasingly

routinized forms of collaborative labour (e.g. clearing, planting, harvesting, and fencing). In traditional societies such activities are typically punctuated by rituals.… If the emergence of agriculture drives an overall increase in the frequency of communal rituals, it also indirectly opens up opportunities for other features of the doctrinal mode to appear … including the homogenization of regional traditions and in time the emergence of professional priesthoods.

This chapter builds on an earlier study suggesting that changes in ritual life at Çatalhöyük were linked with and may have facilitated the shift to large-scale agricultural societies (Whitehouse and Hodder 2010). Of course, Çatalhöyük was always agricultural and the site was always large. But we argued that a shift could be observed from imagistic to doctrinal modes of religiosity. Following Mithen (2004) we suggested that the clearest evidence from Çatalhöyük concerned low-frequency rituals that would have had high-arousal components. Such evidence seemed to predominate in the earlier occupation of the site. The socialized and ritualized interactions with large and dangerous animals, and concomitant feasting, would have occurred relatively infrequently and would have been high-arousal events. Other aspects of the Çatalhöyük data could be interpreted as conforming to the expectations of the imagistic mode. For example, as the hard pointed parts of the animals killed in hunting or teasing and baiting were taken into individual houses there was much variation in the specific interpretations that were made – so there were multivocality and multivalence, as indicated by the great diversity of specific interactions with the bucrania and other animal body parts in individual houses. For example, usually the benches with bull horns occur on the east side of main rooms in houses, but in Building 52 a bench with bull horns occurs on the west side. In the upper levels of the site, Whitehouse and Hodder (2010) argued that the emergence of the doctrinal mode could be discerned not only in the evidence for recurring themes in the construction of acts and artifacts at the site but, more tellingly, in the evidence for an increasingly discursive deployment of those themes in standardized ways and the emergence of authoritative versions.

While Whitehouse and Hodder (2010) noted a concomitant shift from less to more social differentiation in the sequence at Çatalhöyük, little attention was given to possible links among the changing modes of religiosity, community size, and agricultural intensity. Atkinson and Whitehouse's (2010) cross-cultural analysis of contemporary cultures from around the globe found that modes of religiosity are indeed associated with synchronic variation in community size and agricultural intensity. The analysis showed that high-arousal, low-frequency rituals are associated with both hunting/gathering and smaller community size. Conversely, low-arousal, high-frequency rituals are associated with increased agricultural intensity and larger community size. One explanation for this pattern is that ritual is partly a cultural adaptation supporting different scales of cooperation suited to varying challenges of resource extraction and intergroup competition. The aim in this chapter is to move beyond these synchronic data to look in detail at evidence from a single site to see whether the shift to a doctrinal mode of religiosity is linked to increasing agricultural intensity and greater community size and density of population.

In the earlier levels of Çatalhöyük, the best evidence of the imagistic mode is the installations of parts of wild animals within houses. In particular, the horns of bulls and the tusks of wild boar were placed within walls or pedestals; these animals and animal parts seem also to be associated with feasting. After Level South O/P the frequency of such installations declines. In their place are found paintings of people teasing and baiting wild animals. In the material culture inventory there is an increased occurrence of stamp seals and pottery with decoration including representations of bulls. This more discursive and perhaps doctrinal mode occurs from South P to TP. The new recently collected evidence from the site allows evaluation of changes in population size and agricultural intensity through the entire sequence of occupation.

Overall Population Size and Density

Regional survey by Baird (2002, 2005) shows increasing population densities through the Ceramic Neolithic and early Chalcolithic (eighth to sixth millennia BC) on the Çarşamba alluvial fan on the Konya Plain, but also concentration through time into the one large site of Çatalhöyük, followed by dispersal into multiple tells in the Chalcolithic. As far as densities on site are concerned, while we cannot yet map the whole East Mound and each level, there is some evidence to suggest that population gradually rose until Levels South M, N, and O. We know very little of the extent of the earliest occupation of the site, but excavations in the twenty meter by twenty meter area in the South Area found no buildings in the lowest levels, and the midden deposits discovered may have been toward the edge of the site. By Level South J this South Area was more densely populated, and the density of houses increased into Level South N. The number of burials per building is greatest in these middle levels (Cessford 2005), and the densely packed clusters of households (Düring 2006; Düring and Marciniak 2006) suggest that the site's population reached its peak in South M–O and 4040 G. There is also significant change in indicators of human fertility, diet, activity, and disease. Larsen et al. (2013) identify clear evidence for higher levels of fertility in the middle period of occupation (South M and North G). The prevalence of osteoperiostitis among adult individuals is also at its peak in the middle levels (27.9 percent) and declines dramatically in the upper levels (8.6 percent). This evidence suggests heightened conditions of nonspecific stress, especially during the peak population. Evidence of accidental skeletal trauma also suggests a rather more accident-prone population in the middle levels, perhaps linked to the increased workload. The middle period appears to be characterized by higher overall amounts of labor, perhaps stemming from intensified resource exploitation and food production, while in the upper levels there appears to be a decrease in overall workload and an increase in mobility as a wider range of resources was exploited. From South P onward we see more open space between buildings, and habitation seems increasingly dispersed, with contracted settlement in the South Area of the site, sparse settlement in the northern zone, and scattered occupation to the east of the East Mound (Hodder 1996) and in the IST Area. A femoral midshaft index was used (Larsen et al. 2013) to assess the mobility of individuals, and a general trend from less to more mobility through time was noted for both males and females (although only statistically significant for males). Study of long bone cross sections suggested that females show some indication of an increase in mobility through the occupation of the site. All this evidence for increased mobility in the upper levels fits very well with the evidence for increasingly wide use of the landscape for herding sheep and managing domestic cattle (see later discussion).

In summary, population numbers and densities increase into South M–O and then decline or population dispersal occurs. This South M–O period is also the time of greatest fertility and most skeletal evidence of stress on health. In the upper levels this high level of stress is replaced by greater skeletal evidence of mobility.

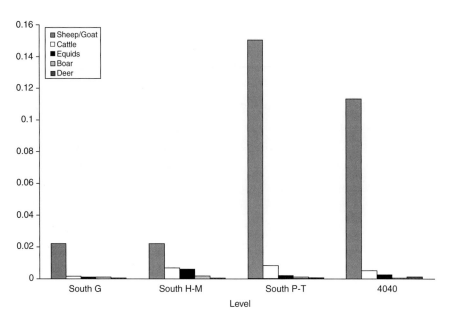

6.1. Midden deposits: density of animal taxa through time.

Agricultural Intensity

The relative proportion of taxa (sheep/goat, cattle, boar, equid, deer) through time shows a rise in sheep/goat in levels South P–T (Russell et al. 2013). But more telling is that the analysis of the densities of faunal remains in midden units by level shows a sharp rise in sheep/goat (Figure 6.1) and a constant level of cattle consumption. The increase in sheep/goat on site from South P onward appears to indicate the intensification of caprine herding in the late levels. It is not clear exactly when this change occurred, as in the South levels the recent excavations have not explored N and O; and in the North we are unsure of the exact chronological relationships with the South levels, but we can say the change occurred somewhere in the South N to P bracket, that is, around 6500 BC.

This increased focus on sheep suggests a major input of labor. There is also evidence for the introduction of domesticated cattle at this time (Russell et al. 2013). Together these shifts suggest a significant increase in the intensification of agricultural production that continues on into the West Mound Chalcolithic. There is some slight indication that this increase in intensification was associated with a shift from collective management of sheep herds to separate house-based control. This argument is based on an interpretation of age and sex profiles in the upper levels (Russell et al. 2013) and on variability in sheep isotopes (Pearson 2013). There is also slight indication (see later discussion) that the shift to herding cattle may have allowed a degree of wealth accumulation, although this always seems to have competed with strong leveling mechanisms at Çatalhöyük.

The botanical remains do not show marked change through the main sequence at Çatalhöyük. Rather they show continuity but with hulled barley introduced as a new, more intensive crop in the uppermost levels and on the West Mound (as seen in both phytolith and macrobotanical remains – Ryan 2013; Bogaard et al. 2013). The clearest evidence of change in the phytolith assemblage is an increase in Australis phragmites in the upper levels, after South P. In general terms phragmites is an indicator of disturbance to the local environment through increased human intervention. Possible causes of the increase are the digging of deeper quarry pits around the mound (in order to provide sandy clays for bricks and pottery), over-wintering of sheep and perhaps local managing of cattle near the site, and the provision of reeds for roofs and mats. The expansion of phragmites would have led to lowered water tables and a decrease in biodiversity. Management of and response to the proliferation of phragmites would have required greater inputs of labor.

Increased Activity in the House and Settlement

The increased evidence for agricultural activity in the post–P South levels can be related to increased intensity of activity in the house. Many aspects of the economy seem to have been organized through a domestic mode. There is much evidence for the intensive processing of sheep bones and meat in the house, using pottery to extract grease and fat as well as to cook meat. We also have much evidence that cereals were stored in the house with spikelets attached. As needed the grains were removed from storage bins, dehusked, and then ground. Given this degree of house processing of sheep and cereal resources it might be expected that as the intensity of animal and plant exploitation in the landscape increased so there should be increased evidence for processing in and around the house. The introduction of pottery and its gradual increase in densities through time (Figure 6.2; a Kruskal Wallis test reported a statistically significant difference between levels) is one indicator of this increased

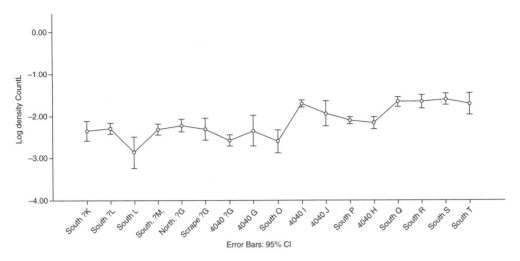

6.2. Density of pottery through time.

processing since the cooking pots were largely used to process sheep meat and fat (Pitter, Yalman, and Evershed 2013); there is also phytolith evidence that pots were used in processing cereals. Ground stone was used to grind and process foods, and there is greater specialization of production of ground stone tools in the upper levels (Wright 2013). There is also incipient small-scale specialization of bone tool manufacture in the upper levels (Russell et al. 2013), and the same can be said of obsidian (Carter and Mili 2013). Mini clay balls, tokens, and stamp seals all increase in the upper levels, and it is possible that all these were used in early forms of accounting (Atalay 2013; Bennison-Chapman 2013). Although not involved in agricultural production, beads demonstrate a greater diversity of raw materials in the upper levels of the site, and greater technical skill was involved in their production (Baines 2013). They thus contributed to the overall increased levels of productive activity.

Since most of these productive activities (final processing of sheep and cereal resources, manufacture of ground stone, bone and obsidian tools, and the production of beads) all took place in the house it might be expected that houses would become larger in the upper levels. Such a trend is clear if we consider the average increase in house size in Çatalhöyük and adjacent sites, incorporating both recent data and the larger sample collected by Mellaart (Figure 6.3). When only the recent excavations are considered, in this smaller set of data the relationship is not found, except for an increase in TP and on the West Mound

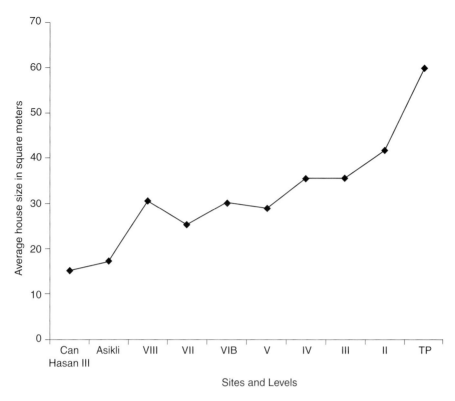

6.3. Average internal area of houses (not including walls) in levels at Çatalhöyük and at two earlier sites in central Anatolia. The Çatalhöyük data include buildings excavated by Mellaart.

(Figure 6.4; a Kruskal Wallis test did not find a statistically significant difference between levels). In the larger data set, the later bigger houses have more storage and side rooms, and there is a very large "farmlike" house that has been excavated on the West Mound (Building 25). While some buildings get larger, there is little evidence of change in the ratio of main rooms to side and storage rooms. The evidence does not suggest substantive social differentiation, but rather a general increase in variation between smaller and larger buildings. The same conclusion is reached by considering the scatterplot in Figure 6.5 that shows floor density in relation to building size and elaboration. While this plot confirms earlier evidence (Hodder and Pels 2010) that more elaborate buildings tend to be larger, there is no evidence of greater or lesser densities of activity on floors of larger or more elaborate buildings.

We have noticed that buildings in the upper levels of the site seem to have cleaner floors. This is perhaps shown in the very slight and gradual

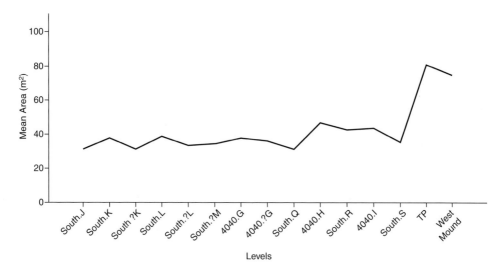

6.4. The area of buildings excavated by the current project in different levels at Çatalhöyük (area calculated from GIS incorporating building walls).

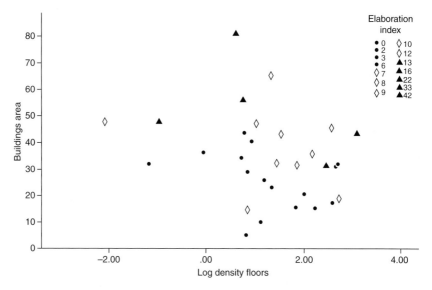

6.5. Scatterplot of logged density on floors (faunal remains, chipped stone, pottery, and ground stone) versus building size, by elaboration index.

change in densities on floors in Figure 6.6 (e.g., a Kruskal Wallis test found a statistically significant difference in pottery densities on floors between levels). On the other hand, there is slight evidence of greater densities of residues in middens in the upper levels (Figure 6.7 and again a Kruskal Wallis test found a statistically significant difference in pottery

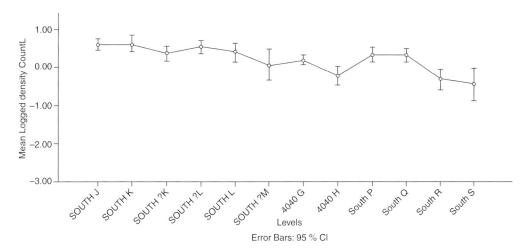

6.6. Density of pottery, chipped stone, faunal remains, and ground stone in floors through levels, 4040 and South for data collected 1995–2008 (botanical remains have been excluded because of missing samples for the early levels).

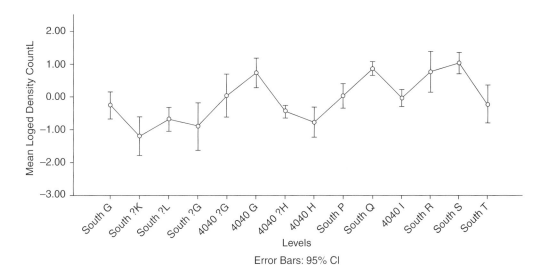

6.7. Density of pottery, chipped stone, faunal remains, and ground stone in middens through levels, 4040 and South for data collected 1995–2008 (botanical remains have been excluded because of missing samples for the early levels).

densities in middens between levels). In the upper levels, then, houses are cleaned out more thoroughly, but also activities that used to take place inside houses now occur more frequently outside – and this is supported by the slight increase in fire spot density in middens in the upper levels (see Figure 6.8) (though with perhaps a final decrease in

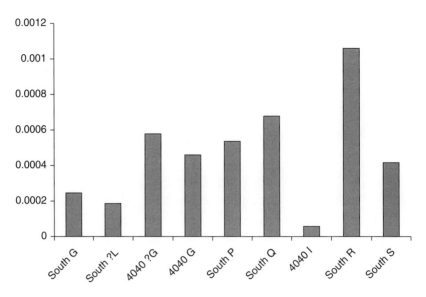

6.8. Densities of fire spots in middens and other external areas by level.

4040 I and South S). As buildings grew bigger and multiroomed they also increasingly made use of adjacent open areas. There seems to be a pattern of increased encroachment onto adjacent midden areas in the 4040 Area of the site, especially onto Sp.60 midden. Similarly ovens and hearths increasingly appear in yards and middens in the South Area from P onward and some buildings (e.g., in the 65-56-44-10 sequence) have openings into adjacent yard or midden areas. The archaeological evidence for increased use of open space between buildings for a range of domestic and productive activities is described elsewhere (Hodder 2013). All the evidence suggests the gradual expansion of the house into a multifunctional productive unit.

Ritual Changes

Overall, therefore, there is evidence for increased productive intensity in the upper levels of Çatalhöyük associated with greater activities in houses and surrounding yards and middens. Settlement both on the site and regionally started to disperse. At the same time there is evidence for greater mobility and the exploitation of a wider range of locales in the landscape for sheep and cattle herding. There is a parallel change in ritual practices in the upper, post–South P levels.

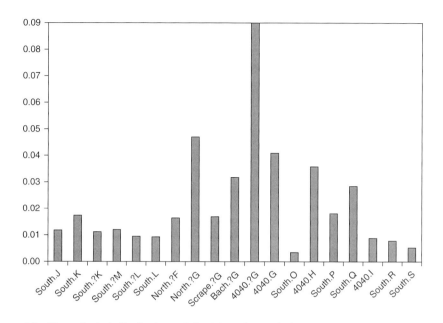

6.9. Chronological distribution of densities of special deposits among all excavated units.

The analysis of faunal deposition has identified special deposits as those with high concentrations of relatively unprocessed large bones. Such special deposits occur, for example, in house abandonment and foundation deposits. In the lower levels of the site such special deposits, as well as feasting deposits, are associated especially with wild bulls (Russell and Martin 2005). The density of these deposits reaches a high point in Level 4040 G, equivalent to South N–O (Figure 6.9). In the upper levels the densities of special deposits decrease again, while sheep/goat proportions increase in special consumption contexts as the overall amounts of sheep/goat increase. Reciprocally, cattle appear to be consumed more often in quotidian settings in the upper levels. A principal component analysis of faunal densities together with pottery, chipped stone, and figurine densities has confirmed these trends. In levels before South P, the special and feasting deposits have less sheep and more cattle, as well as well as less chipped stone. After South P, on the other hand, there is less clear distinction among special, feasting, and daily contexts (Figures 6.10 and 6.11). And indeed cattle now associate with domestic pottery on component 1. So, while feasting and special deposits decline in frequency in the upper levels they are less commonly associated with

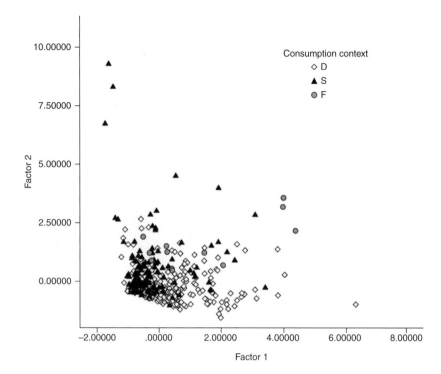

6.10. First two factors resulting from principal components analysis of densities of animal remains, chipped stone, figurines, and pottery in pre–South P level equivalents in the southern and northern parts of the site. Special deposits (S) and feasting deposits (F) cluster on the plot differently from daily consumption deposits (D).

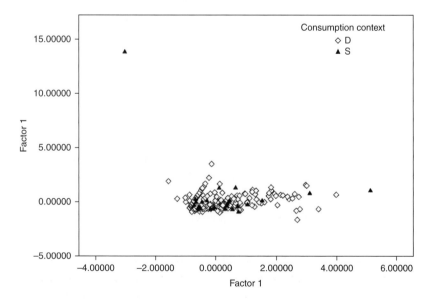

6.11. First two factors resulting from principal components analysis of densities of animal remains, chipped stone, figurines, and pottery in post–South P level equivalents in the southern and northern parts of the site. Special deposits (S) are less distinctive in relation to daily consumption deposits (D) in the upper levels of the site.

wild cattle and other wild animals. As noted previously, the upper levels also see a decline in the use of wild animal parts in installations in houses. There is thus less focus on special events associated with high-arousal experiences and less focus on the direct presencing of dangerous wild animals within the routine practices of everyday life within the house. This confirms the general pattern of a decrease in special events associated with wild cattle and other wild animals and a decrease in installations that memorialize these events.

Burial

The greatest richness and diversity of burial goods occur in South M–O (Nakamura and Meskell 2013), coinciding with the concentration of animal part installations in buildings during the same period. The significance of burial events was perhaps heightened by the incorporation of burial goods in graves. The density of burials, however, changes little through time. In Figure 6.12 the density appears to increase, but the high point of 4040 I is a small sample of baby burials mainly in one building.

There is more focus on foundation burials in the upper levels at the same time as there is less continuity from building to building through time. It is as if continuity of the house building was no longer taken for granted and had to be established through foundation burials of people. There is also increased disturbance of the burials in houses as is seen in an increase in the percentage of primary disturbed loose bones in burials in South S and TP and their absence in the lowest levels (Figure 6.13). In the very uppermost levels of the East Mound there is evidence of major change in burial rites, with "tombs" discovered in the TP Area in which multiple burial and burial of humans with animals now occurred. By the time of the Chalcolithic West Mound there is little evidence of adult burial in houses, and it is possible that separate cemeteries will be discovered.

In general terms, then, as with evidence of installations and special deposits, the role of burial in creating house-based continuities changes after South P, although only gradually. Through the later occupation of the site, burial is increasingly separated from the routines of daily life in the house, where it had earlier aroused notions of continuity. In the

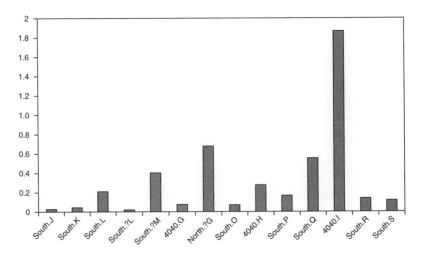

6.12. The density of individuals buried beneath floors in the different levels.

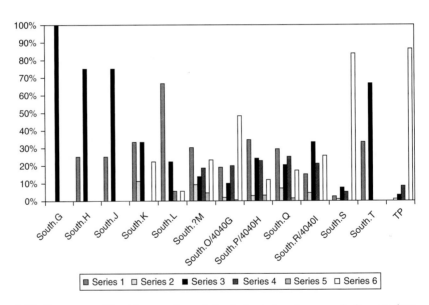

6.13. Percentage of burial types through levels (series1: primary, series2: secondary, series3: tertiary, series4: primary disturbed, series5: unknown, series6: primary disturbed loose).

earlier levels the burial process reaches its apogee in terms of numbers of objects placed in graves in South M–O, but in the upper levels the dead were increasingly disturbed and then distanced and separated from daily life even if they retained an importance, at least on the East Mound, in founding new buildings.

Conclusion

In sum it seems that two trends can be identified that relate to the proposal that a shift to a doctrinal mode of religiosity in the upper levels at Çatalhöyük was linked to increasing agricultural intensity and greater community size and population density.

The first trend identified is increased intensity of agricultural and other forms of production in the upper levels. This shift is associated with a decreased focus on the continuity of the house, fewer installations in the house, and a decrease in special ritual and feasting events focused on the killing of wild animals. It thus appears that these low-frequency rituals, which are likely to elicit high arousal, decreased through time as intensity of production increased. As discussed by Whitehouse and Hodder (2010), there is an increase in the upper levels in discursive mobile symbols as seen on stamp seals and pottery. Feasting or special deposits become more "everyday." The main factor linked to a shift away from high-arousal, low-frequency rituals seems to be productive intensity not community size because we see a decrease in the overall size of the population in the upper levels as houses dispersed and became more separate and independent. Houses do themselves get larger, or some of them do, but the overall density and size of the settlement decrease.

There is a second trend that does relate to the increased density of occupation. Increased population size, density, and fertility occur in South M–O. What we see in South M–O, that is toward the end of what may be a more imagistic mode of religious life in the lower levels, is a heightening of the classic early Çatalhöyük pattern of elaborate symbolism in houses, installations of wild animals, special animal feasting and deposits, and elaborate burial. So, again, the data suggest that settlement size and density are not predicting these changes in ritual form. At Çatalhöyük the highest population size and density are associated with the greatest elaboration of imagistic-type features. There is evidence of stress in the population at this point (South M–O), and it is not until these stresses are relieved with a more intensive and more mobile economy in the upper levels that there is more evidence for aspects of the doctrinal mode. The evidence overall suggests that at Çatalhöyük a shift away from more imagistic, low-frequency high-arousal rituals is linked to increasing intensity of agricultural production rather than population size and density, although this shift may also have entailed a transition of tribal fragmentation toward settlementwide or even regional cultural homogenization and more encompassing forms of group identity. This pattern is broadly consistent with parallel findings from the analysis of ritual variation in contemporary cultures. Doctrinal religious practices are associated with both larger population size and increased agricultural intensity, but in a multiple regression analysis only agricultural intensity remains a significant predictor (Atkinson and Whitehouse 2010).

BIBLIOGRAPHY

Atalay, S. 2013. Clay balls, mini balls and geometric objects. In *Substantive Technologies at Çatalhöyük: Reports from the 2000–2008 Seasons*, ed. I. Hodder. Los Angeles: Cotsen Institute.

Atkinson, Q. D., and Whitehouse, H. 2010. The Cultural Morphospace of Ritual Form: Examining Modes of Religiosity Cross-Culturally. *Evolution and Human Behavior* **32** (1): 50–62.

Baddeley, Alan. 1997. *Human Memory: Theory and Practice*. Rev. ed. Hove: Psychology Press.

Bains, R., Vasić, M., Bar-Yosef Mayer, D. E., Russell, N., Wright, K. I., and Doherty, C. 2013. A technological approach to the study of personal ornamentation and social expression at Çatalhöyük. In *Substantive Technologies at Çatalhöyük: Reports from the 2000–2008 Seasons*, ed. I. Hodder. Los Angeles: Cotsen Institute.

Baird, D. 2002. Early Holocene settlement in Central Anatolia: Problems and prospects as seen from the Konya Plain. In *The Neolithic of Central Anatolia: Internal Developments and External Relations During the 9th-6th Millennia cal BC, Proceedings of the International CANeW Round Table, Istanbul, 23–24 November 2001*, eds. F. Gérard and L. Thissen. Ege Yayınları, Istanbul: Ege Yayınları, 139–159.

2005. The history of settlement and social landscapes in the Early Holocene in the Çatalhöyük area. In *Çatalhöyük Perspectives: Themes from the 1995–1999 Seasons*, ed. I Hodder. Cambridge: McDonald Institute for Archaeological Research/British Institute of Archaeology at Ankara Monograph, 55–74.

Bennison-Chapman, L. 2013. Geometric clay objects. In *Substantive Technologies at Çatalhöyük: Reports from the 2000–2008 Seasons*, ed. I. Hodder. Los Angeles: Cotsen Institute.

Bogaard, A., Charles, M., Livarda, A., Ergun, M., Filipovic, D., and Jones, G. 2013. The archaeobotany of mid-later Neolithic Çatalhöyük. In *Humans and Landscapes of Çatalhöyük: Reports from the 2000–2008 Seasons*, ed. I. Hodde r. Los Angeles: Cotsen Institute.

Carter, T., and Milić, M. 2013. The chipped stone. In *Technologies at Çatalhöyük: Reports from the 2000–2008 Seasons*, ed. I. Hodder. Los Angeles: Cotsen Institute.

Cessford, C. 2005. Estimating the Neolithic population of Çatalhöyük. In *Inhabiting Çatalhöyük: Reports from the 1995–99 seasons*, ed. I. Hodder. McDonald Institute for Archaeological Research, Cambridge, 323–6.

Düring, B. S. 2006. Constructing Communities: Custered Neighbourhood Settlements of the Central Anatolian Neolithic ca. 8500–5500 Cal. BC. Ph.D. Thesis. Leiden University, Nederlands.

Düring, B. S., and Marciniak, A. 2006. Households and Communities in the Central Anatolian Neolithic. *Archaeological Dialogues* **12**:165–187.

Hodder, I., ed. 1996. *On the Surface Çatalhöyük 1993–95*. Cambridge: McDonald Institute for Archaeological Research/London: British Institute of Archaeology at Ankara.

2013. The social geography of Çatalhöyük. In *Integrating Çatalhöyük: Themes from the 2000–2008 Seasons*, ed. I. Hodder. Los Angeles: Cotsen Institute.

Hodder, I., and Pels, P. 2010. History houses: A new interpretation of architectural elaboration at Çatalhöyük. In *Religion in the Emergence of Civilization: Çatalhöyük as a Case Study*, ed. I. Hodder. Cambridge University Press, Cambridge. 163–186.

Ketola, K. 2002. An Indian Guru and His Western Disciples: Representation and Communication of Charisma in the Hare Krishna Movement. Ph.D. Thesis. University of Helsinki, Helsinki.

Larsen, C. S., Hillson, S. W., Ruff, C. B., Sadvari, J. W., and Garofalo, E. M. 2013. The human remains II: Interpreting lifestyle and activity in Neolithic Çatalhöyük. In *Humans and Landscapes of Çatalhöyük: Reports from the 2000–2008 Seasons*, ed. I. Hodder. Los Angeles: Cotsen Institute.

Martin, L. H., and Pachis, P. 2009. *Imagistic Traditions in the Graeco-Roman World*. Thessaloniki: Vanias.

Martin, L. H., and Whitehouse, H., eds. 2005 Implications of Cognitive Science for the Study of Religion, *Special Issue of Method and Theory in the Study of Religion*, Vol. **16**, No. 3.

McCauley, R. N. 2001. Ritual, memory, and emotion: Comparing two cognitive hypotheses. In *Religion in Mind: Cognitive Perspectives on Religious Belief, Ritual, and Experience*, ed. J. Andresen. Cambridge: Cambridge University Press, 115–140.

McCauley, R. N., and Lawson, E. T. 2002. *Bringing Ritual to Mind: Psychological Foundations of Cultural Forms*. Cambridge: Cambridge University Press.

McCauley, R. N., and Whitehouse, H., eds. 2005. *The Psychological and Cognitive Foundations of Religiosity*. special issue of *Journal of Cognition and Culture* **5** Nos. 1–2.

Mishkin, M., and Appenzeller, T. 1987. The anatomy of memory. *Scientific American* **256**(6):80–89.

Mithen, S. 2004. From Ohalo to Çatalhöyük: the development of religiosity during the early prehistory of Western Asia, 20,000–7000 BC. In *Theorizing Religions Past: Historical and Archaeological Perspectives*, ed. H. Whitehouse and L. H. Martin. Walnut Creek, CA: AltaMira Press.

Nakamura, C., and Meskell, L. 2013. The Çatalhöyük burial assemblage. In *Humans and Landscapes of Çatalhöyük: Reports from the 2000–2008 Seasons*, ed. I. Hodder. Los Angeles: Cotsen Institute.

Naumescu, V. 2008. *Modes of Religiosity in Eastern Christianity: Religious Processes and Social Change in Ukraine*. Halle: Lit Verlag.

Pearson, J. 2013. Pearson J.A. 2013. Human and Animal Diet as Evidenced by Stable Carbon and Nitrogen Isotope Analysis. In *Humans and Landscapes of Çatalhöyük: Reports from the 2000–2008 Seasons*, ed. I. Hodder. Los Angeles: Cotsen Institute.

Pitter, S., Yalman, N., and Evershed, R. 2013. Absorbed lipid residues in the Çatalhöyük pottery. In *Substantive Technologies at Çatalhöyük: Reports from the 2000–2008 Seasons*, ed. I. Hodder. Los Angeles: Cotsen Institute.

Richert, R. A., Whitehouse, H., and Stewart, E. E. A. 2005. Memory and analogical thinking in high-arousal rituals. In *Mind and Religion: Psychological and Cognitive Foundations of Religiosity*, eds. H. Whitehouse and R. N. McCauley. Walnut Creek, CA: AltaMira Press.

Russell, N., and Martin, L. 2005. The Çatalhöyük mammal remains. In *Inhabiting Çatalhöyük: Reports from the 1995–1999 Seasons*, ed. I. Hodder. Cambridge: McDonald Institute for Archaeological Research/British Institute of Archaeology at Ankara Monograph, 355–398.

Russell, N., Twiss, C.T. Orton, D. C., and Demirergi, A. 2013. More on the Çatalhöyük mammal remains. In *Humans and Landscapes of Çatalhöyük: Reports from the 2000–2008 Seasons*, ed. I. Hodder. Los Angeles: Cotsen Institute.

Ryan, P. 2013. Plant exploitation from household and landscape perspectives: The phytolith evidence. In *Humans and Landscapes of Çatalhöyük: Reports from the 2000–2008 Seasons*, ed. I. Hodder. Los Angeles: Cotsen Institute.

Swann, William B., Jolanda Jensen, Ángel Gómez, Harvey Whitehouse, and Brock Bastian(2012). When Group Membership Gets Personal: A theory of identity fusion. *Psychological Review*, Vol. **119**, No. 3, pp 441–456.

Whitehouse, H. 1995. *Inside the Cult: Religious Innovation and Transmission in Papua New Guinea*. Oxford: Oxford University Press.

  1996. Rites of Terror: Emotion, Metaphor, and Memory in Melanesian Initiation Cults. *Journal of the Royal Anthropological Institute (N.S.)*, 2:703–715.

  2000. *Arguments and Icons: Divergent Modes of Religiosity*, Oxford: Oxford University Press.

2004. *Modes of Religiosity: A Cognitive Theory of Religious Transmission*, Walnut Creek, CA: AltaMira Press.

Whitehouse, H., and Hodder, I. 2010. Modes of religiosity at Çatalhöyük. In *Religion in the Emergence of Civilization: Çatalhöyük as a Case Study*, ed. I Hodder. Cambridge: Cambridge University Press. 122–145.

Whitehouse, H., and Laidlaw, J. 2004. *Ritual and Memory: Toward a Comparative Anthropology of Religion*. Walnut Creek, CA: AltaMira Press.

Whitehouse, H., and Martin, L. 2004. *Theorizing Religions Past: Archaeology, History, and Cognition*. Walnut Creek, CA: AltaMira Press.

Whitehouse, H., and McCauley, R. N. 2005. *Mind and Religion: Psychological and Cognitive Foundations of Religiosity*. Walnut Creek, CA: AltaMira Press.

Wright, K. 2013. The ground stone technologies of Çatalhöyük. In *Substantive Technologies at Çatalhöyük: Reports from the 2000–2008 Seasons*, ed. I. Hodder. Los Angeles: Cotsen Institute.

Xygalatas, D. 2007. *Firewalking in Northern Greece: A Cognitive Approach to High-Arousal Rituals*. Ph.D. Thesis. Queen's University, Belfast, UK.

PART II

VITAL MATERIALS AT ÇATALHÖYÜK

7

Relational Networks and Religious Sodalities at Çatalhöyük

Barbara J. Mills

Çatalhöyük is often compared to the Pueblos of the North American Southwest. As someone whose work largely focuses on Ancestral Pueblo archaeology, I was intrigued by the possibility of comparing these two areas. My initial reaction upon walking around the site of Çatalhöyük was that it was nothing like the pueblos or the Pueblos of the Southwest.[1] One of the most obvious differences is that the buildings do not share walls, leaving a gap between instead of the villages formed by contiguous rooms that define the aggregated pueblos in the northern Southwest. Buildings at Çatalhöyük were reproduced in the same spaces, creating columns of rooms over time with seemingly little articulation between them. In addition, plazas and other public spaces are difficult to discern, spaces that among the Pueblos are the central focus of villagewide activities. Last is the apparent absence of suprahousehold religious spaces – a paradox that marks Çatalhöyük as different from other Neolithic Anatolian villages as well as from prehispanic and historic Pueblo villages in the Southwest.

The more that I became engaged with the archaeology of Çatalhöyük, however, the greater the similarities with Pueblo societies of the Southwest became. What makes them similar are not the specifics of the architecture, imagery, or artifacts, but the way in which religion was a central part of daily life for those living in both areas and how much of this was made clear through people's interactions with things. At Çatalhöyük, the

---

[1] When used with lowercase, "pueblo" refers to the architectural form, while the uppercase "Pueblo" refers to the social groups. The Pueblos are hardly monolithic, speaking six different languages, with different principles of social and religious organization, and today are spread across an area of several hundred miles of the U.S. Southwest in present-day Arizona and New Mexico.

relationships that people had with other people, animals, plants, buildings, clay, stone, and so on, are evidence for a rich materiality. Like many Southwestern societies, such as the Pueblos, the people who inhabited Çatalhöyük were surrounded by objects and architectural installations that served as reminders of who they were, whom they interacted with, and where they came from. It is the massing of the buildings and the high degree of ritual density (sensu Bell 1997) at Çatalhöyük that make a comparison to the Pueblos of the North American Southwest of interest. In addition, I think that there is much to be learned by such a comparison as a way of looking at how religion shapes relationships, how it intersects with economic and political power, and how relational networks both divide and integrate village societies.

Previous research on religion at Çatalhöyük has underscored several themes that I build upon in this chapter (see especially Hodder 2010). First is the importance of looking at how past practices ranged from the daily and mundane to those that were highly marked and rarely repeated (e.g., Keane 2010; Shults 2010). The archaeology of religion can be elusive, but by focusing on the continua in different practices, and locating those that are more marked than others, it becomes possible to talk about religious practices and their transformation over time. Neolithic people had a spiritual life and there was something transcendent in their lives, although not in the sense of the doctrinal form of religion that we are most familiar with today (Bloch 2010). A second theme in past research on religion at Çatalhöyük is to look beyond the practices themselves to understand why things were important, including their symbolic meaning (Hodder and Meskell 2010). In daily practice at Çatalhöyük there were constant reminders of particularly important spiritual events such as the installation of bucrania and other animal parts in walls, the placement of burials in house platforms, and the creation of wall paintings and reliefs. Even if the enactment of specific rituals was more temporally punctuated, and some events had a higher display quotient than others (Whitehouse and Hodder 2010), the memory of those rituals was constantly present. More subtle are those actions that might have been accompanied by spiritualism, even if they did not seem marked, or publicly performed, such as repeated plastering of walls or careful sweeping of floors prior to room closure. As at Çatalhöyük these are the sorts of ritual activities that in contemporary and historic Pueblos are replete with religion and meaning.

Research on religion at Çatalhöyük also benefits from a relational perspective on the past (Hodder 2011, 2012; Pels 2010). In archaeology such a perspective shifts the zone of interest from objects, people, and buildings to the connections among them (Knappett 2011). Even more generally, we may view this as a shift to a network approach, which emphasizes the connections between nodes rather than one that focuses on the entities themselves. Such an approach emphasizes the ties over categories, that is, the relations between nodes. Objects, burials, houses, and other materials are only important when considered in relation to other objects, burials, houses, and so forth. Whether through genealogies, communities of practice, or "history houses" (Hodder and Pels 2010), it is the connections that are of interest – not simply things. An emphasis on relations rather than entities therefore focuses attention on transmission, practice, and memory. It also affords a perspective that helps to resolve some of the paradoxes that face interpretive projects in archaeology because those paradoxes are often based on erroneous assumptions about what kinds of relationships structured past interaction.

Besides the apparent absence of suprahousehold religious architecture another example of a paradox at Çatalhöyük is our expectation of how people who were interred together in what have been termed "history houses" should be related. We take for granted that individuals who are buried together should have some biological relationship. Recent research by Pilloud and Larsen (2011; see also Hillson et al. 2013) challenges this assumption by showing that burials in the same platforms within Çatalhöyük's most elaborate buildings, or "history houses," were not genetically related. How do we explain religious practices that are not in every structure, that were apparently not transmitted through descent, and that were performed in the same spaces as the full range of domestic activities? Clearly Mellaart's (1967) "shrines" can be discounted because he saw these as spaces exclusively used for religious ritual. As an alternative, Bleda Düring (2005, 2007) applied the House Society concept to interpret the differential distribution of installations, moldings, and wall paintings in buildings at Çatalhöyük. He interpreted the houses at Çatalhöyük as "lineage houses," which he defined as structures for "supra-household social collectivities" (Düring 2011: 116). Several of the participants in the past Templeton project also advocate the idea of a House Society at Çatalhöyük (Bloch 2010; Hodder 2010a; Hodder and Pels 2010; Keane 2010; Whitehouse and Hodder 2010) and the concept of "history houses" was introduced by Hodder and Pels (2010:182) to refer to the "process of differentiation of houses that is universal throughout the settlement and that identifies certain houses as specializing in modes of incorporating 'history.'" While "history house" aptly describes the remarkable continuity in, and elaboration of, certain buildings and practices within Çatalhöyük, like Düring, they have assumed that these were occupied by kin or "nuclear families" (Hodder and Pels 2010: 183). I offer another interpretation that is grounded in a comparative study with Southwestern Pueblos, and particularly Zuni Pueblo, where a variety of cross-cutting societies have been well documented by ethnographers since the late nineteenth century and intersect within the social and physical space of the "house."

There are two major goals to my project. First is to explore how Neolithic societies of the Greater Southwest and Southwest Asia, geographically and temporally far removed from each other, illustrate commonalities in how religion and the relations between people and things intersect. Religious practice imbued daily life at Çatalhöyük as it did and still does in Pueblo societies in the Southwest. One of the ways in which religion structured and still structures interaction in the Southwest was through the formation of religious sodalities, which I argue are a better way of viewing "history houses" at Çatalhöyük. Much of the literature thus far has not parsed out these networks at the settlement or what Whitehouse and Hodder (2010: 134–136) refer to as "religious coalitions." Yet, given the importance of religious sodalities in other village-based societies, we should expect them to be present. The case study of Zuni, in particular, provides an example of how households, societies, and people and their labor flowed through physical and spiritual houses and structured interaction.

My second goal is to bring out how other relational networks at Çatalhöyük have been identified and to contrast how the networks of "history houses" may have intersected with these other networks. What I hope to add to this interpretation is a complementary sense of the different social scales and networks present at the site. I argue that the silolike building construction has, in many ways, anchored relational interpretations to segmentary, nested relational networks rather than to those that are cross-cutting and that intersect. Both were part of the fabric of the Çatalhöyük and I draw on comparisons with the U.S. Southwest in order to bring out the different networks of relations – both nested and cross-cutting.

Whether we think about networks as nested or cross-cutting, they are made up of individuals linked by their participation in a social group. We might also think of these groups as "communities of practice" (Lave and Wenger 1991; Wenger 1998) or communities that are formed through the interaction of people and the transmission of knowledge and materials, including those networks that include religious practices. Communities of practice are particularly interesting to think about in terms of the archaeology of Çatalhöyük because of the vast amount of work that has been done in tracking the flow of materials, the inter-action of people and things, the use of the visible and invisible in the transmission of knowledge and practice, and the different depositional contexts of materials (see especially Hodder 2012). In fact, the very idea of "history houses" is that they represent a network or a community of practice, linking people and things into some form of community, as well as through time. Communities of practice are also memory communities in that they each involve different sets of people in the performance and the transmission of knowledge that has a history and at the same time creates history (Mills and Walker 2008).

Nested Networks at Çatalhöyük

Archaeologists commonly look at relational networks through nested scales and the archaeology of Çatalhöyük is no exception. These are spatially defined but often interpreted socially. The scales discussed for Çatalhöyük range from the region to the individual activity areas. In between are the village itself, divided into North and South areas, neighborhoods, and households (Table 7.1). Each of these networks has a community or communities of practice and each may involve daily as well as more temporally marked religious rituals.

Douglas Baird's work has been the most explicit in showing how religious practices in the broader landscape around Çatalhöyük were structured. The earlier site of Boncuklu (8500–7500 BC cal.) displays many of the memory practices seen later on at Çatalhöyük, including a plastered vessel, a disarticulated human skull, and a decorated stone in the midden area between houses; subfloor burials; a sequence of houses; the

Table 7.1. Nested scales of social networks communities of practice at Çatalhöyük

Social network	Basis for social relations	Archaeological indicators	Relationship to power and property
Çatalhöyük	Residence in village, at least part-time; shared habitus of architecture, depositional practice	Agglomerative, contiguous architecture in a single settlement; communal feasting (extramural); shared habitus of placement of deposits in floors, bins, platforms, etc., that occur throughout the site	Shared use of grazing lands distant from site, hunting areas, wild plant collection areas; identity as different from other large settlements
North/South subareas of town	Residential and potential differential use of surrounding landscape	Mounded areas in North and South of site as a result of longer-term/more intensive occupation with gap in between; isotopic differences between North and South; burial differences not evident; communal feasting (extramural)	Potential subdivision/use of landscape according to North/South areas of settlement representing different hunting, grazing, and collecting areas
Neighborhood	Spatial propinquity, but also suprahousehold groups that share labor, roof spaces, and nearby open areas	Sectors defined architecturally by walls that divide site; adjacent rooftops; shared middens between buildings and in adjacent extramural spaces	Claim over gardens and fields close by, especially for cultivation and grazing; main labor pools for the communal labor needs at critical moments in cycle; potential hosts of communal feasts; potential pool for obsidian and other long-distance procurement drawing on cohorts
Daily sleeping and eating group	Extended or nuclear family in some cases, but membership may be flexible; potential for polygamous families in some buildings	Architecturally defined by the building itself and space available for daily activities; if multiple hearths/ovens in one building then may be interpreted as subgroups and potentially multiple women; different communities of practice in plaster and adobe recipes; figurine discard in middens	Control over intramural storage once taken back to site; multiple hearths suggest more women and control over their labor and their children (by any adult); control over "domestic" ritual, especially through production and use of figurines
Daily food preparation	Subgroup of daily sleeping and eating group, comprising those (women?) engaged in food preparation	Spaces within buildings defined by hearths and ovens; microartifactual and plant (pollen, macro, phytolith) distributions within rooms	Preparation and serving of meals on daily basis – everyday commensal politics (i.e., who is invited to share the meal)
Craft production	Subgroup of daily sleeping and eating group, comprising those engaged in tool production	Different communities of practice in technologies, chaîne opératoires, also microartifactual distributions of production debris	Control over production of items; some production for ritual with resulting power

symbolic use of a large post in the southwest portion of a structure; painted reliefs on a north wall; frequent replasterings; red floors; and a north/south distinction within houses[2] (Baird 2006, 2010). The placement of symbolic objects at Boncuklu between houses suggests that there were already practices that were shared among households as opposed to being restricted to a single house. These practices suggest that many of the religious or marked practices found later at Çatalhöyük were established within the region and perhaps introduced to the site as population in the area coalesced.

The site of Pinarbaşi (Baird et al. 2011), which has levels contemporaneous with Çatalhöyük's Levels V-I (ca. 6500–6000 cal BC), shows how a subset of the population reinterpreted symbolic practices within the region. Animal bones were plastered as they were at Çatalhöyük, but the animals chosen to be plastered were different, as were their depositional contexts. Rather than installations of wild animals that were plastered over, as well documented at Çatalhöyük, the plastered bones at Pinarbaşi were more often sheep and placed on floors or in pits. Baird and his colleagues argue that Pinarbaşi was seasonally occupied by herders and hunters from Çatalhöyük, who reproduced many but not all of the same practices as at the main settlement. When repositioned on the landscape at a different site, a subset of the population engaged with the caretaking of particular species altered their individual religious practices. This analysis clearly shows how the nested scales of region and settlement can be looked at relationally, tying together sites in the region through similar depositional practices.

The next smallest spatial scale is Çatalhöyük itself. Topography and the history of excavations at the site reinforce differences between the North and South areas of the settlement. Isotope studies have shown that sheep and goat were grazed in different areas depending on which areas of the settlement the bones were from and that these areas expanded in diversity over time (Pearson et al. 2007). Distinct grazing areas create different constraints and possibilities for interaction. The contrasts between North and South at the site may also have extended to other practices besides grazing areas, such as differences in the ways in which houses were constructed and where the benches and platforms were

---

[2] Of interest, however, is that at Çatalhöyük it is the southern part of the structure that is dirty (Hodder and Cessford 2004), while at Boncuklu, the northern part is dirty.

placed (Hodder 2006: 100). Love's (2010) analyses of adobe plaster recipes also seem to have been more closely tied to social differences at this social scale. Moreover, the bioarchaeologists have observed differences between the North and the South in terms of their biological distinctiveness (Hillson et al. 2013).

Architectural spaces built close together provide another way of inferring social networks. The neighborhoods at Çatalhöyük identified by Düring in the South Area (2005, 2007) and by the Çatalhöyük project (Hodder 2013) in the North Area all point to groupings of houses into neighborhoods that must have had social significance. The radial pattern that begins at the top of the mound and continues down the hill toward the areas where agricultural fields were most likely located may have a link to property rights that extended into the surrounding areas. Such a radial pattern is common in "fossil" remnants of trails surrounding tells later in the Near East (e.g., Ur 2003; Wilkinson 2010). Ethnographically, in the North American Southwest, Kroeber (1919) identified a radial movement of households outward from the center of Zuni Pueblo as it grew, spatially and socially maintaining links with core households in the central village while moving closer to surrounding fields.

At the next smallest scale are the buildings themselves, thought to represent the social unit of the household. Buildings contain features such as hearths/ovens and storage features, around which daily practices were performed. We may even be able to define smaller communities of practice or task groups, such as the social unit that cooked and prepared food or the obsidian working group, on the basis of the clusters of features such as hearths and ovens, and microartifactual and botanical distributions (Hodder and Cessford 2004).

What the preceding discussion of different nested scales and communities of practice (and summarized in Table 7.2) does not fully bring out are those networks that might crosscut and may have had a strong role in the religious life of Çatalhöyük. These networks, called sodalities, are based on nonkin and nonresidential relationships and are usually restricted to a subset of the community (Ware 2002: 107). I suggest that history houses were in fact sodalities and that these cross-cutting networks were important ways in which the religious life at Çatalhöyük was carried out. As in medicine societies, hunting societies, or other religious networks found in many small-scale societies, the members

Table 7.2. Cross cutting social networks and communities of practice at Çatalhöyük

Social network	Basis for social relations	Archaeological indicators	Relationship to power and property
"Houses"	More flexible networks of house societies – potentially coeval in part with suprahousehold neighborhoods, but also drawing on members from other suprahousehold groups, and potentially those from outside CH	"History houses" – stacked buildings with repeated reconstruction on same footprint; identified by bucrania and other installations; burial areas (archaeological definition is based on accumulation in part, not on synchronic analysis)	Control over labor because it is a suprahousehold group, may have additional power through cross-cutting rituals, such as curing and preparation for the hunt; perpetuation of memories of the group through shared participation in hosting of feasts, burial of individuals who participated in ritual within the network; smaller storage areas suggest dependence on others in surrounding buildings.
Burial cluster	Subgroup of people who were affiliated with house society groups – specific people within suprahousehold groups that may have achieved particular prominence through curing or other rituals	Multiple interments in platforms, apparent lack of genetic relatedness; buildings with subfloor commemorative deposits	Ritual networks of curing, initiation, hunting, etc.; have lasting power as "ancestors of the house" even if not kin relations

would have been linked through shared religious rituals but were not necessarily members of the same nuclear family, descent group, or even neighborhood. And as in other sodalities around the world, each history house would have gained power not just by the number of people who became members but also through the performance of religious rituals that drew together individuals from other social units throughout the village. The ability of different houses to attract individuals from other parts of the community would have been important. This system was replaced at the end of the Çatalhöyük East (i.e., Neolithic) sequence by a more individualized household and more segmentary organization in which the fluidity and flexibility of labor seem to have been more constrained.

Cross-Cutting Networks: A Model Based on Sodalities in the Pueblo Southwest

Religious sodalities are a key part of the history of Pueblo social organization in the Southwest (Ware and Blinman 2000) and religious architecture has been one of the primary ways of identifying them archaeologically. Suprahousehold structures have been recognized from as early as the Early Agricultural period, usually as larger structures and sometimes with different sets of features. These structures are often divided into public architecture (e.g., great kivas, triwall structures) and smaller structures including "oversized pitstructures" and ceremonial rooms (Schachner 2001). The latter two fall into Adler's (1989) category of "low-level integrative facilities," which his cross-cultural analyses show are used for a mix of domestic and religious activities. Importantly, his analyses also show that it is rare for small-scale, sedentary societies to lack any of these structures. Debates about the use of smaller religious structures in the Southwest focus on a number of issues including whether and how often they were used exclusively for religious ritual, the role that they played in the development of inequality and hierarchy, whether they were largely integrative or should be viewed as potentially divisive, and how they relate to ethnographically documented social groups (Adams 1991; Plog and Solemeto 1999; Lekson 2009; McGuire and Saitta 1996; Schachner 2001; Smith 1952). Archaeologists in the Southwest have increasingly seen suprahousehold religious affiliations as a means of creating and maintaining political and economic power even if the hallmarks of the latter are materially masked.[3]

Large-scale religious structures aside, which are more like contemporary Pueblo "kivas" (Lekson 2009), small-scale structures used for a range of domestic and religious activities are widespread throughout the Southwest. Attention on "kivas," and especially their comparison to kivas ethnographically, has mired the discussion of smaller-scale structures that were used for a range of activities. This problem has been recognized in the Southwest for at least two decades (e.g., Adler 1993). Yet, the analogy to kivas seems to have been transferred uncritically to Near Eastern archaeology (see citations in Price and Bar-Yosef 2010 for

---

[3] Examples in which material power was not masked are also recognized in the Southwest, particularly at Chaco Canyon and Casas Grandes.

examples). Instead of kivas, a better comparison are rooms that contain evidence for a mix of both domestic and religious activities, which would be better for understanding the ways in which power, property, and religion intersect.

Ethnographic examples from the Pueblos of the U.S. Southwest offer some important ways of thinking about how the social unit of the house intersected with small-scale religious sodalities. Zuni, one of the Western Pueblos, has a highly complex system of ritual organization and is an interesting comparison because of the view it provides on different forms of ritual relationships and especially those that crosscut households and augment relationships based on descent. Since the late seventeenth century most residents have lived in one major village, which has been continuously occupied for at least six centuries. The total population has ranged widely because of Euro-American diseases but is generally estimated as from two thousand to six thousand during the historic period. Architecture is typically puebloan, with contiguous rooms and entry through ladders as well as doors until the early twentieth century when only kivas remained accessed by ladders. In addition, we know ethnographically that most social units are ranked to each other and that there are hierarchies of social positions within those units, yet there are no outward manifestations of social wealth and prestige outside the ceremonial system.

The "house" at Zuni has a linguistic referent that refers to more than simply the building or an extended household. Late nineteenth and early twentieth century ethnographies have detailed descriptions of different social relationships that make up Zuni, including kin, clan, priesthoods, and fraternities or sodalities (see especially Bunzel 1938; Eggan 1950; Kroeber 1919; Parsons 1939; Stevenson 1904). Watt's (1997) revisionist perspective is particularly helpful to understanding Zuni because she looks at the linguistic roots of Zuni relational terms. She argues that instead of the primacy of descent groups, prominent in Eggan's (1950) work, Zuni's organization is based on a wider definition of relationships within suprahousehold groups. People in these houses are related in a number of different ways including consanguinal, affinal, and fictive kin. She points to three major relations: (1) relative seniority within the suprahousehold group, (2) degree of social proximity, and (3) ceremonial sponsorship. Although Watt specifically addresses Zuni relations, these are principles that coexist in all of the Southwest Pueblos to varying extents.

Seniority structures relations because groups are ranked to each other in most of the Pueblos. At Zuni this applies to the different crosscutting groups of clans, priesthoods, fraternities, and gambling societies. Zuni households are also ranked in relation to each other within household groups. Higher-ranking households are those responsible for the care of fetishes and ceremonial paraphernalia of specific ritual personages and sodalities within the household group. These interlinked suprahousehold groups are the ones that can be relied upon as the maximal pool for agricultural labor and the sponsorship of specific ceremonies and accompanying feasting. The principle of ranking also determines inheritance rights within the household group (Watt 1997: 20–22). This principle is well documented among other Pueblo groups, such as Hopi (Whiteley 1988). These rankings do not mean, however, that there is any external indication of material wealth.

Social proximity, as used by Watt in her work, refers to both spatial and social propinquity. In terms of spatial propinquity, Kroeber (1919) noted that related households have tended to move out in a radial pattern from the core pueblo because of their relationships to each other through the suprahousehold group and because of landownership. The lower-ranked households from the same suprahousehold group were clustered together in order to remain closer together for farming and to maintain claims on land but kept their affiliations with higher-ranked households in the core, which they returned to for ceremonial obligations.

Finally, there is ceremonial sponsorship, which is important because each individual has a ceremonial father or mother outside the parents' clans. Although Zuni and most of the pueblos occupied since the fourteenth century are known for a specific ritual organization known as the Katchina religion, there are other ritual organizations. More well known in the Eastern Pueblos, but with strong presence at the Western Pueblos of Zuni, Acoma, and Laguna, are a group of sodalities more generally known as medicine societies. In fact, Ware (2002) argues that the earliest sodalities in the northern Southwest were the medicine societies, which also include hunting and war societies. Ware (2002) brings out the variation across the Pueblo world in two forms of ritual group membership, descent versus sodality, but underscores that both are nonresidential and crosscut individual households. Descent is more prevalent in the west, especially at Hopi, while sodalities are the basis for ritual societies among the Eastern Pueblos. In between, at Zuni, Acoma, and Laguna, both are important, with the medicine and hunting societies based primarily on crosscutting affiliations.[4]

At Zuni, the medicine societies revolve around specific wild animals called the "beast gods" (Bunzel 1932; Ladd 1979). Each society has different principles of recruitment, its own fetishes, leadership, and rituals. Recruitment into medicine societies is through curing of specific ailments (including witchcraft) and occasionally through trespass (Kroeber 1919). Both men and women may participate, although men more commonly lead the society. The person who cures another is considered to be that individual's ceremonial father, creating a "fictive" kin relationship. There is a range of sacred, magical objects and animals associated with each society – and at Zuni these animals are associated with particular directions.

What is particularly interesting is the way that people, animals, things, and buildings become related as part of these societies. First, there are specific rooms that are designated for their use, but they are not exclusively ritual and when not in use for ceremonies they revert to domestic space. This is a common pattern among many of the Pueblos and particularly so at Zuni.[5] In preparation for the ritual, which may not include all members at each event, the room is usually cleared of most domestic items[6] and an altar erected on the side of the room away from the door. Fresh plaster may be applied before the use of the room for a ceremony, which prepares the room for its alternative purpose and symbolically separates the domestic from ritual use, and wall paintings of animals may be repainted. Objects used in the ceremony are portable and hidden or stored until they are required.

Illustrations of sodality rooms at Zuni in the late nineteenth century show animals painted on walls, including rattlesnakes, mountain lions, bears, badgers, wolves, eagles, and moles, representing different directions. For example, Stevenson (1904: plate CVIII; Figure 7.1) reproduces the room of the (now extinct) medicine society called the

---

[4] In addition, Zuni has multiple ways of figuring descent – every individual has three parents, including a ceremonial parent who is not a member of either of the two birth parents' clans. This system creates an extensive system of ties that crosscuts the village.

[5] There are specialized structures called "kivas" in addition to these rooms, but these are used by different societies at Zuni – those more based on descent rather than on sodality organization.

[6] Although Kroeber (1919) describes how a ceremony may go on at one end while other activities are going on at the other.

7.1. Zuni Hle'wekwe Society Room (after Stevenson 1904: plate CVIII).

Hle'wekwe, or Sword Swallowers, which includes a painting on the floor, the fetishes of each medicine society member arranged on the front of the altar, and other objects of importance laid out between the two. Besides the bear on the wall, two bear paws rest on the bench. During the ceremony, five men impersonate each of these wild animals. Each sodality has a different community of practice that entails the transmission of specific knowledge. Yet, what they share are commonalities in where the art should be placed, the depiction of wild animals with claws and teeth (especially predators), the spatial locations of altars and other ceremonial equipment, the transformation of domestic space into ritual space, the animation of animals parts through human intervention, and the use of many other natural objects during the ritual performance to cure the individual. Objects that belong to the society, its special fetishes, are also generally regarded as important to bury in the room if the society is terminated, as are inalienable objects throughout the Southwest (Mills 2004). Historic period Zuni was still largely a herding and agricultural society, yet domesticated animals and plants are noticeably absent from these ceremonies and imagery. Instead, wild animals, and especially predators, were important to depict.

Medicine societies have leaders who cure through the impersonation or animation of animals. Gifts are required to be given to the healers in order for an individual to join the society. Being cured does not obligate the individual to join, although belonging to one of the medicine fraternities is considered to be desirable. Like participation in all ritual societies at Zuni, wealth is not based on material items, but on one's ceremonial position. Particularly powerful individuals are not only those who lead higher-ranked ritual societies, but those who hold multiple leadership positions. Members of different societies accrue prestige through their participation in different ritual societies, even if they are not leaders. In fact, there are examples of intentional trespass so that an individual may be cured and then able to join a particular society that is high ranked or popular. Popularity was based on societies with many members, who could be drawn upon for different purposes, such as labor, but power was also based on the perceived efficacy of the medicine and its ability to protect its members.

The architectural perpetuation of high-ranking houses within the suprahousehold group is common at Zuni, although individual kivas and especially fraternity rooms may move frequently. Fraternity houses, where medicine society rituals are held, were said to have always been in the same place, but Kroeber (1919: 196) documented considerable turnover in where these societies actually met. Despite all of this movement, buildings were frequently reconstructed in approximately the same place, and prominent families have lived in the same places and have "ceremonial" homes in the core of the pueblo. So, even though people and the society activities themselves flow through these spaces, the architectural spaces remain important because of their association with prominent families.

RETHINKING HISTORY HOUSES AS SODALITIES

Sodalities in the Southwest provide us with several potential lines of comparison for understanding history houses at Çatalhöyük. First is the importance of membership that does not depend solely on biological descent. Second is how some buildings or rooms may become important through the office of one of the household members who practice in that building and/or because the house is the guardian of fetishes and other ritual equipment. These houses become high-ranking within the suprahousehold group as a result of position within the ceremonial cycle. Third, wealth is measured on the basis of ritual power and the efficacy of the rituals performed, but because of payments, the hosting of feasts, and access to agricultural labor there are material benefits. In addition, at Hopi Pueblo, the ownership of fields has been demonstrated to be based on crosscutting ceremonial networks (Whitely 1988). Fourth is the movement of people through the space of a particular room, based on different kinds of networks, and use of it for different purposes ranging from the domestic to the transcendent. And fifth, architecturally these rooms were not necessarily created as specialized spaces; they become different through the accumulation of ritual practices that take place, including the placement of symbolic art on the walls.

I argue that these fields of relations can be more widely applied not just to societies in the Southwest but to those we encounter in the Neolithic of the Near East. They point out ways to augment traditional views of the family and the household to understand how those units fit within relational networks that crosscut individual villages. The principles of seniority, social and spatial proximity, and ritual leadership are key for understanding the networks that created Neolithic communities and intersected with access to people and resources. I would also argue that the striking similarities in ritual art and the relationships among wild animals, people, and particular objects used in Southwest religious sodalities may be analogous to the relationships seen at Çatalhöyük, and that the basis of Çatalhöyük history houses may be productively viewed in this light.

Çatalhöyük's history houses are clearly the result of long-term relational networks because of the accumulation of materials, including animal installations, and burials that define them. In addition, the analyses by Pilloud and Larsen (2011) support an interpretation of "flexible kin." This is exactly what we would expect with intersecting or crosscutting relational networks formed through membership in sodalities that were built upon religious affiliations and not exclusively descent. There may have been specific benefits of association or alliance with a history house, including "wealth in people" through the extension of networks to multiple households who could then participate in labor. Like other religious collectives in Neolithic societies these networks had varied degrees of openness – with labor flowing through the houses and anchored by particularly strong leaders. I think that this is one way of explaining some of the idiosyncrasies that we see across the settlement, such as the figurative art, and especially the fact that history houses have no other material indicators of differences in wealth. When wealth is in people, coupled with ritual or even magical efficacy, there need not be obvious status markers.

There are several archaeological indicators for how history houses may have been used for religious activities that overlapped with curing and hunting, two important activities in the cross-cultural study of sodalities. For example, there are small-scale spaces for retreat or meditation, including platforms with horns. Mellaart (1967) tended to depict these spaces with the horns facing out, as if for an audience, when in fact, they curve inward (Figure 7.2). There are many possible uses of these spaces; among them are retreats for ritual leaders, or spaces for initiates or those who are preparing to embark on a hunting party or about to undergo a particular curing ceremony. Besides the burial platforms, they are one of the few areas within these buildings that seem to be dedicated ritual spaces and they clearly could have only held one or two people at most.

Another line of evidence is the practice of "hiding and revealing" that has been identified at Çatalhöyük, including the intentional placement of animal parts, skulls, and other deposits with ritual symbolism (Hodder

7.2. Building 77. Jason Quinlan and Çatalhöyük Research Project.

2006: 169–184). Hiding and revealing is a typical part of curing rituals. The intentional or "placed" deposits at Çatalhöyük are disproportionately present in history houses, where they were placed in floors, walls, and platforms (Carter 2007; Nakamura 2010; Russell, Martin, and Twiss 2009). There is a very interesting pattern in that of the fifteen buildings completely excavated by the Çatalhöyük Project, eight have commemorative deposits and all of these buildings also contain burials (Russell et al. 2009: 112). Five of these buildings are those that the project has determined to be part of "history houses" (Buildings 23, 44, 56, 59, and 65). The deposits are from different parts of the site (North, South, BACH, 4040, or TP) and from different periods (Levels III-I, IV, V, VI, VIII, X) demonstrating that these communities of practice cross-cut the settlement and show remarkable continuities over time. Several of these deposits may be considered as "bundles" or collections of objects with different kinds of spiritual power (see, e.g., Zedeño 2008). For example, in Building 6 (Space 163, Level VIII Unit 4401), a pit contained "flint, obsidian, ground stone fragments, shell, a drilled cattle incisor, and a badger mandible," which Russell and her colleagues (2009: 108) suggested were originally buried in a bag.[7] The deposition of these objects

[7] Nakamura (2010: table 1.1) reports that this cluster comes from under the oven, but Russell et al. (2009: figure 4) clearly place it on the opposite side of the room.

together suggests that they were part of one individual's personal bundle, perhaps one of the religious leaders of the sodality who lived in or used the space.

Part of the pattern of hiding and revealing is the plastering over of parts of animals, including talons and heads. There is a prominence of wild animals over domesticated fauna in these different deposits. The depiction of wild animals in figurative art increases over time, as consumption of domesticated animals increases. In addition, as Hillson et al. (2013) have summarized, mobility increased in the later levels as herders moved farther away from the main settlement. Figurative representations in the late period include the famous hunting scenes such as a group of figures seemingly "baiting" a bull, where some of the figures are apparently wearing leopard skins (Figure 7.3). I think that this indicates the members of a crosscutting alliance – figures who have been initiated into a particular hunting sodality. As Hodder (2006) has brought out, it is ironic that leopards should figure so prominently in the art of Çatalhöyük when there is only one leopard bone identified from the entire site. People would have known about them, however, and animals need not be ubiquitous to be used as sources of power. In fact, the more rare and dangerous, the more powerful they become. This is the case with the medicine societies at Zuni with the bear being considered the most dangerous and powerful. Like the leopard's, bear faunal remains are rare at Çatalhöyük, even though there are several depictions of bears, including splayed images (Hodder 2006: figure 87). A bear paw with plaster still adhering to it was recovered from Building 24 in the South Area and was probably part of an installation, but those are the only actual bear remains recovered at the site (Russell and Martin 2005: 62). Bears and leopards were likely regarded as sources of power and associated with certain groups who manipulated the imagery for specific events. That this representation should increase when herding and consumption of domestic animals increased may not be the paradox that we think it is. As members of the community spent more time away from the site on the surrounding landscape, the symbolism of community membership through sodalities became more important. A similar pattern has been noted for the emergence of hunting sodalities in the late pre-Hispanic Southwest (Dean 2001; Potter 2000). In the Southwest case, it was increased mobility for hunting rather than for pastoralism that was associated with increased aggregation, but both would have

7.3 Figure from hunting scene with leopard pelt.
Source: Alan Mellaart.

involved age and gender cohorts sharing the landscape, common experiences, and communities of practice.

In addition to the preceding symbolic evidence for medicine and hunting societies through the control of spiritual power, there are biological indicators that may be brought to bear. Important differences between those who were buried in history houses and those who were not include more skeletal pathologies and evidence of trauma among the former. This is what we might expect if individuals were recruited for membership in medicine societies on the basis of some affliction and is a common way in which new members are drawn into these societies within the Pueblos. Members of hunting societies, particularly those who participated in the hunt itself, might be more likely to incur injuries.

It is interesting that other biological indicators suggest that those who were buried in history houses show more evidence of participation in harder work and, among the males, more mobility in comparison to other village members buried elsewhere. Hodder (2013) points out that the former does not conform with the expectation that greater prestige (which we might expect from burial in symbolically charged rooms) would lead to working less or reaping the rewards of others' labor. Instead, he refers to the system as one of "fierce egalitarianism." Differential participation in labor pools also fits the model of sodalities among the Pueblos. As noted earlier for Zuni, membership in medicine societies is often considered to be desirable because one can draw upon wider networks for labor. The evidence that some males were more mobile might not just be the result of pastoralism, but also for hunting wild game or collecting other resources from more distant sources. The history houses may thus be seen as spiritual anchors for individuals who moved through them, as well as networks that could be drawn upon for some longer-distance and labor-intensive tasks.

Discussion

One of the important findings of members of the Çatalhöyük project is the biological unrelatedness of individuals interred in the same buildings (Pilloud and Larsen 2011). The idea that ancestors should evidence some form of lineal descent, and kinship in general should represent "blood ties," ignores alternative networks of affiliation (see Joyce 2000: 191). Instead, the new findings suggest that we should view the burial associations in terms of more flexible networks that made up "history houses." This alternative way of thinking about relatedness is part of a growing interest in "House Societies" in anthropology and archaeology (Carsten and Hugh-Jones 1995; Joyce and Gillespie 2000), and even in rethinking the concept of kinship itself in anthropology. For many of the archaeological applications of the House Society concept, however, its flexibility is both a pitfall and strength. For example, as Susan Gillespie has pointed out, "There is no reference to size or the scale of social complexity, no restriction of specific kin ties, no indication of residential or marital rules" (Gillespie 2007: 38). Yet, Gillespie also suggests that House Societies "tend to appear when property and political power become salient values in organizing social life but in the absence of contractual or class-based relationships binding people to one another" (Gillespie 2007: 40–41).

There is one major problem with the application of the House Society concept to Çatalhöyük, especially as these societies have been described ethnographically. House Societies tend to occur with more evidence of hierarchy than is present at Çatalhöyük, including wealth accumulation and differential house sizes. Applications of the House Society concept to the North American Southwest have been varied; the best case is Chaco Canyon, where great houses, multiple burials, and the burial of heirlooms over centuries speak to the perpetuation of the house as a means of marking claims to land, and creating and maintaining hierarchy (see Heitman 2007; Mills 2008; Wills 2005). Unlike at Chaco, at Çatalhöyük these special places, where multiple interments were found, are small spaces with a small amount of storage and without differentiation in the accumulation of wealth of status (Hodder and Pels 2010). Thus, although they seemed to have spiritual or symbolic power and higher numbers of people who were interred, there are few other material manifestations of property accumulation. Instead, it seems that these houses accrued their power through the intersecting memberships of people who were part of the house network.

The concept of "history house" gets around the preceding problem to some extent but has been tied specifically to lineages in past research. If these social units are not based exclusively on biological relatedness, what constituted the relations, collectivities, or alliances among those who were buried in those houses? What was the material or immaterial property that was inherited through membership in the house and was accumulated in the history house buildings? In order to address these questions I have argued that it is important to see how alternative networks of relatedness might have been constructed and what principles of recruitment may have been present. These networks of relations were clearly part of long-standing religious practices, with important transmission of knowledge, memory, and materiality. I have suggested that it behooves us to look at alternatives such as religious sodalities, which crosscut houses and would have been networks that sustained the transmission of religious practices and organized labor through social networks other than the household itself.

My approach has been a relational one, emphasizing networks or communities of practice. It requires that we think about these relations not just as nested scales, but also as crosscutting. I have argued that history houses are excellent examples of communities of practice based in religious societies that were not exclusively based in residence or descent. The Pueblos of the Southwest offer some interesting examples in the organization of crosscutting ritual sodalities. They are compelling for a number of reasons including their enduring yet changing qualities, their interaction with wild animals (especially within hunting and medicine societies), the rich symbolism of portable and nonportable art, the use of spaces that blur the line between domestic and ritual spheres, and how these societies may have been related to power and property.

The development and transformation of sodalities are among the strongest and most important underlying historical themes in Southwestern archaeology. While history houses seem to help us get beyond thinking about kinship, we may need to go even further to understand the range of variation and the ways in which power and property were intertwined with ritual at Çatalhöyük. In the Southwest some of the complexity of organization was the result of dramatic demographic and social changes that is only beginning to be understood in central Anatolia. Further work on how these factors intersect will be important for untangling the many paradoxes of the Neolithic, especially those intriguingly suggested by the detailed work at Çatalhöyük.

BIBLIOGRAPHY

Adams, E. C. 1991. *The Origin and Development of the Pueblo Katsina Cult.* Tucson: University of Arizona Press.

Adler, M. A. 1989. Ritual facilities and social integration in nonranked societies. In *The Architecture of Social Integration in Prehistoric Pueblos*, eds. W. D. Lipe and M. Hegmon. Cortez, Colorado: Occasional Papers of the Crow Canyon Archaeological Center 1:35–52.

Adler, M. A. 1993. Why Is a Kiva? *Journal of Anthropological Research* 49(4):319–346.

Baird, D. 2006. The Boncuklu Project: The Origins of Sedentism, Cultivation and Herding in Central Anatolia. *Anatolian Archaeology* 12:13–16.

  2010. Ancestral Practices: Pınarbaşı, Boncuklu, from the History of 'History Houses' to Ritual in the Landscape. Paper presented at the conference on "Religion as the Basis for Power and Property in Ancient Near East," Çatalhöyük, Turkey.

Baird, D., D. Carruthers, A. Fairbairn, and J. Pearson. 2011. Ritual in the landscape: Evidence from Pinarbaşi in the Seventh-Millennium cal BC Konya Plain. *Antiquity* 85(328):380–394.

Bell, C. M. 1997. *Ritual: Perspectives and Dimensions.* Oxford: Oxford University Press.

Bloch, M. 2010. Is there religion at Çatalhöyük … or are there just houses? In *Religion in the Emergence of Civilization: Çatalhöyük as a Case Study*, ed. I. Hodder. Cambridge: Cambridge University Press, 146–162.

Bunzel, R. L. 1932. *Introduction to Zuni Ceremonialism.* 47th Annual Report of the Bureau of American Ethnology. Washington, DC: Smithsonian Institution.

Bunzel, R. L. 1938. The economic organization of primitive peoples. In *General Anthropology*, ed. F. Boas. New York: D. C. Heath, 327–408.

Carsten, J., and S. Hugh-Jones, eds. 1995. *About the House: Lévi-Strauss and Beyond.* Cambridge: Cambridge University Press.

Carter, T. 2007. Of blanks and burials: Hoarding obsidian at Neolithic Çatalhöyük. In *Technical Systems and Near Eastern PPN Communities.* Proceedings of the 5th International Workshop. Fréjus 2004, eds. L. Astruc, D. Binder, and F. Briols. Antibes: Éditions APDCA, 343–355.

Cessford, C. 2005. Estimating the Neolithic population at Çatalhöyük. In *Inhabiting Çatalhöyük: Reports from the 1995–1999 Seasons*, ed. I. Hodder. Çatalhöyük Research Project 4. Cambridge: McDonald Institute for Archaeological Research, 221–284.

Dean, R. M. 2001. Social Change and Hunting during the Pueblo III to Pueblo IV Transition, East-Central Arizona. *Journal of Field Archaeology* 28(3/4):271–285.

Düring, B. S. 2005. Building Continuity in the Central Anatolian Neolithic: Exploring the Meaning of Buildings at Askikli Höyük and Çatalhöyük. *Journal of Mediterranean Archaeology* 18:3–29.

Düring, B. S. 2007. The articulation of houses at Neolithic Çatalhöyük, Turkey. In *The Durable House: House Society Models in Archaeology*, ed. R. A. Beck, Jr. Center for Archaeological Investigations Occasional Paper No. 35. Carbondale: CAI, Southern Illinois University, 130–153.

Düring, B. S. 2011. *The Prehistory of Asia Minor: From Complex Hunter-Gatherers to Early Urban Societies.* Cambridge: Cambridge University Press.

Eggan, F. 1950. *Social Organization of the Western Pueblos.* Chicago: University of Chicago Press.

Fowles, S. M. 2010. A people's history of the American Southwest. In *Ancient Complexities: New Perspectives in Pre-Columbian North America*, ed. Susan Alt. Provo: University of Utah Press, 183–204.

Fowles, S. M. 2011. The Southwest in the age of reformation. In *Handbook of North American Archaeology*, ed. T. Pauketat. Oxford: Oxford University Press, 631–644.

Gillespie, S. D. 2007. When is a house? In *The Durable House: House Society Models in Archaeology*, ed. R. A. Beck, Jr. Center for Archaeological Investigations Occasional Paper No. 35. Carbondale: CAI, Southern Illinois University, 25–52.

Heitman, C. H. 2007. Houses great and small: Reevaluating the "house" in Chaco Canyon, New Mexico. In *The Durable House: House Society Models in Archaeology*, ed. R. A. Beck, Jr. Center for Archaeological Investigations Occasional Paper No. 35. Carbondale: CAI, Southern Illinois University, 248–272.

Hillson, S. W., Clark S. Larsen, Başak Boz, Marin A. Pilloud, Joshua W. Sadvari, Sabrina C. Agarwal, Bonnie Glencross, Patrick Beauchesne, Jessica Pearson, Christopher B. Ruff, Evan M. Garofalo, Lori D. Hager, and Scott D. Haddow. 2013. The human remains I: Interpreting community structure, health and diet in Neolithic Çatalhöyük. In *Humans and Landscapes of Çatalhöyük: Reports from the 2000–2008 Seasons*, ed. I. Hodder. Çatalhöyük Research Project Series Volume 8. British Institute at Ankara Monograph No. 47 / Monumenta Archaeologica 30. Los Angeles: Cotsen Institute of Archaeology Press.

Hodder, I. 2006. *The Leopard's Tale: Revealing the Mysteries of Çatalhöyük*. London: Thames and Hudson.

Hodder, I. 2010a. Probing religion at Çatalhöyük: An interdisciplinary experiment. In *Religion in the Emergence of Civilization: Çatalhöyük as a Case Study*, ed. I. Hodder. Cambridge: Cambridge University Press, 1–31.

Hodder, I. 2011. Human-Thing Entanglement: Towards An Integrated Archaeological Perspective. *Journal of the Royal Anthropological Institute* 17:154–177.

2012. *Entangled: An Archaeology of the Relationships between Human and Things*. Malden, MA: Wiley-Blackwell.

Hodder, I. 2013. The social geography of Çatalhöyük. In *Integrating Çatalhöyük: Themes from the 2000–2008 Seasons*, ed. I. Hodder. Los Angeles: Cotsen Institute.

Hodder, I., ed. 2010. *Religion in the Emergence of Civilization: Çatalhöyük as a Case Study*. Cambridge: Cambridge University Press.

Hodder, I., and C. Cessford. 2004. Daily Practice and Social Memory at Çatalhöyük. *American Antiquity* 69(1):17–40.

Hodder, I., and L. M. Meskell. 2010. The symbolism of Çatalhöyük in its regional context. In *Religion in the Emergence of Civilization: Çatalhöyük as a Case Study*, ed. I. Hodder. Cambridge: Cambridge University Press, 32–72.

Hodder, I., and P. Pels. 2010. History houses: A new interpretation of architectural elaboration at Çatalhöyük. In *Religion in the Emergence of Civilization: Çatalhöyük as a Case Study*, ed. I. Hodder. Cambridge: Cambridge University Press, 163–186.

Joyce, R., and S. D. Gillespie, eds. 2000. *Beyond Kinship: Social and Material Reproduction in House Societies*. Philadelphia: University of Pennsylvania Press.

Keane, W. 2010. Marked, absent, habitual: Approaches to Neolithic religion at Çatalhöyük. In *Religion in the Emergence of Civilization: Çatalhöyük as a Case Study*, ed. I. Hodder. Cambridge: Cambridge University Press, 187–219.

Knappett, C. 2011. *An Archaeology of Interaction: Network Perspectives on Material Culture and Society*. Oxford: Oxford University Press.

Kroeber, A. L. 1919. Zuni Kin and Clan. *Anthropological Papers of the American Museum of Natural History* 18(2):39–204.

Ladd, E. J. 1979. Zuni social and political organization. In *Handbook of North American Indians vol. 9, Southwest*, ed. A. Ortiz, pp. 482–491. Washington, D.C.: Smithsoinian Institution.

Lave, J., and E. Wenger. 1991. *Situated Learning. Legitimate Peripheral Participation*. Cambridge: University of Cambridge Press.

Lekson, S. H. 2009. *A History of the Ancient Southwest*. Santa Fe: SAR Press.

Love, S. 2010. How Houses Build People: An Archaeology of Mudbrick Architecture at Çatalhöyük. Ph.D. Dissertation, Department of Anthropology, Stanford University, Palo Alto.

McGuire, R. H., and D. J. Saitta. 1996. Although They Have Petty Captains, They Obey Them Badly: the Dialectics of Prehispanic Western Pueblo Social Organization. *American Antiquity* 61(2):197–216.

Mellaart, J. 1967. *Çatal Hüyük: A Neolithic Town in Anatolia*. New York: Thames & Hudson.

Mills, B. J. 2004. The Establishment and Defeat of Hierarchy: Inalienable Possessions and the History of Collective Prestige Structures in the Puebloan Southwest. *American Anthropologist* 106(2):238–251.

Mills, B. J. 2008. Remembering while forgetting: Depositional practice and social memory at Chaco. In *Memory Work: Archaeologies of Material Practices*, eds. B. J. Mills and W. H. Walker. Santa Fe: SAR Press, 81–108.

Mills, B. J., and W. H. Walker. 2008. Introduction: Memory, materiality, and depositional practice. In *Memory Work: Archaeologies of Material Practices*, eds. B. J. Mills and W. H. Walker. Santa Fe: SAR Press, 3–23.

Nakamura, C. 2010. Magical deposits at Çatalhöyük: A matter of time and place? In *Religion in the Emergence of Civilization: Çatalhöyük as a Case Study*, ed. I. Hodder. Cambridge: Cambridge University Press, 300–331.

Parsons, E. C. 1939. *Pueblo Indian Religion*. 2 vols. Chicago: University of Chicago Press.

Pearson, J. A., H. Buitenhuis, R. E. M. Hedges, L. Martin, N. Russell, and K. C. Twiss. 2007. New Light on Early Caprine Herding Strategies from Isotope Analysis: A Case Study from Neolithic Anatolia. *Journal of Archaeological Science* 34:2170–2179.

Pels, P. 2010. Temporalities of "religion" at Çatalhöyük. In *Religion in the Emergence of Civilization: Çatalhöyük as a Case Study*, ed. I. Hodder. Cambridge: Cambridge University Press, 220–267.

Pilloud, M. A., and C. S. Larsen. 2011. "Official" and "Practical" Kin: Inferring Social and Community Structure from Dental Phenotype at Neolithic Çatalhöyük, Turkey. *American Journal of Physical Anthropology* 145:519–530.

Plog, S., and J. Solemeto. 1999. The Never-Changing and the Ever-Changing: the Evolution of Western Pueblo Ritual. *Cambridge Archaeological Journal* 7:161–182.

Potter, J. M. 2000. Pots, Parties, and Politics: Communal Feasting in the American Southwest. *American Antiquity* 65:471–492.

Price, T. D., and O. Bar-Yosef. 2010. Traces of inequality at the origins of agriculture in the Ancient Near East. In *Pathways to Power*, ed. T. D. Price and G. M. Feinman. New York: Springer, 147–168.

Russell, N., and L. Martin. 2005. Çatalhöyük mammal remains. In *Inhabiting Catalhoyuk: Results from the 1995–1999 Seasons*, ed. I. Hodder. Cambridge: McDonald Institute for Archaeological Research, 33–98.

Russell, N., L. Martin, and K. C. Twiss. 2009. Building memories: Commemorative deposits at Çatalhöyük. In *Zooarchaeology and the Reconstruction of Cultural Systems: Case Studies from the Old World*, eds. B. S. Arbuckle, C. A. Makarewicz, and A. L. Atici. Anthropozoologica, 1. Paris: L'Homme et l'Animal, Société de Recherche Interdisciplinaire, 103–128.

Schachner, G. 2001. Ritual Control and Transformation in Middle-Range Societies: An Example from the American Southwest. *Journal of Anthropological Archaeology* 20:168–194.

Shults, L. 2010. Spiritual entanglement: Transforming religious symbols at Çatalhöyük. In *Religion in the Emergence of Civilization: Çatalhöyük as a Case Study*, ed. Ian Hodder. Cambridge: Cambridge University Press, 73–98.

Smith, W. 1952. *Excavations in Big Hawk Valley, Wupatki National Monument, Arizona*. Flagstaff: Museum of Northern Arizona Bulletin 24.

Stevenson, M. C. 1904. *The Zuni Indians: Their Mythology, Esoteric Fraternities, and Ceremonies*. 23rd Annual Report of the Bureau of American Ethnology, 1901–1902. Washington, DC: Smithsonian Institution.

Ur, J. A. 2003. CORONA Satellite Photography and Ancient Road Networks: a Northern Mesopotamian Case Study. *Antiquity* 77:102–115.

Ware, J. A. 2002. Descent group and sodality: Alternative Pueblo social histories. In *Traditions, Transitions, and Technologies: Themes in Southwestern Archaeology*, ed. S. H. Schlanger. Boulder: University Press of Colorado, 94–112.

Ware, J. A., and E. Blinman. 2000. Cultural collapse and reorganization: The origin and spread of Pueblo ritual sodalities. In *The Archaeology of Regional Interaction: Religion, Warfare & Exchange across the American Southwest & Beyond*, ed. M. Hegmon. Boulder: University Press of Colorado, 381–409.

Watt, L. 1997. Zuni Family Ties and Household-Group Values: A Revisionist Cultural Model of Zuni Social Organization. *Journal of Anthropological Research* 53(1):17–29.

Wenger, E. 1998. *Communities of Practice: Learning, Meaning, and Identity*. New York: Cambridge University Press.

Whitehouse, H., and I. Hodder. 2010. Modes of religiosity at Çatalhöyük. In *Religion in the Emergence of Civilization: Çatalhöyük as a Case Study*, ed. I. Hodder. Cambridge: Cambridge University Press, 122–145.

Whiteley, P. 1988. *Deliberate Acts: Changing Hopi Culture through the Oraibi Split.* Tucson: University of Arizona Press.

Wilkinson, T. 2010. The tell: Social archaeology and territorial space. In *The Development of Pre-State Communities in the Ancient Near East: Studies in Honour of Edgar Peltenburg*, eds. D. Bolger and L. C. Maguire. Oxford: Oxbow Books, 55–62.

Wills, W. H. 2005. Economic competition and agricultural involution in the Precontact North American Southwest. In *A Catalyst for Ideas: Anthropological Archaeology and the Legacy of Douglas W. Schwartz*, ed. V. L. Scarborough. Santa Fe: SAR Press, 41–67.

Zedeño, M. N. 2008. Bundled Worlds: The Roles and Interactions of Complex Objects from the North American Plains. *Journal of Archaeological Method and Theory* 15:362–378.

8

Using "Magic" to Think from the Material: Tracing Distributed Agency, Revelation, and Concealment at Çatalhöyük

Carolyn Nakamura and Peter Pels

Introduction

As the provocative discussions about religious life at Çatalhöyük (Hodder 2006, 2010) have demonstrated, speaking of transcendent forms of sociality in human prehistory is a tricky business. In an earlier volume, Carolyn Nakamura began to address "when" and "where" one can speak of "magic" and whether "magic" could be viewed as something distinct from "religion" in the Neolithic material culture of Çatalhöyük, while Peter Pels elaborated on Webb Keane's suggestion that we try to speak of "religion" at Çatalhöyük in terms of degrees of material articulation (Keane 2010; Nakamura 2010; Pels 2010). The present chapter takes this task further through the explicit confrontation of certain key anthropological ideas and debates about magic to improve archaeological approaches to material interpretation.

The obstacles to such an effort are twofold. First, there is the threat of ethnocentric classification: Çatalhöyük suggests a largely "entangled" material world where certain convenient Western distinctions between functional and symbolic, sacred and secular, nature and culture cannot be maintained. Discerning the more subtle distinction between magic and religion, then, threatens to be even more fraught. While often viewed by many nonarchaeologists as an interpretive morass, the exclusive testimony of the material record, however, pushes us to consider and articulate a more material approach to magic. Archaeologists and anthropologists alike have recentered and theorized materiality as constituting the social (Graves-Brown 2000; Keane 2008; Miller 1987, 2005; Mills and Walker 2008; Meskell 2004, 2005; Meskell and Preucel 2004; Weiner 1992). Many theoretical frameworks now situate embodied practice and materiality as the very stuff of, rather than a secondary factor in social life, thus placing certain concerns of anthropology, sociology, and cultural studies more in line with the core concerns of archaeological inquiry (Berggren and Nilsson Stutz 2010: 173). We think the confrontation between this attention to materiality and spiritual realms often theorized as intellectual and "immaterial" activities will take these discussions further, even if they may not provide us with straightforward "evidence" of either "religion" or "magic."

Precisely this assumption of magic's immaterial, ideal, or illusory quality is the second obstacle: ever since the nineteenth-century evolutionist emphasis on magic as a malfunctioning subjectivity or mythopoetic consciousness (see Hanegraaff 1998), a dominant intellectualist tradition in anthropology has psychologized magic in terms of belief, meaning, and subjectivity (Pels 2003: 31). Instead, we are inspired by another anthropological tradition that focuses on magical acts (Mauss 2001; Malinowski 1925, 1935; Nakamura 2005; Pels 1999: 241–242). Those who, like us, took on ritualized and magicoreligious material practices (rather than beliefs) have either implicitly or explicitly demonstrated how a large part of the discursive genealogies of magic and religion do not in fact lend themselves to socially nuanced understandings of such practices (Gell 1998; Taussig 1998; Meyer and Pels 2003). However, as those studies have moved away from framing such practices in terms of underlying beliefs or meanings and toward analyses of action and practice, they have also highlighted those elements of these discursive genealogies that coincide with and reinforce a renewed attention to the materiality of social relations.

The figure of "magic" thus grows new teeth in this material turn, since it may allow us to situate it within embodied practices that work to actualize an intended desire or outcome, rather than see it as a faulty logic or system of beliefs. Since many such practices leave a material trace, magic becomes a possible subject of archaeological inquiry. However, there remains much work to be done on the problem of how to read references to the occult, the transcendent, or the beyond from material traces. Joining the more materialist theories of ritual, magic, and religion with an archaeological perspective, we begin to explore how we might articulate a new materialist approach to magic, one that "thinks from the material." We argue that this productive confrontation will not only allow us to investigate magic in a Neolithic context, but may also lead us to a critical reconceptualization of a materialist theory of magic more broadly.

Why Magic?

Prehistoric archaeology has all but neglected the topic of magic (but see Gebel et al. 2002; Nakamura 2010; Pinch 1994). The modern idea of magic has become too intimately bound to textual traditions (treatments, spells, and incantations) and intellectualist theories to be conceived as a suitable archaeological subject. Within archaeological circles, significantly more attention has been given to the study of ritual or even religion. Magic, of course, shares an intimate genealogy with these two forms and the triad can rarely be resolved into discrete practices in ancient or modern contexts. Certainly, as we and others have argued previously, "magic" and "religion" should not be regarded as distinct categories of practice in the Neolithic context. Rather they belong to a continuum of ritualized practices that leave traces with a degree of material articulation that stands out, and that cannot be neatly captured in traditional binary forms such as functional and symbolic, corporeal and spiritual, or indeed magical and religious (see esp. Keane, Pels, and Nakamura chapters in Hodder 2010).

Significantly, archaeologies of ritual and religion have made substantial strides in recent years. Many recent studies of prehistoric ritual, spirituality, and religion reflect a critical engagement with practice-based or materialist approaches and move beyond simplistic distinctions between "functional" and "other" values (e.g., sacred vs. profane, symbolic vs. practical, and rational vs. irrational) as a basis for identifying ritual practices in the archaeological record (Bradley 1991, 2003; Brück 1999; Fogelin 2007; Hodder and Cessford 2004; Insoll 2004; Verhoeven 2002a, 2002b, 2011). But within this reinvigorated field, the topic of magic marks a notable absence. Given the obdurate association of magic with particular kinds of ideas, meanings, and beliefs, the term "ritual" is viewed as being more appropriate for research into prehistoric contexts. However, a focus on "ritual" does not address a number of crucial issues of material interpretation that we feel we can find in the corpus of theorizing about "magic."

Therefore, we maintain the use of the word "magic" here to explore distinct kinds of practices that assert human agency and intentionality in a field of social relations (also) governed by nonhuman forces. We acknowledge that any definition of magic is the product of a Protestant Christian genealogy (Pels 2003: 16), but one need not, for example, adopt Durkheim's assumption of an outright (and very Protestant) hostility between religion and magic (1965: 58) to make good interpretive use of some of his other ideas. If religion and social rituals assemble a kind of collective subjectivity and value system, then humans often attribute the creative authorship of spiritual worlds to a nonhuman or abstracted, collective agency, whether gods, spirits, ancestors, or objects. These actions are ritualized in the sense that they become normalized, repeatable, obligatory, or even enacted by rote. As Durkheim argued, they reproduce society in a different register. Acts that we have come to regard as magical, however, seem to assert and address much more individualized or specific desires within the spiritual realm. In this way, they reassert the role of the human and the particular in transformative and transcendent power (see Nakamura 2010). And such acts underscore the human capacity to transform the world and their situations within it. The genealogy of "magic" in anthropology highlights material features of such acts that we feel can become crucial for archaeological interpretation, even when we do not adopt Durkheim's ethnocentric distinction between "magic" and "religion."

It is also important to note that magic and religion may or may not be part of the same system. Modern societies, at least, know forms of magic that contradict other sacred activities and discourses (think, for example, of the uneasy coexistence of commodity fetishism and Christian worship). We take this to indicate that the study of magic and religion as material practices requires us to let go of an assumption that has governed much of the study of religion: that coherent belief systems or cosmologies "underlie" religious practice. This is not to say that, in a certain cultural complex, its magical and religious actions cannot be studied as consistently related to each other, but that both on the conscious and on the unconscious levels of culture, the magical and the religious are primarily related in a historical dialectic of practices in constant interaction, rather than a single cosmology or system of beliefs. A materialist approach to magic (and religion) therefore allows for more fluid and dynamic kinds of relationships among various religious, ritual, and magical ideas and practices and does not require or exclude the possibility that these categories exist as discrete kinds of practice.

Such possibly discrepant complexes of sacralization within a single society can be observed at Çatalhöyük. In an earlier publication, Nakamura has explored the idea of magical and religious practices operating through slightly different material modes composed of specific articulations of place, material, and physical qualities (Nakamura 2010). Her argument starts – significantly, given our present argument – from the material record, by means of the observation that we may take the Çatalhöyük house complex, dominated by the materials of clay, plaster, animal bone (we might also add human bone, given the ubiquity of it throughout the house), and certain household assemblages as both normal and normative. In contrast to this, there are other materialities – involving both common and uncommon materials (obsidian, flint, speleothem, antler, pigment, figurine materials) clustered in seemingly nonrandom combinations, deposited in specific places – that are not necessarily tied into this normative complex. Materially, at least, these two "categories" of materials suggest different kinds of practices or habits. While the latter kinds of practices may not subvert a normative order, they cannot be expected to conform to it fully either.

A focus on materialities of magic thus requires archaeologists to take seriously and interrogate how materials may have been used to mediate between supernatural or spiritual power and human agency and action. Magic is a sociocultural strategy and it operates within a specific field of social relations that includes humans and nonhumans, the living and the dead, the corporeal and the disembodied. Notably, social relations are mediated rather than absolutely given or abstracted and as such contain an irreducibly material dimension (Keane 1997, 1998). The challenge that then remains is how to identify the material entailments of magical (or ritual) acts/relations/events in the prehistoric record and how to understand them within their sociocultural and performative contexts.

Genealogies of Matter and Magic

Scholars interested in such questions have repeatedly turned to the growing literatures on materiality theory and performative action. In earlier works (Pels 1998, 1999, 2003; Nakamura 2004, 2005, 2010), we have explored various anthropological histories and ideas in relation to theories of magic. Many others have also explored, debated, and theorized the relationship between materiality and ritualized practice more generally

(Gell 1998; Gosden 1994, 2005; Graves-Brown 2000; Ingold 2007a, 2007b; Joyce 2000; Keane 1997; Latour 2002; Meskell 2003, 2004; Miller 1998; Mills and Walker 2008; Munn 1986; Nanoglou 2009; Pels 2010; Renfrew, Gosden, DeMarrais 2005; Tilley 2004; and a number of essays in Appadurai 1986; Miller 1993; Myers 2001). Following from these earlier discussions we briefly present what we find to be the three most productive anthropological ideas for translating the anthropology of magic and religion to prehistoric archaeological materials: the first, going back to the genealogy established by Marx and Mauss, emphasizes the distribution of agency across objects (Gell 1998: 133–153). The second translates Malinowski's theory of magical action and its essential focus on manipulating the future by performance to acts of revelation and concealment (Taussig 1998). And the third, following Alfred Gell and Pierre Bourdieu (1977), asserts that ideas of magic (and religion) in prehistoric contexts can be understood only when we think of materials as inherently temporal, and that their meaning cannot be understood unless conceived as social movement. We need to elaborate briefly on these ways of "thinking from the material" before showing how they might help to interpret magic and religion at Çatalhöyük.

The general concept of object agency has been embraced to various degrees by many social archaeologists who explore ideas ranging from Latour's "actants" and "symmetrical" human and nonhuman relations (Latour 2005), to Gell's ideas of distributed or secondary agency (Gell 1998: ch. 7). When speaking of magic, however, Karl Marx's classic text on commodity fetishism provides a particularly relevant starting point (Marx 1976). Marx famously conceived of commodity fetishism as ideology. Rather than recognizing the commodity as a product of human labor (and thus as produced and controlled by humans), consumers mistakenly engaged with commodities as if they were possessed by the things instead. Of course, this was only a specific version of a much more widespread folk theory of industrial society, one that had distinct roots in Protestantism (see Keane 2002: 71). It argued that a true rational or spiritual person should have control over the objects s/he handled, and that to succumb to the attractions of objects – often called, disparagingly, "materialism" – was in effect a reduction of human potential. Yet, the very fact that Marx thought that commodity fetishism was the *Alltagsreligion* (the everyday religion) of capitalist society shows the failure of that modern aspiration to realize itself in everyday practice. True modern people should be in command over the objects they possessed – yet all too often these objects seemed to possess them. This fundamental unease with objects that appear to behave like subjects seems typically modern.

Yet the fetishization of the commodity seems merely one instance of a universal phenomenon: that human beings value things that are useful and important to them and do not feel fully complete as persons when they have to do without them (see Comaroff and Comaroff 1992; Graeber 2001). The distribution of human agency across various material means simply emphasizes the utility of such desires. Rather than being an aberration, commodity fetishism may indicate a normal situation. In contrast, the Protestant ideal that humans show mastery over the things they handle – in trust, that is, of some divine ideal – seems the more exotic practice. As attested at various moments during our earlier discussions about Çatalhöyük, we should not assume a break between utility and sacralization, nor interpret something we think of as exotic or strange as being without use or function for the people who made it. Objects do, routinely, behave like subjects, as Alfred Gell showed beautifully in his *Art and Agency* (1998), and we should not let exotic modern thinking mislead us to think otherwise. Persons are, as a rule, distributed (Gell 1998: ch.7); whether they are distributed over computers, mobile phones, heavy machinery, plants, animals, stocks, or stones is first of all a historical, and only in the second instance an evolutionary issue.

Marcel Mauss's reflections on the gift also make a compelling argument for how given objects carry aspects of persons with them (Mauss 1966; see also Weiner 1992). Both Marx and Mauss can be read as emphasizing the distribution of human agency across objects to such an extent that human beings, in so-called primitive as well as modern societies, cannot live without being animated by objects, just as much as objects are animated by human beings.

The second set of current theories of magic – faintly traceable to Bronislaw Malinowski's theory of magical action – emphasize the crucial role of the acts of revelation and concealment, of hiding things and bringing them forth across certain physical boundaries, and the force of which such acts conjure. Malinowski's "ethnographic theory of the magical word" likens the magical spell to an act similar to the infant's cry for food: in most cases, our earliest experiences of the emission of sound, in the form of cries uttered from want or desire, result in immediate material gratification – a kind of preverbal *Tischlein Deck Dich!* – and it is therefore not remarkable that adults attempt to reproduce this habit in later life (Malinowski 1935: 63). What stands out theoretically in Malinowski's account are the dimensions of material need, expressed in communicative performance, leading to a material response – a theory of magical action by performance.

Drawing on Mauss's insight that magic is made in the moment of the conjuring trick (Mauss 2001: 123), Michael Taussig has taken these ideas about performative action further. Rethinking magic by pointing out that magic does not rely on belief, but on an embodied action sequence of belief and skepticism, he sees the paradigmatic performance as the moment that a shaman materially produces a harmful substance from an ailing body (Taussig 1998). Whether the performance is a trick or an actual moment of healing (or both) is immaterial for the purposes of our "thinking from the material." For our purposes, it is essential to point out, first, that this performance is directed at several human and nonhuman audiences, and second, that – directed at a manipulation of a desirable outcome in the immediate future – it is material in itself. The egress or insertion of substance from or into an ailing body is distributed over two main material components: the substance extracted or ingested and the surface (in the shaman's case, the skin or orifices of the body) through which this movement occurs.

The third set of theories address the inherently temporal and relational nature of things. Alfred Gell's important contribution to the theory of materiality lies in his insistence that aesthetics needs to be subordinated to the social relations between humans and the material objects they confront. In his emphasis on the material object as an index of acts in the past (but also as acts directed toward the future), he has reintroduced temporality into human-object relations, in the sense that the performance of an object in relation to humans in the present is encased in a past-to-future movement, in which the social role of the object is to carry past material qualities into the future for present purposes. (It is important to note here that past and future are both immaterial, and that they can only be social by some material mediation of them in the present.) One could see this as a follow-up on Pierre Bourdieu's insistence that the temporality of gift giving – timing, hesitation and hedging, boldness of performance in relation to an anticipation of a differential return – is far more important than the structuralist rule of reciprocity (the tit-for-tat of the market) can convey (Bourdieu 1977: 5). The insistence on temporality implies not only movement across social boundaries but also repetition. During his fieldwork in the Tanzanian Uluguru Mountains, Pels found that the bark of trees along the footpath, where people had used the trunk time and again to support themselves, had acquired magical power by this simple repetition. As with the Congo *nkisi* (or "nail-fetish": Gell 1998: 62), repetitive use is often synonymous with the building up of magical potency, and repetition leaves traces in the material record.

Thinking from the Material by Means of Theories of Magic

The three discourses on magic and materiality that we analytically separated in the previous section need to be combined in the interpretation of specific cases and sets of materials if they are to help us toward articulating a magical economy in the Neolithic as involving relations between various things: explicit ideas of an extrahuman world, implicit ideas of human-other interaction, the human desire to intervene in this expanded social field, and activities that constitute transcendence by crossing or transforming social boundaries and semiotic modalities. All of these forms are legible to some extent in the material record. Various archaeological accounts of the site point to a fairly distinctive symbolic sphere at Çatalhöyük that was deeply entangled in the daily lives of people and the beings (both living and dead) with whom they shared their world. We might call this sphere of interaction the "transcendent nonhuman world of Çatalhöyük." Certain activities that produce such a world include enduring and widely repeated practices that could correlate to normalized behaviors such as house closure, burial of the dead, and the production of internal space.

The remaining task of identifying material entailments of human intervention aimed at the transcendent nonhuman world and the crossing of material-semiotic boundaries marks rather less well-trodden archaeological territory (but see contributions in Hodder 2010) and requires that we return to the materials. In her 2010 contribution, Nakamura identified certain placed deposits as potentially related to magical practice.[1]

---

[1] Previous to this study, others have also considered the nature of "deliberate deposits" (Cessford 2006; Russell and Meece 2005), which may have been part of magical practices at the site.

In this paper we wish to scrutinize further the material entailments of certain placed deposits and other related acts. Such deposits display a remarkable diversity and range from neonates interred in walls to animal bits embedded into house plaster to rare groupings of various materials buried in a pit or built into a house feature. These kinds of deposits strongly suggest both intentional placement and boundary crossing/marking such that the possibility of their participating in a magical economy becomes compelling.

These archaeological materials and contexts therefore are useful to "think with," as it were, and their closer scrutiny may produce new possibilities for understanding what might constitute "the magical" at the site. While Nakamura has previously detailed certain qualities, locations, and combinations of materials (2010), here we would like to explore specific movements – physical, social, spatial, and temporal – mediated by certain archaeological deposits found at Çatalhöyük. Significantly, the archaeology draws our attention to: 1) how particular materialities and qualities effectively cross social boundaries and semiotic modalities, 2) how these boundaries in turn become more marked (and perhaps more powerful?) through practices of revelation and concealment, and 3) how this material re/ordering of space and time articulates a distinctive kind of agency.

The movement of materials across social boundaries is rather ubiquitous at Çatalhöyük. Wild animal remains and deceased humans are routinely taken into or incorporated into the house structure itself. Traditional binaries of wild/domestic and living/dead become complicated as they come to constitute the same space. These highly visible (animal art and installations) or ritualized practices (burial of the dead) make up what many have called the "religious" or "spiritual" sphere at the site (Hodder 2006, 2010). While we certainly do not exclude the possibility of magical action being part of these practices, we wish to focus on those contexts and materials that depart from these more "normative" practices and instead inhabit a more discrete material register as they work to intertwine the normal with the extraordinary.

Surfaces and Horizons

In the effort to locate spaces of magic, surfaces and horizons were an obvious locus for boundary crossings and interfaces of revelation and

concealment within houses. This distinction between surfaces and horizons is by no means absolute, but rather temporal, since from an archaeological (geological) perspective, horizons can be past surfaces and
surfaces can be future horizons. However, for our present purposes, we
specifically distinguish between construction horizons and occupational
surfaces.

Horizons marked a transition between two things – both a beginning and an ending – but were never surfaces (e.g., foundation layers;
construction and makeup layers of ovens, benches, platforms, etc.; and
infill deposits). As such, they were liminal transitory spaces that remained
apart and unseen from the living activities of the building. Excavators
have found various deposits that appear to mark the transformation of
one thing – a building, platform, oven, or other feature – into another.
Certain buildings had "foundation" burials and/or deposits (e.g., B.1,
B.42, B.54, B.65/56 sequence). And many buildings, upon abandonment, had otherwise clean infill covering deliberately placed deposits and
items (e.g., B.1, B.3, B.49, B.52, B.80, B.65/56/44 sequence). Surfaces,
on the other hand, were directly articulated with residential activities and
occupants; they were part of the fabric of daily life as dynamic interfaces between humans and the structures they inhabited (e.g., building
floors, walls, and platforms; entryways). Inhabitants continually replastered walls and platforms and retrieved materials from burials and older
buildings (Hodder and Cessford 2004). Platforms and floors in particular sustained regular acts of deposition and retrieval.

These two interfaces, we argue, pose different temporal possibilities
that may have sustained different kinds of magical attention and action.
Whereas actions across surfaces (which broker in the play of revelation
and concealment) enable a kind of past to future movement, acts that
mark horizons serve to fix or mark a particular moment that will recede
into the past. The difference between the former and the latter might be
compared to a subtle difference between remembering and commemorating: remembering evokes a more active and creative process of moving something from the past into the present, while commemorating
evokes the active process of placing something into memory. Perhaps
most significantly, these two boundary interfaces likely presuppose different audiences. Acts of revelation and concealment that take place
across surfaces are likely performed for the benefit of a human audience. In a different way, the marking of horizons is likely for the benefit

of a more abstracted audience – for posterity, gods, spirits, ancestors, the unborn, or even the earth itself. We want to emphasize, however, that these two practices are not mutually exclusive. The archaeology provides numerous instances that demonstrate how these two activities are variously intertwined. Moreover, if we take these practices as material mediations between human and nonhuman worlds, this entanglement is not surprising; on the contrary, their specific articulations might be helpful in our pursuit to examine how humans negotiated their own power and agency in relation to a spiritual or supernatural order of things.

READING "MAGIC" FROM CLUSTERS

The materials from Çatalhöyük offer a rich data set to begin to explore these various practices of marking and revelation and concealment. The most germane, yet problematic data set to begin with is the "cluster" category, which is defined as a spatially and temporally "discrete group of artefacts within a unit, i.e., a concentration of pot, bone, lithics etc. or combination thereof" and do not include the surrounding deposit. Given the way this category is defined – as a discrete assemblage of materials within time and space – intentional deposits from more ritualized contexts would likely fall into this data set. Working from the 1995–2008 data available on the Çatalhöyük Database, we selected clusters that comprise a mix of two or more different materials and also included deliberate deposits such as neonate foundation burials and single artifacts, which are found in horizon and surface contexts[2] (Table 8.1). Our current sample totals to 268 cluster (or equivalent) units and includes deposits from building and midden contexts. However, this selection must be regarded as partial and specifically derived using the preceding criteria.

Not all of these units articulate ritualized behavior as they can also represent dumping activities or accidental deposition. Ritualized practices presuppose a certain degree of deliberateness and excavators provide the first line of interpretation of intentional versus accidental placement.

---

[2] Given that these "noncluster" deposits must be tracked down from various specialist databases and reports, our count at the time of publication is incomplete. For instance, many human bone deposits (tertiary burials) and faunal bone deposits (see Russell and Meece 2005; Russell et al. 2009) that might be of interest may not have been included in our database.

Table 8.1. Number of intentional and ritualized deposits in buildings; counts include only most likely clusters and deposits

Building	No. deposits	Level
49	4	4040.G
52	6	4040.G
77	6	4040.?G
45	1	4040.H
55	2	4040.H
58	3	4040.H
60	1	4040.H
67	1	4040.H
3	2	BACH.?G
1	3	North?G
16	1	South.J
18	4	South.J
17	2	South.K
2	5	South.?K
6	1	SOUTH.L
40	2	South.?M
50	2	South.?M
68	1	South.P
65	8	South.Q
56	4	South.R
44	10	South.S
74	1	TP.unasssigned
63	2	IST.unassigned

Impressions of the relative context of deposition, material composition, and integrity of deposits often lend the most compelling evidence for deliberate placement. For instance, Roddy Regan interprets a stamp steal depicting a bearlike figure found face down in the middle of building infill (also in line with an obsidian blade and bone point) as a deliberate placement given that the matrix of the infill was sterile (devoid of artifacts) and the building itself was cleared of almost all materials before infilling (Regan 2013; also see Figure 8.3c).

Using similar criteria, we divided our sample set into nonritualized, possibly ritualized, and likely ritualized deposits. Since this was a very subjective process, we have provided a few examples of various deposits and where they would fall on the deliberate/ritualized spectrum (Table 8.2). Our preliminary analyses show that some materials in cluster deposits appear very rarely (in two or three instances) but always in what we would call deliberate and more ritualized contexts; these include human and animal skeletons, beads, tooth pendants, and pigment lumps

Table 8.2. Examples of deposit types from nonritualized to likely ritualized

	------> Increasing liklihood of ritual associations			
	Not	Maybe	Likely	Descriptive category
Mixed cluster of animal bone, stone, charcoal, and coprolites in room infill or midden that is relatively rich in various materials	-------			N/A
Obsidian debitage on a floor suggesting an activity area	-------			N/A
Clay balls in a scoop near a fire installation	-------			N/A
Various kinds of stone fragments with crystal, fossils, former tools, and grind- and rubstones found in the packing layer of an oven		-------		Horizon
Complete object (such as a stamp seal) found in the middle of sterile room fill		-------	-------	Horizon
Red ochre scatter on the floor near a threshold		-------	-------	Surface
Multiple layers wall painting/plastering episodes on a single wall		-------	-------	Surface
Obsidan cache in platform		-------	-------	Surface
Paired or single objects such as scapulae, obsidian forms, necklaces found deposited in walls, niches, and interstitial spaces			-------	Horizon
Human skull at base of post retrieval pit			-------	Horizon
Cluster of objects found at interface between reconstruction and plastering episodes of a platform			-------	Horizon
Deposit of clustered items on a platform placed right before the building is infilled			-------	Surface/ horizon

(see Table 8.3). Other objects such as antlers, stone tools, animal skulls, flint, axes, figurines, and bone tools occur with much more frequency, and 50 percent of the time in the more deliberate and ritualized contexts (these percentages increase, sometimes dramatically if we include the possibly ritualized deposits). Such materials might have been attributed some kind of power or significance more generally (for a more detailed discussion of various material qualities, see Nakamura 2010). Nevertheless, we want to stress again that what we are investigating as "magic" cannot be reduced to a particular material, location, or attribute, but rather arises from a specific assemblage of these various qualities.

Table 8.3. Materials in clusters: occurrences in all cluster deposits versus deliberate/ritualized deposits

	Percentage occurring in deliberate deposits	All cluster deposits	Possibly ritualized deposits	Likely ritualized deposits
Animal skeletons	100%	1	0	1
Stamp Seal	100%	1	0	1
Beads	100%	5	0	5
Human skeletons	100%	8	0	8
Knuckle bones	100%	2	0	2
Pigment lumps	100%	4	0	4
Tooth pendant/bead	100%	2	0	2
Ochre (nonburial)	80%	5	1	4
Figurines	70%	10	3	7
Axes	69%	13	4	9
Flint	69%	16	4	11
Crystal	67%	9	2	6
Bone tool	65%	23	6	15
Shell objects	63%	8	3	5
Animal skulls	61%	18	6	11
Worked stone/stone tools	55%	20	9	11
Antler	54%	28	12	15
Human bones	50%	6	2	3
Obsidian	46%	87	37	40
Horns/horn cores	44%	18	8	8
Mandibles	44%	16	6	7
Scapulae	39%	33	16	13
Stone	35%	68	31	24
Individual teeth	33%	3	2	1
Bucrania	31%	13	6	4
Pottery	27%	33	20	9
Claws	25%	4	2	1
Owl pellets	25%	4	2	1
Clay balls	13%	16	6	2

Furthermore, as mentioned previously, the line between "surfaces" and "horizons" is very fluid. The distinction becomes especially fraught in contexts of building abandonment, since some floor deposits that mark specific surfaces before the building is infilled effectively function in a similar manner as horizon deposits that mark transitional moments and spaces. So the spectrum of deposits range from those that remain "visible" on surfaces (e.g., ochre scatter on the base of an oven) to those that remain concealed within the fabric of the building and its fundament (e.g., foundation burial under a wall; see Table 8.4)

Table 8.4. Spectrum of surface and horizon deposits

Surface → Horizon				more visible → less visible
	deposits that suggest the *movement across* surfaces	**Revelation and concealment**		
	deposits that *mark* surfaces	**Marking**	deposits that *mark* a distinct transition horizon between features	
		Marking	deposits that are *embedded* directly within the construction layers of a feature or placed within infill and lie in a distinct spatial relation to a feature	

With these heuristic categories, we are trying to focus on particular bundlings of materials, space, and time and to investigate whether particular configurations correspond to possible differences in practice. One obvious starting point would be to look for correlations between certain materials and different kinds of practices. For instance, obsidian is by far the most commonly occurring material found in caches, and we might expect it to be strongly correlated with (surface) contexts that might sustain revelation and concealment. However, obsidian in its various forms is found in diverse contexts and locations and in fact is more ubiquitous in horizon deposits than surface deposits (see Figure 8.1).

We can say, however, that the materials found in surface clusters, possibly associated with activities of revelation and concealment, are a relatively circumscribed group and consist of obsidian, stone, antler, bone tools, horns/horn cores, flint, shell objects, and ochre (surface in Figure 8.2). In contrast, materials related to marking transitional moments and events (surface/horizon and horizon in Figure 8.2) constitute a much broader variety of materials. Notably, there are certain materials that *only* appear in horizon contexts: crystal, pigment lumps, human and animal skeletons, human bones, tooth pendants/beads, and a few other isolated incidences of materials. Most of these materials are not very common on site or are found in rather specific contexts. For instance, pigment lumps are only additionally found in burial contexts, and the occurrence of owl pellets and individual teeth is somewhat rare. It is also intriguing that there appears to be a distinctive correlation between pigment lumps

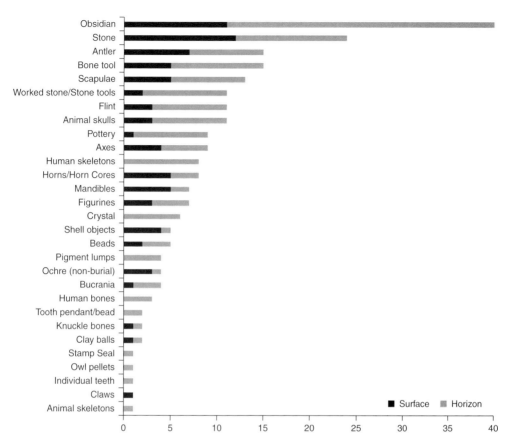

8.1. Occurrences of materials in surface and horizon contexts. NB: These counts include only the most likely surface and horizon clusters from the excavations of 1995–2008 (n = 85).

and crystal objects; the former are always found with the latter, but not vice versa. These materials with their particular spectral qualities might have been given symbolically charged meanings and values (see discussion in Nakamura 2010). Within horizon clusters, pigment lumps and crystal, along with obsidian, bone tools, flint, pottery, human and animal skulls, are strongly associated with packing or makeup layers of various features or construction/abandonment activities. As these materials are embedded within building structures, their inclusion may suggest a specific linkage between a building or feature and a specific object and/or its material quality or social history.

While there are some suggestive associations of particular materials with deposition contexts, the distinction between surface and horizon clusters is one that becomes more apparent when looking at specific

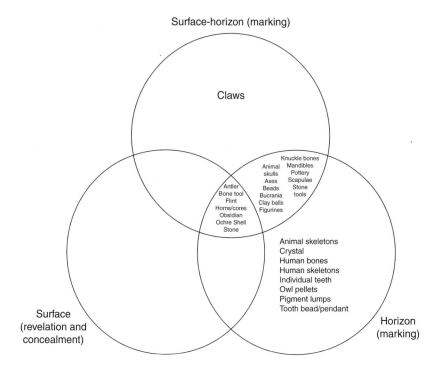

8.2. Materials found in surface and horizon contexts. The additional category of surface/horizon was added to indicate those deposits that are ambiguously placed on surfaces just prior to being concealed, such as in acts of building infill.

cluster examples, which we will describe later. However, one material does seem to draw attention to a distinction between surfaces and horizons: ochre. Distinctive material properties allow ochre to be found in various states: in lumps of raw material, applied to surfaces as paints or scatters, and in various colors ranging from red to brown to yellow. In burials, excavators have found ochre both in yellow-brown lumps (in addition to other mineral pigment lumps) and in scatters of red. Outside burial contexts, ochre occurs in horizon or packing deposits as yellow-brown lumps (included under "pigment lumps" in the chapter tables); whereas on surfaces it occurs as red pigmentation on walls, covering objects, scattered on floors, and lining the base of a bin (N.B. the few instances of red ochre from horizon contexts occur *on the surface of an object* from such a context). Red ochre thus seems to be correlated with the treatment of surfaces more generally, be they building features, bodies, or objects. Perhaps, significantly, while red ochre does occur naturally around the site, yellow-brown ochres also become red when exposed to heat. It would be interesting to investigate whether or not the red ochre pigments were derived from naturally red ochre deposits or from processed yellow ochres. If the latter were the case, then we could imagine that people might have taken the inherently transformative property of ochre into account in their various uses and applications of the material.

MATTERS TAKING PLACE

Activities that appear to mark transitional moments in the life history of a building constitute one of the most provocative practices at the site. Excavators commonly find deposits of materials marking the construction and/or demolition of a building or feature. As such, these deposits are generally referred to as "foundation/abandonment deposits." Given the nature of rebuilding activities at Çatalhöyük, it is often impossible to distinguish between construction and demolition activities. Notably, the prevalence of marking such interfaces with various materials and deposits may suggest a distinct linkage between creation and destruction (Cessford 2007). The makeup of such deposits can be quite varied. There are numerous instances of single or paired objects marking a transitional moment in the life of a house (e.g., 4355 in B.16 and 4205 in B.2), but there are also several cases of mixed deposits that mark and even compose the constructional foundation of a house feature (e.g., 4689 in B.16, 4717 in Sp. 181).

Certain objects that appear repeatedly in such possible contexts include animal parts (scapulae, skulls, mandibles, horns, teeth and claws, antler), obsidian projectiles, bone points, ground stone axes, red ochre (pigment), and human skeletal remains or neonate burials (Table 8.3). Most of these materials are evocative in some way as they possess distinctive physical qualities such as color, hardness, sharpness, shape, and so on, and that easily sustain or condense beliefs, practices, and histories concerning power (Weiner 1995: 66; see also Nakamura 2010). For instance, some have argued that the Neolithic inhabitants likely regarded as powerful certain aggressive or sharp animal parts, such as wild cattle bucrania and various animal claws, given that they were almost always dismantled or defaced when buildings were abandoned (Mellaart 1967; Meskell and Hodder 2011). Alternatively or in addition to these inherent qualities, specific life histories or connections to people or locales can also lend significant power to objects. Cessford (2007) has noted that for the building practices in the North Area, many of the objects found in deliberate deposition have long and complex life histories. The prevalence of pigment and ochre, animal scapulae, skulls, and other human remains might then have tapped into a more historical or biographical power.

Along these lines, Nerissa Russell (2001: 245) has noted that cattle scapulae used as plastering tools are frequently found associated with the demolition of features that such tools were likely used to create. Similarly, Cessford argues that such an interpretation could be applied to ground-stone axes associated with the removal of timber features, and obsidian projectiles found with cattle skulls and horn cores (2007). One might also be able to extend this argument to the occasional placing of neo-nate burials in or underneath structural foundations. These pairings call attention to the coupling of creative with destructive force at moments of transition: the closure of a bin marked by the tool that formed it (scapula tool), the removal of a timber post associated with the axe that shaped it, the dismantled installation of animal remains marked by a pro-jectile point that killed the animal, or the founding of a new house for the death of a person. Such acts of marking and exchange underscore the radical interdependency of cycles of creation and destruction and could have denoted numerous things. They might have signaled the end of a life cycle. They could also have mitigated acts of destruction or creation if such acts were regarded as transgressive. They also could have served to consolidate and/or contain power in a specific location – creating and continuing the social power of the feature or house itself, as it were. In all of these scenarios, the marking of destruction with symbols (and implements) of creation, and vice versa, suggests that not only buildings, but certain features may have been imbued with some sense of power, agency, or being – if not in themselves, then perhaps as extensions of others.

In most of our examples, these and other materials were generally found placed in transitional locations – in vertical construction layers but also spatially liminal spaces such as in between or along walls and in corners (Figures 8.3a, b, d). Not all buildings have such deposits and in those that do, the number can range from one to ten (Table 8.1). Although not a regular practice, unusual deposits have been found in the construction makeup of platforms, hearths, ovens, bins, and benches. Obsidian, various types of stone, and animal bone tools are the most common material in these deposits (see Milić 2004; Carter, Connelly and Spasojević 2005; Russell and Meece 2005). However, some cases reveal human skeletons, figurines, and various other materials. While it

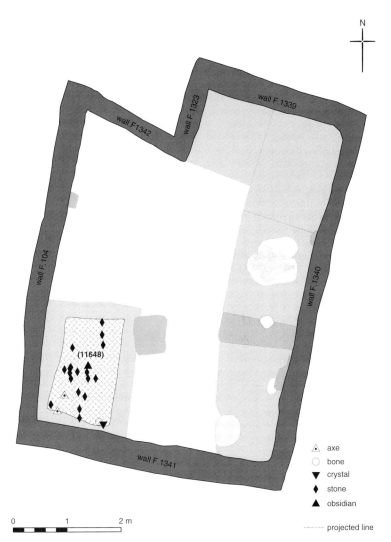

8.3. Plans of B.44–B.56 sequence showing cluster deposits. (a) Construction phase of B.44, SW platform. (b) Occupation phase of B.44. (c) Infill of B.44 before (d) construction of B.56. Occupation phase of B.52.

is possible that there may have been quite practical reasons motivating the deposition of these materials into these features (rebuilding episodes make expedient dumping areas that will be quickly hidden by new features), it is possible or even likely that these inclusions were also symbolically or ritually powerful. The site has demonstrated a long-term and fairly standardized tradition of house cleaning, at least at abandonment. Furthermore, the frequency and makeup of artifact-rich deposits in the construction interfaces of platforms, ovens, and so on, do not suggest

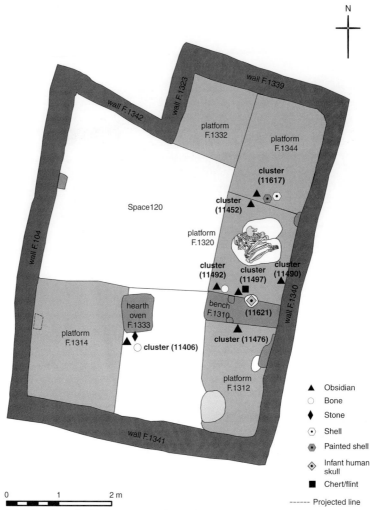

8.3. *(continued).* (b) Occupation phase of B.44.

widespread, regular, or expedient dumping episodes. Rather they are more suggestive of deliberate acts (see later discussion). What might be at work here is the intentional incorporation of materials that in some way articulate a specific event, quality, activity, or person that becomes incorporated into the house or feature.

For instance, B.44 produced a number of interesting obsidian deposits. The makeup layers of eastern platforms F.1320 and F.1321 contained a series of discrete obsidian clusters composed of blade materials; significantly, most of these were end products that appeared to be quite fresh and unused and were likely manufactured off-site (Carter, Kayacan, and

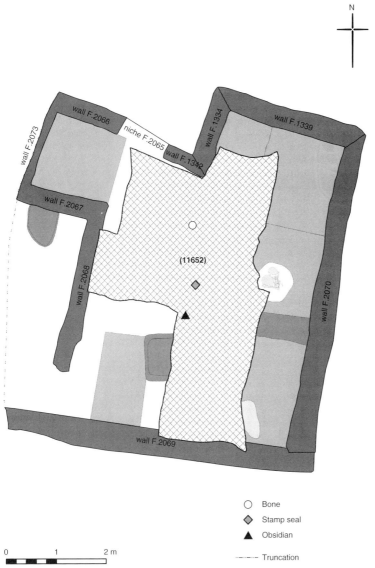

N

8.3. *(continued)*. (c) Infill of B.44 before construction of B.56.

Milić 2005: 199–200). In contrast, the lowest construction fill of a platform (F.1314) in the southwest corner contained notable amounts of
ground stone and large amounts of chipped stone. Carter, Kayacan, and
Milić (2005) suggest that these chipped stone materials were the remnants of knapping activities that took place within the building and had
been gathered up and placed in the platform makeup. These two scenarios underscore rather different kinds of agencies. The first example draws

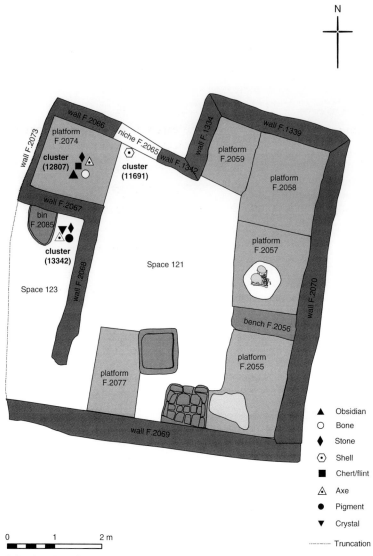

N

▲	Obsidian
○	Bone
◆	Stone
⊙	Shell
■	Chert/flint
△	Axe
●	Pigment
▼	Crystal
----	Truncation

0   1   2 m

8.3. *(continued).* (d) Occupation phase of B.56.

attention to the objects themselves – the obsidian blades that were perhaps highly valued or even fetishized given their lack of use and extramural origin. The second example draws attention to a process: the activities of knapping and tool creation that may have taken place directly within the house. The difference between the agency of objects and the agency of actions is potentially significant. Objects become traces of different worlds depending on the actions that shape them. Thinking along these lines, we might contrast the obsidian blade deposits as a gesture that introduces new or exotic power into the house to the obsidian debitage deposit as a gesture that acts to conserve, consolidate, and contain powers and productive processes already associated with the house.

This apparent concern with both incorporating exotic or "wild" power and conserving existing domestic power within the house on a more hidden register can be seen in other examples as well. Mellaart famously found some plaster protrusions on the east wall of E.VI.8 – what he called "breasts" – all containing lower boar jaws with tusks and teeth (Mellaart 1962: 69). He also found boar jaws in the walls of E. VIB.10 and E.VII.21, two griffon vulture skulls embedded in two wall lumps from E.VIB.10, and one fox and one weasel/badger skull in two vertical lumps. Except for the mandible in E.VIB.10, all of these were found on east walls. The current excavations have also found similar kinds of materials including horn cores and scapulae built into walls in B.1 and Sp.105, and a dog skull in a wall in Sp. 295 (Russell and Meece 2005). Such "hidden" materialities demonstrate the incorporation of various animals into ideas of social or sociospiritual power. The incorporation of various animal parts into wall structures and surfaces may have been compelled by diverse desires. The embedding of sharp animal parts into plaster suggests a kind of muting or blunting action that could have served an apotropaic or protective purpose; it could also have been a memorial gesture marking a particular event or person. However, the action of embedding also suggests integration, such that the powers of various animals (or wild or natural power) become merged with the building form and history. Like the dramatic, highly visible cattle bucrania installations, these materials may have then articulated a specific relationship with the external or nondomestic world. These along with other practices, moreover, undermine any simple opposition between wild and domestic at the site (see Hodder 2006: 82–85).

Another striking example, possibly related to the idea of conserving "domestic" power, can be found in the southwest platform (F.4006) of B.49. This platform was constructed from redeposited burned and used artifacts composed of worked and unworked stone, animal bone, worked bone points, obsidian blades and blanks, red ochre or pigment, a group of clay animal figurines – some of which appear to have been "stabbed" and deformed (see Nakamura and Meskell 2004) – and a broken antler tool. Daniel Eddisford interprets the assemblage as a deliberate collection of a number of artifacts from the house, which were then dumped in the southwest corner and sealed by platform F.4006 (Eddisford 2008: 35). In this case, we may have a mixture of objects (tools) and activities (consumption and procurement rituals) represented in the platform deposit. But again, these all appear to have been specifically associated with the household and thus may have materially signified the various powers or agencies associated with the house. Although there are numerous other examples that we could discuss, these also generally mark transitional episodes and spaces and/or act to distribute or localize various sources of agency.

We will deliberate on the ways in which these "magical" deposits and gestures operated within the social field at Çatalhöyük later. At present we would like to call attention to one potentially significant aspect of these deposits found in buildings. Horizon deposits embedded in the construction layers of buildings and features all asserted a very particular relationship to the human inhabitants: namely, they were placed outside the sphere of direct human engagement. It is possible then that such gestures might have taken on a dedicatory or commemorative aspect, constituting singular, discrete events that inhabited and consolidated power in and of the present. Unlike caching activities, these would not have been explicitly oriented toward the future; that is, they would not have anticipated future human engagements as did caching/retrieving practices. It is to these latter activities that we now turn our attention.

MATTERS OF REVELATION AND CONCEALMENT

Economies of revelation (and concealment) allowed certain powerful things to remain part of the living human world. As much as certain powerful materialities needed to be hidden or set apart from the living household, they also needed to be made a part of that household through periodic revelations or remembrances by a human audience. We suggest that certain practices of object retrieval, wall painting, and figurine making, among others, likely mediated this kind of powerful play between social modalities.

The first two activities compel us to consider more closely the lived surfaces of buildings. Floors and platforms demarcated the boundaries between house and earth, living and dead, the visible and the hidden; they were commonly plastered, sealing the earth below and protecting the living above. Walls similarly delineated and divided living space, but because of their vertical orientation engaged inhabitants in a different manner. All of these surfaces, however, benefited from specific acts of care. People decorated, cleaned, repaired, replastered, and rebuilt house surfaces repeatedly, if not regularly. On floors and platforms, people occasionally dug holes in order to deposit and retrieve things. Notably, however, inhabitants sometimes made an effort to conceal such intrusions by plastering over the scars as if to hide them (e.g., F.1539, F.2389).

1. Caching and Retrieving

Cutting through floor and platform surfaces to store and retrieve buried materials demonstrates the particular memory required for the skilled revelation of concealed things. Such burial and retrieval practices likely anchored specific acts of memory. And it is enticing to consider whether they tapped into the enchanting power of presence and absence, recognizing the agency not only of the boundary crossing, but also of the materials and images to be revealed or hidden. Excavators regularly encounter caches/hoards and retrieval pits, and these constitute obvious interfaces for revelation and concealment. The inhabitants of Çatalhöyük no doubt retained some memory of buildings after they had been abandoned. The building sequences, B.5/1 in the North Area and B.65/56/44 in the South Area, conserved not only the same building layout and plan over three building episodes, but also certain founding and abandonment practices (Hodder and Cessford 2004; Cessford 2007). This memory also extended to the location of certain building elements. In Building 1, an installation or relief had been removed by being dug up after the burned house had been filled in: the retrieval pit (F.17) was dug down very carefully against the wall in the exact location of the sculpture and Hodder and Cessford (2004: 33) estimate that decades may have passed before the sculpture was retrieved.

Obsidian hoards also provide compelling examples of materials stored and retrieved (Carter 2007; Cessford 2007). While not exactly common at the site – fewer than ten obsidian hoards have been identified in the current excavation program – these caches present one of the most striking examples of the practice of revelation and concealment. This idea is further supported by the location of emptied scoops from similar contexts. Cessford describes one example (2007: p. 327).

> The clearest evidence for the deliberate deposition of lithics is the group of 12 obsidian blanks (1460) cached in a small scoop. These were the end product of a complex sequence whereby obsidian was buried and retrieved on several

occasions. As a basin was built directly over them their last deposition was probably intended to be final. Although the blanks are in two sets of six from opposite ends of a core, they do not refit, so although they are in a sense a matching group they are an artificially created one.

Many characteristics of this deposit and sequence are suggestive of a magical presentation, from the distinct and repeated marking of space to the particular arrangement of matched but nonarticulating objects. Here we find the various discourses on magic come together, as distributed agency (of persons, places, and things), revelation and concealment (surface crossing), and repetition (marking through time) appear to constitute a prolonged magical gesture: while the location suggests repeated episodes of deposition and retrieval, this particular assemblage in the final instance served to mark a beginning (of a basin) and ending (of the caching practices).

This assemblage also demonstrates how practices of revelation and concealment (remembering) cannot be easily disentangled from practices of marking (commemorating). Moreover, there seems to be a distinct complementarity between the two practices. In some cases of retrieval or revelation an exchange took place. In some cases, people marked the removal of materials with "offerings" or deposits. Eight of twenty-seven retrieval pits contained some kind of inclusion or deposit. While the deposits are composed of diverse materials, they primarily consisted of plaster, bone and stone tools, and human or animal bones. On the flip side, posthole construction cuts often contained material such as groundstone, which may have lent a supportive function. However, such inclusions could also have participated in acts of marking. A more dramatic example of such marking can be seen in the inclusion of a human female skull (5022) at the bottom of a posthole during the construction phase.

This particular kind of marking practice begs the question: why were certain acts of building and retrieval marked by special deposits while others were not? As mentioned earlier, these sorts of deposits – collections of particular things that appear outside their "normal" contexts of use – are often associated with beginnings and endings and may have targeted a nonhuman or nonliving audience. If the house was regarded as a social being, then such deposits may have been dedicatory in nature or, as Tristan Carter (2007) has suggested for obsidian caches, a gesture that incorporated powerful materials into the house itself.

2. Revealing Figures: Wall Paintings and Clay Figurines

Practices of revelation and concealment were not restricted to the crossing or breaching of surfaces. Some practices involved the transformation of a "surface." The most obvious example can be found in wall-painting practices. Walls hosted periodic painting episodes that were rather quickly covered up with fresh plaster. In this context, the revelatory action required a different kind of skill – that of rendering a new image, rather than revealing an object or group of objects from the past. It is difficult to discern exactly how wall-painting activities operated in the social field. Archaeological analysis tells us that only some buildings had painted surfaces, that in even fewer cases these painted surfaces were decorated (rather than just applied bands of color), and that paintings were visible only intermittently (Hodder 2006: 190). However, from these details we can gather that wall paintings did in fact operate within an economy of revelation (creation) and concealment (plastering over). In addition to the possibility that color itself may have been regarded as magical, an idea that we cannot explore further here (but see Taussig 2009), the temporality of such painting episodes is similar to that of a magical performance. Ephemerality underscores the performance and experience of the painting, rather than the painting itself. And it is this play of presence and absence that conjures force. Furthermore, such play is materially entailed by the wall's specific location and materiality, and by the way the wall and replastering activities come to conceal the painting. The wall thus serves as both a reminder and an effacement of the paintings that lurk underneath its plastered surfaces. In a similar way to the obsidian hoard sequence described previously, such wall-painting sequences – through repeated movements of revelation and concealment – may have served to mark and sacralize particular spaces, at least at particular moments. Alternatively, such marking may have also served to mediate certain social relationships or events and inscribe them in history (time and space). For instance, Barbara Mills (this volume, Chapter 7) argues that certain paintings, such as the bull surrounded by humans dressed in leopard skins, may represent members of a crosscutting alliance, such as initiates into a particular hunting sodality.

In a rather different manner, the abbreviated, expediently made clay figurines most commonly found in rubbish and dumps may also operate under this kind of magical economy of revealing and concealing. Forming a human (or animal) figure from a clay lump, while perhaps requiring minimal skill, does assert a distinctive kind of creative agency through the mimetic act. Some scholars have interpreted these figurine types found primarily in midden and dumping contexts as "wish-vehicles" that were quickly made and perhaps as quickly discarded (Hodder 2006: 190; Pels 2010; Voigt 2000). Again, the focus is on the act of creation or rendering form from an "unformed" surface or medium, rather than the final product. As such, this form of figurine practice could indeed articulate a magical process, whereby the creative and destructive act embodied by the figurine process rendered the human maker a powerful agent in that context (see also Nakamura 2005).

Concluding Remarks

We suggest that these kinds of acts that mark, conceal, and reveal articulate a kind of human-driven economy/technology of social power. It is impossible to know whether the inhabitants of Neolithic Çatalhöyük attributed the creative source of social power to other agents – supernatural or natural, living or dead – or to those among them, but this is, perhaps, beside the point. What is clear is that some idea of a greater collective or abstract power was likely negotiated through materially mediated relationships between living humans and their nonhuman partners: their houses, their dead, various powerful animals and objects. Ian Hodder (2006) and the scholars who participated in the previous Templeton volume (Hodder 2010) have suggested some compelling focal points for spiritual or transcendent practice. The available data come from buildings and suggest complex tensions between, rather than discrete spheres of, wild and domestic, human and animal, and living and dead. That at least some of the dead (primarily human, but occasionally animal) were interred under house floors and various body parts later removed suggests a rather intimate relationship between the living and the dead. The use of animal remains in virtually all realms of social life – to consume, to craft, to hunt, to decorate and incorporate into buildings, and so forth – reveals animals along with clay to be among the most important materials of daily life. Different discourses on magic tell us that such ubiquity does not necessarily translate into their disenchantment, as is often assumed by contemporary Western secularist functionalists. Repetitive articulation can also enhance the power of materials: as modern fetishized commodities show, their very ubiquity may boost rather than deplete their force.

In the latter scenario, it becomes easier to imagine how clay figurines acquire effective agency, or how animal remains embedded in building materials serve to increase the power of a house. In fact, this underscores the point that it makes little sense to try to find evidence for the ethnocentric distinction between magic and religion in the materials themselves. The ubiquity we associate with fetishized commodities can also be found in nonmodern fetishized materials, such as cows among the Tswana (see Comaroff and Comaroff 1992) or, perhaps, the clays and plasters of the Çatalhöyük house.

However, our present focus is less on the power of specific materials and more on investigating possible contexts of magical action through certain material, spatial, temporal, and enacted entailments. In particular we have honed in on practices that mark and empower designated moments and spaces through actions that effectively combine object, human, and other agencies. Some things such as obsidian preforms or (re-)iterations of wall paintings (B.49 and B.80 produced walls with almost identical paintings, one under the other) were meant to be reencountered or recovered, while others were not. Foundation/abandonment burials and deposits, animal parts embedded into walls were not meant to be revealed.

A subtle difference in the nature of certain deposits might hinge on the implicit future act of revelation (or the lack thereof). We might understand this difference in terms of the way in which magical actions conflate or compose distinct temporalities. While some deposits seem primarily to mark events or spaces, others also constitute hidden stores. Although excavators loosely use the term "cache" for both the permanent (unretrieved) and temporary (retrieved) storage of materials in pits or scoops dug into floors and platforms, strictly speaking, a cache – a hidden store – implies the retrieval of its materials at a later date. Materials intended to be left in place might be better described as dedicatory or commemorative deposits. But this distinction is a very evanescent one. In the some postretrieval pits and "emptied" caches, the removal of items apparently precipitated the deposition of others, effecting a kind of exchange: as one thing is revealed something is concealed yet again. In fact, both terms ("cache" and "deposit") are misleading if indeed the act that left these traces has to be thought of as an exchange. We find a similar dynamic in the alternating painting and plastering activities on some walls.

Two points are notable in these acts. First, the different modes of marking (or articulation: Keane 2010) detailed earlier articulate different temporal modalities (cf. Pels 2010). The singular action of placing a deposit "in perpetuity" in a specific location serves to mark a *specific moment* in the present (generally a moment of transition in the Çatalhöyük examples), which, as it recedes into the past, comes to articulate a linear (vertical) historical record. Beyond the present moment at which the space or event became marked, this record would exist for the benefit of those beyond the living realm, those who have come before, those who always persist, and those will come after – in short, it constitutes the realm of myth, folklore, and history. Somewhat differently, the repeated action of concealing and revealing materials, image, or form articulates a *past-to-future movement* in the present. As such, these activities pose a form of active remembering that enables people to maintain an embodied connection to materialities and events in the past. This kind of enacted memory targets living inhabitants as it becomes inscribed in bodily techniques and cultural tradition or guarded knowledge – what Gell once called "technologies of enchantment" (Gell 1992), if the latter term is taken to mean the persuasion needed to convince people of an item's power and importance. Notably, this process of active remembering is also a creative and innovative one, as the past cannot enter into the present unmediated and unchanged. Rather, it becomes inscribed with a new set of social relationships and desires.

Second, both of these forms of "marking" – revelation and concealment and conspicuous marking – that work to sacralize or enchant specific places and moments reveal deposition and retrieval, endings and beginnings as belonging to one in the same gesture. The gesture is the creative power of controlling, shoring up, or exploiting various cracks and gaps in the social fabric. If the confrontation of discourses on magic with the material record at Çatalhöyük produces results, then it will be found in surface economies of revelation and concealment (boundary crossing) and markings that memorialize moments of transformation (boundary inscription). We should not be surprised to find that such oppositional concepts – the making and breaking of boundaries, as it were – might compose a material approach to human-nonhuman transcendent exchanges. Objects and deposits that mark transitions effectively (and paradoxically) memorialize liminality, ephemerality, and ambiguity (Nakamura 2010). Many of these kinds of deposits are regularly but not habitually placed (a notable exception being building "closure" rituals

not discussed in detail here), suggesting a more circumstantial than standardized form of ritualized practice. It thus seems likely that this marking
of liminality was associated with specific events and desires. Yet we cannot fully rely on ritual theory – the source of the concept of liminal states
as moments when established institutions and structures have broken
down – because in ritual theory, liminality is meant to be a *passage* on the
way to restoring stable and normal distributions of power (Turner 1969;
Van Gennep 1960). The emphasis of magical discourse on the uncertainty of the future realization of desire shows why liminal moments are
so dangerous and powerful, since one needs to contain such unregulated
power or take the opportunity to seize control of it. The marking deposits detailed previously then implicate human agency and intentionality in
a rather evocative way: people left traces of their attention, action, and
presence in the very moments and places that would have allowed them
to seize or shore up control and power.

Yet another reason why the articulations that Webb Keane and Peter
Pels started to address in their chapters in the first Templeton volume
(Keane 2010; Pels 2010) cannot be easily "disciplined" by means of
theoretical discourses on religion and ritual is the fact that the placed
deposits and practices of revelation and concealment we have targeted
here – while common to "magic," "religion," and "ritual" – do not
occur in every building; moreover, there are a few intriguing deposits
that occur in midden. In other words, these deliberately placed clusters
invite us to further research whether their frequency and (lack of ubiquity) might be thought of as individual "house magic" instead of the
collective spread we associate with "religion" and "ritual." After all, in
most cases these clusters seem to focus on the structure and life of certain
buildings or building sequences. Time and again, buried and embedded
materials draw our attention to the importance of the house, suggesting
possibly a very specific individual notion of house and household that
does not parse the economic, domestic, and spiritual into discrete categories of thought and practice. Placed deposits evocatively echo certain
aspects of human burial practice on the site (see Russell et al. 2009, and
Mills, this volume), and one potentially productive line of inquiry would
be to explore this relationship more substantively; they also, however,
echo certain expedient practices of storing and dumping. While we may
never gain much insight into how and why certain people, materials,
places, and moments constituted a kind of "magical" force, approaching
such material "bundling" (cf. Keane 2003: 414) through a reinvented

idiom of "magic" may provide a more appropriate frame for understanding a world that was perhaps more concerned with entangling and mixing
than with purifying and separating social experience. Although we have
not discussed all the possible events and contexts of magical egress –
activities in niches, burning, the marking of thresholds with pigment,
to name a few – the cases discussed do suggest that we can significantly
improve our "thinking from the material" by means of such a reinvented
magical idiom, that may even suggest how the building itself appears to
compose a "magical" instrument.

BIBLIOGRAPHY

Appadurai, A., ed. 1986. *The Social Life of Things*. Cambridge: Cambridge
   University Press.
Bell, C. M. 1992. *Ritual Theory, Ritual Practice*. New York: Oxford University
   Press.
Berggren, Å. and L. Nilsson Stutz 2010. From Spectator to Critic and Participant:
   A New Role of Archaeology in Ritual Studies. *Journal of Social Archaeology*
   10(2):171–197.
Bourdieu, P. 1977. *Outline of a Theory of Practice*. Cambridge: Cambridge
   University Press.
Bradley, R. 1991. Ritual, Time and History. *World Archaeology* 23(2):209–219.
   2003. A Life Less Ordinary: The Ritualization of the Domestic Sphere in
   Later Prehistoric Europe. *Cambridge Archaeological Journal* 13(01):5–23.
Brück, J. 1999. Ritual and Rationality: Some Problems of Interpretation in
   European Archaeology. *European Journal of Archaeology* 2:313–344.
Carter, T. 2007. Of blanks and burials: Hoarding obsidian at Neolithic
   Çatalhöyük. In *Technical Systems and Near Eastern PPN Communities.
   Proceedings of the 5th International Worlship. Fréjus 2004*, eds. L. Astruc,
   D. Binder and F. Briols Antibes: Éditions APDCA, 343–355.
Carter, T., Kayacan, N., and M. Milić. 2005 Chipped Stone. In *Çatalhöyük 2005
   Archive Report* Çatalhöyük Research Project.
Carter, T., Conolly, J., Spasojević, A. 2005. The chipped stone. In *Changing
   Materialities at Çatalhöyük: Reports from the 1995–1999 Seasons*, ed. I.
   Hodder. Cambridge: McDonald Institute Monographs and British Institute
   at Ankara, 221–283 and 467–533.
Cessford, C. 2007. Neolithic Excavations in the North Area, East Mound,
   Çatalhöyük. In *Excavating Çatalhöyük: South, North and KOPAL Area
   Reports from the 1995–1999 Seasons*, ed. I. Hodder Cambridge: McDonald
   Institute Monographs British/Institute of Archaeology at Ankara Series.
Comaroff, J., and J. L. Comaroff 1992. Goodly beasts, beastly goods. In
   Ethnography and the Historical Imagination, eds. J. Comaroff and J. L.
   Comaroff. Boulder, CO: Westview Press.

Durkheim, E. [1912]. 1965. *The Elementary Forms of the Religious Life*.London: Allen and Unwin.

Eddisford, D. 2008. Building 49 Archive Report 2008. In *Çatalhöyük 2008 Archive Report*.

Evans-Pritchard, E. E., and Gillies, E. [1937] 1976. *Witchcraft, Oracles, and Magic among the Azande*. Oxford: Clarendon Press.

Fogelin, L. 2007. The Archaeology of Religious Ritual. *Annual Review of Anthropology* 36:55–71.

Gebel, H. G., Hermansen, and Jensen C. H. 2002. *Magic Practices and Ritual in the Near Eastern Neolithic: Proceedings of a Workshop Held at the 2nd International Congress on the Archaeology of the Ancient Near East (ICAANE)*. Copenhagen University, May 2000, Berlin: Ex oriente.

Gell, A. 1992. The enchantment of technology and the technology of enchantment. In *Anthropology, Art and Aesthetics*, eds. J. Coote and A. Shelton Oxford: Oxford University Press, 40–63.

1998. *Art and Agency: An Anthropological Theory*. Oxford: Oxford University Press.

Gosden, C. 1994. *Social Being and Time*. Oxford: Blackwell.

2005. What Do Objects Want? *Journal of Archaeological Method and Theory*, 12(3):193–211.

Gosden, C., and Y. Marshall 1999. The Cultural Biography of Objects. *World Archaeology* 31(2):168–78.

Graeber, D. 2001. *Toward An Anthropological Theory of Value: The False Coin of Our Own Dreams*. New York: Palgrave.

Graves-Brown, P., ed. 2000. *Matter, Materiality, and Modern Culture*. London and New York: Routledge.

Hanegraaff, W. 1998. The Emergence of the Academic Science of Magic: The Occult Philosophy in Tylor and Frazer. In *Religion in the Making: The Emergence of the Sciences of Religion*, eds. A. Molendijk and P. Pels Leiden: Brill.

Hodder, I. 2006. *The Leopard's Tale: Revealing the Mysteries of Çatalhöyük*. London: Thames and Hudson.

ed. 2010. *Religion in in the Emergence of Civilization. Çatalhöyük As a Case Study*. Cambridge: Cambridge University Press.

Hodder, I., and C. Cessford. 2004. Daily practice and social memory at Çatalhöyük. *American Antiquity* 69(1):17–40.

Ingold, T. 2007a. Materials against Materiality. *Archaeological Dialogues* 14(01):1–16.

2007b. Writing Texts, Reading Materials: A Response to My Critics. *Archaeological Dialogues* 14(01):31–8.

Insoll, T. 2004. *Archaeology, Ritual, Religion*. London and New York: Routledge.

Joyce, R. A. 2000. Heirlooms and houses: materiality and social memory. In *Beyond Kinship: Social and Material Reproduction in House Societies*, eds. R. A. Joyce and S. Gillespie Philadelphia: University of Pennsylvania Press, 189–212.

Keane, W. 1997. *Signs of Recognition: Powers and Hazards of Representation in an Indonesian Society.* Berkeley: University of California Press.

1998. Calvin in the tropics: Objects and subjects at the religious frontier. In *Border Fetishisms: Material Objects in Unstable Spaces,* ed. P. Spyer London: Routledge, 13–34.

2002. Sincerity, "Modernity" and the Protestants. *Cultural Anthropology* 17(1):65–92.

2003. Semiotics and the social analysis of material things. *Language and Culture* 23:409–425.

2008. The Evidence of the Senses and the Materiality of Religion. *Journal of the Royal Anthropological Institute* 14(1):110–127.

2010. Marked, absent, habitual: Approaches to Neolithic religion at Çatalhöyük. In *Religion in the Emergence of Civilization. Çatalhöyük as a Case Study,* ed. I. Hodder. Cambridge: Cambridge University Press.

Last, J. 2005. Art. In *Çatalhöyük Perspectives. Reports from the 1995–1999 Seasons,* ed. I. Hodder. Cambridge and London: McDonald Institute for Archaeological Research/British Institute at Ankara.

Latour, B. 2002. What is Iconoclash? Or, is there a world beyond the image wars? In *Iconoclash: Beyond the Image Wars in Science, Religion and Art,* eds. B. Latour and P. Weibel. Karlsruhe/Cambridge, Mass.: ZKM/MIT Press, 16–38.

2005. *Reassembling the Social: An Introduction to Actor-Network-Theory.* Oxford: Oxford University Press.

Malinowski, B. 1925. *Magic, Science and Religion and Other Essays.* New York: Doubleday Anchor Books.

1935. *Coral Gardens and Their Magic.* Vol. II: *The Language of Magic and Gardening.* Bloomington: Indiana University Press.

Marx, K. [1867]1976. *Capital: A Critique of Political Economy, Volume I.* London: Penguin Calssics/New Left Review.

Mauss, M. [1950] 2001. *A General Theory of Magic.* London and New York: Routledge Classics.

1966. *The Gift.* London: Routledge & Kegan Paul.

Mellaart, J. 1962. Excavations at Çatal Hüyük. *Anatolian Studies* 12:41–66.

1967. *Çatal Hüyük: A Neolithic Town in Anatolia.* London: Thames and Hudson.

Meskell, L. M. 2003. Memory's materiality: Ancestral presence, commemorative practice and disjunctive locales. In *Archaeologies of Memory,* eds. S. E. Alcock and R. M. van Dyke Oxford: Blackwell, 34–55.

2004. *Object Worlds from Ancient Egypt: Material Biographies Past and Present.* Oxford: Berg.

ed. 2005. *Archaeologies of Materiality.* Oxford: Blackwell.

Meskell, L. M. and Hodder, I. 2011. A 'Curious and Sometimes a Trifle Macabre Artistry': Some Aspects of the Symbolism of the Neolithic in Anatolia. *Current Anthropology* 52(2):235–263.

Meskell, L. and Preucel, R. W. (eds.). 2004. *Companion to social archaeology.* Oxford: Wiley.

Meyer, B., and Pels, P. (eds.) 2003. *Magic and Modernity. Interfaces of Revelation and Concealment.* Stanford, CA: Stanford University Press.

Milić, 2004. South Summit (Chipped Stone Report). In Çatalhöyük 2004 Archive Report

Miller, D. 1987. *Material Culture and Mass Consumption.* Oxford: Blackwell.

ed. 1993. *Unwrapping Christmas.* Oxford: Clarendon Press.

1998. *A Theory of Shopping.* Cambridge: Polity Press.

ed. 2005. *Materiality.* Durham/London: Duke University Press.

2007. Stone age or plastic age? *Archaeological Dialogues* 14(01):23–7.

Mills, B. J., and W. H. Walker (eds.), (2008). *Memory Work: Archaeologies of Material Practices.* Santa Fe: School for Advanced Research Press.

Munn, N. 1986. *The Fame of Gawa.* Cambridge: Cambridge University Press.

Myers, F. R. 2001. *The Empire of Things: Regimes of Value and Material Culture.* Santa Fe: School of American Research Press.

Nakamura, C. 2004. Dedicating Magic: Neo-Assyrian Apotropaic Figurines and the Protection of Assur. *World Archaeology* 36(1):11–25.

2005. Mastering matters: Magical sense and apotropaic figurines worlds in neo-assyria. In *Archaeologies of Materiality,* ed. L. Meskell Oxford: Blackwell, 18–45.

2010. Magical deposits at Çatalhöyük: A matter of time and place?. In *Religion at the Emergence of Civilization. Çatalhöyük as a Case Study,* ed. I. Hodder Cambridge: Cambridge University Press, 300–331.

Nakamura, C. and Meskell, L. 2004. Figurines and miniature clay objects. In *Çatahöyük 2004 Archive Report.*

Nanoglou, S. 2009. The Materiality of Representation: A Preface. *Journal of Archaeological Method and Theory* 16:157–161.

Pels, P. 1998. The spirit of matter: on fetish, rarity, fact and fancy. In *Border Fetishisms: Material Objects in Unstable Places,* ed. P. Spyder New York: Routledge, 91–121.

1999. *A Politics of Presence. Colonial Contacts between Missionaries and Waluguru in Late Colonial Tanganyika.* Reading and Chur: Harwood.

2003. Introduction. In *Magic and Modernity: Interfaces of Revelation and Concealment,* eds. B. Meyer and P. Pels Stanford, CA: Stanford University Press, 1–38.

2010. Temporalities of Religion at Çatalhöyük. In I. Hodder ed. *Religion at the Emergence of Civilization. Çatalhöyük as a Case Study.* Cambridge: Cambridge University Press, 220–267. .

Pinch, G. 1994. *Magic in Ancient Egypt.* London: British Museum Press.

Regan, R. 2013. The Sequence of Buildings 75, 65, 56, 69, 44 and 10 and External Spaces 119, 129, 130, 144, 299, 314, 319, 329, 333, 339, 367,

371, and 427. In I. Hodder ed. *Çatalhöyük Excavations: the 2000–2008 Seasons.* Los Angeles: Cotsen Institute of Archaeology Press.

Renfrew, C., Gosden, C., and DeMarrais, L. eds. 2005. *Rethinking Materiality.* Cambridge: McDonald Institute for Archaeology.

Russell, N. 2001. The social life of bone: A preliminary assessment of bone tool manufacture and discard at Çatalhöyük. In *Crafting Bone: Skeletal Technologies through Time and Space,* eds. A. M. Choyke and L. Bartosiewicz Oxford: British Archaeological Reports, International Series 937:241–9.

Russell, N., and Meece, S., 2005. Animal representations and animal remains at Çatalhöyük in *Çatalhöyük Perspectives: Themes from the 1995–9 Seasons,* ed. I. Hodder Ankara: McDonald Institute Monographs/British Institute of Archaeology at Ankara, 209–230.

Russell, N., Martin, L., and Twiss, K. C. 2009. Building memories: Commemorative deposits at Çatalhöyük. In *Zooarchaeology and the Reconstruction of Cultural Systems: Case Studies from the Old World,* eds. B. S. Arbuckle, C. A. Makarewicz, and A. L. Atici. Anthropozoologica, 1. Paris: L'Homme et l'Animal, Société de Recherche Interdisciplinaire, 103–128.

Taussig, M. 1998. Viscerality, Faith and Skepticism: Another Theory of Magic. In *In Near Ruins: Cultural Theory at the End of the Century,* ed. N. B. Dirks Minneapolis: University of Minnesota Press, 221–256.

2009. *What Color is the Sacred?* Chicago: University of Chicago Press.

Tilley, C. 2004. *The Materiality of Stone: Explorations in Landscape Phenomenology.* Oxford: Berg.

2007. Materiality in materials. *Archaeological Dialogues* 14(01):16–20.

Turner, V. 1969. *The Ritual Process. Structure and Anti-Structure.* New York: Aldine de Gruyter.

Van Gennep, A. 1960. *The Rites of Passage.* London: Routledge & Kegan Paul.

Verhoeven, M. 2002a. Ritual and Ideology in the Pre-Pottery Neolithic B of the Levant and Southeast Anatolia. *Cambridge Archaeological Journal* 12(2):233–258.

2002b. The Changing Role of Ritual and Symbolism in the PPNB and the PN in the Levant, Syria and South-East Anatolia. *Paléorient* 28(1):5–13.

2011. The many dimensions of ritual. In *Oxford Handbook of the Archaeology of Ritual and Religion,* ed. T. Insoll. Oxford and New York: Oxford University Press, 115–132.

Voigt, M. 2000. Çatal Höyük in context: Ritual at Early Neolithic Sites in Central and Eastern Turkey. In *Life in Neolithic Farming Communities: Social Organization, Identity, and Differentiation,* ed. I. Kuijt New York: Kluwer Academic/Plenum Publishers, 253–293.

Weiner, A. B. 1992. *Inalienable Possessions: The Paradox of Keeping While Giving.* Berkeley: University of California Press.

Weiner, J. 1995. Technology and Techne in Triobrand and Yolungu Art. *Social Analysis* 38: 32–46.

9

"Motherbaby": A Death in Childbirth at Çatalhöyük

Kimberley C. Patton and Lori D. Hager

Introduction

The buried human body is at once both corpse and artifact. As corpse, it is stamped with the biomarkers of a previous existential phase, that is, of animate, gendered, and environmentally situated life, when that body was experienced as "the centre of the world towards which all objects turn their face … the pivot of the world" (Merleau-Ponty 1980: 82; see Meskell 2000: 16). As artifact, it is as much "creation" or ideological representation as any petroglyph, figurine, or built structure. The interred body, physically manipulated and culturally elaborated, is a symbolic entity, a ritualized product of thought. It enacts collective values but also funerary idiosyncrasies: specific responses to the dead individual, both in her past mortal uniqueness and in her new, generic condition. Buried bodies can homologically perform the symbolic structures of their originating society, and vice versa. A skeleton placed in a trapezoidal arrangement from the Late Mesolithic site of Lepenski Vir, and perhaps reiterating the trapezoidal houses there, as Srejovic has suggested, is a dramatic example; this formal mirroring seems to be a kind of mortuary theorem, indicating, as Schulting says, "a powerful metaphor of equivalency between the human body and the structures" (Schulting 1998: 209; Srejovic 1972: 117–118). At Neolithic Çatalhöyük, the funerary-like scouring, caching, sealing, and "burial" of houses, as though they were persons, are hard to construe otherwise. The current excavations show these houses were built in an aggregate, almost-cellular manner, reinscribing the infolded geometric and contiguous spiral patterns of murals on their walls. If the postmortem body remains in any sense "the centre of the world," a static microcosm of the fluid symbolic world it once inhabited, then burials can diagnose key macrocosms – the generative structures of a culture.

When a buried body is that of a late-term pregnant woman, an adult body occulting another complete, miniature human body, the latter ought not to be considered as only an exponent of the former. Both bodies – mother and undelivered child – were almost certainly recognized in some way by the burying community. The anticipated result of maternal labor is birth: the appearance of the newborn, a differentiation of one into two. Before the x-ray or ultrasound, birth was a revelation of what had been invisible. In the case of death in childbirth, the failure of such differentiation does not necessarily mean only one is buried. Depending on the particular culture, any religious ethnography of such burials still might need to account for *both* bodies. Each may have been a focus of mortuary attention; or the two nested bodies, one manifest and the other hidden, may have been construed as a dyadic whole. Here Marilyn Strathern's concept of the *dividual*, the idea, as Lauren Talalay summarizes, "that persons and bodies are not irreducibly unique and bounded units, but composite and divisible entities that interact throughout their lifetimes, creating and defining a variety of shifting relationships," may well be of interpretive usefulness (Strathern 1988: 13, 348–349n; Talalay forthcoming). This may well be extended into the realm of death, especially in the Neolithic, where burials sometimes ritually recombine the remains of more than one individual.

Such attention may not have been identically measured for mother and fetus, and then not in the proportions we might expect. Particularly in prehistoric contexts, interpretively privileging the body of the dead adult mother may reflect uninterrogated, presentist assumptions about the value of an adult over an undelivered full-term fetus. In the case of Çatalhöyük, where fetal (9 percent) and neonatal (41 percent) bodies constitute fully half (50 percent) of foundation burials, with infants accounting for another 14 percent, dead babies were clearly not seen as expendable, but instead as in some important ways vital to the health of the newly built house and thus efficacious for the community.

The potential for impregnation is one of the quintessential markers of female gender in human history; because the production of living infants is necessary for collective survival, pregnancy and childbirth are often highly saturated categories in cultural traditions and their religious hypostases. For example, the colossal, ochre-colored carved monolith depicting the clawed Aztec goddess of night, the underworld, and the dead, Tlaltecuhtli, found at the perimeter of Templo Mayor in 2006 by the team lead by Leonardo López Luján, squats in the birth-giving position above what may be the royal grave of Ahuizotl (d. 1502), seven braided blood flows cascading between her legs (López Luján 2010). Skulls appear at her elbows and knee joints. Çatalhöyük has given prehistory its own icon of divinized childbirth, Mellaart's feline-enthroned clay figurine found in a grain bin, with what seems to be the head of a child – or, alternatively, a skull – emerging between her feet. There are many other examples in the history of religious iconography. These are often theorized within a teleology of fertility. Female childbearing has been mystified in historical anthropology, or even construed as so powerful that blood sacrifice, patrilineally controlled, was universally created by male élites to be its artificial political antidote (Jay 1992).

What may have been a gendered act of power in cultural ideation, however, has always been a state of extreme vulnerability in human lives. Over the course of human evolution, as the size of the fetal cranium and shoulders grew commensurate with the enlarging adult brain and body size, the female human pelvis could correspondingly enlarge only so much, as a result of biomechanics related to bipedalism. Maternal (pelvic)-fetal (head) constraints for modern humans are tight as a result, often leading to complicated labors and deliveries. The ancient dual inhumation that we will explore in this chapter highlights an important contemporary tension, namely, how the medicalization of childbirth and the increasingly high rate of cesarean sections in "developed" nations have obscured the lethal risk that pregnancy and childbirth continue to pose throughout the globe.

Until very recently, maternal mortality threatened every woman everywhere during every pregnancy and childbirth, even through the deadly late nineteenth century in Europe and America, when puerperal fever spread by doctors themselves in hospitals killed hundreds of thousands of women. Maternal death continues to be a killer of women in developing countries, where 99 percent of the 500,000 deaths from childbirth or from complications during pregnancy occur, with 50 percent of women delivering without the assistance of skilled health personnel; one-half of these occur in Sub-Saharan Africa and one-third in South Asia. "A woman in sub-Saharan Africa has a 1 in 16 chance of dying in pregnancy or childbirth, compared to a 1 in 4,000 risk in a [First

World] country – the largest difference between poor and rich countries of any health indicator" (UNICEF 2012; WHO 2012). The most common cause of maternal death in the developing countries is obstetrical hemorrhage (25 percent), followed by deep vein thrombosis and pulmonary embolism (20 percent); in industrialized nations, such forms of venous thromboembolism are the leading cause of maternal death associated with childbirth. The risk to any woman anywhere of developing venous thromboembolism is five to six times greater when she is pregnant (Bourjeily et al. 2010: 500–512). Infections, unsafe abortions, eclampsia, obstructed labor, homicide, indirect factors such as malaria, anemia, HIV/AIDS, and cardiovascular disease account for the balance of causes of maternal death.

We mention such "facts on the ground" to complicate any assumptions about how pregnancy and childbirth were construed in prehistoric cultures. Ethnographic comparanda from classical traditions are far from simple. For example, the ferociously birth-giving Aztec deity Tlaltecuhtli also ate the dead; she was so malignant that her image was always buried face down, looking into her home world, the Templo Mayor vault cover being the lone exception to date. Aztec women who died in childbirth were said to be warriors who had sacrificially "taken a man captive," that is, taken a life – the fetus – on the battlefield of their own wombs. Such women would enjoy a glorious afterlife as hummingbirds, traveling with the solar god Huitzilopochtli each day across the sky. In our view, to claim that pregnancy and live childbirth were always idealized as emblematic of superabundant vitality in Neolithic Çatalhöyük would be greatly to underestimate their attendant ambiguity and danger; their intimate entanglement with dying mothers, dead babies, or both; and the ultimate sterility that death deals. And death in childbirth may well not have been understood as an unambiguous tragedy, but rather, as a catalyst to postmortem heroization: "life in child-death."

An unusual double burial from House B60, found in 2006, seems to magnify and choreograph these tensions. The season's field report lists "One notable burial was that of a pregnant female and with her full-term foetus in the pelvic and abdominal areas. It seems likely they died during childbirth" (Boz et al. 2006: 157). These two were the focus of those who buried them. *How* they were buried is ours.

"Dead Bodies That Were Also Buried Treasure"

In his *Anatomy of the Psyche*, Edward Edinger reports a complicated dream-within-a-dream. The dreamer is attending a party for a dead friend, and the friend is relating a dream he had before his death:

> Its major image was a great circle of grain standing 80 inches high. It grew out of a pit in the earth which contained dead bodies that were also buried treasure. The dreamer [the dead friend] was trying to convey to his friend the importance of the dream. (Edinger 1985: 162)

Our challenge concerns such a pit, a multiple burial in a relatively large albeit eroded house (B60) dating from around 6600/6500 BCE in Ceramic Çatalhöyük. A "history house," in Ian Hodder's designation, because of the evidence for rebuilding and the number of burials – its collective "treasure" – B60 was excavated in 2006 in the 4040 Area of the East Mound. Situated directly on top of House 59, which was itself built atop an earlier house, House 60 contained an oven or hearth installation, a ladder scar, two engaged pillars, a bench, and six platforms. Three burial features were found. To the east, under a relatively large platform (F.2225), were discovered two burial cuts: one containing a crouched infant burial, and the other, a burial pit of eight individuals from multiple burial events, several of which rearranged or disturbed preceding burials (F.2232) (Çatalhöyük Database: Building 60).

The excavation of the pit, the inaugural burial feature in the house, offered a poignant relic at the bottom: the concentric skeletons of a young adult woman (Sk 13162), aged between twenty and thirty years, and her full-term fetus (Sk 13163), with its skull lodged in the birth canal of its mother. The pregnant woman was found on her right side in the crouched position common to Çatalhöyük burials. Her right knee was loosely drawn to her chest while the left one lay against the woman's thorax (Figure 9.1a). Both of her arms were bent, with hands flexed backward at the wrists at an unusual angle, enacting the circular, almost mandalic layout of a typical crouched burial, and reiterating the shape of most of the site's burial pits that contain them.

The presence of an undelivered full-term fetus is not a guarantee of obstetrical death; meningitis or other infectious diseases are also possible candidates. In fact, the B60 mother exhibited a bony spur on one of

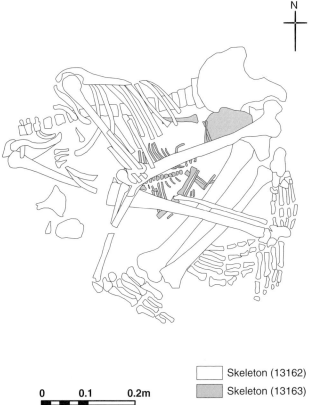

9.1. (a) A pregnant young adult female who died with her full-term fetus engaged in the birth canal. Later, the young woman's head was taken and the upper neck vertebrae displaced (left center); (b) schematic drawing of "motherbaby" in situ by D. Mackie and C. Hall. Courtesy of the Çatalhöyük Research Project. *Source*: Çatalhöyük Research Project.

her pelvic bones that may have impacted success at delivery, and she was suffering from a mild infection. She may well have bled to death from an abrupted placenta or some other-sourced fatal hemorrhaging. Although the infant appeared in a normal cephalic presentation for birth (head-downward), in July 2011, Joseph Hill, MD, an obstetrical specialist, examined the photograph of the position of the fetus and noted the tight flexure of the legs at the hips with the right tibia and fibula extended from the femur toward the fetal skull, which was pressing into the maternal ischial bone: in Hill's words, "an undeliverable lie" (Hill 2011). Mother and baby almost certainly died in the final stages of childbirth.

When the grave of the Building 60 woman was reopened to sever and remove her skull, and perhaps at the same time to inter the adult male near her, the skull and bones of the baby she was unable to deliver would have been revealed at last within her decomposing womb. The schematic drawing in Figure 9.1b gives a sense of how this postmortem "birth" might have looked.

In addition to its status as "first-in" the pit, the burial is ritually distinctive in other ways. The adult female skull is missing, taken after death; this is therefore one of only eighteen headless skeletons of the nearly four hundred individuals found at the site to date. In the process of severing her cranium from her spinal column, the woman's upper cervical vertebrae were displaced, leaving some still scattered in the pit; therefore, skull removal would have occurred after she had been buried for some time, but before full ligamental decomposition was complete, so perhaps a year or so after her death. In addition, there are grave goods of note. A basket (13470.s1) of indeterminate plant remains was found beneath her (Ryan: in press), and green pigment found in close association with a rounded bone point was deposited at her right knee (Meskell and Nakamura: in press).

Also buried in the same pit of Building 60, directly above and to the north of this pregnant woman, was a partial skeleton of some note (Sk 13133). A young adult, probably male, consisting of only the skull and lower jaw, arms, and legs, had been carefully placed in a simulated crouched position, with its head nearly superimposed over the cavity where the woman's skull had been before removal. The deposition of the partial skeleton of the young male and the removal of the woman's head appear to be related events. The excavators comment: "There is no evidence to suggest the dismemberment (of the male) happened in the grave pit. Sk 13133 therefore represents a secondary deposit. That this secondary deposit is related to the female who was headless and died in childbirth is highly probable but this cannot be known with complete certainty." Five other skeletons were interred above these basal three (Çatalhöyük Database: Sk 13133).

This Çatalhöyük woman and her full-term fetus never completed their separation into two bodies and two identities, mother and child. The burial freezes a paradigmatic human event at a liminal moment. One cannot pause too long at the threshold of childbirth and survive. One can call this the burial of a pregnant woman. Or one can see it in a more dynamic and osmotic way. The two were buried as one complex entity, the larger maternal skeleton enfolding the smaller unborn child. The mother's flexed burial position at the same time mirrors her baby's enfolded body during the last two trimesters of pregnancy, when confined and growing fetuses grow too big for major movements.

Why did this unlucky woman receive this kind of postmortem focus? Did the cause of her death figure in the special idioms of her burial, especially the feature of skull removal? The burial of these skeletons in the platform of a house, human remains that would have only been revealed as a twosome after the mother's decomposition, was particular. Meskell has noted that, of those buried under house platforms, "only a few were selected for special treatment" (Meskell 2008: 383). Talalay asks, "Who was selected for postmortem decapitation and were the decapitations hostile or benignly ceremonial (presumably following natural causes of death?)" (Talalay 2004: 152). If we concede that this was a complex rather than a simple burial, a plural as well as a singular event, then any valid interpretation would need to attend to the religious value of both mother *and* infant – both separately and in relation to one another. Such an interpretation would also need to bracket assumptions about which individual was considered more valuable or powerful in the ideologies of death at Çatalhöyük – which individual may have been the focus of any special funerary attention. Was it the mother, the undelivered infant, or both?

High rates of maternal mortality were probable in the Neolithic, particularly for births subsequent to primigravidity. The epidemiological debate on the "Neolithic mortality crisis" aside, sedentary settlement patterns after the development of domestication may well have contributed to shorter child-spacing intervals than found in exclusively hunter-gatherer populations, and thus to maternal nutritive deficiencies and osteodepletion (Caldwell and Caldwell 2003: 153–168). The implications of biological affinity between individuals in shared graves or in graves in the same structure toward parsing the organization of social systems have become vital topics at Çatalhöyük (Pilloud and Larsen 2011). Maternal mortalities, though rare, are significant in that they offer incontrovertible evidence of genetic relationship between interred individuals. Absent DNA analysis (as was recently conducted, for example, for the extracted, mummified fetuses in the tomb of Tutankhamen), such affinity cannot be asserted with certainty between adult females and the neonates, infants, or children in their graves.

Yet only a small proportion of the total number of female skeletons archaeologically recovered have been found with the fetus impacted in the pelvis from among thousands of excavated skeletons from the Neolithic. Interestingly, such cases are also oddly anomalous in the paleopathological record. Citing the very few known prehistoric examples of death in childbirth from across Europe and in pharaonic Egypt, the British obstetrician and medical historian Calvin Wells observed, "The interesting feature of these obstetric calamities is their rarity. The few indubitable examples which have been excavated would make virtually no difference to the sex ratio in any of the populations in which they occurred" (Wells 1975: 1237). The size of fetal bones, even though sometimes heavily mineralized, and the way they are intermingled with the bones of mothers are almost certainly a factor impeding the identification of maternal mortalities. Lori Hager, coauthor of this chapter, who excavated the House 60 platform and burial pit in 2006, comments that "at first it was hard to see" that the adult female skeleton contained another tiny skeleton (Hager 2011). Anna Belfer-Cohen, excavator of Hayonim Cave and Hilazon Tachtit Cave, noted an overlooked fetal skeleton after the Natufian adult female skeleton had been archived in the lab and says the same (Belfer-Cohen 2011). The tiny size and fragility of fetal skeletons, as well as the decomposition of corporeal markers (such as distended abdomen or swollen breasts), may account for a number of "missed diagnoses" of death in childbirth in other Neolithic female skeletons. Nevertheless there remains a puzzling lacuna in the archaeological record, not entirely attributable to poor preservation or oversight. Where are the deaths in childbirth?

As is found elsewhere in the Neolithic period, the inhabitants of Çatalhöyük buried the majority of their dead not outside their living spaces, but rather intimately *within* such spaces, shallowly installed under the floors of their houses; in walls; or in benches, sometimes surrounded by the horns of wild animals. Using razor-sharp obsidian tools, they also practiced a sophisticated dismemberment of the bodies of the "fresh dead," including on occasion the retrieval, recombination, and reinterment of particular bones from older houses into the fabric of newer ones on directly successive levels. Perhaps for the Çatalhöyükians, as the Senegalese poet Birago Ishmael Diop wrote, "Those who are dead are never gone … the dead are not dead" (Diop 1948, trans. John 1961); perhaps the dead were conceived in some sense as living a new life. Their bodies were valuable and potent. It was essential therefore to keep them close at hand – "buried treasure" whose curatorial demands were both precise and constant. The generative power of the dead seems to have been concentrated in their bones. The lengthy later histories of relic veneration in Buddhist, Christian, and Islamic traditions show that the bones of the special dead – mirroring stone in their hardness and permanence – were primary repositories of charisma, vehicles of history making; decomposing flesh was less so, and hence the rarer fleshy relics of the saints and *arhat*s were called incorruptible, that is, like bone (Trainor 2010). To bury the dead into Neolithic houses was, perhaps, then to produce bones that would animate buildings and make them into crucibles of power. Such power could also be transferred through the vehicle of bones, like transferring money between bank accounts, moving batteries, or transplanting organs.

At Çatalhöyük, the separation of flesh, sinews, and ligaments from bones may have been an important metaphorical process. This would have made its acceleration an important goal. Such ideas may anticipate similar concepts in the Bronze Age Mycenaean world, reflected, for example, in how inhumations were sequentially treated in the tholos tombs at Mycenae: revered at first but then chaotically pushed aside after decomposition, or, however anachronistically, in what the Homeric epics sing of heroic cremation, that is, that the destruction of ligaments by fire liberated the *psyche* of the dead to its ultimate destination. Another example would be the rotation of bodies after a year in the shelf graves of imperial era Palestinian family tombs, reflected in the New Testament Passion narratives. In Mediterranean antiquity, then, the soul was entangled in the body only so long as bound to the bones by fleshy ropes. In this liminal condition, the dead might be available to the living as oracles or, more commonly, threatening to them as revenants or pests. If this was Neolithic thinking at Çatalhöyük or elsewhere, it may have been that human beings took control of this process using skull removal and excarnation.

Could bones regenerate flesh? Or was it instead that abundant life's obverse was always the reverse of the familiar, intimate face of death, so that mutable flesh was always understood to be the clothing of powerful, permanent bones? An enigmatic figurine found in 2005 in the Istanbul Area seems to oscillate symbolically between skeleton and extrafleshy female (Özbaşaran 2005: 91; Meskell and Nakamura 2005: 168) (Figure 9.2). It "revolves," like the oval humanoid face–bucranium pot found two years later in a 4040 Area midden and reconstructed by Nurcan Yalman (Hodder 2007: 3, fig. 5).

Ian Hodder described this artifact in the *2005 Archive Report*: "There are full breasts on which the hands rest, and the stomach is extended in the central part.... As one turns the figurine around one notices that the arms are very thin, and then on the back of the figurine one sees a depiction of either a skeleton or the bones of a very thin and depleted human. The ribs and vertebrae are clear, as are the scapulae and the main pelvic bones.... [This] is a unique piece that may force us to change our views of the nature of Çatalhöyük society and imagery" (Hodder 2005: 2, fig. 4). We will consider this figurine later.

Childbearing as Dominant Metaphor at Çatalhöyük

While every burial potentially serves as an interpretive lens on the much wider circles of its cultural matrix, we believe this one may be of particular importance. On the one hand, it is a black swan, with no analogues thus far at the site and extremely few elsewhere in the archaeological record. On the other, a death in childbirth catalyzes preoccupations both prehistoric and modern. The grail of transcendentalized childbirth looms large in Çatalhöyük's status of "firstness" in the history of religion, one of the primary lenses through which the city has become renowned as a religious or symbol-saturated site. This "firstness" was, from the time of James Mellaart's excavation, marked by divine fertility. "The Goddess" whom Mellaart lionized at Çatalhöyük was a goddess who gave birth. Her *live* birth giving he saw ubiquitously as a theme and read it into many of the finds of the first excavation. For decades after the city's

9.2. Headless figurine (12401.x 7) recovered from the Istanbul Area of the East Mound: (a) front, (b) back, and (c) side views.
Source: Çatalhöyük Research Project.

9.2 *(continued)*

rediscovery, it was one of the root metaphors in the reconstructed religious imagination of Çatalhöyük, accepted as such not only by feminist
archaeologists and later neopagan goddess religions, but also by scholars
of classical Mediterranean religion of the caliber of Walter Burkert. The
totem par excellence was Mellaart's famous clay statuette of the grain bin
(Figures 3.2 and 9.3), of which Marija Gimbutas wrote, "This majestic
enthroned Goddess, flanked by felines, is giving birth to the child who
emerges from between her legs" (Gimbutas 2001: 107, fig. 177c). The
geometrically patterned, splayed-figure relief of "Shrine VII.23," with
its protruding herniated umbilicus outlined twice in concentric circles of
red ochre, seemed to be another family portrait of this goddess, similarly
birth-giving. For his part, Burkert saw in the relief and the statuette an
Anatolian predecessor to the Asia Minor Great Mother with her leopard
retinue, and to the early Greek *potnia theron*, "clearly the birth-giving
mother of the animals and of life itself" (Burkert 1985: 12).

That which Paul Ricœur called "the enigma of anteriority" (Ricœur
1998: 100), primordiality has a way of receding, as ever-older instances
of reifications such as "religion," "art," or "abstract thought" appear.
The most recent recension of the story of religious "firstness" dates from

9.3. Detail of object between feet of figurine of an enthroned adult female with felines in Mellaart's "Shrine AII.1." For full figurine see Figure 3.2.
Source: Alan Mellaart and Çatalhöyük Research Project.

1994, when Klaus Schmidt and the Deutsches Archäologisches Institut began to uncover the monumental shrinelike stone edifices of Göbekli Tepe in southeastern Turkey (9600–8200 BCE), carved with fluid programs of giant anthropoids and animals, some ithyphallic, almost all male. "The animals were guardians to the spirit world," comments Schmidt, echoing Jacques Cauvin's "revolution of symbols," which postulated for the first time human consciousness of supernatural beings. "The reliefs on the T-shaped pillars illustrated that other world" (Schmidt in Mann 2011: 57) This intensely masculinized cult site, distinctive for its apparent lack of contiguous settlement and the possibility that it was built by hunter-gatherers who only began to grow einkorn wheat to supply its continual rebuilding, precedes and problematizes the "goddess" iconographies of Çatalhöyük (Banning 2001, esp. discussion). Göbekli Tepe suggests a gendered history of Neolithic religions that is more stippled than the dominant narrative of divinized childbirth, or at least an alternative pantheon seven hundred kilometers away and two millennia earlier.

The Çatalhöyük evidence itself has already undermined this narrative, however, as Meskell has shown (Meskell 1999, 2007). No comparable representations of the seated grain bin goddess have been found. A small terracotta stamp with bear head intact from the fill of a Level V (South P) building in the East Mound may refigure the wall reliefs as bears. If the Istanbul Area figurine does depict pregnancy in some way, it shows impending childbirth as married, not to superabundant life, but to the bone lattice of death.

Because the Building 60 woman is a rare example of a woman who died in the final stages of childbirth, how her burial was handled impacts our understanding of the thought world of Çatalhöyük. As we said earlier, she is both corpse and artifact. As corpse, she belongs to the category of "human remains" or "burial data." But as artifact, we would argue, she and her undelivered child can be considered along with the range of other iconographic evidence from the site pertaining to religious and cultural ideations of pregnancy and childbirth. We can interrogate this now more extended category of evidence, including the group of neonates, infants, and very young children who were often buried in very specific kinds of locations. Our goal is a robust comprehension of how the psychosomatic experience of pregnancy and childbirth, identity-defining and life-threatening for women, manifested in Çatalhöyük, and how such lived experience intersected with local theologies and practices.

Mamatoto: Challenges of Interpreting a Maternal Mortality at Çatalhöyük

In 2008, an American advocate for midwifery noted that "'mamatoto' is a Swahili word meaning 'motherbaby' – reflecting the concept that mother and infant are not two separate people, but an interrelated dyad" (CFM 2008) The umbilicus and highly permeable placental barrier, as well as permanently exchanged cell populations between mother and fetus, biologically reinforce what Swahili culturally iterates. Existential categories that other languages separate can form composite dyads in this Central and East African linguistic system (analogous is the Swahili word "living-dead," which refers to those who are dead but are still alive, both in the memories of the living and in oracular possession to offer advice; one is not fully dead until one is completely forgotten). Whereas the idea of a dyadic human entity, neither strictly singular nor dual, might be palatable in the limited condition of pregnancy, the philosophical

challenges of Siamese twins are starker: Consider the case of the four-
year-old Vancouver twins Krista and Tatiana Hogan, who are conjoined
at the skull and apparently share a neural bridge that allows either twin
literally to feel, see, and hear what the other is experiencing, to think
what the other is thinking. They share not only a brain, but also, apparently, a mind: Are they one or two? (Dominus 2011).

We suggest the term "motherbaby" (*mamatoto*) as a heuristically
valuable lens through which to investigate the woman and fetus buried
in House 60. They represent a complex burial of two skeletons interconnected in death, as they were in life, an assemblage with correlative,
mutually reinforcing semiotic elements, each dependent on the whole
matrix. This burial could instead be viewed concentrically rather than as
an adult female skeleton with impacted fetus, bone pin, and basket. It
is possible that the liminal neonate, dying at the threshold, was thought
to be at the purposive and performative center of the assemblage, with
meaning radiating outward.

The four assemblage elements that distinguish this particular burial
from others at Çatalhöyük are (1) its chronological status as an inaugural burial, the first into the pit of the platform feature in a history house;
(2) the placement of a bone point and green pigment with the pregnant
woman's composite body, an infrequent grave association at Çatalhöyük;
(3) the placement of a woven basket underneath the body/bodies; (4)
the removal of the mother's skull, one of only eighteen headless skeletons out of the nearly four hundred individuals whose remains or partial
remains have been found to date. With the understanding that these elements mutually refract one another, we consider each in turn.

1. INAUGURAL BURIAL IN BUILDING

The initial grave in the house was dug for this "motherbaby," the adult
female and fetus who established the location of the pit in the platform
and its subsequent usage for several more burials over the life of the
house (Figure 9.4).

The partial skeleton, a young male, buried above the "motherbaby"
was the next interment in the house; the relationship between the two
individuals buried within a year of each other is unclear. Was the male
the father of the female's unborn child? Was he her brother or otherwise related to her through biologically- or nonbiologically based, what
Pilloud and Larsen (2011) call "practical" – kinship? As noted earlier,

9.4. A reconstruction of the burial scene for the young woman who died in childbirth in Building 60. By Mesa Schumacher. Note that the basket was found under the belly of the pregnant corpse, not beside it, as depicted.
Source: Çatalhöyük Research Project. Artist: K Killackey.

the secondary skull of the probable male was placed near the void where her skull would have been. Perhaps this represents a kind of "composite" manipulation of bones to create a new, androgynous skeleton. We do have other headless burials where an extraneous skull was introduced; for example, in Building 42 (see later discussion) or in Building 1, where in burial F.29 the articulated skeleton of a mature headless adult male 1466 ("C." in Hodder's discussion) was found with "the skull of an old individual (1928) in the northwest part of the grave under the right elbow of 'C.'; both these elements appear deliberately placed ... "[since] the old individual (1928) is solely represented by a skull" (Hodder 2006: 224).

The first burials in the excavated houses at Çatalhöyük consist of both juveniles and adults, although neonates and infants are commonly found. Foundation layer burials, that is, those not only first-in but found at the construction level, are dominated by neonates followed distantly by infants and fetuses, often placed in the southwest area of the house or space at an early stage of construction. Foundation burials occur more frequently in the upper than the lower levels of the Çatalhöyük sequence

(South Q and later; North G and later), signaling an increased focus over time on placing the neonates in the bases of their houses. Stratigraphically, Building 60 was in use during the upper or later levels of the mound, North Level H, which was characterized by its high number of neonates relative to infants, children, and adults. As we mentioned, of twenty-two foundation burials, 41 percent are neonates; combined juvenile categories account for 73 percent of this type of burial. The prevalence of neonates in the foundation levels was noted in eight buildings in the sequence of houses, including the continuous Buildings 65-56-44-10, dug by Roddy Regan in 2006 and 2007; one of these may represent a set of twins. While juveniles constitute a large body of the inaugural burials, adults were of some significance in these contexts. One foundation burial of an older female from Building 42 was found with a plastered skull of a possible female in her arms. In Building 1, three neonates were buried at the threshold of the central area of the house and a side room. Was the woman in House 60 an inaugural burial because she contained a fetus?

2. ROUNDED BONE POINT WITH GREEN PIGMENT

The second notable feature of the 4040 House 60 "motherbaby" was the presence of a rounded bone point (13147.x1) with green pigment. Located near her right knee, the associated materials were likely placed over her abdomen containing the deceased baby. The bone point was made from a fox foot bone. As noted by Boz and Hager in their recent comprehensive survey and analysis of human remains at Çatalhöyük (2013), the rounded bone point is a relatively rare burial feature. Of the four people buried with green pigment, all are associated with bone tools. Besides the young female and her fetus, an infant from Building 3 had both the green pigment and bone point. Other than the infant, the other individuals with green pigment were adult females. It should be noted that blue pigment is also found infrequently with burials. Three instances of blue pigment occurred in a burial context with two adult females and one infant. One of these adult females also had a rounded bone point. Neonates tend to have fewer pigments overall compared to infants and children. The individuals associated with the blue and green pigments are from the upper levels of the Çatalhöyük sequence (Boz and Hager: in press; Meskell and Nakamura: in press).

Nerissa Russell and Janet Griffits have suggested the round bone point was used on soft materials such as hides or flesh (Russell and Griffits: in press). Specifically, they believe the blunt tools were used to apply pigments or other minerals. Moreover, the individuality of the points is indicated by the varying nature of their bases in conjunction with their rare occurrence with burials. Were the bone point and green pigment grave goods for the unborn infant rather than for the adult mother? Or were these items directly associated with both mother and fetus?

3. BASKET FOUND UNDER SKELETON OF "MOTHERBABY"

The remains of a woven basket were discovered under the mother and child. At Çatalhöyük, burial baskets were used for infants and less frequently for neonates. As a rule, adults were not buried with baskets. Boz and Hager note, "Phytoliths of plant remains that could have been used to prepare the body for interment, including binding, wrapping, or clothing have been found with 53 individuals at Çatalhöyük. Neonates and infants have been found enveloped in phytoliths, suggesting lidded baskets were used to inter them." (Boz and Hager: in press). The use of funerary baskets for infants and very young children has been studied by Arlene Rosen (2005) and Willeke Wendrich (2005), who suggest that in some cases baby baskets were made of plants not used for other items, while in other cases the baskets associated with babies were worn, suggesting use of the basket for other purposes prior to use for interment. Given the extremely high association of baskets with the burials of neonates and infants, the basket beneath the corpse of the woman may have actually been associated more closely with the lost child.

4. HEADLESSNESS/SKULL REMOVAL

Finally, unlike those of the other skeletons in her pit, the pregnant woman's head was removed, severed some time after her initial burial, as indicated by her scattered cervical vertebrae. This makes her one of only eighteen headless skeletons discovered at the site thus far, including adults and juveniles, mostly males but also a few females. As we continue to track the mortuary treatment of infants, it is perhaps worth noting that the only bodiless infant skull of twenty-four, found in Building 44, was given unusual treatment; it was embedded in a bench (Boz and Hager: in press). In the Neolithic period, skull removal was a particular sign of "specialness," memory, and possibly regeneration, as has been eloquently discussed in recent years by Lauren Talalay (2004), Ian Kuijt (2008), and Lynn Meskell (2008: 375–381), among others. Skulls were removed and secondarily treated throughout the Levant, famously at Jericho and 'Ain Ghazal, but there are plastered skulls reminiscent of those at Jericho as well at Koşk Höyük in central Antolia and in one instance at Çatalhöyük. Not every skull in the Neolithic period was removed, but those that were, were often either established at "shrine"-like rooms, like the one reported by Mellaart (his "E.VII.21," currently interpreted as a dwelling that was ritually treated in the context of abandonment; Hodder 2006: 146), or reburied in a position of veneration or cherishing – a classic example being the grave discussed earlier at the foundation of Building 42 when it was built, that of a woman who cradles a skull in her arms; the skull itself is "coated in several layers of plaster, each of which had been painted red" (Hodder 2006: 148 and pll. 13 and 14). Hodder notes the high level of individualization at the site, whereas in similar burials in the Levant and southeastern Turkey, "caches of skulls are often found," "[at] Çatalhöyük the plastered skull is individualized" (Hodder 2006: 148). In discussing a burial from Building 6, in which a wooden plank and phytoliths, evidence of a possible woven cloth cover, were carefully superimposed on a torso later made headless after burial, Hodder has further remarked that such evidence suggests that "when bodies were buried it was known whether the head would later be removed" (Hodder 2006: 147) In most cases, however, there is no indication that the Neolithic people marked the location of the head in anticipation of head removal.

Gender Issues and Maternal Mortality

We began by observing that whereas the gender of human bones cannot always be determined with certainty, a skeleton such as Sk 13162 is easily sexed since she contained the fetus within her. She died in full-term pregnancy, and childbirth almost certainly killed her. We asked whether the most likely cause of the woman's death catalyzed her special ritual treatment in Building 60. In funerary ethnography elsewhere, the cause of death does determine the manner of burial. (To cite only a few examples, in some Native American cultures, the cause of death influences postmortem treatment of the dead; in Jewish and Islamic traditions, martyrs are buried in their bloody garments rather than washed; and in the Roman Church, up until very recently, suicides or unbaptized babies could not be buried in church graveyards.) Was this the case for the Building 60 motherbaby?

In order effectively to interrogate the ritual logic of this evocative burial, it may be necessary first reflexively to interrogate our own ideas about pregnancy, childbearing, and mortality. This approach draws analogously from the theoretical challenge to categories of "gender" made by Marilyn Strathern in *The Gender of the Gift*: "By 'gender' I mean those categorizations of persons, artifacts, events, sequences, on so on which draw upon sexual imagery – upon the ways in which the distinctiveness of male and female relationships make concrete people's ideas about the nature of social relationships. Taken simply to be 'about' men and women, such categorizations have often appeared tautologous" (Strathern 1988: ix–x). Some such questions are suggested here; later, we will review how the data from Çatalhöyük may respond to them in culturally unexpected ways, revealing tautologies equally ingrained by modern Western patterns of thought.

Reflexive Questions

1. Should the identity of a pregnant female from any period be construed as essentially singular, with her fetus as a maternal "attribute," modifying the adult mother? Or, if we believe the fetus is/was construed as separately personified, should we assume that it has/had a value assigned as subordinate to that of the mother?
2. Live childbirth (the birth of a living child) is the fundamental, defining power of the "Great Goddess" contested in Old European religious history; it drives the interpretation of Mellaart's enthroned goddess as giving birth, newborn between her legs.

Is *live* childbirth always to be understood in every culture at every time as a root metaphor for universal fertility? As a corollary, is the production of *living* infants a universally held goal? Should childbearing always be assumed to be the centrifuge of religious awe in any society or community?

3. In death, modern and postmodern anthropologies usually locate some form of pollution, unresolved social tension, or threat to the future viability of the community; it follows that these instabilities must be carefully managed. Is death always to be construed in these ways (polluting and destabilizing)? Is human death always a severe diminishment of human power, extinguishing individual efficacy as well as collective loss, tearing the social fabric?

4. In any given culture, does maternal mortality – the death of a woman in childbirth – necessarily represent a tragic or inauspicious failure of the life cycle?

5. As a corollary, does the preterm death of a fetus or a stillbirth – the production of a dead, rather than a living infant – also invariably constitute a tragedy, a failure of ritual intentionality and of fertility?

6. Are dead babies the ultimate powerless individuals? In all cultural contexts and social ideologies, does the dead fetus or newborn (neonate) represent the nadir of religious efficacy? Can a dead baby ever be powerful or efficacious?

Rethinking Categories through Çatalhöyükian and Comparative Ethnographic Lenses

The classical sinologist Michael Puett has spoken often of "letting data drive theory," rather than the other way around (e.g., Puett 2006). What already emerged at Çatalhöyük, along with the data of comparative ethnography, might drive the preceding questions in different directions. Before we revisit these six questions, two short interventions based on other Çatalhöyük data follow.

Pregnancy and Headlessness

In two teasing/baiting/hunting wall paintings found during the Mellaart excavation, there is a solitary female who is impressively large, in one case disproportionately larger than the depicted male hunters. In the stag-baiting painting found in the 1960s (Hodder 2006: 31, fig. 13), a solitary woman or divine female figure set apart from the action, while typically robust and hourglass-shaped with breasts and hips depicted, does not appear to be pregnant (her arms, bent to rest on her indented waist, seem to indicate this as well). She has a head.

In the wall-painting of an aurochs being baited, teased, and/or hunted found in Level V (South P), however (Hodder 2006: pll. 15 and 16), the large solitary female manifests in blood-red, uninvolved in the action but standing directly in its midst. She towers in height and mass over the males nearby. She holds her arms in roughly the same position as the stag-hunting mural female; like her counterpart, she has breasts, pointing in either direction below her armpits, and the artist(s) has given her prominent hips. Her legs are slightly bent at the knees. But this figure looks pregnant. She has a distended belly on her left side, with a possible herniated umbilicus, the same feature Lynn Meskell observed in the janiform Istanbul Area figurine in 2005. Her right side may represent her backbone, as she may be shown as turning to the viewer to show a side view of her torso, reinforced by the position of her hips, legs, and feet. And unlike that of her counterpart in the first mural, her head is missing, although some kind of neck column (like a dowel?) seems to emerge from her torso in more fugitive color. Perhaps there is a kind of fluidity implied between living body and artifact, as though a woman's actual body, like a figurine, might include a means for the removal and reinsertion of her skull, or someone else's, as in the case of our B60 woman.

Neolithic evidence makes headlessness in corpses and figurines so normal that it is easy to forget that a pregnant woman without a head could not be alive and standing at a hunt. Was headlessness, or detachability of the head, associated with advanced pregnancy? Was pregnancy a phase of a divine female figure? Most fundamentally, was heavily gravid pregnancy a marked state that was sacralized, since the motherbaby in B60 also has no skull, and it was apparently the "special dead" whose skulls were taken? Perhaps the mural figure is another family portrait, the representation of an ideal.

"Reading" Pregnancy; Reading Death

We return briefly to the cryptic Istanbul Area figurine, a janiform that can be revolved in the hand from an image of surplus vitality to one that conjures fatal starvation or death, and back around again. The discovery of an unusual figurine by the Istanbul team confirms that the Çatalhöyük people were familiar with the body after death. On the skeletal ("death") side, Meskell would later write, "the bony, skeletal part that survives death and burial is both embedded and revealed" (Meskell 2007: 152). Several have noticed the artist's familiarity with human bone structure (Boz and Hager: in press). Skeletal parts were carved very precisely at the back of the figurine, indicating that s/he knew ribs connected to the vertebrae and the location of the scapulae and the individual pelvic bones. This particular figurine may also indicate that life and death were viewed as equals. Having what may be a pregnant female on the front side of the figurine with skeletal elements on its back the figurine suggests a consideration of birth and death as events on the same continuum (Boz and Hager: in press).

Is the "vital" side pregnant or corpulent? As Margaret Beck has observed of Upper Paleolithic figurines, referencing the debate about the Willendorf Venus, "pregnancy and obesity are surprisingly difficult to distinguish" (Beck 2000: 214; Delporte 1993: fig. 99). Beck, Meskell, Nakamura, and others have raised the methodological issue of "how literally the physiology of these figurines should be interpreted given the difficulties of working with the raw material" (Beck 2000: 214). Yet there may be a counterargument for the ways in which all somatic artifacts (material representations of the *soma*), including buried corpses, have some objective correlative in physiology. Since death and pregnancy are biologically unambiguous states, they ought not be dismissed as "constructed" in prehistoric aesthetics. We can raise valid questions about how imagined representations of the anthropomorphic, or theoanthropomorphic, form might have their genesis in real bodies.

In the 2005 site report description, Meskell and Nakamura comment that the figurine may, on its "living" side, represent pregnancy: "This figure depicts a human, hybrid representation, perhaps of life and death. The front portrays the typical robust female with large breasts and stomach (provocatively, the navel appears to protrude [umbilical hernia], which sometimes occurs in pregnancy); very thin arms with delineated fingers (see Ankara 79-251-65) fold up to rest on the breasts (see Ankara 79-803-65 and 10475.X2)" (Meskell and Nakamura 2005: 168–169). The report highlights the figurine's anatomical extremity: "We have found no parallel examples for this piece across the site, the Anatolian Neolithic or the European Neolithic for that matter. The skeletal representation indeed seems unique, but even the style of the female body, with its exaggerated breasts and stomach, is different from other known Çatalhöyük examples that portray the female body in more naturalistic proportions." It is possible that this style may not be nonnaturalistic at all, but rather faithful to the temporary distortions that pregnancy imposes on the human body.

A pregnant woman at full term from side view is highly congruous with the figurine seen from the same angle. This supports the initial suggestion that the Istanbul Area figurine portrays a herniated umbilicus, a condition whereby the intestines and other abdominal contents extrude into the thinned wall of the stomach around the umbilicus. Although the famous "splayed-figure" wall reliefs are now thought to depict bears rather than women giving birth, in light of the clay stamp of a bear with head intact found in the fill of a Level V (South P) building beneath the main South shelter on the East Mound (Hodder 2006: pl. 23), both wall reliefs and clay stamp feature a protruding umbilicus, like the figurine. Hager notes that additionally, "the ribs coming off the vertebrae are attached by cartilage, and come around; the two bottom ones free-float. The figure has swollen breasts, with her arms pushing down, signaling that the figurine is pregnant; and a popped-out umbilicus." The figurine's gesture of resting the forearms on enlarged breasts of pregnancy is a universal one, like the rocking gait most women adopt in the third trimester to compensate for a heavy frontal load.

If realism was an aesthetic goal for the bone structure of the woman's back, it could be reasonable to suppose that such a goal obtains to her front. But the figurine's realism is not uncontested; Hodder wonders whether these "vertebrae" are actually cordage or cloth strips used to bind a corpse into the enfolded position favored throughout the graves of the site; and in 2007, Meskell reconsiders her earlier diagnosis of pregnancy for the figurine, aligning her more neutrally with the "fleshy female" type known from the Paleolithic on (Meskell 2007: 152).

It is noteworthy that this hybrid figurine is headless (the report notes that "a prominent dowel hole indicates that originally the piece had a separate, detachable head"), like the pregnant larger-than-life female in the bull-baiting mural, the splayed-figure wall reliefs with red ochre outlining the umbilicus, and the B60 woman who died in childbirth. Many figurines have removable slots for the head; it is not an index of pregnancy. If taken in conjunction with the mural evidence, however, as well as the removable head of the birth-giving grain bin goddess, we might ask whether these testify to an associative matrix whereby the more generic condition of headlessness (or detachability of the head) marks the more particular condition of late pregnancy.

What *are* the poles that are (to contemporary eyes) so radically married in this anomalous figurine? Do the presence of swollen womb or stomach, breasts, and umbilicus on one side and bones on the other signal an effort to "embed" real human anatomy in a "shaped" work, as Meskell asks; in other words, is the Istanbul Area figurine a rendering of an aesthetic composite? Or might the figurine instead enact in clay the volatile nature of particularly late-stage pregnancy and its dangers?

We suggest that the Istanbul Area figurine may be a graphic comment on the potential of superabundant flesh – stretched like a drum over a live human being enfolded within – to become fleshless skeleton when a clot breaks free during hard labor and is thrown to the lungs or brain. This may be the other face of pregnancy and childbirth, the one largely avoided in the care of expectant women in the "First World." That face would have been impossible to avoid at Neolithic Çatalhöyük as woman after woman went from the work of childbirth directly into their graves, many taking their babies with them.

Revisioning Our Questions

Let us revisit and revision our earlier reflexive interrogations, now correcting through the lens of the data at Çatalhöyük, and with reference to other ethnographies.

1. As the Swahili linguistic concept shows, the notion of the pregnant woman as a culturally defined *individual* is far from universal. The pregnant female can be imagined, even in death, as a dyadic entity, a "two-in-one" person or composite "dividual" who has simultaneously singular and plural identities.

2. Pace *Gimbutas*, it is no means a given that pregnancy and childbirth in Old Europe and Asia were associated only with the generation of new life. The experience among women from menarche to menopause in the Neolithic period makes it likely that childbirth was seen as a liminal, dangerous process. The birth-giving mother was caught between bearing a baby and dying herself. Childbirth could always become an endgame, as much a battle to rescue life from the jaws of death as an archetypal act of fertile reproduction. Both possibilities were known at that time; both were religiously represented.

3. Whatever their meaning to the living, the dead of Çatalhöyük, and throughout the Neolithic world, far from being "diminished" persons or entities, were valuable enough to keep very close, within walls, inside storerooms, and under the floors of the living spaces of the house itself. Intimacy and ongoing interaction with human remains appear to have been not only unthreatening, but important and even mandatory; bones were buried, harvested, curated, and

reburied, even recombined, with tremendous social energy. Death may well have represented translation into a more powerful realm that energized and permeated life, existence at every level, and the domestic realm of the house. At the very least, the dead were the locus of heritage and the repository of memory.

4. Death in childbirth may have been valorizing, as has sometimes been the case in other histories. We have mentioned the ancient Aztec apotheosis of maternal mortalities into warrior-hummingbirds to join the daily trajectory of the solar god Huitzilopochtli. Since pregnancy was (and still is, in some parts of the world) not only an exponent of superabundant life but also a one-way ride to an ordeal that could cost everything, it might be necessary to reinterpret its meaning at Çatalhöyük. The Istanbul Area figurine, formed on one side with swollen breasts, heavily gravid belly, and extruding umbilicus, and on the other with skeletal scapulae, vertebrae, and pelvic cradle, may indicate that pregnancy was an exceptional kind of third somatic condition that signaled neither life nor death, but transcended the power of both by uniting or even overcoming what seems from our perspective like their natural polarity. If childbirth was not only the culmination of ideologies of aggressive fertility, then we would need to redescribe it. As pregnancy was a liminal condition, so childbirth might have been understood as a liminal action that placed life and death in lethal proximity: a productive contest. This productivity might have required a ritual response to a woman dying in childbirth that acknowledged the efficacy and sanctity of such death, rather than failure and the abortion of the future.

5. Just as maternal mortality may not have been only a tragedy, if it was one at all, so the event of stillbirth or infant death soon after birth may have been seen with similar ambiguity.

6. Dead newborns (neonates) may well have been received as powerful not powerless newcomers into the world of the living, particularly in relationship to the lives of houses. Neonates have been found in nearly all areas of the house, but they are frequently found in the southern-sector areas, often considered domestic areas; we have already mentioned their predominance in the southwestern corners of foundation cuts. Neonatal inhumation near the ovens would have required digging in the floors in a busy space of the house. The burials in side room, which were used for storage and

near ovens, are nearly all neonates. Two fetuses, one infant, and two adults, both females, have also been found in these closed, possibly private spaces of the Çatalhöyük house. Is there a link between the food storage areas where food is life and the reproductive issues facing the Çatalhöyük woman such as the death of her newborn? Or is it the closeness of the space, the privacy of it, that prompted the interment of newborns here? Or both? Just as childbirth and newborn child care can be seen as an extension of pregnancy, so neonatal burials may have extended the inner domestic sphere of the house and amplified it as an interior mental space (the inner space of women) through the inhumation of dead babies. Diane Gifford-Gonzalez has argued for these neonatal burial patterns in the southern sector as "a discourse on states in the transformative process. . . . Foodstuffs and obsidian rest in the southern sector, literally or figuratively buried in the house floor and its storage bins, until acted upon to produce their final form. The fact that very young children were placed in this zone may signify their unrealized potential as adults" (Gifford-Gonzalez 2007: 106). We might also appreciate these side rooms, ovens, and houses themselves – the graves of tiny bodies – as recapitulating the infolded cellular forms we discussed at the beginning of this paper. These forms are seen in the spiral and aggregative geometric patterning that decorated Çatalhöyük houses, and in the flexed fetus, circular womb, crouched mother, and pit grave of this burial.

The Goddess Revisited

Returning to the famous Mellaart feline-throned figurine in the museum at Ankara, one might consider her belly (Figures 3.2 and 9.3).

It is not that of a pregnant woman but rather, in its resemblance to a deflated sac, more like that of an immediately postpartum woman. The shape of the head of the "baby" between the figure's legs is skulllike, but a close look at the form features two small eyelike indentations on the top and a raised element that may be a nose, as though the neonate is looking up: possibly an occipital posterior stillbirth (Figure 9.3b)? It is possible that the female figure may have just delivered not a living, but a dead infant, perhaps even more valuable in the construction and maintenance of houses.

Late-Term Fetuses, Stillbirths, or Neonatal Mortalities?

The recent discovery of mummified fetuses buried with King Tutankhamun (KV62), from seven and four months' gestation, respectively, reminds us that the value of infants can precede birth (Hawass 2010: 34–61). Millennia later, the Roman sacral Lex Regia of Numa Pompilius (715 BCE; later the Lex Caesarea) required that the child of a woman dead in childbirth be cut from her womb. This in turn seemed to have evolved in Rome into a way of saving the fetus if the mother was ten months pregnant, the assumption being that she would not survive the delivery. This raises, at least hypothetically, the possibility of an older imperative that mothers not be buried pregnant. Might Çatalhöyük dwellers, skilled in the manipulation and dismemberment of human corpses, have sometimes removed neonates from dying or just-dead mothers? Are some of the neonatal burials in foundation cuts and around ovens not neonates, but instead full-term fetuses that were removed dead after maternal death? Some of the female skeletons found at Çatalhöyük may have indicated maternal mortalities, as skeletons only show ligamental evidence of pregnancy, but, if fetuses are absent, no evidence of having died in childbirth. This would make the House 60 burial exceptional, but also possibly account for the infrequency of "motherbaby" skeletal remains throughout the Neolithic if such fetal removal were widespread practice (like skull removal and curating the special dead). If separation of the fetus from the dead mother was Çatalhöyükian practice, why were these two skeletons kept together? If it was not, why is this skeleton with impacted fetus in the pelvis an extremely rare find, not only at this site, but throughout the data of paleopathology? This question remains unanswered.

Life and Death: Duality or Unity?

Hodder has stressed ideas of "mirroring" or "opposition" in the iconography of Çatalhöyük. The artifacts we have seen, including the complex Building 60 skeletons, seem to signify living and dying as more of an oscillating unity than an oppositional dichotomy; this may characterize many prehistoric or even some modern indigenous epistemologies.

We wonder whether the dead woman in House 60, a "history" or heritage house, was specially honored with an inaugural burial, basket, bone pin with green pigment, and the infrequent secondary treatment of skull removal *because* she contained a dead baby, invisibly interred together with her. The grave, a cultural assemblage, thus would have consecrated the bioassemblage that was a pregnant woman, the "motherbaby." Perhaps the "labor" of producing (albeit sequestering) a dead baby, which may have had generative powers in its own right, determined the specialness of her burial and inspired the removal of her skull for ritual installation elsewhere.

It is also possible that the main focus of this special burial *was* the hidden full-term fetus. We have seen that the foundation burials are commonly neonates, and in several houses, inaugural burials are infants. Lidded woven baskets contain infants, not adults. The two rounded bone points with green pigment were found associated with inaugural burials, the mother with child and an infant. As an inaugural burial in its pit, and perhaps also the first in the Building 60, a "history house" of size and multiple burials, is it possible that the grave goods belong primarily to the occulted fetus? The basket was placed below the dead mother's abdomen, where the baby was. The bone point was placed on top of her abdomen, where the baby was. The mother may have been herself a kind of lidded basket for her dead baby, as well as an independent agent. Such treatment may have made the dead baby's powers available to the new collective house. We question Diane Gifford-Gonzalez's notion that "the fact that very young children were placed in this zone may signify their unrealized potential as adults"; it may well have been that the potential of dead babies was viewed as *greater* than it would have been had they survived, with the generative powers of neonates – the "stem cells" of the world of the dead – amplified by death, not diminished by it.

This does not mean that the grief of the Building 60 woman's family was necessarily muted if this were true. Can we nevertheless read maternal mortality through the Çatalhöyükian lens of death as a realm of energy, rich with meaning? As Lynn Meskell has eloquently observed, "life after death" may have implied neither journey nor eschatology. Rather, through the continual reintegration and curating of the powerful dead into the world of living, it was rather, as she puts it, "a way of returning life to the living."

The womb of the dead mother became a kind of grave for her undelivered baby; but she herself was also in some sense recreated in death as a fetus, tightly flexed to fit the womb of her own pit grave. Çatalhöyük graves in their tight circularity, wherein bodies are bound to fit small earthen spaces, resemble pregnancy's morphology. Moving concentrically outward, the houses contained their graves, and the layered settlement contained its buildings and middens interlaced with bone. The ancient city was therefore a skeletal matrix – and at the same time an enfleshed entity, symbolically energized by its dead.

We have suggested that childbirth at Çatalhöyük was always also potential child death, and that we should not assume that this common event was tragic, in our sense. The childbearing "goddess" of Çatalhöyük may have superintended not the abundant realm of fertility attributed to her in the atmosphere of Mellaart's finds, but instead a hybrid, interpenetrating realm of life and death. As each woman's labor began in earnest, existential dice were rolled, and the potential enacted – not only of bringing forth a new life from an existing one, but also of the annihilation of both lives. "First World" obstetrical medicine has lost sight of – or suppressed – what only a few generations ago our great-grandmothers knew all too well, that the risk of death remained close at hand during every childbirth. The pendulum could swing either way, and still can.

But it is possible that at Çatalhöyük, this reality might have been a kind of talisman, rather than an unqualified horror. If dead bodies were a kind of buried treasure, "renewable energy sources" for the living and a way into the future, rather than objects of miasma, so two such bodies, enfolded forever, may have represented a signal power.

BIBLIOGRAPHY

Banning, E. B. 2011. So fair a house: Göbekli Tepe and the identification of temples in the Pre-Pottery Neolithic of the Near East. *Current Anthropology* 52(5):619–660.

Beck, M. 2000. Female figurines in the European Upper Paleolithic: Politics and bias in archaeological interpretation. In *Reading the Body: Representations and Remains in the Archaeological Record*, ed. A. E. Rautman. Philadelphia: University of Pennsylvania Press, 202–214.

Belfer-Cohen, A. 2011. Conversation with Kimberley Patton, July 2011.

Bourjeily, G., Paidas, M., Khalil, H., Rosene-Montella, K., and Rodger, M. 2010. Pulmonary embolism in pregnancy. *The Lancet* 375(9713):500–512.

Boz, B., Hager, L. D., Haddow, S., et al. 2006. Human remains. In *The Çatalhöyük 2006 Archive Report*, Çatalhöyük Research Project, 157, www.catalhoyuk.com/downloads/Archive_Report_2006.pdf.

Boz, B., and Hager, L. D. In Press. Intramural burial practices at Çatalhöyük. In *Humans and Landscapes of Çatalhöyük. Reports from the 2000–2008 seasons* ed. I. Hodder. Los Angeles: Cotsen Institute.

Burkert, W. 1985 (1977, German edition). *Greek Religion*. Trans. J. Raffan. Cambridge, MA: Harvard University Press.

Caldwell, J. C., and Caldwell, B. K. 2003. Was there a neolithic mortality crisis? *Journal of Population Research* 20(2):153–168.

Çatalhöyük Database. http://www.catalhoyuk.com/database/catal/

CFM (Citizens for Midwifery). 2008. http://cfmidwifery.blogspot.com/2008/03/motherbaby.html

Delporte, H. 1993. *L'image de la femme dans l'art préhistorique*. Paris: Picard.

Diop, B. 1948. "Souffles." In *Anthologie de la nouvelle poésie nègre et malgache*, ed. L. Senghor. Trans. J. Jahn, in *Muntu: An Outline of Neo-African Culture*. London: Faber & Faber, 1961.

Dominus, S. 2011. Could conjoined twins share a mind? *New York Times Magazine*, May 29, 2011. http://www.nytimes.com/2011/05/29/magazine/could-conjoined-twins-share-a-mind.html?pagewanted=all

Gifford-Gonzalez, D. 2007. On breasts in beasts: another reading of women, wildness, and danger at Çatalhöyük. *Archaeological Dialogues* 14(1):91–111.

Gimbutas, M. 2001. *The Language of the Goddess: Unearthing the Hidden Symbols of Western Civilization*. London: Thames and Hudson.

Edinger, E. F. 1985. *Anatomy of the Psyche: Alchemical Symbolism in Psychotherapy*. La Salle, IL: Open Court.

Hager, L. D. 2011. Conversation with Kimberley Patton, July 2011.

Hawass, Z. 2010. King Tut's family secrets. *National Geographic* 218(3):34–61.

Hill, J. 2011. Conversation with Kimberley Patton, July 2011.

Hodder, I. 2005. Introduction. In *Çatalhöyük 2005 Archive Report*, Çatalhöyük Research Project, 1–5. http://ancientworldonline.blogspot.com/2010/01/open-access-journal-catalhoyuk-archive.html.

2006. *The Leopard's Tale: Revealing the Mysteries of Çatalhöyük*. London: Thames & Hudson.

"2007 Season review." In *Çatalhöyük 2007 Archive Report*, Çatalhöyük Research Project, 1–6. http://ancientworldonline.blogspot.com/2010/01/open-access-journal-catalhoyuk-archive.html

Jay, N. B. 1992. *Throughout Your Generations Forever: Sacrifice, Religion, and Paternity*. Chicago: University of Chicago Press.

Kuijt, I. 2008. The regeneration of life: neolithic structures of symbolic remembering and forgetting. *Current Anthropology* 49(2):171–195.

López Luján, L. 2010. *Tlaltecuhtli*. Mexico City: Sextil Editores.

Mann, Charles. 2008. The birth of religion. *National Geographic* 219(6):57.

Merleau-Ponty, M. 1980. *The Phenomenology of Perception*. London: Routledge and Kegan Paul.

Meskell, L. 1999. Feminism, paganism, pluralism. In *Archaeology and Folklore*, ed. A. Gazin-Schwartz and C. Holtorf, London and New York: Routledge, 83–89.

2000. Writing the body in archaeology. In *Reading the Body: Representations and Remains in the Archaeological Record*, ed. A. E. Rautman. Philadelphia: University of Pennsylvania Press, 13–21.

2007. Refiguring the corpus at Çatalhöyük. In *Material Beginnings: A Global Prehistory of Figurative Representation*, eds. A. C. Renfrew and I. Morley. Cambridge: McDonald Institute Monographs, 143–156.

2008. The nature of the beast: Curating animals and ancestors at Çatalhöyük. *World Archaeology* 40(3):373–389.

Meskell, L., and Nakamura, C. 2005. Figurines. In *Çatalhöyük 2007 Archive Report*, Çatalhöyük Research Project, 161–88. http://ancientworldonline.blogspot.com/2010/01/open-access-journal-catalhoyuk-archive.html

Meskell, L., and Nakamura, C. In Press. In *Humans and Landscapes of Çatalhöyük: Reports from the 2000–2008 Seasons*, ed. I. Hodder. Los Angeles: UCLA Cotsen Institute of Archaeology Press.

Özbaşaran, M. 2005. IST area. In *Çatalhöyük 2005 Archive Report*, Çatalhöyük Research Project, 89–93. http://ancientworldonline.blogspot.com/2010/01/open-access-journal-catalhoyuk-archive.html

Pilloud, M. A., and Larsen, C. S. 2011. 'Official' and 'practical' kin: Inferring social and community structure from dental phenotype at Neolithic Çatalhöyük, Turkey. *American Journal of Physical Anthropology* 145(4):519–530.

Puett, Michael. Response to lecture by George Rupp, "Religion and the Humanities: A Lovers' Quarrel." Sponsored by the Committee on the Study of Religion, Harvard University, September 2006.

Ricœur, P. 1998. Politics and totalitarianism. In *Critique and Conviction: Conversations with François Azouvi and Marc de Launay*. Trans. K. Blamey, 95–101. Cambridge: Polity Press.

Rosen, A. 2005. Phytolith indicators of plant and land use at Çatalhöyük. In *Inhabiting Çatalhöyük: Reports from the 1995–1999 Seasons*, vol. 4, ed. I. Hodder. Cambridge: MacDonald Institute, Cambridge University, 203–212.

Russell, N., and Griffitts, J. In Press. Çatalhöyük worked bone: South and 4040 Areas. In *Humans and Landscapes of Çatalhöyük: Reports from the 2000–2008 Seasons*, ed. I. Hodder. Los Angeles: UCLA Cotsen Institute of Archaeology Press.

Ryan, P. In Press. Plant exploitation from household and landscape perspectives: The phytolith evidence. In *Humans and Landscapes of Çatalhöyük: Reports from the 2000–2008 Seasons*, ed. I. Hodder. Los Angeles: UCLA Cotsen Institute of Archaeology Press.

Schulting, R. J. 1998. Creativity's coffin: Innovation in the burial record of Mesolithic Europe. In *Creativity in Human Evolution and Prehistory*, ed. S. Mithen. London and New York: Routledge.

Srejovic, D. 1972. *Europe's First Monumental Sculpture: New Discoveries at Lepenski Vir*. London: Thames and Hudson.

Strathern, M. *The Gender of the Gift: Problems with Women and Problems with Society in Melanesia*. Berkeley: University of California, 1988.

Talalay, L. E. 2004. Heady business: Skulls, heads, and decapitation in Neolithic Anatolia and Greece. *Journal of Mediterranean Archaeology* 17(2):139–163.

Talalay, L. E. Forthcoming. "Entangled bodies: Rethinking twins and double images in the Prehistoric Mediterranean." In *Gemini and the Sacred: Twins and Twinship in Religion and Myth*, ed. Kimberley C. Patton. London: I.B.Tauris.

Trainor, K., ed. 2010. Special issue: Relics in comparative perspective. *Numen: International Review for the History of Religions* 57(3–4):267–536.

UNICEF (United Nations Children's Fund). 2012. Maternal and newborn health. http://www.unicef.org/health/index_maternalhealth.html. Accessed June 12, 2012.

Wells, C. 1975. Ancient obstetric hazards and female mortality. *Bulletin of the New York Academy of Medicine* 51(11):1235–1249.

Wendrich, W. 2005. The Çatalhöyük basketry. In *Changing Materialities at Çatalhöyük: Reports from the 1995–99 Seasons*, ed. I. Hodder. Cambridge: MacDonald Institute for Archaeology, 419–424.

WHO (World Health Organization). 2012. Maternal mortality. http://www.who.int/making_pregnancy_safer/topics/maternal_mortality/en/. Accessed June 12, 2012.

10

The *Hau* of the House

Mary J. Weismantel

At the Neolithic site of Çatalhöyük, all architecture is domestic. Earlier sites in the Anatolian region of Turkey, such as the spectacular Göbekli Tepe, boast dramatic public spaces and monumental art. But at Çatalhöyük, despite a very large, very long occupation (perhaps two to eight thousand people from 7400 to 6000 BCE), it appears that no one ever built anything bigger than a house. Maps of the excavations show a mound honeycombed with small rooms, and nothing more (Hodder 2006). This singular fact has inspired lengthy, detailed, insightful studies of the Çatalhöyük house. But even after reading this extensive literature, I still find myself asking a basic question: What – and where – is this house?

The answer is not as obvious as it might seem. Identifying buildings at the site is relatively straightforward, but that does not mean we know the dimensions of "the house" – let alone its ontological status. To begin with, there are several different kinds of houses to be disentangled. Writers on the subject of "the house" tend to erect three different kinds of things on the same semantic terrain – and this is certainly true at Çatalhöyük.

First, there is the "house" at its most concrete: the walls and other features uncovered during excavations, and the evidence for domestic activities that took place within them. A second, more abstract "house," projected onto the first, refers less to the physical structure and more to the social group who inhabits it. This slippage between architecture and social structure produces further slippage between the idea of the "house" and closely related concepts such as "family" and "household" – equally abstract notions that nonetheless sound familiar and real.

Last but not least, hovering somewhere inside or above these first two is the purely conceptual "house": the thing that the people of Çatalhöyük called by a name that meant something like what we mean by "house." That term, like the names of similar entities elsewhere, was presumably capacious, encompassing a building, people, relationships, substances, activities, memories, and beliefs. What held it all together was something we might call the *hau* of the house – a term Marcel Mauss borrowed from the Maori, who used it to refer to "the spirit of things" (1990: 11). We can never recapture the *hau*, but we should pay it careful attention nevertheless. Mistaken assumptions about the conceptual house can lead to misreadings of the archaeological house, and miscalculations of its material and social dimensions.

Box

The Neolithic house has been envisioned as "an enclosed box" (Hodder 1990): a small rectangular building occupied by a nuclear family whose members consider it their private home. This model makes intuitive sense to contemporary researchers, evoking as it does the kind of modern houses depicted in song as "little boxes,"[1] and perhaps reminding them of their own childhood homes. It also seems to fit the site, where excavators have uncovered a seemingly endless series of architectural units, each similar to – but carefully sealed off from – another.

But Çatalhöyük is not a place we can intuitively understand; it is a radically premodern place, where modern concepts like "houses as little boxes" might blind us to the things that are actually there. In this essay, I want to see what happens if we blow up the enclosed box, exploding the walls and lifting the roof to let in the outside world – an iconoclastic impulse inspired by recent writing about Çatalhöyük by Hodder (2012), Hodder and Pels (2010), and Nakamura (2010), as well as Kuijt (2011) and Düring and Marciniak (2006). This demolition should also take out the persons, bodies, and families we have imagined living inside the box: let us replace them, too, with something more lively and open-ended.

Hodder's recent work focuses on the idea of "entanglements" (2012): the long, messy chains of materials, relations, and processes that connect humans and nonhumans, city and landscape. Entanglements broach the

---

[1] In a 1962 song by Malvina Reynolds, made famous by Pete Seeger.

perimeters of the box, and so too do Hodder's recent explorations of various kinds of networks or clusters that might link groups of houses together in neighborhoods or around a central "history house" (Pels and Hodder 2010). I want to push this process one step further, and see what happens if we think of the house itself as a kind of entanglement – or rather, as a node or nexus where particular kinds of entanglements are gathered together and become interlaced into something dense and intimate. This density is at once material and social, and it creates the emotional and conceptual weight that gives the notion of "house" its singular import.

Following the philosopher Jane Bennett, I will use Deleuze's concept of the "assemblage" to refer to this cluster of human and non-human entanglements (Bennett 2010: 23). The house as assemblage is defined by the processes of give and take between it and other entities, which keep it constantly in a state of reinvention, reiteration, and reproduction.

This renovation of the conceptual house provides a new perspective on the material and social "houses" that are its foundation. The first section of this essay, "The Dead in the House," addresses the material house, opening it up vertically to look under the floor and above the missing roof. This move brings a fourth dimension, temporality, into sight as we contemplate the layering of bodies and floors over time.

The second section, "The Gift in the House," addresses the social house or household; it moves from vertical to horizontal perspectives, and from architecture to artifacts. Fragments of plaster, bone, seeds, and clay trace the connections between the house and its surroundings: the cityscape of roofs and middens, and the landscape of wetlands and wild spaces beyond. These links help us conceptualize the house as a social unit that incorporates forms of kin beyond the human, and forms of reproduction beyond the biological. And it returns us to the *hau*, which is not only the spirit of things, but also the spirit of the gift.

The Dead in the House

Anthropologists writing about the symbolic life of houses have repeatedly turned to two powerful ideas, both closely associated with the influential writings of Mary Douglas (1996, 2002). One is the house as human body (C. Hugh-Jones 1979; Guthrie, this volume); the other is the floor plan as a field of structural oppositions (Bourdieu 2003; Cunningham 1964). Both these ideas have been put to good effect at Çatalhöyük (Mills, this volume; Guthrie, this volume), and I will rely on them here – but only as read through Bennett and like-minded authors intent on dissolving modernist ontologies.

As developed by twentieth-century social anthropologists like Douglas, structuralist binarism and homologism rest on deeply essentialist foundations. Houses and bodies alike are seen as modernist monads with unchanging identities, each containing dyads that likewise consist of immutable essences: spirit and matter, mind and body, culture and nature, male and female. Levi-Strauss offers a more dynamic Hegelian formulation, in which the tension between the two halves generates an impulse toward transformation (1963). I want to develop that potential here, moving away from static essences and toward interactive states of becoming (Braidotti 2002). In the process, we can move from a synchronic reading of the floor plan as cognitive map to a diachronic reading of the whole house as embodied and inhabited space – and as an instantiation of history.

DYAD

Mary Douglas beautifully defines the sacred as that which is "set apart" (2002) – a definition the Çatalhöyük house brings vividly to life. During my first visit to the site in 2009, I was forcibly struck by the contrast between comfortable domesticity and unsettling religiosity, a contrast that seemed embedded in the very architecture of the house. Standing on the edge of the pit, I watched the archaeologist Roddy Regan move comfortably around inside the room he had excavated, pointing out features with a trowel. My first thought was how pleasantly domestic it all looked: a hearth, a ladder, white plastered walls, storage bins tucked neatly away in the pantry. The little house did not just look understandable; it looked inhabitable. Its intimate proportions and the traces of mundane activities like building fires and sharpening tools made it homey: *Heimlich*.

But the hearth area told only half the story. The opposite corner was dominated by the enormous, beautiful curves of wild cattle horns, or bucrania, set into low walls surrounding a grave. Here, the sense of familiarity dropped away before a religiosity and an aesthetic entirely alien to a modern sensibility – and much less inviting. The menacing horns – bony, sharp-tipped, inimical to living flesh – cause the body to recoil, as does the thought of dead people under the house: un-*Heimlich*.[2]

Understandably, archaeological interpretation has focused on this dramatic opposition between the northern and southern areas of the floor, which the excavation team talked about as "dirty" and "clean" – terms sharply evocative of Douglas (2002). On one side, a low wall and raised platform mark the space of the sacred and the dead. On the other side, excavators painstakingly recover the unobtrusive traces of living people engaged in utilitarian activities: lithic scatters, ladder scars, a handful of spilled grain.

This is the material evidence for a spatial division between ritual and everyday; from it, anthropologists have read social categories – living and dead, wild and tame, male and female – and conceptual categories – spirit and matter, marked and unmarked (Keane 2010). Bloch, for example, introduces gendered inequality into the house: The woman "crouching by the hearth" occupies a lower, secular, dirty space, in contrast to the sacred "virility" signified by the upraised bucrania (2010). Such allusions recall cosmologies elucidated by anthropologists elsewhere, in which the bones of the dead are masculine agents of the spirit world, powerful and agentive, in contrast to the soft, femininized flesh of the living, who passively obey the dictates of the ancestors.

Unfortunately, recent archaeological data no longer fall neatly into these satisfying dyads. The weakest distinction is between male and female. Meskell and Hodder have convincingly refuted earlier claims that Çatalhöyük was a matriarchal city filled with images of breasts and birth; as they point out, the installations of phallic-looking animal horns are more evocative of a feral, violent masculinity than a benign maternal goddess (Hodder and Meskell 2010). However, a recent study of the bucrania casts doubt on their association with masculinity. Despite the misleading phrase "bull's horns," the horns chosen for installations are not always male – they are just big. The bones found in feasting deposits, too, demonstrate selection for size, but not for sex (Russell, Martin, and Twiss 2009).[3] Unlike in later societies, in Çatalhöyük the sex of animals

---

[2] The classic discussion of *Heimlich*/un-*Heimlich* is in Freud's essay on "The Uncanny" 2003 [1917].

[3] On average, males' larger size resulted in proportionally larger horns, but as is often the case with sexual dimorphism, big females had bigger bones – and bigger horns – than small males.

apparently did not serve as a metaphor for human gender,[4] or the bucrania as synecdoches for the male body.

In fact, there seems to have been a singular lack of interest in gender as a social or symbolic category in any context. The meticulously analyzed mortuary data reveal little patterned relationship between a skeleton's sex and the treatment of the body, in death or in life. Women and men alike performed demanding physical work, ate an abundant and varied diet, and had similar patterns of morbidity and mortality. As Meskell says of the Çatalhöyük figurines, "What seems to have been most salient [was] ... not a specifically gendered person with discrete sexual markers, but an [unsexed] ... human form" (Meskell and Nakamura 2005: 175; Meskell et al. 2008).

The opposition between sacred and profane has also unraveled. What once looked like clear spatial boundaries between "the everyday and the sacred" have been blurred by the discovery of numerous ritual depositions below "even the dirtiest of domestic floors" (Hodder 2010: 16). The ubiquity of these deposits, which Nakamura interprets as remains of magical acts (2010), indicates that the inhabitants found sacred significance in all parts of this house, "dirty" and "clean" alike.

As the evidence for a separation between religiosity and materiality within the house has crumbled, a new consensus has begun to emerge: Meskell, Shults, Pels, and Nakamura all speak of a Çatalhöyük sensibility radically different from the dualism of modernist thought. Rather than neatly segregating ordinary life from the spiritual realm, the inhabitants seem attuned to a house closer to Bennett's notion of "vital matter," or Appadurai's recent call for a return to "the hau of things" (2011). This is a house alive with immanent spirit, yet fully material in its being.

These new readings of the evidence do not allow us simply to collapse the familiar Durkheim/Douglas categories into an undifferentiated mass. The Çatalhöyük house continues to demand a reading that can account for the extraordinary presence of the bucrania and other installations, the careful ritual cleansing of the house at its "death," the ritual depositions inserted into walls and floors, and other practices that acknowledged and reiterated the specificity of the sacred, or what Keane refers to as "marked" (2010). What we need is a more dynamic model for how symbolic dyads might interact – and for this, we need a different model of the body.

---

[4] Twiss, personal comm.

BODY

The idea of the house as body is illuminating – as long as we remember that other people do not see the body, or the self, as we do. Mary Douglas's (1996) insight that the body can be read as a template for the "body politic" is crucial, but there is something inherently modernist (perhaps even particularly British) in her emphasis on bodily boundaries. Ultimately, Douglas's body belongs to modern capitalism, and to a world of autonomous, competitive, unequal individuals whose identities are fixed in their genes, their skin color, and their genitalia. Where people's productive relationships to the world are different, these ontologies of the body and the person will not hold.

Rethinking the Çatalhöyük house, then, requires rethinking the Neolithic body with the help of authors such as Jasbir Puar, who writes of the body as assemblage (2007); Rosi Braidotti (2002), or Marilyn Strathern (1988), whose anthropological theory of the body has come closest to supplanting Douglas's. On the basis of research in twentieth-century Papua New Guinea, Strathern proposes a non-Western concept of the person as "dividual" rather than individual: an entity at once more partial and more expansive than the modernist monad, and constituted through multiple heterogeneous incorporations rather than existing as a unitary essence.

This notion can help us make sense of the sex of the Çatalhöyük body, especially if we concentrate on its parts. Consider the penis. Meskell identified a number of the ceramic and stone figurines at Čatalhöyük as "phallic" – but she notes that these small objects are surprisingly ambiguous. Some are simultaneously male and female: when rotated, a penis and testicles become breasts or buttocks. This visual punning suggests an attitude that emphasizes the mutability, not the fixity, of bodily sex (2011).

The little penises are usually pierced for wearing; they are detached body parts that can be attached to any kind of body, male or female, adult or child. Detachability of body parts and substances is key to Strathern's theory, since it indicates a body that is partible rather than unitary. The detachable penis, like the bucrania, does not inevitably serve as a metonym for a whole gendered person, for masculinity as an abstraction, or for "phallic" power. Instead, elements of maleness and femaleness may be intrinsically partible, inhering in the products of men's and women's labor, as well as in manufactured body parts. These detachable gendered objects and substances can be exchanged, ingested, incorporated, expelled, discarded, or temporarily held by "dividual" persons.

The idea of the body as partible is immensely helpful in understanding Çatalhöyük attitudes toward skeletons. Just as a female child might make and wear a clay penis, so too living persons at Çatalhöyük handled the bones of the dead. The tombs underneath the house were not inviolable – people reopened them periodically not to commune with the souls of the departed, but to interact with the physical remains for specific instrumental ends. They added, mixed, and subtracted bones, especially skulls. In one grave a woman cradles a man's head; another woman's own head has been replaced with that of a man who died long after her (Boz and Hager 2013).

Interfering with the integrity of a corpse is reprehensible in cultural settings where the body represents a unique individual. At Çatalhöyük, burials are like Strathern's dividuals: one scalar unit in a nested series. Not only are individual body parts more significant than intact bodies, but in many graves, several bodies are mixed indiscriminately into a single amorphous unit. After death, these bones entered upon a complex social trajectory in which they figured as entities both larger and smaller than the skeleton.

These practices make sense if we think of the body as an assemblage. In life, the body takes form by repeatedly incorporating substances and parts of other entities, which create a heterogeneous, composite person. After death, this process is slowly reversed as the body is opened, disassembled, and merged with others. Reuse of a bone by a living person or incorporating the skull of an almost-forgotten ancestor into a more recent grave is a means to extend the body's social and material life through interactive processes like those by which it was formed.

In sum, rather than Douglas's indivisible body, Çatalhöyük bodies are divisible assemblages that sported detachable penises in life and traded skulls after death. With this dynamic body as our model, we can see the spatial relationships within the Çatalhöyük house as evidence for an equally dynamic set of relations between old and new houses – and between the present and the past.

HISTORY

Like the body, the Çatalhöyük house may have been a divisible and mutating assemblage. On the face of it, this is an absurd claim, since houses were extremely stable in form, appearance, and location, having been repeatedly rebuilt on the same site over decades or even centuries. But this permanence was achieved through constant, iterative processes like those required to maintain one's gender (Butler 1990), and ironically, maintaining the conceptual integrity of the house apparently required repeatedly violating its physical integrity as a structure. These acts of symbolic maintenance were not lateral alterations of the house footprint in relation to its neighbors; they were vertical intrusions, extractions, and ruptures that created an unstable, interactive relationship between the existing house and its predecessors.

This house is a site of action – like the house we experience during excavation, when field archaeologists take up temporary residence in the spaces we excavate. We remove the trash that has accumulated in the cellar, redig graves and storage pits, and clean out the oven; before long, we are walking on an original floor, sitting down for a cup of coffee, and staring up at odd moments to picture the missing roof. By inserting our own laboring bodies into the spaces built and inhabited by the people we study, we raise the possibility of an embodied understanding of the past (Hodder 2000).

After the field season, this inhabited house vanishes, replaced by inert two-dimensional representations. Here, I want to reverse the process and take the diagrammatic floor plan, in which a series of symbolic oppositions fall onto a single north-south axis, and replace it with a multidimensional analysis of domestic space. This move recuperates some of the concepts that initially seemed important at Çatalhöyük. For example, consider the discovery of ritual deposits throughout the house. These data undermined the two-dimensional, synchronic pattern of "dirty" and "clean" – only to rediscover it as a patterned alternation, enacted not in space but in time. First, during many years of ordinary life, the house was filled with domestic dirt; then an extraordinary phase of ritual cleansing brought that life to an end.

People rarely abandoned decaying houses. Instead of moving on to occupy a new space, they carefully removed the detritus of daily living, inserted ritual depositions throughout, and collapsed the structure inward so that a new house could be constructed on the walls of the old. These acts have several implications: they alter and heighten the significance of being inside a house; they make the house into a dividual; and they change the experience of temporality.

An inhabited house sits on top of earlier houses, just as the inhabitants occupy a space above the graves of previous occupants. The vertical
relationship creates both contrast and congruence between the living
and the dead. Contrast: the quotidian fact of inhabiting a living body in
a living house is constantly thrown into sharp relief by close proximity
to subterranean bodies (of houses and humans) that are no longer alive.
Congruence: the walls of older houses support the walls of the inhabited
house, and by extension, the bodies interred under the floor provide
undergirding support for those living above them.

Judging from the locations of ritual deposits, this support did not
come from the house as a whole so much as from its parts. Depositions
were left at hearths, ovens, platforms, storage bins, pillars, and walls,
ritually marking each of these places and its unique working life within
the collective life of the house. Each was taken to individual closure, and
then recreated in situ within the new structure. With these acts, people
at Çatalhöyük treated the house as they treated human skeletons. They
conceptually dismembered it into individual body parts, each of which
had a material vitality of its own. The house, then, was internally several:
a dividual in which each part is significant in its own right, yet integral
to the whole.

Like the remains of dead humans, the remains of dead houses were
not allowed to rest in peace. The inhabitants habitually dug down into
their floors to take animal skulls from installations, bones from graves,
and artifacts from depositions. The apparent ease with which people
located things left behind by previous generations (or accurately reconstructed a house after a long hiatus) is startling. These acts demonstrate
how very present the remembered past can be, even in the absence of
written histories.

This ease may have been produced by a domestic space that materializes the past. New layouts mimic the old; sacred objects are reinstalled on
new walls. "Now" and "then," experience and memory, cohabitate in a
tense, active relation. The floor separates them, as does the ritual closing
of houses at life's end. And yet they are juxtaposed and knit together:
simply to walk on the floor was to come into contact with the living
membrane between two temporal zones.

The house's inhabitants recognized the vitality of these floors by plastering them repeatedly and with care. But just as often as they created
smooth, unbroken surfaces, people broke through them – piercing the

plaster and puncturing the present. The past was an accessible resource: one could reach down for a piece of it, or remix history by adding something to a grave. Like a giant amorphous body, this past could be disarticulated and rearranged as needed.

Surprisingly, the effect of all this dynamism was great continuity over a very long period (Hodder and Cessford 2004). Individual acts of rupture were undertaken conservatively, infrequently, repetitively; each opening was followed with a renewed closure. This very attentiveness to repetition speaks to a sense of the past as dangerously unfixed: a mobile, vital, unpredictable assemblage intimately entangled with who we are now – and who we might become.

FUTURE

The houses at Çatalhöyük famously have no doors. The buildings are crammed together, their exterior walls contiguous; as a result, Çatalhöyük also lacks streets. These absences call our attention upward, to the roofs we can no longer see, but about which we can adduce certain facts. Roofs provided access to the house and supported paths that linked houses to one another, to the open areas within the city, and ultimately to the wetlands, fields, and pastureland beyond.

The first time I stood on the floor of a Çatalhöyük house, I found myself looking upward, imagining this space of sociality, light, and air. The place where I stood felt like a basement: a windowless bunker filled with storage bins, dried food, and dead things. These interiors, which we have called "houses," are only fragments of domestic space. Microartifacts found near ladder scars indicate that people worked above, in the light; some cooking was not done at the interior hearths, but elsewhere, on the roofs or second stories and/or in the middens shared between clusters of houses.

The word "house" may have included these exterior places, as is true in many indigenous agricultural communities of the Americas. There, "house" is understood to include the patios and work areas where most waking hours are spent, as well as the small dark buildings used for sleeping and storage (Robin 2002; Weismantel 1988). At Çatalhöyük, this New World duo of interior and patio may have been stacked vertically, with the weight bearing roofs supporting activity areas, cooking hearths, even shelters, rooms, or second stories.

Space creates time. Seasonality is implicit in these two levels: open areas belong to warmer weather and daylight, the protected interior to winter and night (Pels 2010). Longer temporalities are also layered into the house, bifurcating the present. The lower rooms contain things associated with the immediate past: in the unfinished rooms at the perimeter, seeds, dried foods, and stored tools; in the highly finished main room, graves and animal-bone installations commemorating past feasts. Interior rooms might also house the elderly, no longer able to climb the ladder. These lower, enclosed rooms evoke hibernation, burrowing, waiting, potentialities: pasts that contain the seeds of the future.

The outside areas are different: here, active adults process newly harvested or gathered plants and recently killed animals. Outside areas are public areas, where people see one another coming and going, working and resting – especially at Çatalhöyük, where roofs were roads that linked houses and people. Archaeological attention has recently turned to the middens between house clusters, revealing intensive activity there: cooking, feasting, even areas with finished floors. At these active, open sites, the house finds its future: these are places of generative possibility, where social and reproductive links between houses are forged.

This perspective makes it difficult to see the Çatalhöyük house as a stable, clearly demarcated entity, created at one point in time, inhabited for a set period afterward, and finally abandoned. What we see instead is a composite series of houses, partial and complete, abandoned and inhabited, expanding through space and time. This house was always, and by design, incomplete. Its upper and outer limits were open to social and material entanglements with others; its lower boundaries were blurred by entanglement with its own past. This house is a composite in another sense, too: Its inhabitants treated it as a collection of separate parts rather than a single entity – perhaps because they themselves were internally heterogeneous, their own identities composed of pieces of other individuals, living and dead.

Having explored the vertical dimensions of the house, it is time to expand its horizontal limits. We turn now to the making of this composite house, which was assembled through material entanglements with other bodies and things that entered and left the house through processes of exchange.

The Gift in the House

When I began my ethnographic research in Zumbagua, an agricultural community of the Ecuadorian Andes, I was confused by the physical configuration of buildings and courtyards, and the social configurations in which people ate, slept, and worked. Finally I stopped looking for the limits of the house and started following its heartbeat: the movements of people and things (Weismantel 1988: 168–195).

This new focus let me see the house in action. Meals were centrifugal forces that gathered people together: small, sleepy groups around the hearth in the predawn darkness; larger groups who ate together at outdoor work sites during the day; and, rarely, enormous gatherings in the patio for weddings and feast days. Equally important were the centripetal movements of things between households. Little pots of soup, daily carried by children between houses; bags of raw materials like potatoes or wool, intermittently delivered by adults: these gifts reinforced or redefined links between social and biological kin. The whole entity changed form as it pulsed to overlapping cycles, frequent and infrequent, predictable and sporadic, festive and workaday.

The house is in motion because it is a machine. The great modernist architect Corbusier called it "a machine for living," a phrase that is even more apt for premodern houses, which served as sites of production and processing. As I learned in Zumbagua, a farmer's house is as much launching pad or base camp as domicile.

The house is also a site of reproduction – a term I do not mean reductively to refer to a private place where people "make babies." Our cultural biases lead us to think of reproduction as biological, a matter of birth and blood (Schneider 1980), but feminist anthropologists define it more accurately as a social and material phenomenon (Ginsburg and Rapp 1995). The production of bare biological life – an activity that may or may not take place within house walls – is a relatively unimportant phase in the long process of raising a human being that is in turn capable of reproducing itself. The manufacture of shelter, stability, sociality, and culture matters more. Social reproduction also necessitates exchange: material exchanges of necessary things, and social exchanges that bring new people in, and give others away.

To understand the house as reproducing machine, we look not at architecture but at artifacts. As I found in Zumbagua, this change of focus produces a very different map, not of floors and walls but of lines radiating outward in a dense tanglegram (Hodder 2012). Each fragment, cluster, or scatter evokes a distinct social and productive history; each connects the house to other houses nearby, and to nonhuman assemblages of animals, plants, water, and soil beyond. Caprine bone and seed fragments contain traces of the fields and corrals on the edges of the community; the abundance of plaster and clay is a material record of frequent visits to the surrounding wetlands; rare things like obsidian hint at long-distance exchange networks.

Most of these are mundane materials associated with workaday tasks, but one class of artifacts stands out: the bucrania and other assemblages of animal bone mounted on house walls. These are the most spectacular objects in the house – and the most enigmatic. These displays are clearly expressive in intent, but the message is lost to us today. We can partially recover it, however, by following the social and material histories of these skulls and horns. Although they originate far from the house, the bucrania hold the key to its *hau*.

ANIMAL

The aurochs in the house evokes a powerful set of symbolic oppositions: animal/human, wild/domestic,[5] and nature/culture. Wild cattle were enormous, ferocious, and untamed; other installations featured bear claws or the teeth of foxes and weasels. Even the round protuberances once thought to represent human breasts contain the jaws and teeth of wild boars, covered with layers of plaster (Hodder and Meskell 2010). By mounting these things in close proximity to human burials, the residents of the house appear to mobilize a dramatic contrast between ancestors and animals.

But according to recent scholarship in animal studies, not all societies recognize the duality of man and beast (Weismantel and Pearson 2010: 20–22). For many indigenous societies, humans are merely one species among many (Vivieros de Castro 1998); similarly, Western Europe before Descartes lacked a monolithic ontological category of "the animal" (Shannon 2009). These ethnographic analogies suggest that the same might be true at Çatalhöyük – as does the archaeological evidence.

The displays assemble horn, tooth, and bones of different sizes, shapes, and kinds. They are idiosyncratic, opportunistic creations, rather like the figurines studied by Meskell, albeit more permanent and on a

---

[5] Space precludes a discussion of the domestic/wild opposition, as exemplified in the contrast between aurochs and caprines. I hope to explore this question in a subsequent publication.

grander scale. Instead of representations of an abstraction, these are bodily presences that materialized an animistic sociality, immersing the house's human occupants in a lively multispecies world.

This interpretation makes the animals more like the humans buried below them – who, it turns out, are also a surprisingly heterogeneous bunch. We might assume that a group of people buried together in the same house share biological ancestry, but the data say otherwise. "Intracemetery biological distance analysis indicates that interment within a house was only minimally related to biological affinity" (Pilloud and Larson 2011: 519).

In sum, rather than two homogeneous categories, "wild animals" and "our ancestors," we have two heterogeneous groups. Having failed to establish biological links between them, or to the house, we must, as Pilloud and Larson suggest, look for "an alternate and more fluid definition of 'kin'" (2011: 519).

KIN

The absence of genetic relatedness is not really surprising: in many ethnographically documented societies, biological distance analyses of the bodies of "family" or "lineage" members would provide similar results. In Zumbagua, kinship was all-important in producing the dense set of social linkages upon which material life depended – but as I gradually discovered, these networks had only the loosest connections to biological ties of birth (Weismantel 1988, 1995). Cross-culturally, actual ties between people are built through everyday sociality, and shaped over time by affinities and accidents; once in place, these links are renamed to conform to powerful biological fictions.

At Çatalhöyük, the data show that links between people and houses were primarily social in origin: created not through the accident of birth, but through repeated deliberate acts that resulted in shared labor, shared meals, shared sleep. The sequence of events that led to *these* people being buried in *this* house was a contingent history, neither natural nor inevitable. As in Zumbagua, we can deduce that centripetal social forces came into play between these people, drawing them together until they belonged to the same house, and ultimately became its dead.

A similar focus on contingent histories clarifies the link between the bucrania and the house. These bones, like those of the humans, are here as a result of a particular chain of events: a hunt, a death, and a feast.

Excavations of the open spaces or middens between house clusters indicate that feasts were key centripetal events in Çatalhöyük social life. A successful hunt was celebrated publicly and communally, creating a festive occasion when a household could host others, placing themselves at the center of a network of gift giving that indebted others to them – and made future kin (Dietler and Hayden 2001; Weismantel 2002). The distinctive horns, claws, or teeth displayed within Çatalhöyük houses served as memorials to these signal events (Keane 2010; Russell et al. 2009). Residents of Çatalhöyük houses could trace their genesis as a family or a household to the series of feasts commemorated on their walls – almost like the framed photographs of weddings that adorn modern homes.

Displays of bucrania, bear claws, or boar jaws also commemorated another vital link: to the "family" of aurochs, bears, or boars that had given up one of its members. Unlike the modern hunt, which celebrates human (masculine) power over lesser beings, the hunt in small-scale precapitalist societies is understood to be a delicate, carefully cultivated relationship between two sentient beings and their respective kin, which culminates in the gift of the animal's body (Marvin 2006).

GIFT

This brings us full circle to the word *hau*, which signifies not merely "the spirit of things," but "the spirit of things *given*" (Mauss 1990: 11, emphasis added). Nothing embodies the spirit of the gift so completely as a hunted animal and the rituals that surround its death (Ingold 1994; Marvin 2006); and nothing so beautifully instantiates that gift as the installations on Çatalhöyük walls, which memorialize it in all its material and spiritual fullness.

Each display within the house is literally a unique assemblage made from body parts chosen for their unusual shapes or remarkable size (Russell, pers. comm., Çatalhöyük 2011). Each is an assemblage in another sense, too. It materializes and entangles a series of social and material histories receding back in time, each of which involved a series of gifts. The most recent was the feast, when gifts of meat radiated out from this household to others; before the feast, there was social drama of the hunt.

Preceding these human stories, the very first assemblage was that of the animal itself, its social life shaped by the herd, its body fed by the grasses and waters of its homeland. The ability of the ruminant body to ingest these elements and then in turn to be ingested is its great gift to its hunters. Although permanently embedded within the house, the bucrania were still living members of another ecosystem: according to Mauss, "the thing given ... is invested with life"; it "is animated by the *hau* of its forest, its native hearth and soil" (1990: 13).

Far from being dead matter, the gift from the wild is actively volitional: it seeks to "produce, on behalf of the clan and the native soil from which it sprang, an equivalent to replace it" (1990: 13). The bucrania are a visible promise: their insistent will to generate continued relations between their new home and their "native hearth" ensures that the house will continue to be entangled in life-giving relations with others.

As with the other dyads discussed here, we have dismantled the animal/human divide only to rediscover it in a new, more active form, as an unstable and productive relationship enacted over time as well as in space. Aurochs, bears, and boars had a spatial and social origin outsidethe human community; this alterity is expressed in their disposition within the house, where their bones are placed near human graves but somewhat apart. In this, they resemble affines, who are simultaneously strangers and kin. And in fact, many hunting societies conceptualize animals in this way: in Native American myths, horses become husbands and jaguars become wives. Over time, affinity becomes descent: in other tales, dolphins and deer are ancestors.

And so with the aurochs. Born into another, nonhuman "family" in another place, they nonetheless come to be fully incorporated into the house in the most literal possible sense: their flesh consumed by its inhabitants, their bones built into its walls. Displays of the teeth, claws, and horns – the only parts of the skeleton that are visible during life – slyly suggest that the rest of the bones are invisibly present under the plaster. (This is literally true of the bucrania, where the horns are exposed, but the skull is hidden, as though enfleshed by its plaster covering.) These installations proclaim that the supporting armature of the house, the vital core that ensures its continued survival, is its active relationship with the outside world: with the strangers and animals who bring gifts and become kin.

An Open End

This essay has attempted to replace the house as enclosed box with the house as an assemblage of vital matter. It explored new models of the body as vital, partible, and multiple and applied this insight to a series of dyads – male/female, sacred/secular, animal/human, stranger/kin – and to a consideration of the house as a material and temporal construct, and as a spatial and social one.

In its vertical dimension, the house is expansive. The current house rests on the remains of earlier houses: its immediate predecessor forms an integral, load-bearing part of its architecture; that house, recently inhabited and still remembered, is intermixed with the inchoate remains of previous, forgotten houses, expanding downward from memory to myth.

Its horizontal dimensions are likewise expansive and entangled, structured by ongoing relations of exchange to strangers and future kin, human and nonhuman. Like the communal roofs – an open structure of roads and doorways – the house is open to the future, as well as to the past. This openness is instantiated in the bucrania, living gifts; for as Bourdieu (1997) explains, the gift at its heart is an open-ended, unfinished transaction.

This house has an identity, a spirit, a *hau* – but not an immutable and timeless essence. Instead, its *hau* is its history: a history of things, animals, and people that went in and went out, dismembered into parts or assembled into pluralities. As an assemblage of "things given," the Çatalhöyük house is a living machine composed of animate elements, each alive with productive desire. By digging in, opening it up, and setting its disarticulated parts into new circulation as artifacts, the archaeologists at Çatalhöyük have unwittingly become the latest humans to satisfy that never-ending desire for sociality and continued life.

BIBLIOGRAPHY

Appadurai, A. 2011. The social life of things. Keynote address presented at *The Life of Things* Conference, Franke Institute for the Humanities. April 30, 2011.

Bennett, J. 2010. *Vibrant Matter: A Political Ecology of Things*. Durham, NC: Duke University Press.

Bloch, M. 2010. Is there religion at Çatalhöyük…or are there just houses? In *Religion in the Emergence of Civilization: Çatalhöyük as a Case Study*, ed. I. Hodder. New York: Cambridge University Press, 146–162.

Bourdieu, P. 1997. Marginalia – some additional notes on the gift. In *The Logic of the Gift: Toward an Ethic of Generosity*, ed. A. D. Schrift. New York: Routledge, 231–244.

Bourdieu, P. 2003. The Berber house. In *The Anthropology of Space and Place: Locating Culture*, eds. S. M. Low and D. Lawrence-Zuniga. Malden, MA: Blackwell, 131–141.

Boz, B. and Hager, L. 2013. Intramural burial practices at Çatalhöyük. In *Humans and Landscapes of Çatalhöyük: Reports from the 2000–2008 Seasons*, ed. I. Hodder. Los Angeles: Cotsen Institute.

Braidotti, R. 2002. *Metamorphoses: Towards a Materialist Theory of Becoming*. Cambridge: Polity Press.

Butler, J. 1990. *Gender Trouble: Feminism and the Subversion of Identity*. New York: Routledge.

Cunningham, C. E. 1964. Order in the Atoni house. In *Bijdragen tot de Taal-, Lanen Volenkunde*, Deel 120, 1ste Afl., *Anthropologica* VI, 34–68.

Dietler, M. and Hayden, B., eds. 2001. *Feats: Archaeological and Ethnographic Perspectives on Food, Politics, and Power*. Washington, DC: Smithsonian Institution Press.

Douglas, M. 1996. *Natural Symbols: Explorations in Cosmology*. New York: Routledge.

  2002. *Purity and Danger: An Analysis of Concept of Pollution and Taboo*. New York: Routledge.

Düring, B. S. and Marciniak, A. 2006. Households and Communities in the Central Anatolian Neolithic. *Archaeological Dialogues* 12(2), 165–187.

Freud, S. 2003. *The Uncanny*. New York: Penguin Classics.

Ginsburg, F. D. and Rapp, R., eds. 1995. *Conceiving the New World Order: The Global Politics of Reproduction*. Berkeley: University of California Press.

Haraway, D. 2003. *The Companion Species Manifesto: Dogs, People, and Significant Otherness*. Chicago: Prickly Paradigm Press.

Hodder, I. 1990. *The Domestication of Europe*. Oxford: Blackwell.

  2006. *The Leopard's Tale: Revealing the Mysteries of Çatalhöyük*. London: Thames and Hudson.

Hodder, I. 2010. Probing religion at Çatalhöyük: an interdisciplinary experiment. In *Religion in the Emergence of Civilization: Çatalhöyük as a Case Study*, ed. I. Hodder. New York: Cambridge University Press, 1–31.

Hodder, I. 2012. *Entangled: An Archaeology of the Relationships between Humans and Things*. Oxford: Wiley-Blackwell.

Hodder, I, ed. 2000. *Towards Reflexive Method in Archaeology: the Example at Çatalhöyük: by Members of the Çatalhöyük Teams*. Cambridge: McDonald Institute Monographs and the British Institute of Archaeology at Ankara.

  ed. 2010. *Religion in the Emergence of Civilization: Çatalhöyük as a Case Study*. New York: Cambridge University Press.

Hodder, I. and Cessford, C. 2004. Daily Practice and Social Memory at Çatalhöyük. *American Antiquity* 69(1), 17–40.

Hodder, I. and Meskell, L. 2010. The symbolism of Çatalhöyük in its regional context. In *Religion in the Emergence of Civilization: Çatalhöyük as a Case Study*, ed. I. Hodder. New York: Cambridge University Press, 32–72.

Hodder, I. and Pels, P. 2010. History houses: A new interpretation of architectural elaboration at Çatalhöyük. In *Religion in the Emergence of Civilization: Çatalhöyük as a Case Study*, ed. I. Hodder. New York: Cambridge University Press, 163–186.

Hugh-Jones, C. 1979. *From the Milk River: Spatial and Temporal Processes in Northwest Amazonia*. Cambridge: Cambridge University Press.

Ingold, T. 1994. From trust to domination: An alternative history of human-animal relations. In *Animals and Human Society: Changing Perspectives*, eds. A. Manning and J. Serpell. London: Routledge, 1–22.

Keane, W. 2010. Marked, absent, habitual: Approaches to Neolithic religion at Çatalhöyük. In *Religion in the Emergence of Civilization: Çatalhöyük as a Case Study*, ed. I. Hodder. New York: Cambridge University Press, 187–219.

Kuijt, I. 2011. Thinking about the household: Building clusters, history houses, and spatial organization at Çatalhöyük. Presentation. Çatalhöyük, Turkey. July 1, 2011.

Levi-Strauss, C. 1963. *Structural Anthropology*. New York: Basic Books.

Marvin, G. 2006. Wild killing: Contesting the animal in hunting. In *Killing Animals*. Urbana: University of Illinois Press, 10–29.

Mauss, M. 1990 [1923]. *The Gift: The Form and Reason for Exchange in Archaic Societies*. Trans. W. D. Halls. London: Routledge.

Meskell, L. 2011. Dirty, pretty things: On archaeology and prehistoric materialities. Paper presented at *The Life of Things* Conference, Franke Institute for the Humanities. April 30, 2011.

Meskell, L. and Nakamura, C. 2005. Çatalhöyük figurines. In *Çatalhöyük: Archive Report, 2005*. figurines.stanford.edu/files/Catal_Figurine_Archive_Report_2005.pdf.

Meskell, L., Nakamura, C., King, R., and Farid, S. 2008. Figured Lifeworlds and Depositional Practices at Çatalhöyük. *Cambridge Archaeological Journal* 18(2):139–161.

Nakamura, C. 2010. Magical deposits at Çatalhöyük: A matter of time and place? In *Religion in the Emergence of Civilization: Çatalhöyük as a Case Study*, ed. I. Hodder. New York: Cambridge University Press, 300–331.

Nakamura, C. and Meskell, L. 2009. Articulate bodies: Forms and figures at Çatalhöyük. In *Journal of Archaeological Method and Theory* 16, 205–230.

Pearson, S. J. and Weismantel, M. 2010. Does 'the animal' exist: Toward a theory of social life with animals. In *Beastly Natures: Animals, Humans, and the Study of History*, ed. D. Brantz. Charlottesville: University of Virginia Press, 17–37.

Pels, P. 2010. Temporalities of 'religion' at Çatalhöyük. In *Religion in the Emergence of Civilization: Çatalhöyük as a Case Study*, ed. I. Hodder. New York: Cambridge University Press, 220–267.

Pilloud, M. A. and Larsen, C. S. 2011. 'Official' and 'Practical' Kin: Inferring Social and Community Structure from Dental Phenotype at Neolithic Çatalhöyük, Turkey. *American Journal of Physical Anthropology* 145(4):519–530.

Puar, J. 2007. *Terrorist Assemblages: Homonationalism in Queer Times*. Durham, NC: Duke University Press.

Robin, C. 2002. Outside of Houses: The Practices of Everyday Life at Chan Noohol, Belize. *Journal of Social Archaeology* 2(2), 245–268.

Russell, N., Martin, L., and Twiss, K. C. 2009. Building memories: Commemorative deposits at Çatalhöyük. In *Zooarchaeology and the Reconstruction of Cultural Systems: Case Studies from the Old World*, eds. B. S. Arbuckle, C. A. Makarewicz, and A. L. Atici. Paris: L'Homme et l'Animal, Société de Recherch Interdisciplinaire, 103–128.

Schneider, D. M. 1980. *American Kinship: A Cultural Account*. Chicago: University of Chicago Press.

Shannon, L. 2009. The Eight Animals in Shakespeare; or, before the Human. *PMLA* 124(2), 472–479.

Strathern, M. 1988. *The Gender of the Gift*. Berkeley: University of California Press.

Twiss, K. and Russell, N. 2010. Taking the Bull by the Horns: Ideology, Masculinity, and Cattle Horns at Çatalhöyük. *Paléorient* 35(2):19–32.

Viveiros de Castro, E. 1998. Cosmological Deixis and Amerindian Perspectivism. *The Journal of the Royal Anthropological Institute* 4(3):469–488.

Weismantel, M. 1988. *Food, Gender, and Poverty in the Ecuadorian Andes*. Prospect Heights, IL: Waveland Press.

1995. Making Kin: Kinship Theory and Zumbagua Adoptions. *American Ethnologist* 22(4), 685–704.

Weismantel, M. 2002. Embarrassment of Riches. Review of Feasts: Archaeological and Ethnographic Perspectives on Food, Politics and Power, eds. Michael Dietler and Brian Hayden. *Current Anthropology* 44, 141–2.

Weismantel, M. 2004. Moche Sex Pots: Reproduction and Temporality in Ancient South America. *American Anthropologist* 106(3), 495–505.

11

Material Register, Surface, and Form at Çatalhöyük

Victor Buchli

The tradition of research on the Neolithic settlement of Çatalhöyük has emphasized the importance of sedentism in relation to the rise of the domestic as the key locus for social and ritual life. The settlement itself is referred to in terms of an agglomeration of "houses" with the elicitations of settled domestic life and individual households based on common kin affiliation that the notion of the "house" entails. In fact it is the notion of "house societies" derived from the work of Claude Lévi-Strauss and further articulated in the collection of Carsten and Hugh-Jones and subsequent work that has held a strong hold on the interpretative imagination at Çatalhöyük. To an anthropologist with a specialization in material culture studies with a long-standing interest in the domestic and architectural form, the structures encountered at Çatalhöyük are indeed beguiling in regard to what they might be able to say in terms of the nature of dwelling and the appearance of what might seem to be the origin of the domestic. The trope of house societies has certainly taken hold (Bloch 2010) and has evolved more recently in terms of the notion of "history houses" (Hodder and Pels 2010). Indeed the relation of the houses to the production of persons is a long-standing association (see Preston-Blier 1987). As Carsten and Hugh-Jones famously noted, it is in fact difficult to disentangle bodies from houses, and houses from bodies, meaningfully. At Çatalhöyük this imbrication of bodies and buildings is profoundly entangled as dead bodies are interred in household platforms; bones of the dead are rearranged, dug out, and reinterred at later dates by later people (Boz and Hager 2013); neonates are buried in walls, adults and the aged in floors and platforms and the body parts of various wild beasts such as aurochs horns are decorated and plastered into walls; and the plastering itself seems to be performed using the scapulae of aurochs, while a whole range of wild animals are represented on wall murals (and notably domesticated animals such as sheep are absent). The bodies of beasts and of humans and architectural forms are all wildly mixed up in terms of modernist ontologies.

More recently the presumption that these structures were dwellings where kin groups resided is contradicted by dental evidence from skeletons at the site that indicates that there is no discernible genetic connection between human skeletons buried in individual structures at the site (Pilloud and Larsen 2011). The jumble of human and animals bones is even further complicated.

In light of these complications to our understanding of these structures at Çatalhöyük, I would like to propose that our preoccupation with architectural forms that lead us to identify "houses" implicating forms of kinship and gender and its attendant meanings are problematic and misleading. We see "floor plans" with hearths and platforms with burials and we imagine "domestic" spaces where "families" live and are buried for several generations.

I would like to suggest that what I like to refer to as our modernist preoccupation with form serves us well in our modernist endeavors, especially those that seek cross-cultural comparisons and analogues in reference to similarities in material form. Such formal preoccupations are typologizing and subsume many disparate things according to the logic of the type. They assume the understanding of a house and concomitant notions of kinship, gender, and cosmology across a vast range of otherwise heterogeneous objects here subsumed under the formal characteristics of a "house." However, it would appear that the origin point of our first settlements where we might see the ancestors of our sedentary institutions is increasingly less and less recognizable and more confusing as research at Çatalhöyük progresses (Düring and Marciniak 2006; Last 1996).

I would like to propose rather that our preoccupation with form give way to a preoccupation with surfaces and their engagement. And thereby propose that rather than being "history houses" or "houses" at all (at least not in any conventional sense), these structures serve to contain, harness, and curate powerful substances both sublime and prosaic for the benefit of corporate groups (see Weismantel, this volume, and Kuijt pers.comm. in seminar discussions; Bogaard et al. 2009; Düring and Marciniak 2006). In particular I want to suggest that a deep time perspective imparted by archaeology allows us to investigate shifts in material registers that should wean us away from our preoccupation with form and the productive power of formal typologies such as the primacy of the house form and be sensitive instead to shifts in material registers and in fact the dominance of certain registers over others in different places and at different times.

The elaborately decorated structures at Çatalhöyük with their murals, bucrania, and burial platforms, though most celebrated, are not the norm at Çatalhöyük. Only some structures possess these elaborate features and not always at the same time. Some structures of roughly the same size receive little or no elaboration at all. The celebrated decorations only appear intermittently within the same level at different times. The celebrated murals are often replastered and disappear and are then painted again differently at a distant time. Later levels (notably on the West Mound) show less elaboration of decorative wall elements and an increase in decorative pottery. A shift over time seems to indicate an irregular articulation of elaborate wall surfaces that gradually gives way to a preoccupation with decorated ceramics, where before there was no interest in elaborate decorated ceramic ware (Düring and Marciniak 2006; Hodder 2006; Last 1996). The articulation of surfaces switches from the surfaces of walls to the surfaces of pots. Expressive material registers are inconsistent and over time shift.

In other parts of the Neolithic Middle East, there seem to be similar inconsistencies. At the earlier site of Aşıklı Höyük, the structures though similar in form are even more distinctive in their treatment of surfaces by virtue of the complete absence of any surface decoration, no murals, no bucrania, just clean walls (see Düring and Marciniak 2006). Similarly, Göbekli Tepe Level III could not be more distinctive materially with its regularly rebuilt phallic monumental stellae arranged in open circles compared to the conglomeration of small cramped enclosed rectangular structures at Çatalhöyük. As is more recently noted, the Neolithic in the Middle East saw many responses to the rise of the domestication of animals and plants with differing material responses (Düring and Marciniak 2006; Hodder 2006).

Our preoccupation with form can be misleading as a productive typology in a setting of such heterogeneous responses. In this regard I would like to move away from form and engage with surface, in part through a reengagement with the writings of Gottfried Semper, the nineteenth century theorist of architecture and the decorative arts, who took issue with his protomodernist contemporaries such as Ruskin, Violet le Duc, and Pugin (Malgrave 1989): those protomodernists who avowed the honesty of structure and form and eschewed the superfluousness of decoration. Semper, on the contrary, argued that form and structure were anterior to enclosure. Walls merely existed to support surfaces, and it was at the surfaces that humans engaged with built forms through decorative elements and their wide-ranging effects.

> Hanging carpets remained the true walls, the visible boundaries of space. The often solid walls behind them were necessary for reasons that had nothing to do with the creation of space; they were needed for security, for supporting a load, for their permanence, and so on. Wherever the need for these secondary functions did not arise, the carpets remained the original means separating space. Even where building solid walls became necessary, the latter were only the inner, invisible structure hidden behind the true and legitimate representatives of the wall, the colorful woven carpets. (Semper 1989: 104)

One should not take Semper literally about the primacy of carpets, especially in relation to Çatalhöyük, where others have suggested unconvincingly that the wall decorations resembled the patterns of kilims many thousands of years later (Mellaart 1967: 152). Rather, Semper was arguing for the primacy of the *Wandbereiter* (the wall fitter) and the primacy of wall dressings, comprising woven textiles, carpets, stucco, painted decoration, and so on, over walls themselves. Semper was a product of his time and his discussion of decorative elements, particularly wall elements, was part of a larger project investigating the evolution of built and decorative form. The inadequacies of such investigations into origins have been long rehearsed. But I would like to retrieve Semper's emphasis on surface over form against his protomodernist contemporaries as his approach has a certain resonance with more recent attempts to steer away from those very same modernist legacies (see Heynen 1999; Vidler 2000), because if one considers surfaces as primary, then we might be able to consider different kinds of surfaces, the surfaces of walls, the surfaces of pots (burnished and decorated), and other such surfaces that might be elaborated, decorated, and engaged with. This might help to find a framework with which to consider different material registers not bound by form and modern typologies and to consider their social effects, especially if we begin to see walls giving way to pots as the sites of elaborate surfaces and engagement.

With this focus I want to direct attention to the important aspect of embodiment and daily practice that surfaces are intimately entailed with. Regular cleaning, sweeping, airing, washing, replastering, painting, polishing, burnishing, rebuilding, reburial are all profoundly intimate bodily practices that engage the inhabitants of these sites on a regular basis, engaging scales as diverse as the quotidian to the eternal. As Mary Douglas noted, the dwelling has an innate capacity to encompass all of these diverse scales through their varying embodied practices (Douglas 1991). The profoundly detailed quality of empirical data produced at the Çatalhöyük excavations makes these embodied intimacies visible while interpellating the excavator and analyst within these cyclical embodied practices that I would like to suggest point to a certain limited but enduring "truth" to the efficacy of these repetitive embodied material practices, as their materiality then as now produces a certain kind of enduring social engagement and form of knowledge. It is at this point that I want to direct this discussion also to the question of religiosity and ritual practice that has been the preoccupation of the Templeton project, because it is here that a very different sense of religiosity seems to suggest itself in contrast to the monumentality of Göbekli Tepe, which is famously considered the first religious architecture. I want to suggest that the embodied quotidian aspects of surface engagement produce an intimate and intensive mode of religiosity that is nondoctrinal but embodied and materially sustained by the requirements of surface engagement at varying scales of consciousness, and bodily and social activity. In particular I want to suggest that surface engagement, polishing, brilliance, and decay produce a sense of revelation and transcendence (see Keane 2010; Miller 2009) within the nested practices of surface engagements from the quotidian sweeping of floors, the plastering and replastering of floors and walls, to the burial and reburial of bodies and destruction and construction of structures. The materials within these material registers produce oscillations between two worlds, through polishing, excavation, whitewashing, and repainting, suggesting and invoking the quotidian along with the transcendent and in fact making the two inseparable from one another so that one spills over into the other and is actually "revealed" through these practices (see Keane 2010; Hodder and Pels 2010 on revelation). This is an intimate, embodied practice, and I would suspect a largely nondiscursive one, distinct from the episodic and monumental practices one might associate with Göbekli Tepe (Schmidt 2010).

It is on the basis of these observations that I would like to propose, and particularly in light of very recent data, that the structures at Çatalhöyük are not houses in the conventional sense, or "history houses" or even "power houses," and certainly not "house societies" but rather containers of powerful generative substances, both prosaic (seed, foodstuffs, etc.) and sublime (human bones, wild animal parts), that are necessary for the sustenance of life and the moral worlds sustained therein. What is taken as evidence of daily life, the hearths and their respective waste products, are the activities associated with the small number of people who could have possibly lived there. It has been noted that the burials at some structures are too numerous to have been the actual occupants of the same house. Actual inhabitants might possibly be considered caretakers, possibly elderly caretakers who cared for (judging by the smoke filled lungs that carbon residues on the ribs of the aged suggest), supervised, possibly maintained, but more generally probably curated these powerful generative substances and whose power and efficacy waxed and waned with the fortunes of the corporate groups associated with the individual structures.

As subsistence changed, after level South P and again later with a move to the West Mound from the East, new means of engaging with the sustenance of social and moral life emerged, that become more extensive, certainly not as extensive as at Göbekli Tepe, but more than it had been previously at Çatalhöyük. With this the sorts of embodied surface engagements sustaining structural social and moral worlds through their embodied, regularized, and cyclical engagements shifted from the intimate scales produced through these sensuous engagements with walls, in decoration, maintenance, cleaning, and burial practices to more extensive forms. These extensive forms saw burials increasingly outside, and there was a shift to more elaboration of technically sophisticated burnished pottery wares and their decorative surfaces that seems to echo the decorative motifs of earlier murals (Hodder 2006; Last 1996).

In the following sections I would like to discuss a number of activities related to the social engagement with surfaces that might be useful in assessing the shifts in material register that one sees on the site.

Storage

Bogaard et al. (2009) discuss recent findings concerning storage bins and their contents in the structures at Çatalhöyük. They argue for a contrast between more invidualized and private storage of grains and seeds at the "houses" of Çatalhöyük as compared to more communalistic activities such as the hunting of aurochs. Storage bins are decidedly undecorated especially compared with regional ethnoarchaeological evidence while the platforms depicting animal hunts and the modeling of bucrania indicate a more public and elaborate engagement with communal hunting. Grains and wild animals seem to be in opposition. I would like to suggest otherwise that the structures unite both, as "containers" (in the manner suggested by Warnier 2007, 2006) of powerful substances. The generative power of seeds and grains is literally stored, while, rather than seeing bucrania and murals as "representations" to be "read" regarding communal activities, these murals serve through a process of mimetic contagion to "contain" or rather harness the power of these activities (see Hodder 2006 on Lewis-Williams's observations). A hunt and its productive capacities cannot literally be stored or contained, but its lingering and extended effects and power in the form of bucrania can be mimetically indexed and harnessed and "stored" through the elaborate images that punctuate the use of these structures over time – they are literally stored and contained as the power of seeds and grain is stored, as the power of the dead is stored, and remembered and stored again. That is why the images can be obscured by layers of white stucco; they are stored, remembered, and then augmented again at later dates after subsequent plastering and later mural painting (see Matthews et al. 2013). The remains of the power of the dead are stored, plastered over, contained, remembered, excavated, reinterred, and "stored" at later dates for later generations. Furthermore, Bogaard et al. suggest that the cattle representations and remains serve as "storing up" the memories of such events (2009: 656). These are mimetic acts not symbolic acts – embodied practices not discursive ones. These images are meant to be "felt" not "seen," or rather "seeing" should be understood in more haptic terms as a form of touch, contact, and contagion. To seal an image with plaster is to contain it and limit the circulation of its powers. I would suggest that their visibility compared to the relative invisibility of the storage bins (though as Bogaard et al. 2009 suggest this pattern does have exceptions) is a function of how the power effects of both can be meaningfully stored. In any case, all the contents of these structures are effectively not visible outside the few individuals who could actually enter, in a dimly lit smoke filled room where the images are only periodically visible as they are plastered over and "stored" again to be rearticulated and whose power could be augmented and "topped up" with later images. Such images had no "public" audience; in fact, they were not representations for a public at all, but mimetic stores as the earlier part of Bogaard et al.'s analysis suggests. Bogaard et al. also note that the storage bins represented only a portion of potential storage at the site. There is evidence of other more ephemeral (and one might note more transportable) forms of storage (2009: 660) in potentially other locations, intramurally, on roofs, in abandoned structures, and so on. The bin volumes on the whole at the site represent a capacity of one cubic meter, enough to feed a group of five to seven people for a year (2009: 661), and as such they represent only a portion of what would have been used for a wider population.

Seals

Türkcan (2013) reports on the numerous seals found at the site (a total of fifty-nine at Çatalhöyük). They invoke geometric motifs and animal motifs of various kinds, bears, leopards, hands, and so-called Goddess (splayed figure) motifs. It is believed that they could have been used on a wide range of media, clay, walls, leather, cloth, human skin, and more (see also Mellaart 1967). Hodder (2006: 231; Türkcan 2013) notes that these seals emerge with greater frequency in the upper layers of the site, suggesting a shift in decorative media from walls to seals, and a shift in scale from the intensive scale of murals within structures to the more mobile and dynamic scale of seals that could be applied to many different kinds of surfaces, both static and mobile, in short, an extensive use of decorative motifs that exploit similar powerful animal motifs such as those found on murals (e.g., leopards, aurochs, bears; see Hodder 2006: 233). I would like to suggest that this represents a shift in the way generative power is distributed in space and time and in terms of its embodied experience (see also Kamerman, this volume). As Hodder notes, the geometric and animal motifs of seals are closely associated with the "houses," but the designs extend the decorative motifs of the "houses" outward (Hodder 2006: 177), attaching these motifs to other mobile things (as suggested on bodies, cloth, movable objects, etc.) Later in the late Neolithic and Chalcolithic at Çatalhöyük West the designs are seen on pottery. Hodder interprets these as indicating a concern with ownership and individuation. I would like to consider these more in terms of the extension across media, scales, and space of the mimetic capacity of seals. Through their physical contact they enable magical contagion and the extension of generative powers, both prosaic and sublime. As Marciniak and Czerniak (2007) have noted, from level South P onward, the neighborhood based associations of corporate life seem to give way to more individual and individuated structures with vertical doors on walls that open on to space (as opposed to roof entrances) that could more feasibly be understood in terms of autonomous, possibly kin based households in the more conventional sense. Within this more attenuated and relatively individualized setting the intensive material registers in effect earlier at lower levels would give way to more extensive, distributed, and mobile material registers such as those enabled through stamping.

The subtle shift in registers from wall murals to decorated pots might hesitatingly be linked to the subtle yet significant earlier shift in ceramic technology on the site (see Last 1996). If one considers the shift from rough wares to more sophisticated ones suitable for cooking around South M, then one might hazard to suggest a certain interruption in the intensification of activities within these structures. As heated clay balls requiring constant attention give way to pots that can be left alone to cook (Hodder 2006), a certain attenuation of activities subtly begins. As Hodder notes, individuals are freed to do other things; an intensive engagement with the materiality of the structures subtly shifts to give way to more attenuated activities. Ceramics develop a certain virtual agency, as suggested by Hodder, that eases the task of food preparation by enabling preparers to do other things. Finer ceramics begin to have an unexpected agency and one might argue an emerging incipient importance (if the subsequent investment in their specialized and elaborate production is anything to go by) in terms of their material affordances that enable a certain attenuation of material engagements. Eventually decorated ceramics might just seem to be the more pragmatic and effective means by which to effect certain forms of sociality materially within changing contingencies.

Murals, Plastering, and Ceramics

Modern conventional archaeological typologies tend to separate things according to modern analytical categories; bones are distinct from ceramics, art work is distinct from botanical remains, and houses are distinct from pots. But such modern Euro-American categories tend to obscure the relations categories of objects might have to one another in non-Euro-American settings. Nancy Munn's (1977) work among the Gawa shows how there are certain semantic fields that logically gather what might seem to be disparate things from a Euro-American perspective into functional unities such as "redness" and others (what she refers to in terms of Peircean semiotics syntagmatically as "qualisigns"). Similarly Marilyn Strathern's (1999) work on Melanesia speaks to certain categories of substance that unite otherwise empirically disparate elements such as whiteness for semen, pig fat, cowrie shells, and so on, that are responsible for social and bodily generative processes (see also Knauft 1999). In this section I would like to consider the surfaces of walls in relation to the surfaces of ceramics to suggest a common semantic field along an anaphoric chain of associations. The philosopher of science Joseph Rouse (Rouse 2002) describes such slippages along such chains in terms of the way pronouns work. Pronouns enable us to retain commitments to previous statements without having to reiterate their content. "Anaphoric expressions such as pronouns enable a discursive performance to inherit the inferential commitments and entitlements of another performance without having to articulate its specific content. Such expressions are crucial to keeping track of discursive commitments, because one can use them to talk about whatever someone else is talking about, without having to understand or endorse the concepts she used to talk about it. Anaphora are the linguistic expressions that enable communication to proceed in the absence of shared meanings" (Rouse 2002: 202). Furthermore within Rouse's discussion is the suggestion that rather than thinking of anaphora in linguistic terms it can be understood in distinctly material and embodied terms. It is this emphasis on contact or touch between anaphoric chains that is relevant to this discussion here. In this regard Rouse cites Brandom: "One can grasp an anaphoric chain as one grasps a stick; direct contact is achieved only with one end of it, and there may be much about what is beyond that direct contact of which one is unaware. But direct contact with one end gives genuine if indirect contact with what is attached to the other end … incorporates, as two sides of one coin, both the possibility of ignorance of and error about our own concepts and the possibility of genuine aboutness of those concepts and genuine knowledge of the [phenomena]" (Brandom in Rouse 2002: 296). In a similar way seemingly unrelated material phenomena can be considered in concert where some registers are foregrounded and some are backgrounded. The registers nonetheless coexist in a complex nonarbitrary relation to one another. They slip from one register to the next within a very specific historical trajectory and genealogy and within contracting and expanding notions of time and space (following Munn 1977). Their productive capacities also slip between these different anaphoric chains but are nonetheless entailed in relation to one another. Thus an overall shared commitment emerges that might be hazarded as a "tradition." It is useful to consider empirically through observations regarding polishing, cleaning, replastering, and decoration the social engagements these materials and their treatments entail. Rather than seeing these things as analytically disparate, they might be considered as analytically united in terms of an intensive embodied relation to surface and the curation of generative powers along anaphoric chains of otherwise empirically disparate media.

Warnier's (2007) example of Cameroonian kingship shows how the generative powers of social life are literally contained in the king within his rounded corpulent body, which he distributes through his circulation of raffia wine at ceremonial occasions. The kingly blessings are bestowed either through spewing of this liquid from his mouth onto recipients or distributing it more widely in containers of wine. Similarly his monopoly of many wives and the distribution of his semen among these wives are part of his monopoly of generative powers, both prosaic and sublime, that consolidate and distribute power. As his corpulent body is the locus and index of these generative powers, which are in turn housed within his palace and then further contained within the ceremonial limits of his city, one can see what might appear like a nested set of Russian dolls in which an intensive hierarchy of generative powers are consolidated, distributed, and maintained. Thus one has a semantic field or chain of anaphoric associations that would meaningfully unite the corpulent body with the walls of the palace, with the boundaries of the city, and with the containers of raffia wine that constitute this political economy – hence Warnier's characterization of the "pot-king." These otherwise empirically distinct categories are meaningfully and transformatively united within this same semantic field, which brings together what might otherwise seem to be very different material registers. One might speculate about the corpulent figurines from Çatalhöyük, which are ambiguously gendered by virtue (Keane 2010; Nakamura and Meskell 2013) of their distinctive obesity, particularly in a population that rarely exhibited such bodily qualities according to the dietary and osteological evidence. (Larsen et al. 2013 show how the inhabitants were physically fit much as North American hunter-gatherers were.) Such bodies could be seen as containing or monopolizing generative powers within their flesh. Marilyn Strathern has shown in other contexts how a fat baby must be killed by his agonized mother because the baby is born a "witch," who "unnaturally" is monopolizing generative powers as indexed by his notable fatness (Strathern 1999). As Nakamura and Meskell (2013) suggest, figurines found at the site seem to emphasize abstracted capacities in relation to buttocks and bellies and not necessarily reproductive or sexual characteristics, and they indicate as well that these somewhat "obese" representations do not square with the osteological evidence at the site.

"Power Cleaning, Curating Power"

In addition I want to consider here the activities of burnishing, plastering, and wall painting that occurred frequently, undertaken by individuals and groups and entailing a direct, sustained, and intimate embodied encounter in a manner suggested earlier by anaphoric chains.

It has been noted that the plastering of walls and floors occurred on a regular basis. An almost endless process of plastering, at yearly, seasonal, and even monthly intervals (Hodder 2006: 252; Matthews et al. 2013) took place. In the upper levels, plastering is less frequent; layers are thicker but less frequently applied, indicating an apparent disinvestment in the surfaces of the structures (Hodder 2006: 252). The frequent plasterings in the lower levels of occupation are linked to the frequent burials within the floor platforms, which require replastering after burial.

As Matthews et al. note that, the wall paintings associated with the structures at Çatalhöyük happened at periodic intervals during their use over time and were covered by many plaster layers and that the plastering over of these paintings might be a way "to preserve or seal the memory and/or potency of the events or periods associated with them" (Matthews et al. 2013: 132)

However, as Hodder and others note, these famous murals that have been so often reproduced and dominated the modern imagination in numerous reproductions – from Mellaart's widely read and published volume (Mellaart 1967) to Hodder's more recent volume (Hodder

2006) and in other media such as the permanent long-standing experimental reconstruction at the site, which, like an earlier reconstruction at the Museum of Anatolian Civilizations at Ankara, has these murals on view continuously – never in fact enjoyed the peculiar visibility ascribed to them now and produced by modern sensibilities. They were rarely ever seen by the communities that produced them. They were seen intermittently and then covered over by white plaster; Hodder notes, "But the paintings were seen only intermittently. Through most of the life of any particular house, the walls were white or sooty. But for short periods of time they became transformed into a blaze of colour and activity, either as figurative or geometric paintings" (Hodder 2006: 190).

I would like to suggest that the memories of these images were retained either in terms of an actual obscured image (similar to the destroyed sculptural images associated with the Malangaan of New Ireland described by Susanne Kuechler) or anaphorically in terms of a deferred contact and engagement reminiscent of distinctly contemporary urban and modern practices in twenty-first century mural painting. The work of the Turner Prize–winning artist Richard Wright is instructive here. For the 2009 Turner Prize, he painted an elaborate wall mural in radiant pure gold, which was covered over in white paint after a few months of exhibition. The art historian Sarah Lowndes writes: "An interesting aspect of Richard's installations for the Turner Prize exhibition is that he was returning to a space where he had previously made a painting (for the group exhibition 'Intelligence' [2000]). Although that older work was submerged under layers of white paint, the afterlife of that earlier piece (a delicate black and dark blue gothic work, painted just beneath the ceiling) reverberated in the coils and tendrils of the vast golden painting Richard made in the space of early autumn of 2009" (Lowndes 2009: 60). In this respect twenty-first century mural painting seems less modern than one might imagine in comparison with the murals of Çatalhöyük.

The painting of images and their obscuring suggests a resource that can be remembered, and reanimated with subsequent painting, at appropriate moments and in appropriate intervals (see Hodder 2006 on David Lewis-Williams on the power associated with imagery at Çatalhöyük). The brilliantly polished white rooms in certain structures were saturated with vibrant images whose vibrance indexed and reanimated subsequent ones, typically in conjunction with what must have been an auspicious burial. And similarly these burials were also plastered over, and their power permeated these white brilliantly polished plasterings. What might at most times appear alternately as either a brilliantly austere white or sooty room depending on the cycle of replastering was seething under the surface with powerful images and bones, constantly available for rearticulation or whose powers were constantly indexed, presenced, and literally felt and sensuously brought into contact through the multiple replasterings that further contained and curated the power of the images and bones buried deep within as material anaphora As Matthews et al. (2013: 132) suggest these replasterings could "preserve or seal the memory/and or potency" of these images. The quotidian practices of cleaning, polishing, and plastering served in an embodied fashion to engage the person directly, placing him or her into direct apotropaic and contagious contact with powerful forces contained, curated, and activated through these actions The materiality of delicate whiteness in relation to constant sootiness required a nondiscursive and embodied response to engage regularly and thereby have contact and invoke these stores of power – sootiness required this rearticulation and was in effect generative of these engagements. In reference to the elements of touch and contact that characterize the anaphoric chains, to paraphrase Christopher Tilley in reference to Merleau-Ponty, one is touched by the object and the object touches you. This mutual engagement creates a zone of contact where powerful elements are accessed and where two realms seemingly distinct – the quotidian and the transcendent – come into contact and are sustained through the seemingly mundane practices of cleaning, polishing, and plastering. One might speculate that the use of wild cattle scapulae for the plastering of walls also linked through magical contagion and contact the powers of the wild beasts outside with the powerful materials contained inside the multiple replasterings.

Matthews et al. (2013) note in a manner reminiscent of Gottfried Semper how interior surfaces are quite distinct in social significance and material engagement from the architectural frames in which they occur. Furthermore, Matthews et al. (2013) observe how fine white plasters seem to be associated with the eastern and "ritually" significant section of the structures as opposed to the less fine and darker plastering associated with the oven areas. Matthews et al. note how some plasters such as the ultrawhite plasters are associated with sources six kilometers from the site and in particular landscapes, suggesting a specific importance placed on the plaster in relation to the structure and the landscape it indexes.

Carbon residues found on long-term occupants suggest that these structures might very well have been primarily occupied by the elderly (Hodder 2006). These potentially revered individuals not only held the memories of the events, foodstuffs, images, objects, animal parts, human bodies, and other powerful images and substances of these structures but tended and maintained them through their daily practices as caretakers and curators of the powerful substances cached within. Revered elders could very well be the ideal occupants and caretakers of these structures. Their own relative immobility due to age and infirmity made them that much closer to the realm of the dead and transcendent spheres. It is worthwhile to consider McKinnon (2000) on Indonesian ancestral houses where elders are liminally placed between the realm of the living and the realm of the ancestors, and whose bodies are seen as on the verge of merging with the structural elements of the house.

The reliefs of leopards were replastered, painted, and replastered again, or the installations of animal bones in the walls were plastered and replastered again to create protuberances that were continuously plastered. Mellaart interpreted such protuberances as breasts containing animal parts (Mellaart 1967: 106), but one might more meaningfully see them as not representational but merely the result of containment, replastering, and further containment over time.

The notable shift in structures after South O and P and the rise of what seem to be more independent households increasingly reliant on domesticated sheep and domesticated cattle suggest a radical shift in subsistence and social life. However, the continued use of decorative motifs that reference the murals of earlier structures suggests a continuity (see Last 1996 on ceramics and continuity from the East to the West Mound). If social life and subsistence were regulated within structures that stored and curated the powerful substances that sustained social and reproductive life, then a shift to a less intensive and more dispersed mode of social life and production does not necessarily suggest a stark rupture. The proliferation of decorated pottery and the noticeable preponderance of portable figurines suggest that sublime and prosaic generative powers needed to be engaged with more extensively rather than intensively as before. More widely distributed and independent "households" could not be sustained as easily within the intensive material engagements of earlier structures. Those powers could not be concentrated to be effective within such a setting; rather they would need to be more extensive and distributive to be effective. Stamps, decorated pots, and figurines were more mobile and partible means of extending and distributing the generative powers that had such a long tradition at the site. The material register and its anaphoric associations would have to shift in order for these powers to be effective within a new reproductive setting. McKinnon (2000) notes – regarding the power of ancestral forests legitimating aristocratic families in Indonesia – a series of anaphoric chains. She observes how the generative powers derived from the forests and their productive capacities – to the houses as the extension and embodiment of those capacities, to the ancestral jewelry stored within these houses, and to the subsequent loss of such houses and even those ancestral adornments – could be even further sustained in the names of those jewels alone reaching back to the ancient forest claims they invoked in the modern period and in the wake of modernity and colonization and decolonization. From a forest to a name to all the various instantiations of these generative and ancestral claims through wildly divergent material registers (forests, houses, bones, jewels, names), an effective continuity is established. This is done within different registers to sustain, support, and extend those claims under extremely different political and economic conditions. Thus one might consider how, albeit over a decidedly extended time scale, a similar set of anaphoric associations could sustain claims to generative powers both prosaic and sublime within the new material registers of stamps, decorated pots, and mobile figurines.

On the other hand, the intensive concentration and curation of generative powers in the levels prior to South O may not be as immobile and intensive as one might imagine. Certain material objects needed to be dynamic and move. As Marciniak and Czerniak (2007) note, every sixty years or so structures were rebuilt on top of and with reference to each other with most of the portable artifacts removed and reinstated. Within burial platforms of individual structures bones would move up, excavated in prehistory and reinterred in subsequent layers as secondary burials. Mellaart noted how the heads and paws of leopard or bear reliefs would be removed, and famously the heads of the dead would be removed and reburied later on (consider also the discussion of the heads of figurines in Nakamura and Meskell (2013)). It has also been observed that wooden posts would be removed and reinstated. When circumstances dictated, the intensively curated powerful objects and substances would move "upward" diachronically rather than "outward" synchronically in later periods.

Exhaustion

Matthews et al. (2013: 135) also suggest through their detailed micromorphological analysis of building surfaces that the later layers of plastering in any one building tend to be less frequent. There is a greater presence of dirt between layers just before the structure is abandoned or destroyed. The greater investment in layering, plastering, and mural decoration with cleaner surfaces occurs earlier on in the foundation of the structure. This might suggest an "exhaustion" of the powerful resources of the structure over time that would lead to its eventual abandonment. A structure's generative powers could be dissipated or possibly superseded. Before deliberate destruction "structures" are also noted to have been cleaned, with portable artifacts removed before being destroyed, and a new structure built on top. Rather than seeing this as a purely destructive process, one might see it as a means of sealing an "exhausted" structure (just as plastering does not destroy so much as seal the image below) whose exhausted and remembered powers are residually felt and could be harnessed and indexed for the benefit of the foundation of a new structure or through the circulation of powerful mobile artifacts. Matthews et al. suggest a built landscape with several abandoned or "exhausted" houses among others still vibrant and potent. Similarly, Nakamura and Meskell's (2013) observations regarding the quick disposability and extensive distribution of figurines, easily made; quickly, crudely, and widely distributed; but significantly mostly found in middens, might suggest that figurines could similarly be "exhausted" of their efficacy.

There are a number of ethnographic contexts that suggest how different kinds of material registers produce different kinds of social relations. It is often observed how in some traditions certain architectural elements are associated with vertical and spatially intensive male lineages and other household elements with other kin relations and spatially extensive connections. Rebecca Empson (2007) shows how yurts associated with agnatic relations are complemented by the more ephemeral objects (cloth, hair, etc.) associated with these other kin relations. Similarly Anna

Hoare observes the importance of foregrounded agnatic relations at the expense of other kin relations among modern Irish travelers (Anna Hoare, personal communication). The point to consider here is that certain material registers highlight dominant or foregrounded social relations that often coexist in a complementary fashion with backgrounded relations expressed in different material registers. One might consider the proliferation of small figurines at Çatalhöyük less as a subaltern practice of "magic" counterpoised to the "official" religiosity of murals, platform burials, and bucrania (Nakamura 2010) than as "backgrounded" practices in a different, more extensive, mobile, and partible material register. These easily used, disposed of, proliferating, and individualistic figurines are eminently partible and broken up with their heads removed and circulated (Nakamura and Meskell 2013). Their relative crudeness technically is precisely what enables these social effects – made up on the spot by one person instantly available for use and immediately disposable upon exhaustion. Nakaumura and Meskell (2013) suggest a relation between the headlessness of human and animal remains and animal representations and the detachability of heads from small intimate figurines. Their analysis suggests a preoccupation with the head as a site of "identity." I would further like to consider the head in terms of power more broadly, power that can be detached and transmitted, extended or attenuated over various networks, distances, and scales and through various media (skulls human and nonhuman, representations of heads removed and circulated, figurines with heads removed and circulated, etc.; see also Knauft 1999 regarding the circulation of body parts, notably heads and their relation to power). These mobile partible figurines are at times associated with storage bins (Mellaart 1967; Nakamura and Meskell 2013: 214–15). Figurines, grain, and foodstuffs, detachable as they are, are eminently partible, circulating in what might appear to be baskets (Bogaard et al. 2009). Horns too are found in bins (Bogaard et al. 2009). This would seem to belie the interpretation of bins as containing purely prosaic and "economic" things rather than symbolic ones (see Keane 2010 on the difficulty of separating the prosaic from the religious). Rather the generative power of partible things produces exchange and debt, those powerful sinews of social life (Leach 1954) that make up people and socialities.

The importance of surfaces, notably building surfaces, has only recently received sustained attention within the social sciences.

Graham and Thrift (2007) have discussed the much-neglected study of building maintenance over time in terms of the wider political economy that such seemingly mundane practices sustain. Similarly Young (2004) has shown how the color "white" for the surfaces of interiors in early twenty-first century economies creates an economy of "fluid" and "extensive" and thereby more valuable property, while McCracken (1989) focuses on the articulation and intensification of domestic surfaces through the layering of materials, patterns, and objects that produce "homeyness" as the material means by which relations are intensified within the dwelling. By way of contrast, "nonhomey" minimalist strategies of whiteness produce extensive, universal, and exchangeable forms of value, as demonstrated by Young. Similarly, under the conditions of Soviet modernism whiteness enabled detachment and the deintensification of early twentieth century domestic practices in favor of more extensive and attenuated relations at larger revolutionary social scales: the scales of the socialist collective rather than the individual bourgeois domestic (Buchli 1999). In more recent contexts, Nicholas Rose (2006) suggests that frequent home decoration is not important in terms of what it signifies but in terms of a continuous sensuous practice that constantly marshals psychic and bodily energies toward the production, management, and generation of the self-managing neoliberal self.

In light of these observations I would like to suggest that increasing material entanglements do not necessarily mean that there is a cumulative quasi-evolutionary intensification. Rather one register and its attendant entanglements give way to another; the emphasis is more pragmatic than evolutionary, and certainly local when compared to other Neolithic and Chalcolithic sites (Düring and Marciniak 2006). Certain material registers simply expand human capacities and are then superseded by others within a cosmopolitan universe of differentially efficacious registers. The suggestion that figurines might represent a form of unofficial "magic" in the face of more "official" religious practices (Nakamura 2010) indicates a pragmatic practice of limited range, more intimate and individual. The figurines are less about the dead, corporate lineages, and deeper scales of time and space, and possibly more about a range of "cosmopolitan" pragmatic practices effective at different scales, just as decorative ceramics are more effective at certain pragmatic scales of extensive interaction as opposed to the more intensive practices surrounding the dwelling.

More succinctly it is worthwhile focusing attention again on Warnier's "pot-king," where the slippage between buildings and pots is more clearly described (Warnier 2007). Pots, buildings, and the body of the king are all repositories of generative substances and are regulated effectively, extensively, and intensively through the elision of bodies/pots/buildings. In the context of Çatalhöyük, the efficacy of structures as containers and curators of powerful substances and forces is made more extensive with pots and stamps. Pots and stamps are eminently transportable, dynamic, promiscuous, and extensive – more so than architectural structures. After all, there are very good reasons why museums are filled with pots and stamps and not with houses. The former are eminently mobile and transportable, whereas the latter are notoriously immovable (as the French term *immeuble* for a building suggests). This is why the Templeton scholars are all gathered at the site of Çatalhöyük and not in a museum collection. The intensive nature of this material register is as effective and interpellative and entangling then as it is now. The structures at the site as they emerge archaeologically require an intensification and entangling of focus and activities in relation to them. One might also hazard to suggest that such intensive engagements are more "expensive" – many more resources need to be deployed and tightly managed in comparison to the "extensive" and less "expensive" practices associated with mobile decorations on pots and stamps.

In short, this is not an attempt to elaborate an evolutionary principle in aid of an explanation toward the rise of "civilization." The evidence from the Neolithic in the Middle East seems to suggest that paths to what are considered to be the rise of such "civilization" are numerous, not lineal and certainly hybrid and heterogeneous (Düring and Marciniak 2006). There seems to be a variety of responses with varying degrees of efficacy as local contingencies change. The contemporary examples offered here are not intended to serve as ethnographic analogues but as examples of similarly creative human endeavors involving shifting material registers. The examples are not analogues of each other, and they cannot be reduced to an evolutionary principle; rather they testify to an enduring protean capacity to refigure the material world subtly in creative registers to sustain social life in all its various forms and to serve its constantly changing needs.

BIBLIOGRAPHY

Bloch, M. 2010. Is there Religion at Çatalhöyük ... or are there just houses? In *Religion in the Emergence of Civilization: Çatalhöyük as a Case Study*, ed. I. Hodder. Cambridge: Cambridge University Press, 146–162.

Bogaard, A., Charles, M., Twiss, K. C., Fairbairn, A., Yalman, N., Filipovic, D., Russell, N., and Henecke, J. 2009. Private Pantries and Celebrated Surplus: Storing and Sharing of Food at Neolithic Çatalhöyük, Central Anatolia. *Antiquity* 83:649–668.

Buchli, V. 1999. *An Archaeology of Socialism*. Oxford: Berg.

Carsten, J., and Hugh-Jones S., eds. 1995. *About the House*. Cambridge: Cambridge University Press.

Douglas, M. 1991. The Idea of a Home: A Kind of Space. *Social Research* 58(1):287–307.

Düring, B., and Marciniak, A. 2006. Households and Communities in the Central Anatolian Neolithic. *Archaeological Dialogues* 12(2):1–23.

Edensor, T. 2005. *Industrial Ruins: Space, Aesthetics and Materiality*. Oxford: Berg.

Empson, R. 2007. Separating and containing people and things in Mongolia. In *Thinking through Things*, eds. A. J. M. Henare, M. Holbraad, and S. Wastell. London: Routledge Press, 113–140.

Graham, S., and Thrift, N. 2007. Out of Order: Understanding Repair and Maintenance. *Theory, Culture and Society* 24(3):1–25.

Boz, B., and Hager, L.D. 2013 Intramural Burial Practices at Çatalhöyük. In Hodder, I. (ed) *Humans and landscapes of Çatalhöyük: reports from the 2000–2008 seasons*. Çatalhöyük Reseach Project Series Volume 8. British Institute at Ankara Monograph No. 47 / Monumenta Archaeologica 30. Los Angeles: Cotsen Institute of Archaeology Press. 413–440.

Heynen, H. 1999. *Architecture and Modernity: A Critique*. Cambridge, MA: MIT Press.

Hodder, I. 2006. *The Leopard's Tale: Revealing the Mysteries of Çatalhöyük*. London: Thames and Hudson.

Hodder, I., ed. 1996. *On the Surface: Çatalhöyük 1993–95*, London: MacDonald Institute for Archaeological Research and the British Institute of Archaeology at Ankara/Oxbow Books.

2010. *Religion in the Emergence of Civilization: Çatalhöyük as a Case Study*. Cambridge: Cambridge University Press.

Hodder, I., and Pels, P. 2010. History houses: A new interpretation of architectural elaboration at Çatalhöyük. In *Religion in the Emergence of Civilization: Çatalhöyük as a Case Study*, ed. I. Hodder. Cambridge: Cambridge University Press, 163–186.

Hodder, I., and Whitehouse, H. 2010. Modes of religiosity at Çatalhöyük. In *Religion in the Emergence of Civilization: Çatalhöyük as a Case Study*, ed. I. Hodder. Cambridge: Cambridge University Press, 122–145.

Humphrey, C., and Laidlaw, J. 1994. *The Archetypal Action of Ritual*. Oxford: Oxford University Press.

Joyce, R., and Gillespie, S. 2000. *After Kinship: Social and Material Reproduction in House Societies*. Philadelphia: University of Pennsylvania Press

Keane, W. 2010. Marked, absent, habitual: Approaches to Neolithic religion at Çatalhöyük. In *Religion in the Emergence of Civilization: Çatalhöyük as a Case Study*, ed. I. Hodder. Cambridge: Cambridge University Press, 187–219.

Knauft, B. M. 1999. Bodily images in Melanesia: Cultural substances and natural metaphors. In *From Primitive to Postcolonial in Melanesia and Anthropology*, ed. B. M. Knauft. Ann Arbor: University of Michigan, 21–88.

Larsen, C.S., Hillson, S.W., Ruff, C.B., Sadvari, J.W., and Garofalo, E.M. 2013. The Human Remains II: Interpreting Lifestyle and Activity in Neolithic Çatalhöyük. In Hodder, I. (ed) *Humans and landscapes of Çatalhöyük: reports from the 2000–2008 seasons*. Çatalhöyük Reseach Project Series Volume 8. British Institute at Ankara Monograph No. 47 / Monumenta Archaeologica 30. Los Angeles: Cotsen Institute of Archaeology Press. 397–412.

Last, J. 1998. A Design for Life: Interpreting the Art of Çatalhöyük. *Journal of Material Culture*.

Last, J. 1996. Surface pottery at Çatalhöyük. In *On the Surface: Çatalhöyük 1993–95*, ed. I. Hodder. London: MacDonald Institute for Archaeological Research and the British Institute of Archaeology at Ankara/Oxbow Books.

Leach, E. 1954. *Political Systems of Highland Burma*. London: The Athlone Press.

Lowndes, S. 2009. Learned by heart: The paintings of Richard Wright. In *Richard Wright*, ed. K. Pallister. New York: Gagosian Gallery/Rizzoli.

Malgrave, H. F. 1989. Introduction. In G. Semper, *The Four Elements of Architecture*. Cambridge: Cambridge University Press.

Marciniak, A., and Czerniak, L. 2007. Social Transformations in the Late Neolithic and the Early Chalcolithic Periods in Anatolia. *Anatolian Studies* 57:115–130.

Matthews, W., Almond, M.J., Anderson, E., Wiles, J., Williams, H., and Rowe, J. 2013. Biographies of Architectural Materials and Buildings: Integrating High–resolution Micro–analysis and Geochemistry. In Hodder, I. (ed) *Substantive technologies at Çatalhöyük: reports from the 2000–2008 seasons*. Çatalhöyük Reseach Project Series Volume 9. British Institute at Ankara Monograph No. 48 / Monumenta Archaeologica 31. Los Angeles: Cotsen Institute of Archaeology Press. 115–136.

McCracken, G. 1989. Homeyness. In *Interpretive Consumer Research*, ed. E. Hirschman. Provo: Association for Consumer Research.

McKinnon, S. 2000. The Tanimbarese Tavu: The ideology of growth and the material configurations of houses and hierarchy in an Indonesian society. In

Beyond Kinship: Social and Material Reproduction in House Societies, eds. R. Joyce and S. Gillespie. Philadelphia: University of Pennsylvania Press, 161–176.

Mellaart, J. 1967. *Çatalhöyük: A Neolithic Town in Anatolia*. New York: McGraw-Hill.

Miller, P. C. 2009. *The Corporeal Imagination*. Philadelphia: University of Pennsylvania Press.

Munn, N. D. 1977. The Spatiotemporal Transformations of Gawa Canoes. *Journal de la Société des océanistes* 33(54–55):39–53.

Nakamura, C. 2010. Magical deposits at Çatalhöyük: A matter of time and place? In *Religion in the Emergence of Civilization: Çatalhöyük as a Case Study*, ed. I. Hodder. Cambridge: Cambridge University Press, 300–331.

Nakamura, C., and Meskell, L. 2013. Figurine Worlds at Çatalhöyük. In Hodder, I. (ed) *Substantive technologies at Çatalhöyük: reports from the 2000–2008 seasons*. Çatalhöyük Reseach Project Series Volume 9. British Institute at Ankara Monograph No. 48 / Monumenta Archaeologica 31. Los Angeles: Cotsen Institute of Archaeology Press. 201–234.

Pilloud, M., and Larson, C. S. 2011. 'Official' and 'Practical' Kin: Inferring Social and Community Structure from Dental Phenotype at Neolithic Çatalhöyük, Turkey, *American Journal of Physical Anthropology* 145(4):519–530.

Preston Blier, S. 1987. *The Anatomy of Architecture: Ontology and Metaphor in Batammaliba Architectural Expression*. Cambridge: Cambridge University Press.

Rose, N. 2006. *Politics of Life Itself: Biomedicine, Power and Subjectivity in the Twenty-First Century*. Princeton, NJ: Princeton University Press.

Rouse, J. 2002. *How Scientific Practices Matter: Reclaiming Philosophical Naturalism*. Chicago: University of Chicago Press.

Sahlins, M. 2011. What Is Kinship? (part 1). *Journal of the Royal Anthropological Institute* 17(1):2–19.

Schmidt, K. 2010. Göbekli Tepe – the Stone Age Sanctuaries. New Results of ongoing excavations with a special focus on sculptures and high reliefs. *Documenta Praehistorica* XXXVII: 239–256.

Semper, G. 1989. *The Four Elements of Architecture*. Cambridge: Cambridge University Press.

Strathern, M. 1999. *Property, Substance and Effect*. London: Athlone.

Türkcan, A.U. 2013. Çatalhöyük Stamp Seals from 2000 to 2008. In Hodder, I. (ed) *Substantive technologies at Çatalhöyük: reports from the 2000–2008 seasons*. Çatalhöyük Reseach Project Series Volume 9. British Institute at Ankara Monograph No. 48 / Monumenta Archaeologica 31. Los Angeles: Cotsen Institute of Archaeology Press. 235–246.

Vidler, A. 2000. Diagrams of Diagrams: Architectural Abstraction and Modern Representation. *Representations* 72:1–20.

Warnier, J. 2006. Inside and outside: Surfaces and containers. In *The Handbook of Material Culture*, ed. C. Tilley. London: Sage.

Warnier, J. 2007. *The Pot-King: The Body and Technologies of Power*. Leiden: Brill.

Young, D. 2004. The Material Value of Colour: the Estate Agent's Tale. *Home Cultures* 1(1):5–22.

12

The Use of Spatial Order in Çatalhöyük Material Culture

Anke Kamerman

From the first moment I laid eyes on the representations of the "leopard" reliefs from Çatalhöyük they attracted me by what seems a contradiction. On the one hand, there is the rigidity of their formal position: By pose, proportions, and the mirroring of the painted figures on their bodies, the "leopards" show strong reflection symmetry. On the other hand, the figures differ in kind and in pattern from layer to plastered layer and by stratigraphic level (Hodder 2006: 10; Mellaart 1967: 119). When the "leopards" are compared to other paintings in the same stratigraphic levels, the contradiction becomes even stronger: In the "vulture" paintings, for example, the central figure is asymmetric and figures are positioned much more freely. Why are these reliefs so rigid by their positioning and pose, while the skin patterns differ by layer and level and other paintings are asymmetrical and much more freely positioned? My curiosity was aroused and I wanted to analyze them in more detail.

Returning, in the course of this essay, to the themes of the position of the observer, the changing of the pattern on the skin, the focus on the navel, and the continuities between "leopard" and "bear" reliefs, and related seals used in later phases of the settlement, I will try to show how spatial patterns of formal and more free positioning function with these two kinds of artifacts and can be analyzed as means of identification and communication.

Like most others who study patterns and schemata in artistic expressions, Ernst Gombrich and Alfred Gell concentrate on the notion of style and focus on the identification of large geographical and historical continuities and discontinuities. They make a distinction between representational schemata of style and nonrepresentational ordering in decorative patterns. Hereby they tend to treat small-scale patterning as mere adornment. Such an opposition is not helpful in analyzing material artifacts in Çatalhöyük, because it tends to restrict the notion of pattern to formal, geometrical forms (ignoring freer positioning), because its opposition of representational schemata and decorative pattern is value-laden, and because the multiplication of patterns is reduced to nonrepresentational functions of ordering and orientation. In this Neolithic context (and in many others), schemata and patterns cannot be as easily distinguished and may share representational and nonrepresentational functions. A much broader concept of pattern, therefore, is needed to interpret the formal and freer forms of positioning in Çatalhöyük material culture. Moreover, in order to interpret patterns that cross the boundaries between objects and bodies, and create continuities between them, a notion of patterning that can encompass spatial organization in general, whether within or between artifacts, or between the observer and the artifact, is needed, and I find this in the work of Rudolf Arnheim (1974).

However, I am also inspired by Gombrich (1996, 2006) and Gell (1998), particularly by their argument that artworks in "primitive" societies should not be primarily interpreted aesthetically, but as means of persuasion and action. I will try to show how patterns on different scales can be understood as persuasion devices in daily life. The possibilities for persuasion of an image or artifact inhere in the ways its patterning and spatial organization can direct the attention of producers and observers, whether in the act of looking at it, producing it, or acting upon it. I will show that the persuasive spatial patterns of formal and freer positioning, and their repetition and variation, can help us classify clusters of artifacts, and, by overlap of patterns, can also associate different types of artifacts like reliefs and seals with each other. Even if it is never immediately obvious what such patterns mean, I think it is possible to argue, by showing the contrast in patterning between "leopard" reliefs and "bear" reliefs, that in the "bear" relief the displacement of a spatial pattern beyond the physical shape of the body is a possible sign of transcendence. I will focus initially on "leopard" and "bear" reliefs in Mellaart's stratigraphic Levels VI and VII (South O–M). In the last part of the paper, I will shift attention to the seals found in later levels, because I want to show that there is an iconic continuity between spatial patterning in reliefs and seals. First, however, I will discuss how I deal with the problem of the division between schemata and pattern and explain how I use the concept of pattern in the further development of my argument.

Schemata versus Pattern

In *Art and Illusion*, Ernst Gombrich states that the most important characteristic of styles is that they restrict themselves to specific "schemata." According to him schemata are formats by which a specific representation or "illusion of reality" is constructed. Gombrich uses the concept of schemata to identify styles and artifacts within styles to be able to locate them and to place them in a historical context. Schemata have representational qualities: they refer to "prototypes." Schemata are based on restrictions: not everything is possible within a style. Gombrich sees the history of style, like the history of artistic innovations, as expressing a succession of different phases in representing reality. These phases are characterized by the use of different schemata. In the Middle Ages, for instance, the schemata are formed by the outlines of (living) things, and these things are constructed by the use of geometrical figures. In impressionism the schemata are formed by patterns of color referring to things and their surroundings, while sharp outlines of physical shape are neglected (Gombrich 1996: 44–45). "Neolithic art is characterized by a rigid style and geometric schemata" (Gombrich 1996: 92–93). According to him, this required something of a constructor's engineering skill. This skill and habit may have developed together with the needs of settled communities and the development of agriculture and its technology (Gombrich 1996: 93, 100). Gombrich rejects the evolutionist idea that rigidity in patterning is an index of a "primitive" stage in art history by the argument that the animal paintings found in Lascaux, which are much older, lack this rigidity completely. How these geometrical schemata are connected to technical stages of human evolution is not a main focus of his attention; yet, as we shall see, this grand historical vision is not always helpful for the analysis of formal patterns.

After the Middle Ages the formal orientation devices of the schemata of "primitive" civilizations, like rigidity and the use of symmetries, disappear according to Gombrich from most representational art. Rigidity of ordering and the use of symmetries became predominantly restricted to decoration and ornament. In *The Sense of Order*, a study in the psychology of decorative art, Gombrich makes a sharp division between the schemata found in styles, which have prototypes and are representational, and decorative patterns that have their origin in orientation and can by this reason be nonrepresentational. In the context of decorative art, he shows that by multiplying an individual motif, for instance, a human face, the informative quality of the individual motif decreases. This can be a reason why in decoration, motives with prototypes are only marginally representational.

Although anyone familiar with Çatalhöyük will raise eyebrows at reading Gombrich's diagnosis of the Neolithic as "geometric" and "rigid," and, as we shall see, there are, indeed, a number of problems with some of Gombrich's core assumptions, his work is nevertheless very instructive: he gives examples of a wide range of different kinds of decorative patterns, analyzes the working of formal patterning, and shows a broad range of possibilities for communication within patterns. He shows how positioning can achieve the focusing of attention, for instance, by isolating a motif, echoing of forms by encircling, using reflection symmetry, or articulating the center. Not only can it be used to focus the view and attract attention, the contrary effect can also be created: by radiating and shattering motifs, they can be marginalized, and by multiplying, their meaning can be diminished (Gombrich 2006: 73, 229, 235). Also, his assumption that design is rooted in movement will turn out to be useful in the third part of this essay (Gombrich 2006: 10).

However, if Gombrich's argument points to a number of important dimensions of analyzing formal and freer forms of positioning, his distinction of schemata and pattern is tied to a value-laden identification of long-term historical continuities. Gombrich himself describes *Art and Illusion* as a book about the change in the course of history from a schematic to a naturalistic style. Likewise, his target in *The Sense of Order* is a more or less linear evolution toward a world where geometric patterns are mostly banished to the marginal role of decoration (Gombrich 2006: ix). He compares the ordering, regularity, and overview that decorations provide to animal patterns: means for recognition and communication that are not essential to representation. Patterns in the animal world function, according to Gombrich, as instruments for spatial orientation (Gombrich 2006: 2). He assumes that decoration and ornament have developed from this need. Ordering is a characteristic that patterns in the animal world and decorative patterns share, and these characteristics account for the fact that in decorative patterns, representation is absent. However, in the animal world patterns still function within the context of action, as devices for recognition, for focusing attention, for conspicuous marking, and for hiding by camouflage. What distinguishes these plant and animal patterns and decorative patterns is that patterns in nature are less formal, but more importantly, that decorative patterns have for the most part lost their function in the context of action. In decorative patterns the organization of parts is only used to fill up frameworks and embellish shapes (Gombrich 2006: 65). Alfred Gell's comparable insistence that patterns are decorative and nonrepresentational seems directly inspired by Gombrich (Gell 1998: 73).

Gombrich's grand historical vision hinders analysis, because it predominantly positions representational schemata in opposition to decorative patterns, as a result of which both he and Gell judge geometrical patterns to be nonrepresentational and decorative. Gell assumes, influenced by Arnheim´s idea of visual forces, that these patterns have more than decorative functions: by their suggestion of movement, by repetition and symmetries, they create unsolved visual puzzles that create attachments between persons and things and can therefore be used as defensive screens or demon traps (Gell 1998: 82–84). Despite these additional functions of decorative patterns, Gell's definition nevertheless leads, like Gombrich's, to a notion of pattern that is too restricted (even when compared to some of Gombrich's own examples). Second, it also introduces a value-judgment in the opposition of representation and decoration that is not helpful in analyzing the material culture of Çatalhöyük. Third, the multiplication of patterns characteristic of decoration is too quickly regarded as nonrepresentational. Fourth and perhaps most importantly, both Gombrich and Gell confine the study of patterns to physical objects and bodies, while it is perhaps one of the most powerful aspects of patterning that it can blur and overlap physical boundaries and connect things across them. I will discuss these four points of critique briefly to show what kind of alternative notion of pattern is needed to analyze the material culture of Çatalhöyük.

First, by reducing pattern to geometry and decoration, Gombrich and Gell restrict their analysis to such an extent that they would not have been able to analyze the "leopard" reliefs had they wanted to. The notion of pattern encompasses much more: it is, for example, employed in geometrical models, in graphical representations of the movements of a dancer, or in depicting a face. It can refer to the spatial organization shared by two different icons of Madonna with child as well as to the organization of repetitive symmetrical motifs in wallpaper. Taking Gombrich's own analysis of a medieval text illustrated by Albrecht Dürer

(Gombrich 2006: 252–253), the decoration of the margins of a formal representation (a regular text) can even be composed of elements of a freely drawn fantasy, just as the spatial organization of the formal representation itself forms a more rigid pattern. I will, therefore, need a broader and more flexible concept of pattern, with which one can describe the relations between wholes and parts and changes in spatial configuration, regardless of the motifs employed. Following the work of Rudolf Arnheim, who will be discussed further later, I shall use the word "pattern" as a coherent spatial organization of parts, the meaning of which depends on its context, which can be dictated by a range of factors varying from geometric rules to rules of social behavior. This definition is deliberately vague, since that allows me to interpret how patterns can be made to fulfill different goals and to adopt different, even contrary, forms (such as formal versus freer positioning), and to avoid studying patterns as exclusively geometrical (as Gell seems to do), or as either representational or decorative (as sometimes seems to be the case with Gombrich).

Second, such an approach is also needed because the separation of representational schemata and decorative patterns is of problematic value when analyzing the material artifacts of Çatalhöyük. Especially in societies that lack a written language (but in many literate contexts too), it is difficult to decide whether a certain figure is decorative or representational, and it is certainly not possible to make that decision about the spots on the "leopard" reliefs or the diamond patterns on the "bear" reliefs before analyzing the pattern as a whole. That indeterminacy, however, is not the only problem with this separation. Both Gombrich and Gell think that patterns have their origin in movement and orientation, and both think that this makes geometrical patterning primarily indexical, decorative, and nonrepresentational (Gell 1998: 73). If we consider the relations among patterns and orientation and movement, there is a difference between a pattern as an index – a trace of former movement and motor activity – and a pattern as a representation – an abstraction of a prototype (Wright 2004). Patterns that depict direction, movement, or paths (such as the geometrical drawings that Yolngu use as ritual decorations, but also as maps of their rights to the land or sea: Morphy 1980; Morphy and Morphy 2006) represent as well as trace movement and orientation, and translate between the two as well. Moreover, the visual field itself can be patterned in such a way as to become a representation, as when (as Gombrich himself shows) the schemata of impressionism and of paintings by Van Gogh use patterns of shadow, light, and color as illusions of atmospheric changes in nature (Gombrich 1996: 49, 309). All examples show that the tendency of Gombrich and Gell to place "pattern" in the second, less valued half of binary oppositions – such as meaning opposed to pure form or order, art opposed to decoration, culture opposed to nature, or regularity opposed to chaos (Gell 1998: 73; Gombrich 2006: XI, XII, 2, 7) – does not make the analysis of images or artifacts more productive.

This is directly related to the third problem: it is, of course, true that motifs with prototypes, by multiplication, can lose part of their information value. That, however, depends on context: In our world, for example, with its extensive possibilities for reproduction, it might seem more likely to happen than in a Neolithic settlement. But even in a world with such possibilities for reproduction, the multiplication of a pattern is not straightforwardly tied to the loss of representational content: the multiplication of a football club's shirt color, or that of a swastika or the picture of an African head of state during a political rally, seems to strengthen rather than reduce its meaning. This observation is reinforced when we realize that the multiplication of an individual motif on a large number of artifacts is not the same as the multiplication of associated motifs on a single artifact. An example from the anthropologist Adrian Gerbrands's work with Asmat woodcarvers illustrates this variability: he was repeatedly assured by his informant that what he initially saw as sheer ornamental geometrical patterns on Asmat shields were in fact stylized chains of ancestors, images produced by the transformations of abstracting, multiplying, and merging the images of the praying mantis, the most powerful symbol of head-hunting and the ancestors (Gerbrands 1967: 33–35). Here, the multiplication of patterns represents the generalized group of the ancestors and raises the power they can give their descendants. But it also shows that by abstraction and multiplication the access to powerful information can be controlled, as Gerbrands himself had experienced before his informant had let him in on the secret.

A fourth and final defect of Gombrich's and Gell's approach to formal and freer patterning is perhaps the most important: the fact that they implicitly assume that patterns can only be studied as confined to specific bodies or objects. A group of spots can be set in a regular relation to each other – and thus form a pattern – without needing an outline or a boundary to become a pattern. In fact, this is one of the more powerful aspects of patterning, as we can see from the real (not the Çatalhöyük) leopard's spots. By reflecting the surroundings of light and shade and the color of dry grass in its pattern of spots, the leopard has the capacity to merge with its surrounding, and it is for its prey and even for an experienced hunter very difficult to identify its body until the leopard explodes into attack. Research on camouflage has taught us why the leopard's spot pattern can dissolve the boundary between its body and the environment by disruptive coloration, countershading, and background matching, in a three-dimensional play of shadow and light (Stevens 2008: 3). A workable definition of pattern, therefore, whether geometrical or free, human or animal, rigid or based in motion, cannot restrict it, as Gombrich and Gell seem to do, to a picture frame or the outlines of the shape of an object or body, since the power of the pattern might precisely be its capacity to dissolve or cross such boundaries, or resonate with patterns on other bodies or objects and thus draw them together. The work of Rudolf Arnheim shows how we can conceptualize the working of such patterns. While the first three points of critique mentioned will return in the analysis of the Çatalhöyük material later, the fourth point of critique sets the stage for all the others and requires further elaboration before we turn to the material itself.

Building Blocks of Spatial Patterns

Physical shape is expressed by the boundaries that are formed on the edges of empty space and that occupied by bodies. Physical bodies can be perceived by touch, by hearing (i.e., echolocation), and by vision – seen by contour lines, cues of light and shadow, and variations in color, which make the difference between empty space and space occupied by bodies. How we represent physical shape is not universal. The art historian Rudolf Arnheim gives the example of a dominant Western style of painting, created by the Renaissance, that restricted shape to what can be seen from a fixed point of observation. The Egyptians, the American Indians, and the Cubists, among others, ignored this restriction. Perhaps more importantly, Arnheim identifies other spatial aspects besides physical boundaries, aspects that are not generally considered to be properties of shape – such as whether the object is placed right-side-up or upside-down, whether objects are present or nearby, or whether they are turned toward us by front, side, or back (Arnheim 1974: 47). These other spatial aspects of positioning and orientation are crucial for my argument, because they form the *spatial context* of physical bodies, which contributes to their meaning and provides important clues for interpreting formal and freer forms of positioning.

Arnheim illustrates the fact that the same spatial organization may be differently perceived and even signify radically different meanings when positioned in a different context with an example from Wittgenstein: the line drawing of a triangle can be seen as a triangular hole, a solid, a mountain, a wedge, an arrow, or a pointer (Arnheim 1974: 96). To identify its meaning we have to know the position of the observer, not only toward the form itself, but also in regard to the broader context of the form, to decide its shape, size, and content: to decide whether it is a figure in itself or a ground for something else, whether it is a whole or a part, whether it is up there in the distance or right in front of us, and so on.

In Arnheim's view, we have learned to identify things by wholes and parts, which are the building blocks of patterns, and this works regardless of the scale or size of the physical boundaries of the object or body perceived. As in the perception of a human face, an overall pattern of essential elements is grasped – eyes, nose, mouth, head, hair – into which further detail can be fitted. And if we decide to concentrate on a person's eye, that eye, too, will be perceived as a whole pattern. These wholes and parts are, therefore, by themselves not self-evident building blocks. They can only be perceived as such by *framing*. While looking, the observer assigns certain patterns the role of framework, on which other patterns seem to depend. The visual field of the observer represents a complex hierarchy of such dependencies (Arnheim 1974: 380). It is the contrast between patterns at different scales that makes framing easier. For instance, the wall of a specific Çatalhöyük house works as the frame of the "leopard" relief, the body of the "leopard" as the frame for its body decorations, and the decorative pattern as the frame of the individual motif (the representation of a leopard's spot). Frame and physical shape can coincide, but this need not be the case (this will turn out to be important in interpreting the "decorations" on one of the "bear" reliefs). Apart from saying that wholes and parts are, in their application, rather flexible concepts, Arnheim writes that the interplay between whole or part is not self-evidently universal. He mentions the fact that in groups unfamiliar with "realistic" photography people had trouble identifying human figures in pictures, because they had not learned as we have to decipher their shape. In this case, contrasts of patterns were not naturally perceived because they were not self-evidently conceived.

Arnheim hands us the instruments for pattern recognition and explains its building blocks, but possibly because he is preoccupied with Gestalt psychology, in which form and shape are the dominant concepts, patterns are for him not a special point of attention. I therefore want to systematize Arnheim's insights on patterns a few steps further. There is a difference between pattern organization as a whole and as a physical shape. A coherent pattern organization does not require the clear boundaries that a physical shape usually has. The coherence of its pattern organization is formed by the distance between the different parts, their relation to its imaginary center, and the angles at which the parts are positioned in relation to each other. A pattern does not need to have the same characteristics as a physical shape (or the visual representation of a physical shape) because the basis of a pattern is not formed by its boundaries but by the relations between its parts. A pattern can find itself within the boundary of a physical shape but can also cross that boundary into another space or object and connect the two. A pattern can also be formed by the spatial relationship between different artifacts.

The frame is not a physical grid or a picture frame but a frame of reference. It works as the ground against which figures are contrasted *by an observer*. The angles according to which we move and relate to the things around us are constantly changing. But we are usually aware (also because of our biological equipment) whether a plane is horizontal or slanted, whether we are standing straight up, or whether there is something directly in front of us. These relatively stable coordinates can be formalized by stereometry: the concept of the X axis can be used to describe the horizontal dimension of perception (analogous to the horizon); the Y axis can be used to describe the vertical dimension (our sense of "up" and "down"); and when depth has to be described, the Z axis can be used to convey our sense of distance to what is perceived or our perception of the volume of the object. Besides depending on these axes of perception, our sensing of location and orientation depends on what we have learned about size and what we know about proportions – but they are always realized within an X-Y-Z framework.

12.1. The four "leopards" look rather rigidly fixed in place by their formal positioning. *Source*: Hodder 2006: 10, 91, 151, 152.

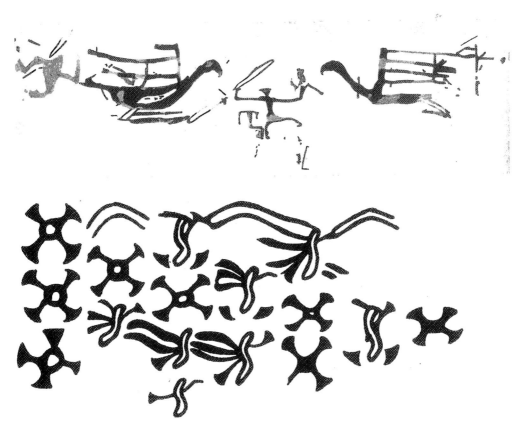

12.2. (a) In this "vulture" painting a human figure swinging some kind of stick is running toward us along a Z axis. (Mellaart 1967: 94); (b) painting interpreted by Mellaart as showing bees. (Mellaart 1967:163).

I will call the patterning of the motifs of an artistic expression by positioning them on straight X, Y, and Z axes formal positioning. I distinguish this from a freer, "dynamic" positioning of figures. Symmetry, which can be defined as rotations and reflections that transpose patterns as a whole, is therefore a form of formal positioning. In two-dimensional planes, it knows three different types: translation symmetry, rotation symmetry, and reflection symmetry. Its stereometric analysis will prove useful in interpreting the reliefs in Çatalhöyük. The "leopards" on the reliefs are both positioned upon a horizontal line – an imaginary X axis. Their proportions and size and the patterns within their bodies are doubled by reflection symmetry. The "leopards" look rather rigidly fixed in place by their formal positioning when we compare them with images like the contemporary "bees" or "vulture" paintings (Figures 12.1 and 12.2).

In the latter, we see a human figure that, swinging some kind of stick, is running toward us along a Z axis. This kind of formal spatial analysis will be the basis of the interpretation of Çatalhöyük figures in the rest of this essay.

Formal Patterns Relating Artifacts

If we temporarily ignore the clearly visible differences in pattern and proportions among the four "leopards" reliefs, we can assume that they belong to the same group of (persuasive) devices, not only because they have roughly the same proportions but also because they have the same formal positioning in common. (I will return to the importance of the differences later.) Formal patterns, however, can also make connections between groups of artifacts or images of an unmistakably different type. At first glance, it did not strike me that the "bear" reliefs and the "leopard" reliefs had more in common than just being reliefs. By analyzing the resemblances among the four "leopard" reliefs in more detail, it struck me that the "bear" reliefs, like the "leopards," are treated similarly according to their formal positioning. The bears, while single creatures, had their limbs positioned in angles of approximately 90 degrees and are therefore also represented in reflection symmetry on a horizontal and vertical axis, even if their pose was completely different from that of the "leopards."

"FACING"

The importance of difference in pose between the "leopard" and "bear" reliefs can be explained by the theme of "facing." Human bodies or faces are only symmetrical when people are facing each other, when they stand on level ground (an imaginary horizontal X axis combined with a vertical Y axis) and meet each others' gaze on the Z axis. This positioning goes together with proximity and the possibility of reflecting each other's conduct. Reflection symmetry, therefore, is not only a way of formal positioning; it has also an iconic (re-presentative) relation with human behavior. Condon and Ogston postulate that it is a characteristic of human beings that they obtain their knowledge about their fellow humans mostly by eye contact. Kendon recognized these and other functions that are also served by implicit behaviors, particularly eye contact. He noted that looking at another person helps gain information about how that person is behaving in regulating the initiation and termination of speech, and in conveying emotionality or intimacy (Kendon 1967a in Mehrabian 2009: 4). The crux of interpreting such formal positioning in terms of "facing" is that it implies that the persuasive device potentially enables two-way traffic. Not only can I get information of the other, but the other can get information about me. This aspect of facing is stressed by both Gombrich and Gell in their analyses of art. Both have identified the importance of eyes in worshipping because of this quality. Both refer to the "magical" fact that certain portraits seem to look at us, and Gell elaborates on the example of the Hindu notion of *darshan*, where divine images can be treated as real persons and agency and animation are transferred by eyes (Gombrich 1996: 96, 97; Gell 1998: 116–121). However, although Gombrich and Gell both stress the importance of facing, they do not acknowledge how dependent facing is on formal positioning.

Facing takes place along a Z axis, shared by two people facing each other. The Z axis is therefore the social axis because along this axis social contact and agency take place. However, this is not restricted to the contact between people. The persuasiveness of images and artifacts – what Gell emphasizes as the social part of human interactions with things – takes place along a Z axis, the axis that can relate people to the things around them when they are facing them; it is the axis of the onlooker. Because the Z axis is the axis of depth, it also determines the extent to which onlooker and image share physical space (Figure 12.1). When we apply this insight to the four "leopard" reliefs, we see some interesting differences: in only one of them, the "naked leopard" relief, the bodies of the "leopard" are rather thin and merely face each other. At first sight, the bodies of the three other "leopard" reliefs, which are decorated with spots, are also represented in a side view, similarly emphasizing the horizontal plane on which they stand and the vertical one along which they are symmetrically reflected. However, in all three "decorated" images, both heads of the "leopards" are positioned according to the Z axis, articulated in shape by making the heads stick out considerably from the plane of the bodies and deliberately turning them toward the onlooker. In the decorated "leopard" reliefs, therefore, the contact between the "leopards" and the observer is articulated.

Facing is also articulated, both positively and negatively, in the "bear" reliefs: the bears are positioned on the Z axis, with their face toward the observer. This is strengthened further by the position of

12.3. Defaced bear relief positioned on X, Y, and Z axes covered by patterns. *Source*: Hodder 2006: 157.

limbs, which are opened to the viewer. In a reconstruction by Mellaart of the so-called twin goddess (a male and female bear relief, placed next to each other) it seems that in the drawing their faces and paws are intact although the drawing is not very clear (Mellaart 1967: 109), but in the other reliefs, where their face and opened paws have been broken off at a certain moment in the history of the house, we can see facing articulated negatively, reinforcing the suggestion that facing conveys, like the example of *darshan* discussed by Gell, a certain power. Whereas the formal positioning of both "leopard" and "bear" reliefs on the X-Y-Z axes relates the two to each other, they both also articulate the theme of facing, if in different ways: defacing only happens with the "bear" reliefs, increasing the suggestion of the "bears'" power vis-á-vis the "leopards" (Figure 12.3).

An example from the study of Göbekli Tepe may illustrate how significant this analysis of formal positioning and facing may be. In his book *Sie bauten die ersten Tempel*, Klaus Schmidt makes a comparison between a sculpture of a reptile found in Göbekli and the so-called Mother Goddess – the "bear" relief – found in Çatalhöyük, and he is right in joining those who have questioned whether it is a goddess at all (Schmidt 2008: 95–97) (Figure 12.4). Schmidt also plausibly suggests that the sculpture dug up in Göbekli Tepe is a reptile because of its resemblance to a "crocodile" sculpture now in the museum of Urfa. However, even if the iconic resemblance – the splayed body – between

12.4. So-called reptile found in Göbekli.
Source: Schmidt 2008: 96, 97.

the so-called reptile and what is now called a "bear" relief is striking,
their meaning is unlikely to be similar: Schmidt does not tell us how his
"reptile" (said to be a fragment of an "installation") was incorporated
in that installation, but "it was probably placed vertically with its head
down at the top of a T-shaped stele." In terms of formal positioning,
the onlooker either looks up the stele facing the reptile (in which case
the Z-axis runs through it from head to tail along its spine, and its claws
are on the horizontal (X) axis), or looks at its top – looking at the stele
from the front – (in which case the Z-axis crosses the spine – or Y axis –
at right angles) but with the head in the reverse position as compared
to the "bear" relief. In the former case, we are talking about "facing,"
but with a completely different sculpture: not a wall mounting like the
"bear" but one that stretches all along the spine of the animal depicted.
In the latter case, the symmetry that goes together with a viewpoint from
above, while superficially similar to that of the "bear" reliefs, expresses a
completely different relation to the human onlookers, since "facing" is
impossible in that formal position.

STRIPPING AND CHANGING THE SKIN

Apart from the heads, there is another part of the "leopards'" bodies
that is conspicuously and differently articulated, namely, their skins and
spots. Again, at first sight there seem to be significant overlaps with persuasive devices used at later levels: there are wall paintings of hunters

who seem to be wearing skins with the tail and the spots of leopards, and figurines of women wearing skins or fabrics with spots. However, it seems important that, in the "leopard" reliefs, we can distinguish between the kernel or body of clay and the surface, which consists of layers of plaster and paint. A significant difference with wall paintings and figurines found at later levels, therefore, apart from the formalized positioning of the moldings on the wall, is that while the paintings are visible only for a short period, the kernel of the "leopard" reliefs continues to be visible despite the fact that the surfaces of both reliefs and paintings are painted and plastered over and over again. In the "leopard" reliefs the painted patterns change by layer, but the two animals continue to face each other and wear in each layer the same pattern of spots. These patterns always remain within the contours of the animal. In each layer of the relief there is a mirroring of the same spots on the two bodies, but with each new layer the "leopards" are stripped by the act of putting a uniform layer of plaster on top of the previous one, and subsequently "dressed up" with a new pattern of spots. So it appears that, in the reliefs, the articulated "skin" is relatively detached from the body.

What can we say about this? The material evidence suggests the act of stripping the skin and adopting a new one. This might be compared to the later paintings of the hunting scenes and the figurines (if it is indeed probable that it is a leopard skin that is depicted), for after all, the humans have to strip the skin off the leopard to be able to wear it. But how can we interpret the painted patterns on the "leopard" reliefs? Why would they employ different leopard spots in each layer? First of all, leopards and other wild cats occurred in historical times (Hodder 2006: 12, 28). It appears that the four "leopard" reliefs have roughly the same catlike outlines and body proportions as leopards in real life; they have a round head, small ears, and a flexible tail, although the evidence is not conclusive (Hodder 2006: 10, 11, 91, 153). On three "leopard" pairs, the surfaces have "decorative" patterns that are identical within the pair, but differ between the pairs. Two pairs have patterns that have a vague resemblance to leopard spots. One pair is blank (Hodder 2006: 91). But the fourth pair has a pattern that is constructed out of squares filled with diagonal crosses, which have no iconic reference whatsoever to the actual spots of leopards (Hodder 2006: 153). Whatever might be said about the patterns of the spots themselves, it seems clear that (at least some) Çatalhöyük people were preoccupied with changing the "leopard's" spots.

As mentioned, we know only recently how camouflage by patterning works. In Çatalhöyük in prehistoric times, one can imagine experienced hunters, who were not familiar with the workings of camouflage, still could observe the "magic" and the efficiency of camouflage as effected by the leopard's spots. They may have had the impression that leopards, while one moment clearly visible by their conspicuously marked patterns and the next moment dissolving within their surroundings, mimicked their environment, and thereby increased their hunting prowess, by the capacity of changing their spots. If this remains speculation, at least at this stage of our knowledge, it does suggest that the pattern as it was painted on the "leopard" reliefs' "skins" was an articulation of a certain power, just like the face of the "bear."

Patterns as Persuasive Devices

Gombrich, Gell, and Arnheim were conscious of the possible function of artifacts as practical instruments, tools to achieve certain goals. As Arnheim writes: "Primitive images ... spring neither from the detached curiosity about the appearance of the world nor from the 'creative' response for its own sake. They are not made to produce pleasurable illusions. Primitive art is a practical instrument for the important business of daily life; it gives body to superhuman power so that they may become partners in concrete undertakings. It replaces real objects, animals, or humans, and thus takes over their jobs of rendering all kinds of services. It records and transmits information. It makes it possible to exercise 'magic influences' on creatures and things that are absent" (Arnheim 1974: 146; see also Gombrich 1996: 94). Contrary to Arnheim and Gombrich, Gell does not seem to think that "decorative" patterns can be used as communicative devices. However, he does shed light on what patterns can accomplish, especially in complex patterns that may form "traps" where their framing of figure and ground is not stable and images oscillate in the eyes of onlookers (Gell 1998: 79). While Arnheim, Gell, and Gombrich seem to assume the practical value of representational art, they do not seem to take abstract or nonrepresentational patterns sufficiently into account. In the present section, I try to use overlaps and relations between so-called decorative patterns to explore the use of positioning as a persuasion device by the creators of these Çatalhöyük images and artifacts.

As with all acts of repetition, reflection, translation, or rotation symmetry has the power of attracting attention of those (whether makers or observers) who interact with the artifact. As the number of motifs (whether referential or abstract) in a pattern is multiplied, the individual figure can be devaluated (Gombrich 2006: 152). In such cases, attention is focused less on the individual shapes and more on their interrelationships by the creation of series. Although Gell points to the phenomenon of articulation of relations in geometrical patterns by the multiplication of motifs, he assumes that it is caused in the absence of representation (1998: 76). The repression of the individual figures by multiplication and the reduction of size can, indeed, articulate them as ornament. However, while it is possible that the patterns of the "leopard" reliefs could be "mere" ornaments to articulate the body, it is premature to assign them such a meaning before the patterns in the material evidence have been fully studied. Earlier in this chapter I mentioned the case of the Asmat shields, where the symmetrical repetition of geometrical patterns, which Gerbrands initially saw as sheer abstract ornament, turned out to be abstractions and transformations of ancestors – not just ornaments to orient the onlooker, but powerful means of persuading the prototypes of the images as well. Similarly powerful motifs may be identified in the Çatalhöyük archaeological record.

THE FOCUS ON THE NAVEL

I have already noted that the variations in the patterns of the "leopard" spots suggested a preoccupation with these spots that superseded mere ornament. This is reinforced in the "bear" reliefs (Figure 12.3). Only one "bear" relief is covered by patterns, and the parts or figures of the pattern are scattered and placed much more freely. More importantly, they go far beyond the body outlines of the "bear." It is obvious that the application of these patterns to the body is clearly different from the "leopard" reliefs. The patterns of the "leopards" were systematically drawn to stay within the outlines of the body.

If the whole shape of the bear had been covered by the same chaotically drawn pattern that negates the outlines of the shape of the bear, it could have been interpreted as an expression of iconoclasm. However, this seems not to be the case when we look more closely at the pattern on the relief of the " bear." One can clearly notice significant differences within the pattern. Diamond-shaped figures with clear outlines, repeated by means of translation symmetry, are positioned next to each other and form some sort of chain because they are placed directly above the navel on the Y axis of the "bear" figure as a whole.

The pattern's dominant characteristic, however, seems to revolve around the positioning of the navel. Positioning the navel on the central Y axis of the figure's reflection symmetry makes it a magnet to the eye, since it is the only area that is not doubled by symmetry (Gombrich 2006: 126). Moreover, the navel is articulated by its place in the center of the rectangle between the "elbows" and "knees" of the figure, formed in particular when breaking off the head, hands, and feet. The navel is also articulated by two concentric circles around it. Last but not least, chaotically blurred diamond-shaped patterns cover the complete body of the "bear," even going far beyond its outline, but do not cover the navel.

This is reinforced by the formal and freer positioning of the diamond-shaped figures – formal, on the Y axis directly above the navel on the relief, and freer on other parts of the bear. At a distance from the navel, the pattern becomes a more dense crossing of irregular lines, as if the diamond-shaped figures were written on top of each other. The motifs are painted over the outlines of the bear and spread irregularly far beyond its skin. The farther away from the navel, the looser, freer, and more irregular they are. It looked as if the concentric circles around the navel were echoed by waves of diamond-shaped motifs traveling away from it, with the navel seeming to be the generating force behind the spreading and shattering of the diamond-shaped forms. We might be able to see similar patterns of displacement and transformation when turning to the "seals" found mostly in later phases of the settlement.

PATTERNS IN "SEALS"

Although there is no positive evidence that the objects discussed were actually used as seals or stamps, I adopt the common way of discussing them (Türkcan 1997: 2). Despite the fact that they are mostly found in very different stratigraphic levels, there is a strong connection between "seals" and reliefs, because images of "bear" and "leopard" are the only images of animals found on both (Türkcan 2003: 4; Türkcan 2005: 3) (Figure 12.5) – although a possible boar has been identified in recent

12.5. Similarity of motifs on leopard relief and seals (illustrations of separate seals from Türkcan 1997: 3).
Source: Çatalhöyük Research Project.

work (Türkcan 2003). The seals and reliefs are also similar in the way bears and leopards are positioned. Only one "leopard" is represented on a "seal," but positioned in the same side view as in the reliefs. The "bear" on the seal sits in the same spread-eagled position with its limbs upright. The limbs of the bear form a square and the navel is articulated at the center. Compared to the "bear" relief the articulation of the navel takes another form. It can be described as a double embrace of the navel from opposite directions, in which the two halves of the embrace are positioned in relation to each other in rotation and translation symmetry. Just as in the "bear" relief discussed previously, the navel seems to radiate a centrifugal power by being the center of the seal and by being articulated by rotation symmetry, while the spreading of the limbs also makes the navel the center of a centripetal force. The twirl in the seal appears to symbolize these opposing forces from the inside out and from the outside in. The diamond shape on the bear relief closely resembles the pattern by which the articulation in the navel in the "bear seal" is accomplished.

When we compare the "leopard" seal with the "leopard" relief, its symmetrical counterpart is missing. However, if they were really used as seals, the reflection symmetry might have been restored in the act of stamping. Although the "leopard" seal is rather damaged and its head and parts of the feet are missing, it is evident that the leopard's spots are strongly articulated (Türkcan 2003: 4). There is also an iconographic resemblance between the spots of the "leopards" on the reliefs and patterns on the seals and the seals and the navel on the "bear" relief (Figures 12.5 and 12.6).

It is also possible to associate the spots of the "leopards" on the reliefs, the patterns on the seals, and the navel on the "bear" relief in a different way: in some seals, the outlines coincide with the outlines of the pattern, but in others the pattern may suggest an infinite elaboration of it beyond the boundaries of the seal. In the latter, although the seals are still intact, the pattern on the seal is purposely broken off, suggesting a continuation that passes beyond the boundaries of its "body" (Türkcan 1997: 3) (Figure 12.7). I was particularly encouraged by the last observation to place the patterns next to each other. Moreover, it is possible to connect the individual stamps, following the same principles as the pattern by which the seal is ordered, by elaborating further and further on the same pattern and thereby creating a never-ending pattern (Figure 12.8). I can imagine that such playing with patterns and ordering by means of the printing of the seals made the development of more complicated patterns possible. If such associations are correct, they suggest a movement from the articulation of the navel (in both "bear" reliefs and seals) to the multiplication of their representation in the seals and the stamping of the seals, leading to their dissolution in an abstract pattern – a dissolution that may, however, signal an augmentation of vital force rather than a reduction of representational meaning, as the Asmat example suggests (Figure 12.9). When, however, formal positioning in terms of reflection, rotation, and translation symmetries and positioning under discrete angles is absent, there is only a vague association between motifs and the pattern is more difficult to establish.

FIXED FORMAL POSITIONING AS AN INDEX OF CONTROL

Persuasion is an attempt at control. The positioning of patterns in the seals is still restricted by means of symmetries and positioning under discrete angles, but compared to the reliefs, the seals allow for more freedom within the formal possibilities of positioning on axes and the rotation, translation, and reflection along them. This applies to the organization of the pattern in each seal. Most seals are different. The resemblances and differences of the "navel" pattern on the different seals refer

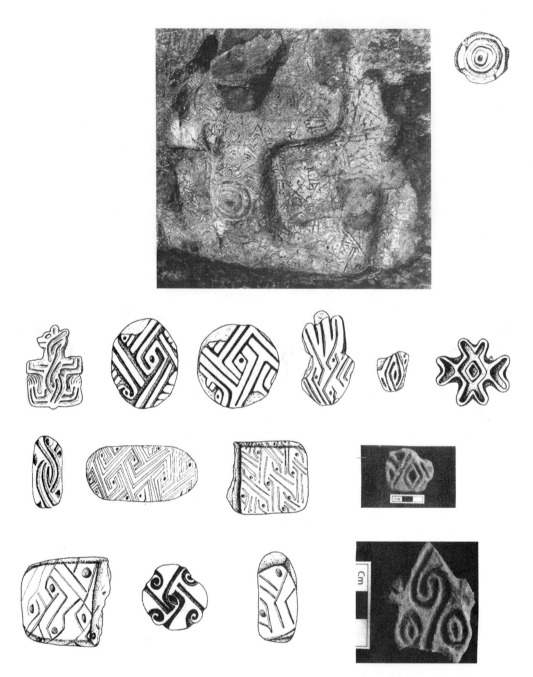

12.6. (a and b) Similarity of motifs on bear reliefs and seals (illustrations of separate seals from Türkcan 1997: 3).
Source: Çatalhöyük Research Project.

  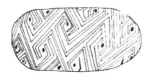 

12.7. The bear seal and other stamp seals (illustrations of separate seals from Türkcan 1997: 3).
Source: Çatalhöyük Research Project.

to each other as members of the same family. While in the "bear" reliefs the positioning and pose of the bear are fixed according to the X, Y, and Z axis and the way the limbs are set under angles of approximately 90 degrees, there is much more freedom of movement in varying on the pattern for each seal. But the freedom of movement is still restricted: one cannot do much more with the pattern (or parts of it) than elaborate, remove, connect, open, close, multiply, and/or scatter it. This relative freedom also possibly applies to the act of stamping, if these are really seals. One can make one print, but making the next print on the same surface implies decisions about whether to do so on the same angles as are available in the pattern on the seal. The seal might also be used more loosely and freely, since there is no restriction on the angles at which the stamp is placed for a new print. Without evidence of stamping and the materials on which stamps were used, however, this will remain a puzzle.

However, despite the fact that the number of possibilities of manipulating positions is, as I have tried to show, huge, this does not mean that we have exhausted all possibilities for thinking about restriction as persuasive control. Fixing formal positioning can tell us more than that because it may also fulfill a dual goal. According to Gell, there are countless possibilities in the production, reception, and circulation of artworks of the entanglement with power relations, which will have an impact on the way the artwork is produced or used (Gell 1998: 29). Gell sheds light on the power exerted by the visual representation of identical images: like naming, the representation of a person can "bind" the prototype and fix and imprison it within the index (Gell 1998: 102). So limiting possibilities by positioning could in the case of the "bear" and the "leopard" possibly be a practical instrument to fix the prototype within the index. However, this necessity of controlling the image by positioning seems to

12.8. Stamping the seals next to each other in the direction of their formal positioning creates a never-ending pattern (illustrations of separate seals from Türkcan 1997: 3). *Source*: Çatalhöyük Research Project.

12.9. The navel dissolves in the multiplying patterns (illustrations of separate seals from Türkcan 1997: 3).
Source: Çatalhöyük Research Project.

have decreased in the seals, with the isolation of powerful elements like spots and navel.

Conclusion

Gombrich is convinced that in "primitive" societies artworks function within contexts of action, and Gell has elaborated that vision for an anthropology of art. However, their analyses do not satisfy the demands for a small-scale study of Çatalhöyük material culture, because they separate schemata of representation within long-term continuities of style from patterns, confine patterns within the outlines of bodies and objects, and reduce patterns predominantly to motion. Arnheim's flexible definition of a pattern as an organization of wholes and parts is more suited for the explanation of patterns as we can find them in Çatalhöyük. By the analysis of "leopard" and "bear" reliefs, I have shown that patterns can be perceived by framing and contrast, that patterns are not restricted within the outlines of shapes and can be rather loosely organized. Moreover, patterns can, by their way of organizing, focus attention by repetition and echoing and the use of reflection symmetry. The cohesion between their parts can be strengthened by contraction, and loosened by spreading and shattering. Also, there is the possibility that patterns fade or shatter across permeable outlines. The latter generates possibilities for transformation, but also makes patterns sometimes more difficult to recognize. I have tried to show some of the effects of the multiplication of motifs in a pattern of spatial organization and how it might be regulated by geometrical principles, by using the formal positioning of images and artifacts on X, Y, and Z axes and including its symmetries in the analysis. The latter I have called formal positioning. By repetition, the pattern attracts attention, but by multiplication the repetition suppresses information and shifts the focus to another scale, from the pattern of the individual motif to the patterning of relations between the individual motifs.

By utilizing this more flexible definition of patterns in art I have tried to answer the questions posed at the beginning of this paper: How can we start interpreting the fact that these reliefs are so rigid by their positioning and pose, while people evidently also had the choice of a much freer positioning, as in the paintings? This rigidity recurred mainly in "bear" and "leopard" reliefs, and the analysis of how it was constructed revealed a formal spatial pattern of reflection symmetry and positioning along the Z axis – the communication axis that implicates the onlooker within the pattern. Thereby I showed that the "leopards" and "bears" required an onlooker. I tried to show that this forced a "facing" relationship on the onlooker and that this relationship was literally broken off in the case of the "bears" by defacing the moldings and removing the hands and feet. In the case of the "leopards," this formal positioning emphasized not only "facing" but also the mirroring of the figures themselves, strengthening the focus on the adoption of each other's outlook. The two "leopards" in the reliefs mimic each other's pose and patterns, and it is probably not a coincidence that the parts on the "leopard" reliefs (the spot patterns) share in the reflection symmetry of their wholes. However, that also suggests that onlookers not only faced the "leopards" but were persuaded to duplicate this mirroring by some kind of identification with the "leopards" themselves. This is reinforced by the fact that in later levels one finds that hunters in paintings seem to have adopted the outlook of the "leopards" by wearing their skins, or at least some cloth mimicking them. Whereas the "bears" also articulate "facing," this does not seem to be reinforced by the theme of mirroring present in the "leopards." The question why such formal patterning is found with the "leopard" reliefs only might be speculatively answered: I have argued that the patterns on the skin of a real leopard are a bit like "mirrors," reflecting the animal's surroundings to such an extent that the animal itself can adopt the outlook of its environment. This changeability – both an asset and a danger to the leopard's human rivals' hunting – seems to be confirmed by the "leopard" reliefs, which in each layer of plaster mirror each other while changing from layer to layer as time passes. Moreover, mirroring water surfaces in Çatalhöyük's swampy environment must have made such a natural process familiar. However, there is no direct relationship of mimicry between the real leopard's spots and those in the patterns on the reliefs, so the possibility that they are "mere" decoration remains open.

If the "leopard" reliefs articulate mirroring as a persuasive device, in the "bear" reliefs facing is articulated, not least by defacing and the removal of other points of potential contact – the paws. However, at least one of the "bear" reliefs provides more decisive clues that the patterns on the body were not merely ornamental, but "vital matters" for those whose painted them. At first glance, the patterns on this "bear" relief could be interpreted as a form of iconoclasm: chaotic figures painted on a relief that erase its outlines. However, looking more closely at different spatial patterns as parts, and depending on the framing of the whole that I choose to emphasize, the navel appears to be repeatedly articulated and the figures painted on the "bear" relief appear to become much more freely positioned as they were placed farther from the navel. The navel seemed the radiating force behind the shattered pattern that passed out of the body of the "bear." These patterns seemed to gain a force beyond the body of the "bear, suggesting they are, indeed, "vital matters" – elements that can accomplish some kind of transcendence.

The interpretation of such visual signs in terms of vitality seems to be confirmed by the continuity between seals and reliefs that is suggested by the recurrence of depictions of "leopard" and "bear" in the seals, and reinforce the idea that these motifs and their associated patterns were important to Çatalhöyük people also at later stages of the occupation of the settlement. It seems as if some characteristics that were articulated in both types of reliefs (the navel and the spots) could be abstracted from the bodies of "leopard" and "bear" and transferred to the seals, allowing them to be used on artifacts found in mostly later levels of Çatalhöyük's stratigraphy when the reliefs themselves had gone out of fashion. On the one hand, the fact that these patterns, despite their resemblance to those on the reliefs, have become much more mobile for not being fixed on walls and can be much more freely positioned if indeed they were used as seals or prints in clay or cloth suggests major changes in the use of persuasive devices in the settlement. On the other hand, however, the resemblance itself, and the fact that these patterns were associated with demonstrable forms of facing, mirroring, and therefore identification at earlier stages strongly suggests that the possible use of these patterns in a never-ending reproduction of wholes and parts was not "mere decoration" and continued to give life to the relationships between Çatalhöyük people and their environment.

BIBLIOGRAPHY

Arnheim, Rudolf. 1974 [1954]. *Art and Visual Perception: A Psychology of the Creative Eye*. Berkeley: University of California Press.

Gell, Alfred. 1998. *Art and Agency, An Anthropological Theory*. New York: Oxford University Press.

Gerbrands, Adriaan. 1967. *Wow-Ipits. Eight Asmat Woodcarvers of New –Guinea*. The Hague ans Paris: Mouton.

Gombrich, Ernst. 1996 [1959]. *Art and Illusion: A Study in the Psychology of Pictorial Representation*. London: Phaidon Press.

2006 [1979]. *The Sense of Order, a Study in the Psychology of Decorative Art*. London: Phaidon Press.

Hodder, Ian. 2006. *The Leopard's Tale*. London: Thames and Hudson.

Mehrabian, Albert. 2009 [1972]. *Nonverbal Communication*. New Brunswick, NJ: Transaction.

Mellaart, James. 1967. *Catal Huyuk, a Neolithic Town in Anatolia*. Londen: Thames and Hudson.

Morphy, Frances, and Howard Morphy. 2006. Tasting the Waters: Discriminating Identities in the Waters of Blue Mud Bay. *Journal of Material Culture* 1(1/2):67–85.

Morphy, Howard. 1980. What Circles Look Like. *Canberra Anthropology* (1):17–36.

Schmidt, Klaus. 2008. *Sie bauten die ersten Tempel. Das ratselhafte Heiligtum der Steinzeitjager*. München: DTV Deutcher Taschenbuch.

Stevens, Martin and Sami Merilaita. 2008. Animal camouflage: current issues and new perspective. http://rstb.royalsocietypublishing.org/content/364/1516/423.short (accessed January 5, 2012).

Top, Jaap. 2008. Symmetrie (lectures). www.math.rug.nl (accessed January 1, 2010).

Türkcan, Ali Umut. 1997. Stamp seals. In *Catalhöyük 1997 archive report*. http://www.catalhoyuk.com/archive_reports/19!.

2003. Stamp seals and clay figures in *Catalhöyük 2003 Archive Report* http://www.catalhoyuk.com/archive_reports/20| (accessed May 2012).

2005. Clay stamps seals. In *Catalhöyük 2005 Archive Report*, cultural and environmental materials reports. http://www.catalhoyuk.com/archive_reports/20| (accessed May 2012).

Wright, Craig. 2004 [2001]. *The Maze and the Warrior, Symbols in Architecture, Theology, and Music*. Cambridge, MA: Harvard University Press.

PART III

VITAL DATA

13

Theories and Their Data: Interdisciplinary Interactions at Çatalhöyük

Ian Hodder, with Contributions from Project Participants

As noted in Chapter 1, the project that resulted in this volume had initially explored the notion that the role of religion in the early farming societies of the Middle East and Anatolia could be explained in terms of power and property. It was assumed that religion was produced by the need to create communities, explain power, and justify differentiation and specialization. But the evidence from Çatalhöyük did not support these assumptions; neither did a critical evaluation of the evidence from many other Neolithic sites in the Middle East. While religion undoubtedly played such roles and had many other instrumental functions, as the chapters in this volume demonstrate, it cannot be fully explained in these terms. More generally, while religion has evolutionary significance at many scales it can also be understood as a cognitive by-product of other distinctly human processes and mechanisms.

The Universality of Vital Matter

Several of the authors, especially in the first part of the volume, explore the question of the evolutionary significance of religion. Religion is as vital for humans as food because it is tied to fundamental cognitive and social capacities. But what is this tie? Van Huyssteen considers the question of whether religion is an evolutionary adaptation related to reproductive fitness, or a by-product of various cognitive capacities of the human mind (such as attachment or altered states of consciousness). Following Wesley Wildman he suggests that some mixture of both views best supports the evidence. Religion is evolutionarily conditioned and specific religious traits have adaptive value, but many aspects of religion can be seen as side effects of traits adapted for some other nonreligious purpose.

337

Shults and Guthrie see religion as born out of a particular adaptive trait – the overactive human tendency to detect agency. Guthrie's important contribution to the notion of anthropomorphism is summarized in Chapter 4. He sees a cognitive continuity between religious and everyday thought and action. For him religion derives from our tendency to anthropomorphize. We are predisposed to detect disembodied agents. For example, at Çatalhöyük the house was born, had a life, and then died and was buried. Shults takes up the theme of anthropomorphism when he argues that there is an evolutionary default toward anthropomorphic promiscuity and sociographic prudery. By this he means that the human religious tendency is toward the detection of supernatural agency in the world around us while protecting social coalitions. This is because (following Guthrie) in early human evolution there was a selective advantage for individuals with cognitive capacities that enabled them quickly to detect predators, prey, protectors, and partners in the natural environment. But there were also selective advantages for individuals who maintained the social norms of the social environment. For Shults, religion could have played a number of social roles at Çatalhöyük, including the role most often cited by the authors in this volume – that religion held the social group together in common cause. But Shults also suggests other functions – for example, that the watchful eye of supernatural agents might inhibit cheats and free-riders. The ever-present bucrania and other images on the walls of houses could have enforced a moral code – and indeed it is remarkable how little archaeological evidence there is for internal conflict within the community (Hillson et al. 2013). Shults also suggests that the bucrania and other symbols of dangerous animals may have been a costly way to signal commitment to the norms of the social group.

Shults sees religion as a cognitive by-product of the human tendency to anthropomorphize (which itself has evolutionary origins), but he also shows that this tendency came to have adaptive and functional value of its own, including the protection of coalitions and the maintenance of social norms. Mills provides an insight into how these social coalitions could have been produced at Çatalhöyük by drawing comparisons with the pueblo societies of the American Southwest. She sees the history houses as creating social networks through crosscutting sodalities such as medicine or hunting societies. The memory networks surrounding leopard and bear reliefs and interred human remains produced a complex web of social interactions; indeed the flow of materials and symbols took the place of kinship in forming social relations. The handing down and participation in these symbols were vital in forming social relations centered around history houses. The dense network of interactions and dependencies allowed society to be resilient in an environment that is today marginal for rain-fed agriculture.

But through time at Çatalhöyük, the density of occupation changed and the intensity of agricultural production transformed. Whitehouse et al. argue that there were changes in religion as societies and degrees of sociality transformed. They propose an increased frequency of rituals during the course of the occupation of Çatalhöyük and suggest that this increase fulfilled an important function in the development of complex societies. In an evolutionary vein they argue for a link between modes of religiosity and the intensity of agricultural production. They suggest on the basis of cross-cultural data that the exploitation of wild resources requires only sporadic group cooperation (e.g., in hunting larger game), whereas the domestication of animals and plants leads to routinized forms of collaborative labor (e.g., clearing, planting, harvesting, and fencing). An imagistic mode of religiosity (entailing infrequent and high-arousal rituals) is effective at creating strong social bonds within small groups facing daunting but sporadic collective action problems, whereas the doctrinal mode (entailing frequent and low-arousal rituals) allows larger-scale communities to engage in less risky and more routinized forms of cooperation. Whitehouse et al. show that the variable that most clearly correlates with a shift away from the imagistic mode at Çatalhöyük is not population size and density but intensity of agricultural production.

Many of the rituals at Çatalhöyük are connected to the creation of memories and histories, and van Huyssteen sees these as having another vital function for humans – the creation of a sense of self. Following Paul Ricoeur, he argues that it is narratives of time and history that are central to changing notions of personhood, including in the Neolithic. Van Huyssteen suggests that with the passing of generations, personal memories tied to individual skulls that were circulated at Çatalhöyük became transformed into general collective memories (Kuijt 2008). It is particularly in secondary mortuary practices such as skull and other body part removal and relocation that personhood becomes mutable and multiple. The increased entanglements that people found themselves in at Çatalhöyük and elsewhere in the Neolithic also led to increased ownership and partitioning so that a separate sense of a historical self emerged, itself tied to notions of the transcendent. So religion was also involved in this development of a sense of historical self. A transcendent meaning for self was increasingly sought within the complex material entanglements that were emerging. This observation suggests a larger-scale neural-biological link between humans and the transcendent. Indeed, van Huyssteen follows Fuchs in seeing the mind as quintessentially relational, located within specific material and social contexts. The mind is entangled with the world. As noted previously, van Huyssteen argues that this link between embodied entanglements and religiosity is a product of a complex mix of cognitive and adaptational processes.

Vital Substances

We can go further in arguing that while there are evolutionary and universal cognitive components in the human potential to engage with a world that has transcendent components, the specific forms of that engagement are relational and diverse. So religion is vital for humans and their sociality in general, but it is sufficiently plastic to play a vital role in the ways in which specific societies are produced and reproduced historically. Most authors in this volume aim to break out of our Western assumptions and to understand the specifics of religion and ritual at Çatalhöyük. For example, Kamerman critiques the work of Gombrich and Gell on style and decoration, and through careful contextual interpretation of the art she proposes very different roles for the adornment on the walls at the site. Nakamura and Pels adopt a broad and general distinction between religion and magic in terms of normalized and nonnormative sacralization, while recognizing multiple ways in which magic and religion can be constructed in varied contexts.

As another example of the tendency among the authors to explore specific forms of religiosity, van Huyssteen argues on the basis of the work of a number of authors including Wesley Wildman that embodiment is central to any understanding of general human religious capacities; that forms of religion emerge within specific material entanglements and embodiments. Different forms of self and the transcendent are produced in different settings, sometimes more individualized and sometimes more partible. In the context of Çatalhöyük, Patton and Hager argue for the relevance of Marilyn Strathern's concept of the dividual.

Persons and bodies are not always separate and bounded units; they can be composite and divisible entities that transform throughout their lifetimes. Patton and Hager argue in reference to the burial in B.60 of a mother with unborn fetus that we cannot assume that the mother and child were seen as separate identities. Rather, they may have been seen as a "two-in-one" person or composite dividual.

Perhaps most obviously at Çatalhöyük, dead bodies and bones seemed to have been partible vital substances – that is, substances that had agentful power necessary for human life. Patton and Hager argue that the dead were not dead at Çatalhöyük but continued to live in the house and in the lives of the inhabitants. They show how juveniles were the predominant type of burial used in founding houses, especially in the upper levels. This type of body seems to have been necessary for founding houses. The death of a "motherbaby" may have had a special power. Patton and Hager suggest that a woman's dying in childbirth might not have been seen as a failure and an abortion of the future but as having a sanctity derived from the productivity of the contest between life and death in pregnancy and childbirth.

The role of the dead and of skulls at Çatalhöyük has to be set within wider traditions in the Middle East, as is shown by Goring-Morris and Belfer-Cohen in Chapter 2. Skull removal and decoration has a long tradition in the Middle East, being well documented by the Early Natufian from the thirteenth millennium BC and continuing into the late PPNB. But there are differences across time and space in the specific practices. For example, there is more grouping and caching of skulls in the southern Levant than at Çatalhöyük; and in burial practices more generally animals are found in burials in the southern Levant but not at Çatalhöyük except in the one case of one sheep burial (Russell and Düring 2006).

In comparing Çatalhöyük with the earlier Neolithic in the northern and southern Levant, Hodder and Meskell (2011) have argued for an understanding of Neolithic symbolism that is less couched in fertility and motherhood and more in an ithyphallic world of wild animals. But in their chapter in this volume, Patton and Hager explore this complex set of intersections and argue that indeed childbirth did play a central role at Çatalhöyük. They suggest that pregnancy and childbirth in Old Europe and Asia were not so much associated with the generation of new life. Rather, childbirth may have been seen as a liminal, dangerous process. Their revisionist discussion of the so-called Mother Goddess figurine found by Mellaart as having a stillborn child between her legs casts a new light on these accepted icons.

Certainly there is much evidence for an active role for skeletal remains at Çatalhöyük. As noted in Chapter 1 there are examples of skulls and human body parts being curated and handed down and sometimes reburied. The social fabric at Çatalhöyük was to some degree produced and held together by secondary burial and the circulation of human (as well as animal) bones. For Shults, the treatment of the dead at Çatalhöyük and the circulation of skulls indicate that the bones were perceived as having some form of supernatural agency. The human skull with plastered facial features found in Building 42 (Hodder 2006) certainly suggests a form of reanimation. A figurine of a woman, perhaps pregnant but with a skeletal back, found in the IST Area of the site and discussed by Patton and Hager in this volume suggests again the vital force of human bones at Çatalhöyük.

More generally, Nakamura and Pels discuss how materials may have been used to mediate between supernatural or spiritual power and human agency. They discuss theoretical frameworks regarding the animation of objects including the Marxist emphasis of fetishization in which consumers mistakenly engage with objects as if the objects controlled them. Nakamura and Pels broaden such notions to all cases in which humans come to value things they think they need. Objects often behave like subjects and have secondary forms of agency, as argued by Gell. Persons are often distributed over things, and, following Mauss, humans and objects animate each other in exchange and in the social process. As one example, Nakamura and Pels follow Taussig in arguing that performative material action can produce healing.

It is particularly the house at Çatalhöyük that seems to have had vital force. The dead, wild animals, and the house were tied up with each other in the reproduction of social life. The house was animated in a number of specific ways. Patton and Hager suggest that the large amount of fetal and neonatal bodies buried in house foundation contexts suggests they may have given a vitality to the house. For Guthrie, the sharp animal parts installed in the house embodied energy and power and contributed animacy to the house. The animal parts were a "condensation of animal power" (Nakamura 2010: 321). The house was situated within a network of power substances.

Weismantel explores recent work by the philosopher Jane Bennett (2010) and uses Deleuze's concept of the "assemblage" to describe the house as a process of give and take between it and other entities, so that it is continually being reinvented, reiterated, and reproduced. Weismantel takes her lead from Puar (2007), Braidotti (2002), and Strathern (1988) in arguing that the body and the house in nonmodern contexts are constituted through multiple heterogeneous processes. As noted previously, the body is seen as dividual: that is, partible and extendable. So too the house. Weismantel eloquently envisages the numerous and complex ways in which houses were linked to each other through the exchange of gifts and the movement of spirit and *hau*. Animal body parts were circulated along with the prestige of feasts and of kills of large wild animals, and there was a fluid notion of kin as indicated by new biodistance research (Pilloud and Larsen 2011). There has thus been an important shift in the way that the Çatalhöyük project has understood the house. Weismantel shows that the notion of the house as made up of a series of structural oppositions (north-south, clean-dirty, ritual-domestic, death-life) has gradually been replaced by the notion of the house as materially alive, as infused with spirit and being. This is partly the result of new data. We have increasingly found examples of ritual practices and burial even in the southern "dirty" parts of houses, and we have more evidence now of the sharing, especially of meat, between houses (Demirergi et al. 2013). But it is also the result of the new theoretical perspectives introduced within the Templeton project.

Buchli sees the house as container of powerful generative substances. The house has a life of generative potential that becomes "exhausted" through time, leading to the need for rebuilding and renewal. Again, the Çatalhöyük project had tended to see abandonment and foundation rituals in structural terms, as simply marking the beginning and ending of the house. But Buchli's insights provide new explanatory force. House walls may have started to collapse and plaster to fall off walls and burials to become too dense, requiring abandonment and renewal. But this material exhaustion may have been linked to a generative exhaustion, itself requiring reconstruction.

Different parts of the house may have had different forms of generative role. Buchli suggests that different kinds of material register might be related to different kinds of social relations. In some ethnographic contexts the fixed parts of the house may have more to do with agnatic relations while figurines and later pottery, along with exchanges of grain, may have been more related to affinal relations. Certainly there is much evidence that certain parts of houses, especially the wooden posts and sculptural installations (bucrania), were retrieved and were probably reused in later buildings, and human skeletons played similar roles. On the other hand, there is much evidence of sharing of meat and a range of manufactured goods (beads, obsidian, ground stone) between houses. As noted, Mills identifies sodality relationships that connect houses in relation to history houses through the exchange of symbols and rituals.

Nakamura and Pels too explore how different types of material interface might relate to different forms of social process. They make a distinction between horizon and surface. Horizons are interfaces that mark transitions, whereas surfaces were produced by residential activity. Horizons are seen as marking (through abandonment and foundation deposits) a particular moment that will recede into the past, linked to commemoration, whereas actions across surfaces (such as revelation and concealment) enable past to future movement, linked to remembering. They show how the data on cluster deposits at the site indicate differences between these two types of interface, suggesting different types of "magical" action within house-based practices.

The white plasters on the internal walls of main rooms were important surfaces for the generation of vitality. Kamerman suggests that the paintings at Çatalhöyük are not just passively aesthetic but actively persuasive. She suggests that the stripping and changing of plaster "skins" on the leopard reliefs are paralleled by the wearing and removing of leopard skins by humans shown in later paintings. She further argues that the changing spot patterns mimicked the ability of the leopard to merge into the environment and thus had a certain power. She notes how the organization of pattern on and over a bear relief acts as a magnet to the eye, at the same time giving a symbolic importance to the navel. In a bear stamp seal and in the paintings over a bear relief, the navel is seen as creating a centripetal force. The paintings have a vitality that produces transcendence. She also suggests that the images of bear and leopards in the reliefs are more fixed and controlled than the later use of stamp seal designs, which are freer – relating in an interesting way to other changes between earlier and later levels (Hodder 2013 and see Whitehouse et al. in Chapter 6). Her identification of the "facing relationship" of the bear and leopard reliefs with the onlooker is of interest as, on other grounds, it can be argued that these are perhaps the most likely candidates for symbols or emblems of social groupings within the settlement, such as clans or secret societies, as argued by Mills in Chapter 7.

Buchli suggests that the intermittent wall paintings reanimated earlier paintings that had occurred on the same walls. He talks of the white walls and white platforms as "seething under the surface with powerful images and bones." The mundane acts of cleaning sooty walls, replastering, and polishing plaster walls are thus infused with both the quotidian and the transcendent. Buchli also discusses how the intense concentration of generative powers within the house in the pre–South P levels was increasingly replaced in the upper levels of occupation with a focus on the new material registers of stamps, decorated pots, and mobile figurines. There is a neat link to all the evidence collected by the current project for change in the upper levels, involving greater house independence, increased mobility, and less focus on house-based installations of wild animals.

Theories "Confront" Data?

Overall, then, the interactions between Templeton scholars and the archaeologists at Çatalhöyük have led to a new perspective on the role of religion at the site. We have shown that religious practices there are not sufficiently explained in terms of the control of production and material power. We have also shown that structural approaches to the symbolism in the houses in terms of south/north, dirty/clean, mundane/ritual are inadequate. So too are arguments that understand the house rituals in terms of beginnings and endings, foundations and abandonments. Instead we have come to see the house as infused with vital matter and by an animacy that, on the one hand, derives from specific networks of agentful objects and, on the other hand, from broader and deeper human evolutionary and cognitive mechanisms.

This successful transformation of theories about Çatalhöyük has come about through an interactive and interdisciplinary process in close association with large amounts of data collected from a complex and rich archaeological site. But how has the engagement between theory and data come about in this case? I have long argued that while archaeologists habitually talk of testing theories against data, what they actually do is accommodate theories and data in a hermeneutic spiral (Hodder

1999). The hermeneutic spiral is not a circle of self-fulfilling relativism because the accommodation has to deal with the physical objectness of what is found. The material that is found by archaeologists is not just constructed; it also "objects," even if that objection is itself understood by the archaeologist within a specific theoretical perspective. The interdisciplinary context of the project described in this volume provides a way of evaluating these claims. Did the interdisciplinary scholars who spent part of each summer over three years at the site simply take their pet theories off the shelf and impose them on Çatalhöyük, or did they accommodate and change their points of view, their pet theories in confrontation with the "big data" from the site. Did the complex interconnections of data cause theorists to change their minds?

More generally, it is of interest to engage in a dialogue with the participants in the Templeton project in order to understand the processes at work as theory and data interact, and in order to provide a basis for future interdisciplinary collaboration involving archaeological data. As part of the evaluation of the Templeton project I asked the participants to write about their experiences. The following is based on their responses, often given as direct quotes.

Having one's own pet theories with one as new data and ideas are confronted is of course a necessary initial step. The strange experience of being recruited to discuss a site about which much had been written and much data collected was often dealt with by "finding a way in" – finding things familiar that allowed understanding and initiated dialogue. The participants found the theories they had on their shelves comforting and helpful as a starting point; they sought points of familiarity and connection.

For example, Anke Kamerman had previously worked as an architect, and she leaned on this background in approaching the material from Çatalhöyük.

> I couldn't have imagined the excitement which I felt, when shown how patterns existed of very slight differences in substance and colour of earth, of the levels which had yet to be uncovered, crystallized, during the process of digging, in bricks, walls, platforms or floors. Getting the opportunity to unravel the material substance without the existence of a language, a practice which I exercise in my work as an architect, I had an affinity with the digging process, starting with certain clues for patterns, continuously peeling of layer after layer while the pattern or the outlines of form grew in clearness.

Mary Weismantel too found herself going back in order to go forward.

> The strongest emotions came from encountering the actual excavations themselves, which evoked an unexpectedly vivid nostalgia for my own past, and for the experiences that made me fall in love with anthropology. I had not known that Çatalhöyük would bring back half-forgotten, suddenly visceral kinesthetic and sensory memories of past lives: the year and a half I spent excavating Mississippian houses in the Midwest as a "shovel bum" between college and graduate school, and the years 1984–5, when I lived in an impoverished indigenous community in Ecuador called Zumbagua. Like the Neolithic houses at Çatalhöyük, those houses of the indigenous Americas – the ancient Midwest and the twentieth century Andes – were windowless, one-room structures made of timbers, mud brick and plaster, inhabited by farmers, filled with agricultural implements, seeds and animal bone – houses I had spent long hours, days and months recording in meticulous detail and struggling to understand as living entities.

Stewart Guthrie had a similar initial response.

> My feelings on receiving the invitation to this project mixed surprise and pleasure with doubt that, as a non-archaeologist, I would have anything to contribute. This doubt survived my arriving in Konya, meeting other non-archaeologists in our cohort, and even learning the outlines of Çatalhöyük from the archaeological team. My confidence began to return, however, when we learned that Çatalhöyük may well have been a house society, a type familiar from my fieldwork in another house society, Japan.

Comparison is of course a fundamental principle of science, and in particular of anthropology. The study of the anthropology and archaeology of religion is built from the comparative study of a wide range of societies and of their changes through time. As noted earlier, many of the papers in this volume take an evolutionary approach based on the comparison of similarities and differences. It is thus not surprising that participants in the project initially sought similarities with what they knew, but these initial impressions and off-the-shelf moments quickly gave way to more nuanced evaluations of difference in context. As Barbara Mills commented,

> For me, what was particularly interesting was the opportunity to think about the archaeology of another part of the world that has often been compared to my own area, the North American Southwest. Although my own contribution takes one direction, there are many others that could be made. My notebook

has many marginal comments where specific facts about Çatalhöyük seem to resonate with certain times and places in the Southwest sequence, or do not. Even other areas of the Near East during the Neolithic are very different from Çatalhöyük and I think that may be what makes the site so interesting. Like Chaco Canyon in the Southwest, Çatalhöyük sticks out in many ways from other contemporary settlements because of its "ritual density."

Kimberley Patton wrote of how the data from the site changed her and other people's assumptions about the roles of religion and ritual.

Neolithic Çatalhöyük – and what it was said to mean – was a kind of immovable icon during my graduate education; the matriarchal "start" of the history of classical Mediterranean religion and archaeology, one whose interpretation we took at face value. The evidence revealed by the new excavations, and the new models used to assess both the first and second phases of work on the site, have almost entirely displaced and repainted that icon. To offer only one example, our dominant paradigm cleaved to the dichotomy between domestic and cultic spaces. The new paradigm, which during the seminar we heard from our first day, was "that "there are no shrines that are not houses, and no houses that are not shrines." This idea alone, born from the discovery of cooking ovens in Mellaart's "shrines" and auroch horns guarding the dead beneath the floors of ordinary houses, changes everything in how we ought to consider not only inhabited space in the Neolithic, but the assumed divide between "sacred" and "secular" experience and knowledge at that time.

As the sure ground of the theories on the shelf is left behind, and as familiarity with the archaeological data from Çatalhöyük increased, so new ideas seemed to emerge unexpectedly. We were a diverse group. As Barbara Mills noted,

One of the results of the process for me, personally, was a deeper appreciation of the different ways that religion is being approached in other disciplines other than anthropology – and even the diversity of approaches within anthropology, from magic to modes of religiosity. The group was quite heterogeneous in their interests and I am not sure that we convinced each other of our own interpretations, as there are some clear disjunctures among us.

And yet a good number in the group managed to reach a degree of apparent consensus on a number of issues. For example, as Barbara Mills again observed,

I was thinking about commonalities or themes that run through our papers – or at least that ran through our presentations as they evolved each summer. One of these was the degree to which many of us agreed on the idea that history houses, at least, seem to have been regarded as animate. The installations, burials, object placement, replastering, cleaning, decorating, commemorating, and decommissioning all have parallels with ethnographic and archaeological examples elsewhere in which architectural spaces become alive (and then are buried or deanimated). What is different in our interpretations, however, is just what that animacy means in terms of the social groups who moved through those spaces.

Out of the heterogeneity, as people allow themselves to leave their comfortable bookcases with their shelves of familiar theories, there is an uncertainty and there remain differences, but new ideas and a degree of consensus appear to emerge. For example, in the first Templeton project (Hodder 2010), the idea of "history houses" seemed to emerge out of the blue, and it immediately appeared attractive and useful for many members of the group – even though the group members were very divided in terms of their starting positions. That emergent idea has come to dominate much of our research at Çatalhöyük. In the second Templeton project that led to the current volume, there was a gradual and unpredicted coalescing around the idea of vitality. The idea seemed to emerge in the interstices between our different backgrounds and interests. After all, on the one hand, the idea resonated with theories concerning the evolutionary and adaptive role of anthropomorphism and the human attribution of agency to things, while, on the other hand, it resonated with current theories of materiality and distributed personhood. The idea, then, joined different interests and seemed to emerge as a "third way" between project members.

The interactions between the Templeton scholars and the thirty-six different specialisms within the Çatalhöyük Research Project created a diverse yet relatively "flat" (nonhierarchical) work environment. In such interdisciplinary contexts, knowledge often seems to be produced opportunistically by the assembly of parts. Within philosophy and social theory, the term "assemblage" is often used, as a result of the work of authors such as Deleuze and Guattari (2004), DeLanda (2006), and Bennett (2010) to refer to the contingent ways in which juxtapositions of usually separated elements lead to the emergence of new knowledge. The arguments that emerge do not come about solely from the top-down testing of hypotheses and expectations worked out beforehand or taken off the shelf; rather the arguments emerge through the process of interlacing and braiding across and between domains. These bootstrapping operations can lead to dissonance as the different types of data are shown to be misaligned, or they can lead to strong and robust arguments as different perspectives coalesce around specific assemblages of data. Certainly the notion of history houses has taken a firm hold for the moment, and the idea of vital matters may provide a new example.

The project participants described the process by which a new or third form of knowledge emerged from the assemblages of researchers and data. Mary Weismantel noted first how different researchers interacted with the site in different ways. She observed,

> The theologian and the religious studies scholar, hushed and alert in the presence of the sacred – a reminder that we anthropologists can be too facile, too thoughtless, in our assessments of religion, magic, etc; the archaeologists who work in the region: always putting the site in comparative context, temporally and spatially – so useful to have conversations with them, since I knew so little – I was grateful to the Israeli couple for their patience in answering my inane questions; Victor Buchli, his attention to textures, surfaces, made me realize the importance of the plaster.

Kimberley Patton too noted the initial differences between participants and went on to describe the emergence of new knowledge regarding animacy, the role of the dead, and concepts of time.

> Some of the most interesting projects with which I have been involved as a scholar have been the most interdisciplinary, wherein even the most basic assumptions were not comfortably shared, but instead forcibly vetted or outright challenged by the collective. Since in this seminar we were stuck with one another in central Anatolia for a week at a time or more each summer, such difficult conversations among archaeologists, anthropologists, historians of religions, and theologians could not be politely dropped, but had to continue, like a stone polishing machine continuously grinding, until some kind of détente, an agreement to disagree, emerged.
>
> What often came of such "no exit" discourse, however, was not détente, but instead a 'third' path through the questions, a kind of recombinant idea. This new generative concept would then itself be subjected to triage by the archaeological team who joined our sessions, gave generously of their time and their longstanding, intimate knowledge of the site's data, which changed (literally) daily; by the material evidence that surrounded us; by Fork Mound, always visible from every window and which we visited from time to time to hear and see what it had lately revealed – a painted spiral, an ochre hand, a burnt house – ; by the quiet, enigmatic presence of the dead of millennia ago, enjoying their first dawn of human attention after such a long sleep, interlaced in the earth and forgotten.

The anthropologist Victor Turner spoke of communitas, which he defined as the temporary but powerful cohesion of a group of people who gather for a common purpose, often in a place that is foreign to most or all of them. Deracinated from their everyday lives and environments, such people are often able in this short-lived crucible of time to communicate and to learn in a radical way. They are stripped of the normally heavy matrix of social inflection or intellectual defense that might characterize their conversations at their respective homes. Pilgrims are a classic example, but so, perhaps, were we, a group of scholars from different institutions, disciplines, and countries. As Turner has it, those who experience communitas are almost always changed. This was very true, I would say, of our own group.

If the "house/shrine" dichotomy was broken apart by what we learned at Çatalhöyük, so too, perhaps, was the arbitrary distinction between past, present, and future, already wryly dashed by William Faulkner: "The past is never dead; it's not even past." What Ian Hodder has called "the production of memory" seems to have been as huge a cultural focus at Çatalhöyük as the production of food. This occurred through the history houses, large communal generators of meaning, most obviously realized in their role as sources of ancestral bone to be harvested and shared out. But it also occurred in everyday houses and everyday lives. The so-called "survival" imperative clearly included, on a daily basis and in quotidian thinking, all that had not survived.

Perhaps those who lived in this city did not simply move from the present on into the future; perhaps these terms are inadequate for explaining the Çatalhöyük concept of time. It was not so much that the people of this city lived looking backward. It was that time itself may have always been experienced as more of an integrated continuum than as a linear march. Perhaps the past did not continually recede, as we have it, but rather was always available in the here and now, like the Australian aboriginal Dreamtime. In the form of burial platforms, wall paintings, and ever-growing earlier levels of occupation, the Çatalhöyük past existed in a striated platform that made present life possible. But it not only existed; it hummed like a generator under the floors and all around. This supporting platform of the past had both existential and literal dimensions; one lived directly on the multiple levels of the not-dead past, directly over the bones, even retrieving those bones to "start up" the present levels, like batteries. This was process seemed not to have been morbid or enervating; rather, it was necessary and life-giving. As time went forward at Çatalhöyük, the past seems to have grown stronger and more alive, not weaker and more dead.

What the members of our group found so interesting, however, was that the past could not do so without help. It needed constant human intervention to remain stronger and more alive, consuming ever-increasing amounts of human energy. So it was not only that the mud-brick walls needed more and more reinforcement and trips to places further away as resources were depleted, part of an imperative that Ian calls "entanglement" in materiality; it was that the world of the past as it literally built and grew up from the earliest levels similarly required upkeep. This had to be done in order to continue to re-charge and empower the present and to make the future possible. The skeletons needed further disarticulation and re-arranging; the leopard paintings needed re-painting; the bull and ram bucrania guarding platform graves needed re-plastering. More black, glassy obsidian had to be gathered from the far-off mountains of Cappadocia. There was little or no respite from this continuous, life-giving but also draining imperative.

Thus the maintenance of the powerful past and the heavily populated world of the powerful dead, of memories of communal events, and of animal relics and representations – of what might be called spiritual or cognitive realities – had to be undertaken on a material plane. When Çatalhöyük houses died, they were given funerary deposits of special assembled objects, just as humans are, cleaned and sealed. Like human beings, they received a funerary platform, beneath which they themselves continued to exist in the not-dead past. What animated the houses – human bones – perhaps did the same for the new houses above them, their descendants. The dead houses became dynamic ancestors of sorts, their bodies stacked up along vertical axes of memory. The dead were, in some real sense, always alive in the present; the past was always available to the future.

Stewart Guthrie talked of how interdisciplinary projects, while "posing difficult questions about the distant past to both local experts and outside specialists, can find answers from unexpected quarters. It also enriches the participants – including those seemingly unprepared for the endeavor." In creating *communitas* the diverse group assembled bits and pieces of data that appeared to support arguments that produced new but coherent ideas. Some of the new knowledge emerged from the interstices between perspectives and theories, filling gaps and edges that had been missing – perhaps this is true of the history house idea, which seemed to be an entirely novel creation; history making had been little discussed in previous accounts of the Neolithic of the Middle East or of early religion. Another process that produced consensus seemed more Hegelian in that the participants moved to levels of abstraction that subsumed differences. If we could not reach agreement on specifics, we could find ways of talking to each other at higher and more abstract levels. Thus, in both Templeton projects participants disagreed about the use of the term "religion" in prehistory, but there seemed more consensus about the use of more abstract terms such as "the beyond," "the marked," "the transcendent," "animacy," and "vitality." There was disagreement about whether Çatalhöyük could be described as a Levi-Straussian House Society, but the more general idea of history houses and the production of history seemed more acceptable. And the impetus to seek these various forms of consensus was undoubtedly spurred on by the search for *communitas* itself. On the whole the visiting group of scholars sought the community of social consensus.

So, in retrospect, this book makes a number of new claims about the role of religion in early farming societies. It argues that religion is a necessary and emergent component of what it is to be human, and that notions of animacy and vitality were central building blocks of human-material interactions as humans settled down and became ever more entangled in the material worlds they had fashioned. At Çatalhöyük in particular something very special happened. There was an especially high density of ritual engagement. This drew in a particularly high density of closely packed people, all attracted by and then held together by the vitality of the place. As Kimberley Patton put it, the place was charged; it seemed to buzz or hum. Such vitalities were central to the social processes that accompanied agglomeration, and indeed they were productive of the high densities of people that ultimately spread out from Anatolia and across Europe (Renfrew 1987). But the book also describes how that same vitality of place drew together a diverse group of scholars, and it shows how they too sought consensus and community as they assembled new arguments. The interdisciplinary process "at the trowel's edge" was difficult and complex, and knowledge seemed to emerge in unpredictable and contingent ways. Çatalhöyük past and present acted as a node, generated by but also generating new knowledge.

Perhaps we can leave the last words to Mary Weismantel. Her account is an example of what many in the group felt as they looked back over their experiences in the project.

> My encounter with Çatalhöyük was rather like an illicit love affair: an exhilarating episode that begins unexpectedly, awakens old desires, arouses new ones – and ends as abruptly as it began. It was a curious interlude, after all, in a decades-long scholarly relationship with the Andes: three summers that plunged me into an intense (but intermittent) intellectual relationship with an enigmatic and celebrated archaeological site. The romance was sweet, the end predictable.... But I've already found bits and pieces of Çatalhöyük creeping into some of my writing and thinking, and hope it will continue to do so.

BIBLIOGRAPHY

Bennett, J. 2010. *Vibrant Matter: A Political Ecology of Things*. Durham, NC: Duke University Press.

Braidotti, R. 2002. *Metamorphoses: Towards a Materialist Theory of Becoming*. Cambridge: Polity Press.

DeLanda, M. 2006. *A New Philosophy of Society*. London: Continuum.

Deleuze, G. and F. Guattari 2004. *A Thousand Plateaus*, trans. B. Massumi. London: Continuum.

Demirergi, G. A., Bogaard, A., Green, L., Twiss, K. C., Ryan, P., and Farid, S. 2013. Of bins, basins and banquets: Storing, handling and sharing at Neolithic Çatalhöyük. In *Integrating Çatalhöyük: Themes from the 2000–2008 Seasons*, ed. I. Hodder. Los Angeles: Cotsen Institute.

Hillson, S. W., Larsen, C. S., Boz, B., Pilloud, M. A., Sadvari, J. W., Agarway, S. C., Glencross, B., Beauchesne, P., Pearson, J., Ruff, C. B., Garofalo, E. M., Hager, L. D., and Haddow, S. C. 2013. The Human Remains I: Interpreting Community Structure, Health and Diet in Neolithic Çatalhöyük. In *Humans and Landscapes of Çatalhöyük: Reports from the 2000–2008 seasons*, ed. I. Hodder. Los Angeles: Cotsen Institute.

Hodder, I. 1999. *The Archaeological Process*. Oxford: Blackwell.

  2006. *The Leopard's Tale: Revealing the Mysteries of Çatalhöyük*, London: Thames and Hudson.

  ed. 2010. *Religion in the Emergence of Civilization: Çatalhöyük as a Case Study*. Cambridge: Cambridge University Press.

Hodder, I. 2013. Temporal trends: The shapes and narratives of cultural change at Çatalhöyük. In *Integrating Çatalhöyük: Themes from the 2000–2008 Seasons* ed. I. Hodder. Los Angeles: Cotsen Institute.

Hodder, I. and Meskell, L. 2011. A 'Curious and Sometimes a Trifle Macabre Artistry': Some Aspects of Symbolism in Neolithic Turkey. *Current Anthropology* 52(2):235–263.

Kuijt, I. 2008. The Regeneration of Life: Neolithic Structures of Symbolic Remembering and Forgetting. *Current Anthropology* 49(2):171–197.

Nakamura, C. 2010. Magical deposits at Çatalhöyük: A matter of time and place? In *Religion in the Emergence of Civilization: Çatalhöyük as a Case Study* ed. I. Hodder. 300–331. Cambridge: Cambridge University Press.

Pilloud, M. A. and Larsen, C. S. 2011. 'Official' and 'Practical' Kin: Inferring Social and Community Structure from Dental Phenotype at Neolithic Çatalhöyük, Turkey. *American Journal of Physical Anthropology*. http://onlinelibrary.wiley.com/doi/10.1002/ajpa.21520/abstract (accessed June 24, 2011).

Puar, J. 2007. *Terrorist Assemblages: Homonationalism in Queer Times*. Durham, NC: Duke University Press.

Renfrew, C. 1987. *Archaeology and Language: The Puzzle of Indo-European Origins.* Cambridge: Cambridge University Press.

Russell, N. and Düring, B. 2006. Worthy is the lamb: A double burial at Neolithic Çatalhöyük (Turkey). *Paléorient* **32**(1), 73–84.

Strathern, M. 1988. *The Gender of the Gift.* Berkeley: University of California Press.

Postscript: On Devotion at Çatalhöyük

Alejandro Garcia-Rivera

I am convinced that devotion is certainly at work at Çatalhöyük and may help us answer questions about the process of recognizing a religious significance in the material culture of the site.

I would rather use the term "devotion" than "religion" for reasons I cannot get into here. Having said that, I have to confess that I would be foolish to try to define devotion. Devotion, as many scholars point out, is easier recognized than defined. If you were to ask me for a brief description of devotion, however, I would say that it involves living out a powerful imagination with surprising destructive tendencies that if disciplined can also be incredibly life-giving and creative.

Being a totally naïve observer of archaeological method has paradoxically made me a good candidate to detect devotion at Çatalhöyük. Being naïve has advantages. In fact, I was immediately struck by the devotion displayed by the architectural team. Those of you who work here are a great example of what devotion is all about. What are its symptoms? Let me make a few observations.

A first observation has to do with the power such material objects have on the imagination of the researchers. The material culture of Çatalhöyük is on the tip of every tongue. Whether at lunch or at break or listening to the researchers at the labs, it is obvious that a great power has a grip on the researchers' imagination. Something vital and supremely valuable about Çatalhöyük is felt by each person here. It appears to have an erotic power, that is, *eros* in its most wide sense, that at times is difficult to control. It is striking to observe how much more the researchers wish to go beyond the bare facts but restrict themselves to remaining at the edge of a powerful imagination. I believe this erotic power is part of the religious significance at Çatalhöyük.

A second observation: I have also been impressed by the discipline shown by the archaeological team in taming the imagination raised by the erotic power that seems to come from the material culture at Çatalhöyük. I saw very professional and talented individuals barely able to contain their speculative imagination. Yet they managed to do so but at a price. That price is the risk of understating the significance of the very evidence before them and hesitating to pursue the many hypothetical possibilities the evidence itself suggests, possibilities that might lead to a fertile research track.

Finally a third observation: I also observed that the staff, while greatly disciplined, are also quite imaginative. Indeed, they rely on that imagination to guide the research. Without it, they would not only be digging blindly, mechanically, but, more important, they would not be able to recognize a figurine or a piece of clay pot in some misshapen clump of clay or shattered stone. Without imagination, research at Çatalhöyük would cease. Yet such imagination is often blunted or buried beneath a great mound (so to speak) of facts.

Thus, I see the research at Çatalhöyük faced with a paradox. The imagination of the researchers is both a help and an obstacle to their research. The paradox becomes more acute because it is raised by another imagination that arises from the material culture found in Çatalhöyük itself. In trying to understand the imagination that created Çatalhöyük, the staff's own imagination is powerfully affected and must find a way to discipline itself without losing itself in the process.

This triple play of imaginations then is one of the great methodological issues at Çatalhöyük. It points to the crux of the very question Templeton asks about recognizing the religious significance in the material culture of Çatalhöyük. The religious significance at Çatalhöyük is to be found in a marvelous imagination still viable and able to affect us today. Yet Çatalhöyük's imagination must be allowed to interpenetrate and inform the imagination of those who wish to know it. Such interpenetration, however, can only be fruitfully done with some sort of discipline that prevents the overpowering of one imagination by another. What is this discipline? One must understand, I think, the nature of Çatalhöyük's imagination. Let me suggest it is very close to what might be called the devotional imagination.

So what is the nature of the devotional imagination? It is imagination understood in a special and dynamic way. It is not an imagination mentally observed but an imagination fully entered into. In other words, it is not an imagination to be imagined but an imagination to be lived.

Such an imagination has these characteristics. It is provoked by a debilitating tragic sense felt by all people at some time. It is the sense that things are not what they should be. We may call such a sense "suffering" or "the human condition." However you may refer to it, the sense is mysterious, for it can only have come about by an experience of the way things should have been. Yet those of us stricken by this tragic sense would be the first to agree that we have never actually had such an experience. It is this mysterious knowledge that provokes and guides our special imagination.

Through this imagination, the bearer of the tragic sense enters into a world with the hope of finding the experience that provoked that tragic sense – an experience where no pain or suffering was ever felt or tear ever shed. It is the job of this imagination to reveal such a world of experience so that the pilgrim traveling in this imagination finds a way to be united to that world.

Such imagination, however, carries great power, and it can easily overwhelm and take over a person. Indeed, such an imagination is imperialistic. It can devour the person who enters into it. This is why wise practitioners of a living faith never enter such an imagination unprepared. They undergo a spiritual discipline to tame and limit the destructive tendencies of such an imagination.

This, in my opinion, is what the researchers at Çatalhöyük seeking its religious dimension are up against – an imagination of great erotic power, engaging the tragic sense that is the common lot of human existence yet must have been disciplined in some way to avoid its destructive tendency.

It is, then, not only this imagination but its discipline that must be attended to if we are to understand the so-called religious dimension at Çatalhöyük.

But how to do that? There is a kind of reasoning that studies the nature of a disciplined imagination. I am referring to aesthetics. Aesthetics attempts to understand the principles that allow an imagination to give an experience of great erotic power without being consumed by it. In living faith traditions this imagination is best seen in what is known as devotional practice. As I said before, devotion is easier to recognize than to define. Yet such recognition is not insuperably difficult. Where there is devotion, there is materiality and it is of an aesthetic nature. Devotion is inextricably connected to what is known as devotional art. I do not have time to try to give an account of what makes for devotional art, but it might help to contrast it to what today is called fine art or just simply art. Fine art is art that is "looked at," but devotional art is art that is "lived with."

Devotional art is meant to be touched, kissed, paraded around, put in pockets, displayed in kitchens, dressed up, buried, and a thousand other things. What is constant is that devotional art shares a life that is ordinary yet is a door into an imagination that queries and envisions something beyond the ordinary.

It seems to me that it might be a fertile approach to look for examples of devotional art at Çatalhöyük. In the short time I've been here, I have seen some objects that appear to be good candidates for classification as devotional art. From figurines, to wall paintings, to the structure of the space of these houses one can make a reasonable hypothesis that some of these were used in devotional practices.

Assuming this to be the case, I have done some very tentative speculation based on a very primitive aesthetic analysis of some objects we have seen. An aesthetic analysis of devotional works of art does not follow contemporary theories of aesthetics. Art that is "lived with" must be looked at with a different set of lenses than art that is "looked at." Art that is "lived with" is best looked at through an aesthetics of drama or a dramatics (see Garcia-River 2008).

A key concept in a dramatics is the dramatic horizon. A certain magic happens when we watch a good drama. There comes a time in a good drama when the distance between stage and audience suddenly disappears and one finds oneself right in the middle of the action of the stage. This moment is the dramatic horizon. Unlike a regular horizon that keeps its distance from us as we approach it, a dramatic horizon dissolves the distance. A dramatic horizon unites us and takes us into itself. A preliminary aesthetic analysis of potential objects of devotional art then means trying to find such dramatic horizons.

One easy way to find devotional art is to find that art that is in the form of *istoria* or story. This is the basic comic book form where a series of frames and panels tell a story (McCloud 1999). Much devotional art takes this form.

When I saw the wall painting reconstruction (from Mellaart's F.V.1 "Hunting Shrine") in the visitor's center it immediately suggested to me that it was a comic book or *istoria* form. I began to count the number of people in the painting and it seems there are three sections. There appear to be fifteen people in each section so we have an *istoria* or comic book form in three panels or frames. If reading from right to left one notices two striking formal elements. The rightmost panel is straight as an arrow and orderly; the remaining leftmost panels consist of round forms and are chaotic.

The chaotic, round forms of the leftmost panels are marked by two foci of attention – two animals quite large in proportion to the people chaotically surrounding them. I do not understand the wall painting simply as a scene of baiting or teasing the animals. First of all, the people "baiting" the animals are disproportionately smaller. One person, for example, is as big as the deer's tongue he is presumably pulling out of the deer's mouth! I wonder whether the animals are the Çatalhöyük people themselves. If so, then the people in the painting may be attackers of the Çatalhöyük people and the wall painting is telling some sort of story of a previous attack, or of some significant tragic event. In any case, it is possible to conclude that the animals themselves are the real story. They are surrounded by circles of annoying "teasers" and are visually dominant. If so, one could read the transition between the two leftmost panels as a transformation of the animals themselves. If the animals somehow represent Çatalhöyük, then the animals were transformed by the event. The "middle panel," for example, shows great dynamism and chaos. The last "panel" shows a marked sense of dynamism especially in the people surrounding the animal suggesting some sort of resolution. The large size of the deerlike form visually suggests its significance. What that may be I do not know, but one might reasonably expect to see devotional significance to deer animal parts or forms. This wall painting suggests to me the presence of a dramatic horizon. What I would need to look at further is the living context in which the wall painting was found.

A second candidate for devotional art might be the space that holds a burial site in B.77: a space set aside by a pair of cattle skulls enfleshed in clay and orthogonal to each other. This space also contained a calf's head enfleshed in clay. When we visited the site on Saturday, I stood for a while at that site. I was deeply moved by it. It drew me into itself. This, I am willing to bet, is the site of a dramatic horizon.

I puzzled about this until I saw the figurine from the IST Area of the site that is a skeleton in the back and a full-fleshed woman on the front.

Bones generate life. The source of life is literally the bones. It seems to me from all I have heard and seen here, the Çatalhöyük might very well have had a belief that the soul, understood as the source of life and identity, is literally the skeleton itself. This might explain the vulture symbolism found at Çatalhöyük. If vultures eat away the flesh and leave behind the skeleton, then vultures reveal the "soul" of Çatalhöyük. They are revelatory agents in the devotional practices that might be going on at Çatalhöyük. In other words, vultures may function as the Scriptures do in Christianity: they reveal something about ourselves we could not have known by ordinary means.

In terms of the skeleton itself, I believe the skull might have been believed to be the seat of the soul. I came to this hypothesis because it is reasonable to deduce that if the skeleton is the soul, then something like Ezekiel's vision might have been at work at Çatalhöyük. Ezekiel's vision, if you are not familiar, is a vision of a field of skeletal remains becoming enfleshed and alive and rising from the ground. It is a powerful image of a people defeated returning from defeat to a position of strength.

In any case, the enfleshing of a bone is to reconstitute the person or animal. In the case of the skull, its enfleshment would result in a face and I can imagine that the face would be seen as the very window into the soul.

Having said that, I can see why the Çatalhöyük people might have symbolically enfleshed the skull of cattle and calf to take them back symbolically to a kind of living presence. Objects that communicate a sense of a living presence are definitively devotional in nature. So this burial site seems to me to be a particularly important devotional site with a powerful dramatic horizon.

Following the suggestiveness of this imagination, it is possible that the clay at Çatalhöyük may have been felt to be spiritually potent. Applied to the "soul," that is, the skeletal remains of humans and animals, a spiritual or rather devotional presence could be evoked or reconstituted. This would affirm the hypothesis I heard many times that houses may be considered living entities. Yet that does not seem to give clarity to an important datum: people lived in these "living entities." If these dwellings were alive, then what does it mean to live within a living space?

Perhaps the answer lies in the arrangement of the cattle skulls and the calf's head around the burial platform. If this is a devotional site, then it begs to be approached. Could this space have been a place where an individual entered to commune with the dead? Or could it be that the site is empty because the empty space is a dynamo that reconstitutes its imagination in the spatial arrangement of the dwelling? Or could it be yet that this empty space was a place for visions, visions to be painted on the walls? Perhaps this is why some houses were so concerned about keeping the space arranged a certain way. The arrangement was dictated through some vision experienced at the site and reproduced somehow in the space. It may be then that living within a spiritually alive space may have created a powerful unitive experience with the sources of life and death: indeed, a way of living at the threshold between life and death that illumined the tragic sense that is the heart of the devotional imagination. In any case, this spot in B.77 is another good candidate for what I have been calling a dramatic horizon.

These are my very brief observations. I realize I am a newcomer to Çatalhöyük and have much to learn. Yet, as I said earlier, being naïve has its advantages and you may regard my observations in that light. I hope my observations may become more sophisticated as I learn more about the mysteries found here at Çatalhöyük.

BIBLIOGRAPHY

Garcia-Rivera, A. 2008. On a new list of aesthetic categories. In *Theological Aesthetics beyond von Balthasar* (ed) O.V. Bychkov and J. Fodor. 169–186. Aldershot: Ashgate.

McCloud, S. 1999. *Understanding Comics.* New York: Paradox Press.

Index